My Dearest Friend

~⌾~ *My Dearest Friend* ⌾~

LETTERS OF ABIGAIL AND JOHN ADAMS

Edited by Margaret A. Hogan and C. James Taylor

THE BELKNAP PRESS OF
HARVARD UNIVERSITY PRESS
Cambridge, Massachusetts
London, England
2007

Designed by Annamarie McMahon Why

Library of Congress Cataloging-in-Publication Data
Adams, John, 1735–1826.
[Correspondence. Selections.]
My dearest friend : letters of Abigail and John Adams /
edited by Margaret A. Hogan and C. James Taylor.
p.   cm.
Includes index.
ISBN-13: 978-0-674-02606-3 (alk. paper)
ISBN-10: 0-674-02606-3 (alk. paper)
1. Adams, John, 1735–1826—Correspondence.   2. Adams, Abigail, 1744–1818—
Correspondence.   3. Presidents—United States—Correspondence.   4. Presidents'
spouses—United States—Correspondence.   5. Married people—United States—
Correspondence.   6. Couples—United States—Correspondence.   7. United States—
History—Revolution, 1775–1783—Sources.   8. United States—History—1783–1815—
Sources.   9. Love letters—United States.   10. American letters.   I. Hogan, Margaret A.
II. Taylor, C. James, 1945–   III. Title.
E322.A4 2007
973.4′4092—dc2   2007004380

Contents

Illustrations follow p. 236

Foreword

JOSEPH J. ELLIS

My two favorite scenes of John and Abigail Adams come from their retirement years at Quincy. In the first John is out in the fields working alongside his hired hands, swinging the scythe as he murmurs curses under his breath against Tom Paine and Alexander Hamilton. Abigail is duly recording his murmurings, seconding his denunciations, noting that Thomas Jefferson should also be added to the rogues' gallery. In the second scene, Abigail has descended to the basement of the Quincy house to shell peas. John accompanies her, bringing along a copy of Descartes to read to her while she prepares dinner.

It is the combination of pungency and intimacy embodied in these two scenes that gives the correspondence between John and Abigail such enduring significance, though a few other factors contribute to the ultimate impact. They happened to be living through the most tumultuous and consequential chapter in America's birth as a nation, when the core values were declared and the abiding institutions created. They happened to be centrally involved in these declarations and creations. They happened to preserve about 1,160 letters between them, recording their thoughts and feelings with uncommon candor. (Martha Washington destroyed all but three of the letters she and George exchanged.) And both of them happened to be, each in their own distinctive ways, prose stylists of equally uncommon felicity. If you want to understand how the American republic was improvised on the run, this is a seminal source. If you want to understand how a husband and wife can sustain their love over a lifetime of struggle and tragedy, this is a splendid story of an emotional and intellectual partnership that endured to the end. It is an epic tale about the making of American history and a great love story all rolled into one.

One of the most ironic features of their correspondence is that we get the clearest glimpse of their intimacies when they are apart. This means that the record is richest when John is in Philadelphia at the Continental Congress in the 1770s, when he is ensconced in Paris as the American negotiator of the peace treaty with Great Britain in the 1780s, and when he is vice president in the Washington administration in the 1790s. Previous editions of the correspondence have covered the first chapter in this story and bits of the second with admirable diligence. But this edition of letters is the first to include material beyond 1784 and to cover the Adams vice presidency and presidency.

Toward the end of his life John liked to tell anyone who would listen that the true story of the American Revolution would never get into the history books, predicting that a gloss of coherence and inevitability would be laid over the much messier realities. In his view, a historically correct account of the American Revolution would emphasize the utter confusion of the actors in the drama, including himself, who were making it up as they went along.

These letters, most especially during the wartime years and the Adams presidency, recover the messiness of history-as-it-happens, providing the kind of experiential perspective that Tolstoy captured in *War and Peace*. Abigail's first-person account of the Battle of Bunker Hill, for example, accurately conveys the sense of chaos—the swirling mix of rumors, the deafening thunder of a cannon, the obscuring clouds of smoke over the battlefield—that gives her narrative an immediacy and psychological authenticity lost in most standard accounts of battle.

Similarly, John's letters from Philadelphia expose the abiding uncertainty within the Continental Congress as the delegates groped toward the realization that the unthinkable—a war for American independence against the greatest military power on the planet—was becoming inevitable. John sensed where history was headed before most of

the other delegates, but his letters to Abigail capture the prevailing be-
fuddlement, the widespread mood of desperation and denial, the frequent backpedaling and incessant pettiness that dominated the deliberations. Eventually, by July of 1776, the cacophony became a chorus,
but the process of getting there was very untidy, a back-and-forth
story with melodramatic interludes when all was in the balance. John's
letters provide the clearest window that we have into the zigzaggy
course of a revolution in the making.

The exchange during the 1770s also reveals how great public events,
like the decision to appoint George Washington as commander-in-
chief, or the request for all the colonies to draft new constitutions as
states—a *de facto* declaration of independence that John correctly regarded as his most consequential contribution—were invariably mixed
together with very private and highly personal concerns, like the inoculation of Abigail and her children against smallpox. Once again, the
letters permit the recovery of the layered mentality and complex con-
sciousness of a married couple juggling their roles as prominent political actors and parents, engaged in a conversation that shifts seamlessly
from an assessment of British military strategy to a discussion of John
Quincy's reading habits. In most histories these personal factors are
airbrushed out, leaving the outstanding public events to stand alone as
the spine of the story. But the real story, told here, has multiple dimen-
sions that defy any purely linear narrative.

In part the size of the full correspondence makes it the most revealing exchange between a publicly prominent husband and wife in all of
American history. But the literary quality of the letters, and the sustained emotional and intellectual sophistication of the conversation, elevate these letters above all others as historical documents of a marriage and a crucial era.

It is also a lost era. Predating the telegraph and the telephone, much
more the cell phone and email, letter-writing in the late eighteenth
century was a more deliberative process, less an exchange of information than an exchange of *personae*, more a crafted verbal composition
than a merely factual memorandum. Both time and space were experi-

enced differently back then, with the former felt more leisurely than now, and the latter regarded as a more formidable obstacle that delayed the reception of your words and thoughts for weeks or months. Both Abigail and John were master practitioners of letter-writing in the eighteenth-century style, more self-consciously literary—Abigail even more so in this regard—more committed to digested opinions than immediate impressions. They took letter-writing more seriously than we do today. That said, some of the most poignant letters—Abigail's report between contractions of what proved to be a still-born child, and John's effusive reaction to the vote on American independence on July 2, 1776—were spontaneous expressions of the moment memorable for their immediacy.

Although several generations of scholars have read them in manuscript, few of the letters from the 1790s have ever been published before. They constitute the record of a political partnership in which Abigail served as John's chief advisor and confidante. During his vice presidency her main task was to calm him down as he fidgeted and raged against the "splendid miseries" of his office, then to assure him that his position on such controversial issues as the National Bank and the Jay Treaty had her blessing. As the election of 1796 approached, Abigail soothed his savage breast when John worried to her about his ambition for the presidency, then worried that his ambition would go unfulfilled. Abigail was the designated vote counter—John regarded such self-interested behavior as unbecoming—and she was the one to apprise him that the New York electoral votes put him over the top.

Before there was Eleanor Roosevelt or Hillary Clinton, there was Abigail Adams. The term "First Lady" had yet to be coined, but its implication of a wife devoted primarily to matters of social etiquette does not accurately describe Abigail's role, which was more substantive than ceremonial. Abigail and John were commonly regarded as a team, and as Fisher Ames, the Federalist sage, put it, "the good Lady his wife . . . is as complete a politician as any body in the old French Court." Because they were together in Philadelphia for much of this time, the only surviving letters date from those occasions when Abi-

gail was back at Quincy. But those letters show that John correctly regarded his Cabinet as disloyal and Abigail as his only trustworthy political advisor.

Indeed, it is clear that she played a major role in the two land-
mark decisions of the Adams presidency. The first, which provoked a
firestorm of criticism and disbelief in both the Federalist and Republican camps, was the decision to send a peace commission to Paris and
thereby end the "quasi war" with France. Critics speculated that the
president had lost his senses because his wife was back at Quincy and
therefore unable to temper his outbursts. In truth, Abigail endorsed
the decision as a brilliant stroke and relished the rumors that her absence had contributed to her husband's impetuous behavior. History
has shown that the Adams decision put American foreign policy on the
correct course, though its unpopularity at the time was probably responsible for his failure to win re-election in 1800.

The second decision, which turned out to be the greatest blunder of
the Adams presidency, was his endorsement and signing of the Alien
and Sedition Acts. John eventually came to realize that this repressive
legislation was a monumental mistake, and it has become a tin can tied
to his legacy ever since. Abigail strongly supported the Alien and Sedition Acts, mostly because she wanted to silence her husband's critics
in the press. It was one instance when her love for him clouded her political judgment.

Her involvement in policy-making continued to the end. In the last
line of the last letter in the correspondence, written when she was traveling back to Quincy while John remained at Washington, Abigail observed: "I want to see the list of judges." She was referring to the last
judicial appointments of the Adams presidency, subsequently known
as "the midnight judges." The most prominent of these appointments
was John Marshall as Chief Justice of the Supreme Court, which
turned out to be one of John's most consequential legacies. It would
seem that Abigail had a hand in that decision, too.

Abigail lived on until 1818, John until his exquisitely timed death on
July 4, 1826. We can catch glimpses of their retirement years at

Quincy through letters they wrote to others. But letters to each other were unnecessary, since they spent every day in each other's company. They regarded their children and the enduring American republic as their greatest legacies and would probably be surprised to know that their own correspondence has become a worthy third entry on the list. This selection is the most judicious, most revealing, and most comprehensive ever published.

Joseph J. Ellis
Amherst, Massachusetts
January 2007

Introduction

Abigail and John Adams's correspondence, spanning the years 1762 to 1801, covers the most important forty years in American history. The monumental topics of revolution, independence, and nation building, with comments on many of the major personalities of the age, are woven into the fabric of these letters. John recognized that they lived "in an Age of Tryal." As early as July 1774, he addressed Abigail as "my dear Partner in all the Joys and sorrows, Prosperity and Adversity of my Life" and entreated her "to take a Part with me in the struggle." She responded with both support and encouragement: "I long impatiently to have you upon the Stage of action." But the Revolution and all the "Tryal" it entailed was only the backdrop; what remains central is the enduring relationship between these two American icons. Their misfortune—to be separated frequently, and often for extended periods—has proved the good fortune of subsequent generations who have marveled at their literate, sensitive, and revealing letters.

From the time John left Braintree to represent Massachusetts at the First Continental Congress in August 1774 until he returned home to the renamed Quincy in 1801 upon the completion of his single presidential term, he spent twenty-seven years in almost uninterrupted public service. Abigail's constant support, encouragement, and advice made that contribution possible. Scholars will continue to debate the significance of his legacy, but no one can question Abigail and John's personal sacrifice.

Abigail and John formed the best-known husband and wife partnership in American history. In 2006, a television dramatization of their relationship aptly promoted them as "America's first power couple." But when the minister's 14-year-old middle daughter met the farmer's 23-year-old eldest son in 1759, no one could have guessed that they would be so immortalized. While much of that fame stems from their important role in American history, some also arises from the survival of nearly twelve hundred of their letters—a remarkable window into their world and a testament to the importance written correspondence played in the lives of people before the modern era of rapid travel and communication.

The earliest extant letter is John's playful note to his teenage "Miss Adorable" in October 1762, insisting that she remained in his debt "for the Kisses as I have given two or three Millions at least." Through their courtship this flirtatious and sweet mode continued. In later years the address became more formal but never less affectionate. "My Dearest Friend" was their most common salutation, meant quite literally. The final letter of theirs to survive was written by Abigail in February 1801, while making her way home to Quincy from Washington, D.C., after Thomas Jefferson had defeated her husband in the recent presidential election. Four decades after the first lighthearted notes, the now sophisticated 56-year-old international traveler, who had met kings and queens and moved in the highest European and American society, returned to her modest Massachusetts home and farm. But her thoughts stayed with her husband, expressing both her great love for him and her continuing involvement in his important political decisions: "Adieu my dear Friend. I wish you well through the remainder of your political journey. I want to see the list of judges." Throughout those years and in the numerous roles she filled, Abigail remained John's greatest supporter and most trusted advisor.

Their correspondence provides a view of a world long gone. Time and distance restricted communication in ways that are beyond modern minds' comprehension. During his public service at Philadelphia and New York, John had to allot several days to get to or from his Massachusetts home. The difficulty and uncertainty of travel combined with his dedication to work made six-month separations from his family common and those of longer duration not unusual. His diplomatic missions to Europe resulted in years away from Abigail and their children and sometimes months between communications. Consequently their relationship had to be sustained by love and letters.

John's delight at what he discovered during his travels, however, occasionally moved him to write with something less than sensitivity to Abigail's needs and concerns. After he sailed for France from Boston in February 1778, Abigail did not receive her first letter from John until June: "Shall I tell my dearest that tears of joy filld my Eyes this morning at the sight of his well known hand the first line which has bless my Sight since his four months absence." One can imagine that tears prompted by another emotion may have flowed as she read on. "To tell you the Truth," John mused, "I admire the Ladies here. Dont be jealous. They are Handsome, and very well educated. Their Accomplishments, are exceedingly brilliant." To make matters worse, he noted how the French women not only allowed his fellow diplomat Benjamin Franklin "to embrace them as often as he pleases, but they are perpetually embracing him." Abigail's reply chastised him for not writing more about how he and their son John Quincy had fared on the voyage, what reception he met, "and a thousand circumstances which I wish to know." Then, rather than giving him news of family and farm, which he always loved to read, she devoted the bulk of her letter to defending American women and making a strong case for female education. In his 26 July reply, a now more alert husband did not mention the French ladies. He assured her instead that while France "is a delicious Country" there "are no Enchantments for me."

Among the differences in the style and content of their exchanges, Abigail wrote longer, more emotional, and more personally revealing letters. In her accounts of the management of the farm she clearly prided herself on her skills. John in turn confided in her about the many people, events, and problems that seemed constantly to frustrate him, but his letters were frequently shorter and less expressive. Abigail complained about this, but John excused himself by explaining that public business consumed his time and that much of what he wished to write could not be trusted to the post. Many of his letters took a didactic turn, as he discussed what she must do for the children's education or instructed her on what she should read for self-improvement. The health and educational progress of their children remained a primary interest of both parents, and their later correspondence reveals the disappointment and sorrow they shared for the problems and failures of their adult children.

The fear of contagious disease, especially smallpox, was a constant worry and frequent topic. Reports of sickness and death among friends, neighbors, and family permeate the letters. Reminders of human mortality abound and add a sober tinge. The state of their own health along with that of the children remained the most constant subject of John and Abigail's letters. Long periods—weeks and in some cases months—between letters created anxieties and heightened fears that a loved one might be dead or dying, while the distant spouse had no way of knowing until well after the event. This also meant that the person facing the crisis, usually Abigail, had no partner close by on whom she could lean for support. Her letters during these wrenching periods of loss are truly pathetic and underscore the great sacrifice she made while her husband served the nation.

Two of the most traumatic events in her life occurred while John attended the Continental Congress. In the fall of 1775, Elizabeth Quincy Smith, Abigail's mother, died during a dysentery epidemic that plagued eastern Massachusetts. Abigail, exhausted from ministering to her own sick household and recently ill herself, took up her pen only hours after her mother succumbed. On the verge of despair, she wrote, "At times I almost am ready to faint under this severe and heavy stroke, seperated from *thee* who used to be a comfortar towards me in affliction." In July 1777, again alone, she delivered a stillborn daughter. During the later stages of the pregnancy she sensed a problem with the fetus. She shared her anxieties in a letter: "I keep up some spirits yet, tho I would have you prepaird for any Event." On this and other troubling occasions, she employed her pen to express and relieve her pain. John wrote to convey his encouragement and, when needed, consolation. But writing about her personal afflictions also became Abigail's means of coping. In September 1776, between these two devastating losses, she expressed perfectly the significance the correspondence had for her: "There are perticuliar times when I feel such an uneasiness such a rest less ness, as neither company Books family Cares or any other thing will remove. My Pen is my only pleasure, and writing to you the composure of my mind."

The letters held an importance that transcended the information they contained. When on more than one occasion Abigail wrote caustically about well-known personalities or institutions, she begged her husband to destroy the letters. While some of the letters miscarried, were lost in transit, or even were intercepted during wartime, there is no evidence that John ever destroyed a letter from his "Portia." Likewise it is unimaginable that she would have considered burning his. As John himself replied to one such request, "You bid me burn your Letters. But I must forget you first."

This is the third edition of Abigail and John's correspondence transcribed from the original manuscripts. When their grandson Charles Francis Adams published his 1876 *Familiar Letters of John Adams and His Wife, During the Revolution,* in honor of the centennial of the nation, the family still held these and tens of thousands of other letters and documents chronicling a century of the nation's as well as the family's history. Early in the twentieth century the Adams family placed the letters on deposit at the Massachusetts Historical Society in Boston. In 1956 the Historical Society took formal possession of the collection and began a long-term commitment to publish a modern edition under the direction of Lyman H. Butterfield. The Adams Papers project has completed forty volumes to date and will in time publish some one hundred from this unparalleled collection. Butterfield and his colleagues took time from the multi-volume edition in 1975 to publish *The Book of Abigail and John: Selected Letters of the Adams Family, 1762–1784* in celebration of the bicentennial.

These first two editions, despite their use of many of the same manuscripts, differed dramatically. The 1876 edition contains 284 letters written between 1774 and 1783. The 1975 edition includes 207 letters from a slightly longer period. Abigail and John's circumspect grandson Charles Francis carefully redacted anything that might be considered trivial or mundane, along with topics or comments deemed unsuitable for publication, such as discussions of Abigail's pregnancy or issues that he believed failed to serve the family's reputation. He corrected unusual or regional spellings that he feared might show his grandmother to be less literate than she in fact was. Lyman Butterfield and his co-editors selected fewer letters but did not alter them other than to modernize capitalization and punctuation. Butterfield also, in addition to some brief contextual commentary, inserted diary entries and letters from other correspondents to create a framework for the letters.

This volume includes 289 letters and is selected from the entire corpus of John and Abigail's correspondence. It is meant to show both the consistency of their relationship and the evolution of the family through the entire founding era. The letters have not been edited for content or to modernize or correct spellings, which tell us much about regional pronunciations and eighteenth-century style. Selections have occasionally been made, however, from long letters written in journal-like fashion with more than one date entry. In order to include as much of the correspondence as possible, no additional documents are printed in this edition. It is our belief that Abigail and John said it best.

Note to the Reader
and Acknowledgments

The editors have designed this volume to be read and enjoyed, not necessarily studied. For fully annotated versions of the letters dated between 1762 and 1789, readers should consult the same material as published in the *Adams Family Correspondence*, volumes 1–8 (Cambridge: Harvard University Press, 1963–2007). These books also include additional letters between John and Abigail, as well as copious correspondence among many different members of their extended families. Readers seeking to learn more about the Adams family's story should turn to these volumes and consult the indexes first for specific topics.

The texts presented here are generally given in complete form with the following exceptions: (1) When a letter was written on two or more days, the editors have felt free to omit silently whole dated sections, but not to omit portions of a dated section. (2) Brief and negligible postscripts have been omitted.

Texts are given literally with no regularization of spelling and only minimal regularization of punctuation and capitalization for readability. Missing or illegible material is supplied by the editors in square brackets; bracketed comments in italics are editorial insertions included to clarify the author's meaning or to identify names and places. An ellipsis in brackets indicates an unreadable word or words. Words printed struck through represent cancellations in the original that the editors have restored because of their interest.

Whether or not these items have been previously published, the manuscript originals of the letters are in the Adams Family Papers manuscript collection, given by the Adams family in 1956 to the Massachusetts Historical Society. Digital images of the letters—and of all of John and Abigail's correspondence—are also available through the Historical Society's website (www.masshist.org) at "The Adams Family Papers: An Electronic Archive." The three exceptions are as follows:

(1) John's letter of 24 July 1775, one of his "intercepted" letters, is reprinted here from the *Massachusetts Gazette and Boston Weekly News-Letter* of 17 August 1775. The original has been lost, probably destroyed by the printer.

(2) Abigail's letter of 23 April 1797 was first printed in Caroline Smith de Windt, ed., *Correspondence of Miss Adams, Daughter of John Adams, Second President of the United States,* New York, 1842, vol. 2, pp. 149–150. Sadly, all of the manuscript letters used for that edited collection of Abigail Adams 2d's correspondence, prepared by her daughter Caroline Smith de Windt, were destroyed in a fire in the mid-nineteenth century.

(3) Abigail's letter of 26 April 1797 has been reprinted from Charles Francis Adams, ed., *Letters of Mrs. Adams,* 4th edition, Boston, 1848, pp. 376–377. The location of the original is unknown.

The editors gratefully acknowledge Jennifer Snodgrass of Harvard University Press for her enthusiastic support and the entire Adams Papers staff for their encouragement of and assistance with this project.

Courtship and Marriage

"Now Letter-Writing is, to me, the most agreable Amusement:
and Writing to you the most entertaining and Agreable of
all Letter-Writing."

—*John Adams*

"And—then Sir if you please you may take me."

—*Abigail Smith*

"It gives me more Pleasure than I can express to learn that you sustain
with so much Fortitude, the Shocks and Terrors of the Times.
You are really brave, my dear, you are an Heroine."

—*John Adams*

"My pen is always freer than my tongue. I have wrote many things
to you that I suppose I never could have talk'd."

—*Abigail Adams*

"Love Sweetens Life"

OCTOBER 1762–JULY 1774

John first mentioned Abigail Smith in a Diary entry from the summer of 1759, in which he was less than overwhelmed by her charms—"Not fond, not frank, not candid" was his overall assessment. Quite possibly John's good friend Richard Cranch introduced him to the Smith family. Richard had been spending time in their household in Weymouth, where the Rev. William Smith served as minister, and would eventually marry Abigail's older sister Mary in 1762.

Despite his poor first impression, John continued to visit the family and obviously grew increasingly enamored of Abigail. By 1762, the date of their first extant letter, they had become intimates if not yet formally engaged. John's mother, Susanna Boylston Adams, initially objected to the relationship but "brought herself to acquiesce" in the face of John's persistence. Once John had successfully established his law career sufficient to support a family, they were free to marry; the ceremony, officiated by Abigail's father, took place in October 1764.

Even in these early years of courtship and marriage, before John became an important national figure in the Revolution, the couple spent considerable time apart. John's work as a lawyer required him to "ride the circuit," attending courts held at various towns throughout Massachusetts and Maine, which took him away from Abigail and their young family for weeks at a time.

John Adams to Abigail Smith

Miss Adorable   Octr 4th. 1762

By the same Token that the Bearer hereof *satt up* with you last night I hereby order you to give him, as many Kisses, and as many Hours of your Company after 9 OClock as he shall please to Demand and charge them to my Account: This Order, or Requisition call it which you will is in Consideration of a similar order Upon Aurelia for the like favour, and I presume I have good Right to draw upon you for the Kisses as I have given two or three Millions at least, when one has been recd, and of Consequence the Account between us is immensely in favour of yours

John Adams

John Adams to Abigail Smith

Dear Madam   Braintree Feby 14th 1763

Accidents are often more Friendly to us, than our own Prudence. I intended to have been at Weymouth Yesterday, but a storm prevented. Cruel, Yet perhaps blessed storm! Cruel for detaining me from so much friendly, social Company, and perhaps blessed to you, or me or both, for keeping me at *my Distance*. For every experimental Phylosopher knows, that the steel and the Magnet or the Glass and feather will not fly together with more Celerity, than somebody And somebody, when brought within the striking Distance. And, Itches, Aches, Agues, and Repentance might be the Consequences of a Contact in present Circumstances. Even the Divines pronounce casuistically, I hear "unfit to be touched these three Weeks."

I mount this moment for that noisy, dirty Town of Boston, where Parade, Pomp, Nonsense Frippery, Folly, Foppery, Luxury, Polliticks, and the soul-Confounding Wrangles of the Law will give me the Higher Relish for Spirit Taste and sense, at Weymouth, next sunday.

My Duty, were owing! My Love to Mr Cranch And Lady, tell them

I love them, I love them better than any Mortals who have no other Title to my Love than Friendship gives and that I hope he is in perfect Health and she in all the Qualms that necessarily attend, Pregnancy, in all other Respects very happy.

Your—(all the rest is inexpressible)

John Adams

John Adams to Abigail Smith

Diana   April 20th. 1763

Love sweetens Life, and Life sometimes destroys Love. Beauty is desirable and Deformity detestible; Therefore Beauty is not Deformity nor Deformity, Beauty. Hope springs eternal in the human Breast, I hope to be happyer next Fall than I am at present, and this Hope makes me happyer now than I should be without it. I am at Braintree but I wish I was at Weymouth! What strange Revolutions take Place in our Breasts, and what curious Vicissitudes in every Part of human Life. This summer I shall like Weymouth better than Braintree but something prompts me to believe I shall like Braintree next Winter better than Weymouth. Writers who procure Reputation by flattering human Nature, tell us that Mankind grows wiser and wiser: whether they lie, or speak the Truth, I know I like it, better and better. I would feign make an original, an Exemplar, of this Letter but I fear I have not an original Genius. Ned. Brooks is gone to ordination, I know. I have not seen him, nor heard of him, but I am sure that nothing less than the Inspiration of his Dæmon, that I suppose revolted from him somewhere, near the foot of Pens-Hill could have given me Understanding to write this Letter. This is better Reasoning than any I learned at Colledge.

Patience my Dear! Learn to conquer your Appetites and Passions! Know thyself, came down from Heaven, and the Government of ones own soul requires greater Parts and Virtues than the Management of

Kingdoms, and the Conquest of the disorderly rebellious Principles in our Nature, is more glorious than the acquisition of Universal Dominion. Did you ever read Epictetus? He was a sensible Man. I advise you to read him: and indeed I should have given this advice, before you undertook to read this.

It is a silly affectation for modern statesmen to Act or descant upon Ancient Principles of Morals and Civility. The Beauty of Virtue, The Love of ones Country, a sense of Liberty, a Feeling for our Fellow Men, are Ideas that the Brains of Men now a Days can not contemplate: It is a better Way to substitute in the Place of them, The Beauty of a Lady, the Love of Cards and Horse Races, a Taste in Dress, Musick, and Dancing, The Feeling of a pretty Girl or Fellow and a genteel Delicacy and Complaisance to all who have Power to abuse us.

I begin to find that an increasing affection for a certain Lady, (you know who my Dr) quickens my affections for every Body Else, that does not deserve my Hatred. A Wonder if the Fires of Patriotism, do not soon begin to burn! And now I think of it, there is no possible Way of diminishing the Misery of Man kind so effectually as by printing this Letter.

It is an intolerable Grievance and Oppression upon poor literary Mortals, to set wasting their Spirits And wearing out that great Gland the Brain, in the study of order and Connection, in f[ix]ing every Part of their Compositions to [. . .] certain scope. This keeps them besides [fr]om the Joys of seeing their Productions in Print, several days longer than is needful, (not nine years indeed, according to those fools the Ancients): We are to our Honor grown a good deal wiser than they.

Now I can demonstrate that a Man [might?] write three score years and ten, after the Model of this Letter, without the least Necesity of Revisal, Emendation or Correction, and all that he should write in that time would be worth Printing too. I find the Torrent Hurries me down, but I will make a great Effort to swim ashore to the Name of

Philander

To the great Goddess Diana

Abigail Smith to John Adams

My Friend   Weymouth August th 11 1763

If I was sure your absence to day was occasioned, by what it generally is, either to wait upon Company, or promote some good work, I
freely confess my Mind would be much more at ease than at present it
is. Yet this uneasiness does not arise from any apprehension of Slight
or neglect, but a fear least you are indisposed for that you said should
be your only hindrance.

Humanity obliges us to be affected with the distresses and miserys
of our fellow creatures. Friendship is a band yet Stronger, which
causes us to feel with greater tenderness the afflictions of our Friends.

And there is a tye more binding than Humanity, and stronger than
Friendship, which makes us anxious for the happiness and welfare of
those to whom it binds us. It makes their Misfortunes Sorrows and afflictions, our own. Unite these, and there is a threefold cord—by this
cord I am not ashamed to own myself bound, nor do I believe that you
are wholly free from it. Judge [you] then for your Diana has she not
this day had Sufficient cause for pain and anxiety of mind?

She bids me tell you that Seneca, for the sake of his Paulina was
careful and tender of his health. The health and happiness of Seneca she
says was not dearer to his Paulina, than that of Lysander to his Diana.

The Fabrick often wants repairing and if we neglect it the Deity
will not long inhabit it, yet after all our care and solisitude to preserve
it, it is a tottering Building, and often reminds us that it will finally fall.

Adieu may this find you in better health than I fear it will, and
happy as your Diana wishes you.

Accept this hasty Scrawl warm from the Heart of your Sincere

Diana

In 1764, an outbreak of smallpox occurred in Boston. Because John rode the court circuits, he needed to be inoculated, a process that took a month or more and required that the patient be infected with a mild case of the disease under controlled circumstances. This gave the individual an immunity from taking the disease "in the natural way," which was far more dangerous.

Abigail would endure the same procedure with all of her children in the summer of 1776 while John served in Congress in Philadelphia.

Abigail Smith to John Adams

Sir   Weymouth April 7. 1764

How do you now? For my part, I feel much easier than I did an hour ago, My Unkle haveing given me a more particuliar, and favorable account of the small pox, or rather the operation of the preparation, than I have had before. He speaks greatly in favor of Dr Perkins who has not, as he has heard lost one patient. He has had since he has been in Town frequent opportunities of visiting in the families where the Doctor practises, and he is full in the persuaision that he understands the Distemper, full as well if not better than any Physician in Town, and knows better what to do in case of any dificulty. He allows his Patients greater liberty with regard to their Diet, than several other physicians. Some of them (Dr Lord for one) forbid their patients a mouthful of Bread. My unkle Says they are all agreed that tis best to abstain from Butter, and Salt—And most of them from meat.

I hope you will have reason to be well Satisfied with the Dr—and advise you to follow his prescriptions as nigh as you find your Health will permit. I send by my unkle some balm. Let me know certainly what Day you design to go to town, Pappa Says Tom shall go that Day and bring your Horse back.

Keep your Spirits up, and I make no doubt you will do well eno'.

Shall I come and see you before you go. No I wont, for I want not again, to experience what I this morning felt, when you left.

Your

A. Smith

John Adams to Abigail Smith

My dear Diana   Saturday Evening Eight O'Clock [*7 April 1764*]

For many Years past, I have not felt more serenely than I do this Evening. My Head is clear, and my Heart is at ease. Business, of every Kind, I have banished from my Thoughts. My Room is prepared for a Seven Days, Retirement, and my Plan is digested for 4 or 5 Weeks. My Brother retreats with me, to our preparatory Hospital, and is determined to keep me Company, through the Small Pox. Your Unkle, by his agreable Account of the Dr. and your Brother, their Strength their Spirits, and their happy Prospects, but especially, by the Favour he left me from you, has contributed very much to the Felicity of my present Frame of Mind. For, I assure you Sincerely, that, (as Nothing which I before expected from the Distemper gave me more Concern, than the Thought of a six Weeks Separation from my Diana) my Departure from your House this Morning made an Impression upon me that was severely painfull. I thought I left you, in Tears and Anxiety. And was very glad to hear by your Letter, that your Fears were abated. For my own Part, I believe no Man ever undertook to prepare himself for the Small Pox, with fewer than I have at present. I have considered thoughrououghly, the Diet and Medicine prescribed me, and am fully satisfyed that no durable Evil can result from Either, and any other Fear from the small Pox or it's Appurtenances, in the modern Way of Inoculation I never had in my Life. Thanks for my Balm. Present my Duty and Gratitude to Pappa, for his kind offer of Tom. Next Fryday, for certain, with suitable submission, We take our Departure for Boston. To Captn. Cunninghams We go—And I have not the least doubt of a pleasant 3 Weeks, notwithstanding the Distemper. Dr Savil has no Antimony—So I must beg your Care, that John Jenks makes the Pills and sends them by the Bearer. I enclose the Drs Directions. We shall want about 10 I suppose for my Brother and me. Other Things we have of Savil.

Good Night, my Dear, I'm a going to Bed!

Sunday Morning 1/2 After 10. The People all gone to Meeting, but my self, and Companion, who are enjoying, a Pipe in great Tranquility, after the operation of our Ipichac. Did you ever see two Persons in one Room Iphichacuana'd together? (I hope I have not Spelled that ineffable Word amiss!) I assure you they make merry Diversion. We took turns to be sick and to laugh. When my Companion was sick I laughed at him, and when I was sick he laughed at me. Once however and once only we were both sick together, and then all Laughter and good Humour deserted the Room. Upon my Word we both felt very sober. But all is now easy and agreable, We have had our Breakfast of, Pottage without salt, or Spice or Butter, as the Drs. would have it, and are seated to our Pipes and our Books, as happily as Mortals, preparing for the small Pox, can desire.

John Adams to Abigail Smith

My ever dear Diana   Braintree Ap. 11th. 1764

The Room which I thought would have been an Hospital or a Musæum, has really proved a Den of Thieves, and a scene of Money Changers. More Persons have been with me about Business, since I, *shut up,* than a few, and many more than I was glad to see, for it is a sort of Business that I get nothing by, but Vanity and Vexation of Spirit. If my Imprisonment had been in Consequence of Bankruptcy, I should not have endured much more Mortification and Disquiet. I wish this Day was a Fast, as well as Tomorrow, that I might be sure of two Days Tranquility, before my Departure. I am not very impatient at present: Yet I wish I was at Boston. Am somewhat fearful of foul weather on Fryday. If it should be, the very first fair Opportunity, must be embraced.

Abstinence from all, but the cool and the soft has hitherto agreed with me very well, and I have not once transgressed, in a single Iota. The Medicine we have taken is far from being loathsome or painful or troublesome, as I own I expected. And if I could but enjoy my Retreat in silence and solitude, there would be nothing Wanting but Obliviscence of your Ladyship, to make me as Happy as a Monk in a Cloyster or an Hermit in his Cell. You will wonder, perhaps at my calling in Monks and Hermits, on this Occasion, and may doubt about the Happiness of their situations: Yet give me leave to tell you freely, the former of these are so tottally absorbed in Devotion and the latter in Meditation, and such an Appetite such a Passion for their Respective Employments and Pleasures grows habitually up in their Minds, that no Mortals (excepting him who hopes to be bound to your Ladyship in the soft Ligaments of Matrimony) has a better security for Happiness than they.

Hitherto I have written with the Air and in the style of Rattle and Frolick but now I am about to shift to the sober and the Grave. My Mamma, is as easy and composed, and I think much more so than I expected. She sees We are determined, and that opposition would be not only fruitless, but vexatious, and has therefore brought herself to acquiesce, and to assist in preparing all Things, as conveniently and comfortably as she can. Heaven reward her, for her kind Care, and her Labours of Love!

I long to come once more to Weymouth before I go to Boston. I could, well enough. I am as well as ever, and better too. Why should not I come? Shall I come and keep fast with you? Or will you come and see me? I should be glad to see you in this House, but there is another very near it, where I should rejoice much more to see you, and to live with you, till we shall have lived enough to ourselves, to Glory,

Virtue and Mankind, and till both of us shall be desirous of Translation to a wiser, fairer, better World.

I am, and till then, and forever after will be your Admirer and Friend, and Lover

John Adams

Abigail Smith to John Adams

My Dearest Friend   Weymouth April 12, 1764

Here am I all alone, in my Chamber, a mere Nun I assure you, after professing myself thus will it not be out of Character to confess that my thoughts are often Employ'd about Lysander, "out of the abundance of the Heart, the mouth Speaketh," and why Not the Mind thinketh.

Received the pacquet you so generously bestowed upon me. To say I Fasted after such an entertainment, would be wronging my Conscience and wounding Truth. How kind is it in you, thus by frequent tokens of remembrance to alleviate the pangs of absence, by this I am convinced that I am often in your Thoughts, which is a satisfaction to me, notwithstanding you tell me that you Sometimes view the dark side of your Diana, and there no doubt you discover many Spots— which I rather wish were erased, than conceal'd from you. Do not judge by this, that your opinion is an indifferent thing to me, (were it so, I should look forward with a heavey Heart,) but it is far otherways, for I had rather Stand fair there, and be thought well of by Lysander than by the greater part of the world besides. I would fain hope that those faults which you discover, proceed more, from a wrong Head, than a bad Heart. E'er long May I be connected with a Friend from whose Example I may form a more faultless conduct, and whose benevolent mind will lead him to pardon, what he cannot amend.

The Nest of Letters which you so undervalue, were to me a much more welcome present than a Nest of Baskets, tho every stran of those had been gold and Silver. I do not estimate everything according to the price the world set upon it, but according to the value it is of to me, thus that which was cheapest to you I look upon as highly valuable.

You ask whether you shall send a History of the whole voyage, characters, visits conversations &c &c. It is the very thing that I designd this Evening to have requested of you, but you have prevented my asking, by kindly offering it. You will greatly oblige me by it, and it will be no small amusement to me in my State of Seperation. Among the many who will visit, I expect Arpasia will be one, I want her character drawn by your pen (Aurelia says she appears most agreable in her Letters). I know you are a critical observer, and your judgment of people generally plases me. Sometimes you know, I think you too severe, and that you do not make quite so many allowances as Humane Nature requires, but perhaps this may be oweing to my unacquainedness with the World. Your Business Naturly leads you to a nearer inspection of Mankind, and to see the corruptions of the Heart, which believe you often find desperately wicked and deceitful.

Me thinks I have abundance to say to you. What is next? O that I should have been extreemly glad to have seen you to Day. Last Fast Day, if you remember, we spent to gether, and why might we not this? Why I can tell you, we might, if we had been together, have been led into temptation. I dont mean to commit any Evil, unless setting up late, and thereby injuring our Health, may be called so. To that I could have Submitted without much remorse of Conscience. That would have had but little weight with me, had you not bid me adieu, the last time I saw you. The reflexion of what I that forenoon endured, has been ever since sufficient to deter me from wishing to see you again, till you can come and go, as you formerly used to.

Betsy sends her Love to you, says she designd to have kissed you before you went away, but you made no advances, and she never haveing been guilty of such an action, knew not how to attempt it. Know you of any figure in the Mathematicks whereby you can convey one to her? Inclining lines that meet in the same center, will not that figure come as nigh as any?

What think you of the weather. We have had a very promising afternoon, tho the forenoon threatned a Storm. I am in great hopes that Sol will not refuse his benign influence tomorrow.

To-Morrow you leave Braintree. My best wishes attend you, with Marcia I say

> "O ye immortal powers! that guard the just
> Watch round his Head, and Soften the Disease
> Banish all Sorrow from his Mind
> Becalm his Soul with pleasing thoughts
> And Shew Mankind that virtue is your care."

Thus for Lysander prays his

A Smith

John Adams to Abigail Smith

my dearest   [*Boston, 13 April 1764*]

We arrived at Captn. Cunninghams, about Twelve O'Clock and sent our Compliments to Dr Perkins. The Courrier, returned with Answer that the Dr was determined to inocualate no more without a Preparation preevious to Inoculation. That We should have written to him and have recd Directions from him, and Medicine, before We came into Town. I was surprized and chagrined. I wrote, instantly, a Letter to him, and informed him we had been under a Preparation of his prescribing, and that I presumed Dr Tufts had informed him, that We depended on him, in Preference to any other Gentn. The Dr came, immediately with Dr Warren, in a Chaise—And after an Apology, for his not Recollecting—(I am obliged to break off, my Narration, in order to swallow a Porringer of Hasty Pudding and Milk. I have done my Dinner)—for not recollecting what Dr Tufts had told him, Dr Perkins demanded my left Arm and Dr Warren my Brothers. They took their Launcetts and with their Points divided the skin for about a

Quarter of an Inch and just suffering the Blood to appear, buried a Thread about a Quarter of an Inch long in the Channell. A little Lint was then laid over the scratch and a Piece of a Ragg pressed on, and then a Bandage bound over all. My Coat and waistcoat put on, and I was bid to go where and do what I pleased. (Dont you think the Dr has a good deal of Confidence in my Discretion, thus to leave me to it?)

The Doctors have left us Pills red and black to take Night and Morning. But they looked very sagaciously and importantly at us, and ordered my Brother, larger Doses than me, on Account of the Difference in our Constitutions. Dr Perkins is a short, thick sett dark Complexioned, Yet pale Faced, Man, (Pale faced I say, which I was glad to see, because I have a great Regard for a Pale Face, in any Gentn of Physick, Divinity or Law. It indicates search and study). Gives himself the alert, chearful Air and Behaviour of a Physician, not forgeting the solemn, important and wise. Warren is a pretty, tall, Genteel, fair faced young Gentn. Not quite so much Assurance in his Address, as Perkins, (perhaps because Perkins was present) Yet shewing fully that he knows the Utility thereof, and that he will soon, practice it in full Perfection.

The Doctors, having finished the Operation and left Us, their Directions and Medicines, took their Departure in infinite Haste, depend ont.

I have one Request to make, which is that you would be very careful in making Tom, Smoke all the Letters from me, very faithfully, before you, or any of the Family reads them, For, altho I shall never fail to smoke them myself before sealing, Yet I fear the Air of this House will be too much infected, soon, to be absolutely without Danger—and I would not you should take the Distemper, by Letter from me, for Millions. I write at a Desk far removed from any sick Room, and shall use all the Care I can, but too much cannot be used. I have written thus far, and it is 45 Minutes Past one O Clock and no more.

My Love to all. My hearty Thanks to Mamma for her kind Wishes. My Regards as due to Pappa, and should request his Prayers, which are always becoming, and especially at such Times, when We are undertaking any Thing of Consequence as the small Pox, undoubtedly, tho, I have not the Least Apprehension att all of what is called Danger.

I am as ever Yr

John Adams

Abigail Smith to John Adams

My Friend   Weymouth April th 16 1764

I think I write to you every Day. Shall not I make my Letters very cheep; don't you light your pipe with them? I care not if you do, tis a pleasure to me to write, yet I wonder I write to you with so little restraint, for as a critick I fear you more than any other person on Earth, and tis the only character, in which I ever did, or ever will fear you. What say you? Do you approve of that Speach? Dont you think me a Courageous Being? Courage is a laudable, a Glorious virtue in your Sex, why not in mine? (For my part, I think you ought to applaud me for mine.) Exit Rattle.

Solus your Diana.

And now pray tell me how you do, do you feel any venom working in your veins, did you ever before experience such a feeling? This Letter will be made up with questions I fancy—not set in order before you neither. How do you employ yourself? Do you go abroad yet? Is it not cruel to bestow those favours upon others which I should rejoice to receive, yet must be deprived of?

I have lately been thinking whether my Mamma—when I write again I will tell you Something. Did not you receive a Letter to Day by Hones? This is a right Girls Letter, but I will turn to the other side and be sober, if I can—but what is bred in the bone will never be out of the flesh, (as Lord M would have said).

As I have a good opportunity to send some Milk, I have not waited for your *orders;* least if I should miss this, I should not catch such an other. If you want more balm, I can supply you.

Adieu, evermore remember me with the tenderest affection, which is also borne unto you by your—

A Smith

Abigail Smith to John Adams

[*The letter begins on 19 April 1764.*]
Fryday Morning April th 20 [*1764*]

What does it Signify, why may not I visit you a Days as well as Nights? I no sooner close my Eyes than some invisible Being, Swift as the Alborack of Mahomet bears me to you. I see you, but cannot make my self visible to you. That tortures me, but it is still worse when I do not come for I am then haunted by half a dozen ugly Sprights. One will catch me and leep into the Sea, an other will carry me up a precipice (like that which Edgar describes to Lear,) then toss me down, and were I not then light as the Gosemore I should shiver into atoms. An other will be pouring down my throat stuff worse than the witches Broth in Macbeth. Where I shall be carried Next I know not, but I had rather have the small pox by inoculation half a dozen times, than be sprighted about as I am. What say you can you give me any encouragement to come? By the time you receive this hope from experience you will be able to say that the distemper is but a triffle. Think you I would not endure a triffle for the pleasure of seeing Lysander, yes were it ten times that triffle I would. But my own inclinations must not be followed—to Duty I sacrifice them. Yet O my Mamma forgive me if I say, you have forgot, or never knew—but hush. And do you Lysander excuse me that something I promis'd you, since it was a Speach more undutifull than that which I Just now stop'd my self in. For the present good by.

Fryday Evening

I hope you Smoke your Letters well, before you deliver them. Mamma is so fearful least I should catch the distemper, that she hardly ever thinks the Letters are Sufficently purified. Did you never rob a Birds nest? Do you remember how the poor Bird would fly round and round, fearful to come nigh, yet not know how to leave the place— just so they say I hover round Tom whilst he is smokeing my Letters.

But heigh day Mr, whats your Name? Who taught you to threaten so vehemently "A Character besides that of critick, in which if I never did, I always hereafter shall fear you."

Thou canst not prove a villan, imposible. I therefore still insist upon it, that I neither do, nor can fear thee. For my part I know not that there is any pleasure in being feard, but if there is, I hope you will be so generous as to fear your Diana that she may at least be made sensible of the pleasure. Mr Ayers will bring you this Letter—and the *Bag*. Do not repine—it is fill'd with Balm.

Here is Love, respects, regards, good wishes—a whole waggon load of them Sent you from all the good folks in the Neighbourhood.

To morrow makes the 14th Day. How many more are to come? I dare not trust my self with the thought. Adieu. Let me hear from you by mr Ayers—and excuse this very bad writing, if you had mended my pen it would have been better, once more adieu. Gold and Silver have I none, but such as I have, give I unto thee—which is the affectionate Regard of your—

A Smith

John Adams to Abigail Smith

Boston May 7th. 1764

I promised you, Sometime agone, a Catalogue of your Faults, Imperfections, Defects—or whatever you please to call them. I feel at present, pretty much at Leisure, and in a very suitable Frame of Mind to perform my Promise. But I must caution you, before I proceed to recollect yourself, and instead of being vexed or fretted or thrown into a Passion, to resolve upon a Reformation—for this is my sincere Aim, in laying before you, this Picture of yourself.

In the first Place, then, give me leave to say, you have been extreamly negligent, in attending so little to Cards. You have very litle Inclination, to that noble and elegant Diversion, and whenever you have taken an Hand you have held it but awkwardly and played it, with a very uncourtly, and indifferent, Air. Now I have Confidence enough in your good sense, to rely upon it, you will for the future endeavour to make a better Figure in this elegant and necessary Accomplishment.

Another Thing, which ought to be mentioned, and by all means amended, is, the Effect of a Country Life and Education, I mean, a certain Modesty, sensibility, Bashfulness, call it by which of these Names you will, that enkindles Blushes forsooth at every Violation of Decency, in Company, and lays a most insupportable Constraint on the freedom of Behaviour. Thanks to the late Refinements of modern manners, Hypocrisy, superstition, and Formality have lost all Reputation in the World and the Utmost sublimation of Politeness and Gentility lies, in Ease, and Freedom, or in other Words in a natural Air and Behaviour, and in expressing a satisfaction at whatever is suggested and prompted by Nature, which the aforesaid Violations of Decency, most certainly are.

In the Third Place, you could never yet be prevail'd on to learn to sing. This I take very soberly to be an Imperfection of the most moment of any. An Ear for Musick would be a source of much Pleasure, and a Voice and skill, would be a private solitary Amusement, of great Value when no other could be had. You must have remarked an Example of this in Mrs Cranch, who must in all probability have been deafened to Death with the Cries of her Betcy, if she had not drowned them in Musick *of her* own.

In the Fourth Place you very often hang your Head like a Bulrush.

You do not sit, erected as you ought by which Means, it happens that you appear too short for a Beauty, and the Company looses the sweet smiles of that Countenance and the bright sparkles of those Eyes. This Fault is the Effect and Consequence of another, still more inexcusable in a Lady, I mean an Habit of Reading, Writing and Thinking. But both the Cause and the Effect ought to be repented and amended as soon as, possible.

Another Fault, which seems to have been obstinately persisted in, after frequent Remonstrances, Advices and Admonitions of your Friends, is that of sitting with the Leggs across. This ruins the figure and the Air this injures the Health. And springs I fear from the former source vizt too much Thinking. These Things ought not to be!

A sixth Imperfection is that of Walking, with the Toes bending inward. This Imperfection is commonly called Parrot-toed, I think, I know not for what Reason. But it gives an Idea, the reverse of a bold and noble Air, the Reverse of the stately strutt, and the sublime Deportment.

Thus have I given a faithful Portraiture of all the Spotts, I have hitherto discerned in this Luminary. Have not regarded order, but have painted them as they arose in my Memory. Near Three Weeks have I conned and studied for more, but more are not to be discovered. All the rest is bright and luminous.

Having finished the Picture I finish my Letter, lest while I am recounting Faults, I should commit the greatest in a Letter, that of tedious and excessive Length. There's a prettily turned Conclusion for You! from yr

Lysander

Abigail Smith to John Adams

Weymouth May th 9 1764

Welcome, Welcome thrice welcome is Lysander to Braintree, but ten times more so would he be at Weymouth, whither you are affraid to come—Once it was not so. May not I come and see you, at least look thro a window at you? Should you not be glad to see your Diana? I flatter myself you would.

Your Brother brought your Letter, tho he did not let me see him, deliverd it the Doctor from whom received it safe. I thank you for your Catalogue, but must confess I was so hardned as to read over most of my Faults with as much pleasure, as an other person would have read their perfections. And Lysander must excuse me if I still persist in some of them, at least till I am convinced that an alteration would contribute to his happiness. Especially may I avoid that Freedom of Behaviour which according to the plan given, consists in Voilations of Decency, and which would render me unfit to Herd even with the Brutes. And permit me to tell you Sir, nor disdain to be a learner that there is Such a thing as Modesty without either Hypocricy or Formality.

As to a neglect of Singing, that I acknowledg to be a Fault which if posible shall not be complaind of a second time, nor should you have had occasion for it now, if I had not a voice harsh as the Screech of a Peacock.

The Capotal fault Shall be rectified, tho not with any hopes of being lookd upon as a Beauty, to appear agreeable in the Eyes of Lysander, has been for Years past, and still is the height of my ambition.

The 5th fault, will endeavour to amend of it, but you know I think that a gentleman has no business to concern himself about the Leggs of a Lady. For my part I do not apprehend any bad effects from the practise, yet since you desire it, and that you may not for the future trouble yourself so much about it, will reform.

The Sixth and last can be cured only by a Dancing School.

But I must not write more. I borrow a hint from you, therefore will not add to my faults that of a tedious Letter—a fault I never yet had reason to complain of in you, for however long, they never were otherways than agreeable to your own

A Smith

As John and Abigail prepared for marriage, they faced the task of establishing their own household. John had inherited from his father in 1761 a saltbox cottage and accompanying farm land near Penn's Hill in Braintree. Besides furnishing this home, they also had to locate appropriate servants to assist Abigail in managing the home and farm hands to work the lands, particularly during John's absences for his court rounds. To this home—later known as the John Quincy Adams Birthplace—Abigail and John "went to housekeeping" and began their family. Over the next eight years, Abigail gave birth to five children: Abigail 2d (Nabby, b. 1765), John Quincy (b. 1767), Susanna (b. 1768, d. 1770), Charles (b. 1770), and Thomas Boylston (b. 1772).

John Adams to Abigail Smith

My dear Diana   Septr. 30th. 1764

I have this Evening been to see the Girl. What Girl? Pray, what Right have you to go after Girls? Why, my Dear, the Girl I mentioned to you Miss Alice Brackett. But Miss has hitherto acted in the Character of an House-Keeper, and her noble aspiring Spirit had rather rise to be a Wife than descend to be a Maid.

To be serious, however, she says her Uncle, whose House she keeps cannot possibly Spare her, these two Months, if then, and she has no Thoughts of leaving him till the Spring, when she intends for Boston to become a Mantua Maker.

So that We are still to seek. Girls enough from fourteen to four and Twenty, are mentioned to me, but the Character of every Mothers Daughter of them is as yet problematical to me. Hannah Crane (pray dont you want to have her, my Dear) has sent several Messages to my Mother, that she will live with you as cheap, as any Girl in the Country. She is stout and able and for what I know willing, but I fear not honest, for which Reason I presume you will think of her no more.

Another Girl, one Rachael Marsh, has been recommended to me as a clever, Girl, and a neat one, and one that wants a Place. She was bred in the Family of one of our substantial Farmers and it is likely understands Country Business, But whether she would answer your Purposes, so well as another, I am somewhat in Doubt.

I have heard of a Number of younger Girls of Fourteen and thereabout, but these I suppose you would not choose.

It must therefore be left with you to make Enquiry, and determine for yourself. If you could hear of a suitable Person at Mistick or Newtown, on many Accounts she would be preferable to one, nearer home.

So much for Maids—now for the Man. I shall leave orders for Brackett, to go to Town, Wednesday or Thursday with an Horse Cart. You will get ready by that Time and ship aboard, as many Things as you think proper.

It happens very unfortunately that my Business calls me away at this Juncture for two Weeks together, so that I can take no Care at all about Help or Furniture or any Thing else. But Necessity has no Law.

Tomorrow Morning I embark for Plymouth—with a disordered stomach, a pale Face, an Aching Head and an Anxious Heart. And What Company shall I find there? Why a Number of bauling Lawyers, drunken Squires, and impertinent and stingy Clients. If you realize this, my Dear, since you have agreed to run fortunes with me, you will submit with less Reluctance to any little Disappointments and Anxieties you may meet in the Conduct of your own Affairs.

I have a great Mind to keep a Register of all the stories Squibbs, Gibes, and Compliments, I shall hear thro the whole Week. If I should I could entertain you with as much Wit, Humour, smut, Filth Delicacy,

Modesty and Decency, tho not with so exact Mimickry, as a certain Gentn. did the other Evening. Do you wonder, my Dear, why that Gentn. does not succeed in Business, when his whole study and Attention has so manifestly been engaged in the nobler Arts of smutt, Double Ententre, and Mimickry of Dutchmen and Negroes? I have heard that Imitators, tho they imitate well, Master Pieces in elegant and valuable Arts, are a servile Cattle. And that Mimicks are the lowest Species of Imitators, and I should think that Mimicks of Dutchmen and Negroes were the most sordid of Mimicks. If so, to what a Depth of the Profound have we plunged, that Gentns. Character. Pardon me, my dear, you know that Candour is my Characteristick—as it is undoubtedly of all the Ladies who are entertained with that Gents Conversation.

Oh my dear Girl, I thank Heaven that another Fortnight will restore you to me—after so long a separation. My soul and Body have both been thrown into Disorder, by your Absence, and a Month or two more would make me the most insufferable Cynick, in the World. I see nothing but Faults, Follies, Frailties and Defects in any Body, lately. People have lost all their good Properties or I my Justice, or Discernment.

But you who have always softened and warmed my Heart, shall restore my Benevolence as well as my Health and Tranquility of mind. You shall polish and refine my sentiments of Life and Manners, banish all the unsocial and ill natured Particles in my Composition, and form me to that happy Temper, that can reconcile, a quick Discernment with a perfect Candour.

Believe me, now and ever yr faithful

Lysander

P.S. My Duty to my worthy Aunt. Oh! I forget myself. My Prophetick Imagination has rap'd me into future Times. I mean, make my Compliments to Mrs Smith. And tell Betcy I wont expose her Midnight Walks to her Mamma, if she will be a good Girl.

Since the enclosed was written my Mother has informed me, that Molly Nash and her Mother too asked her to get a Place for Molly with me. She is a pretty, neat, Girl, and I believe has been well bred. Her Mother is a very clever Woman. The Girl is about 17.

But my Mother Says that Judah will do very well for your service this Winter. She is able to do a good deal of Business. And my mother farther says that she shall have no Occasion for her this Winter and that you may take her if you please and return her in the Spring, when it is likely she will have Occasion again for some Help and you will it is likely want some better Help.

This last Project is the most saving one. And Parcimony is a virtue that you and I must study. However I will submit to any Expence, for your Ease and Conveniency that I can possibly afford.

All these Things I mention to you, that you may weigh them [. . .] I shall acquiesce with Pleasure in your D[eterminat]ion.

Abigail Adams to John Adams

Sunday Eveng.

My Dearest Friend   Weymouth Sepbr 14 [*13*] 1767

The Doctor talks of Setting out tomorrow for New Braintree. I did not know but that he might chance to see you, in his way there. I know from the tender affection you bear me, and our little one's that you will rejoice to hear that we are well. Our Son is much better than when you left home, and our Daughter rock's him to Sleep, with the Song of "Come pappa come home to Brother Johnny." Sunday seems a more Lonesome Day to me than any other when you are absent, For tho I may be compared to those climates which are deprived of the sun half the year, yet upon a Sunday you commonly afforded us your benign influence. I am now at weymouth. My Father brought me here last night. To morrow I return home, where I hope soon to receive the Dearest of Friends and the tenderest of Husbands, with that unabated affection which has for years past, and will whilst the vital spark lasts, burn in the Bosom of your affectionate

A Adams

John Adams to Abigail Adams

My Dear   Septr. 17. 1771

There is no Business here—And I presume as little at Braintree. The Pause in the English Trade, has made Husbandmen and Manufacturers, and increased Industry and Frugality, and thereby diminished the Number of Debts and Debtors, and Suits and Suiters.

But the hourly Arrival of Ships from England deeply loaden with dry Goods, and the extravagant Credit that is dayly given to Country Traders, opens a Prospect very melancholly to the public, tho profitable to Us, of a Speedy revival of the suing Spirit. At present I feel, very easy and comfortable, at Leisure to read, and think. I hope all are well, shall come up tomorrow after noon, if Mr Austin comes down in the Morning.

Yr

John Adams

John Adams to Abigail Adams

My Dr   Plymouth May. Saturday 1772

I take an opportunity by Mr Kent, to let you know that I am at Plymouth, and pretty well. Shall not go for Barnstable untill Monday.

There are now signs of a gathering Storm, So I shall make my self easy here for the Sabbath. I wish myself at Braintree. This wandering, itinerating Life, grows more and more disagreable to me. I want to see my Wife and Children every Day, I want to see my Grass and Blossoms and Corn, &c every Day. I want to see my Workmen, nay I almost want to go and see the Bosse Calfs's as often as Charles does. But above all except the Wife and Children I want to See my Books.

None of these Amusements are to be had. The Company we have is not agreable to me. In Coll Warren and his Lady I find Friends, Mr Angier is very good, but farther than these, I have very little Pleasure in Conversation. Dont expect me, before Saturday. Perhaps Mrs. Hutchinson may call upon you, in her Return to Boston, the later End of next Week or beginning of the Week after.

Pray let the People take Care of the Caterpillars. Let them go over and over, all the Trees, till there is not the appearance of a nest, or Worm left.

John Adams

Abigail Adams to John Adams

Weymouth December 30 1773

Alass! How many snow banks devide thee and me and my warmest wishes to see thee will not melt one of them. I have not heard one word from thee, or our Little ones since I left home. I did not take any cold comeing down, and find myself in better Health than I was. I wish to hear the same account from you. The Time I proposed to tarry has Elapsed. I shall soon be home Sick. The Roads at present are impassible with any carriage. I shall not know how to content myself longer than the begining of Next week. I never left so large a flock of little ones before. You must write me how they all do. Tis now so near the Court that I have no expectation of seeing you here. My daily thoughts and Nightly slumbers visit thee—and thine. I feel gratified with the immagination at the close of the Day in seeing the little flock round you inquiring when Mamma will come home—as they often do for thee in thy absence.

If you have any news in Town which the papers do not communicate, pray be so good as to write it. We have not heard one Word respecting the Tea at the Cape or else where.

I have deliverd John the Bearer of this the key of your linnen. I hope you have been able to come at some by taking the Draw above it out. I should be obliged if you would send me that Book of mr Pembertons upon the classicks and the progress of Dullness which is at mr Cranchs.

You will not faill in remembring me to our little ones and telling Johnny that his Grand mama has sent him a pair of mittins—and charlly that I shall bring his when I come home. Our little Tommy you must kiss for Mamma, and bid Nabby write to me. Dont dissapoint me and let John return without a few lines to comfort the heart of your affectionate

Abigail Adams

Growing political tensions with Great Britain led to economic difficulties for Americans, particularly throughout New England. In the wake of the Boston Tea Party, the British Parliament acted quickly to punish Bostonians by closing Boston's port to all trade and enacting a series of so-called Coercive Acts that sought to reinforce Great Britain's control over Massachusetts. These acts galvanized opposition to Britain and spurred representatives from all of the American colonies to meet in Philadelphia in a Continental Congress. For John and Abigail, it meant a sharp reduction in John's law business but also a new opportunity: to represent Massachusetts on the national stage.

John Adams to Abigail Adams

My Dear   Boston May 12. 1774

I am extreamly afflicted, with the Relation your Father gave me, of the Return of your Disorder. I fear you have taken Some Cold. We have had a most pernicious Air, a great Part of this Spring. I am sure I have Reason to remember it—my Cold is the most obstinate and threatning one, I ever had in my Life: However, I am unwearied in my Endeavours to subdue it, and have the Pleasure to think I have had some Success. I rise at 5, walk 3 Miles, keep the Air all day and walk again in the Afternoon. These Walks have done me more good than any Thing—tho I have been constantly plied with Teas, and your Specific. My own Infirmities, the Account of the Return of yours, and the public News, coming alltogether have put my Utmost Phylosophy to the Tryal.

We live my dear Soul, in an Age of Tryal. What will be the Consequence I know not. The Town of Boston, for ought I can See, must Suffer Martyrdom: It must expire. And our principal Consolation is, that it dies in a noble Cause. The Cause of Truth, of Virtue, of Liberty and of Humanity, and that it will probably have a glorious Reformation, to greater Wealth, Splendor and Power than ever.

Let me know what is best for us to do. It is expensive keeping a Family here. And there is no Prospect of any Business in my Way in this Town this whole Summer. I dont receive a shilling a Week.

We must contrive as many Ways as we can, to save Expences—for We may have Calls to contribute, very largely in Proportion to our Circumstances, to prevent other very honest, worthy People from suffering for Want, besides our own Loss in Point of Business and Profit.

Dont imagine from all this that I am, in the Dumps. Far otherwise, I can truly say, that I have felt more Spirits and Activity, since the Arrival of this News, than I had done before for years. I look upon this, as the last Effort of Lord Norths Despair. And he will as surely be defeated in it, as he was in the Project of the Tea. I am, with great Anxiety for your Health your

John Adams

John Adams to Abigail Adams

My Dr   Ipswich June 23. 1774

I had a tollerable Journey hither, but my Horse trotted too hard. I miss my own Mare—however I must make the best of it.

I send with this an whole Packett of Letters, which are upon a Subject of great Importance, and therefore must intreat the earliest Conveyance of them.

There is but little Business here, and whether there will be more at York or Falmouth is uncertain, but I must take the Chance of them.

My Time, in these tedious Peregrinations, hangs heavily upon me. One half of it is always spent without Business, or Pleasure, or Diversion, or Books or Conversation. My Fancy and Wishes and Desires, are at Braintree, among my Fields, Pastures and Meadows, as much as those of the Israelites were among the Leeks, Garleeks and onions of the Land of Goshen.

My Sons and Daughter too are missing, as well as their Mother and I find nothing in any of my Rambles to supply their Place.

We have had a vast Abundance of Rain here this Week, and hope you have had a sufficiency with you. But the Plenty of it, will render, the Making of Hay the more critical, and you must exhort Bracket to be vigilant, and not let any of the Grass suffer, if he can help it.

I wish you would converse with Brackett, and Mr Hayden and Mr Belcher about a proper Time to get me a few freights of Marsh Mud, Flatts, or Creek Mudd. I must have some If I pay the Cash for getting it, at almost any Price. But I wont be answerable again to Dn Palmer, for the Schough. Whoever undertakes shall, hire that— and I will be chargeable to no Man but the Undertaker, and Labourers. I want a freight or two, soon, that it may be laid by the Wall and mixed with Dust and Dung that it may ferment and mix as soon as may be, now the hot Weather is coming on.

I want to be at Home, at this Time, to consider about Dress, Servant, Carriage, Horses &c &c for a Journey.

But—Kiss my sweet ones for me. Your

John Adams

John Adams to Abigail Adams

York July 1st: 1774

I am so idle, that I have not an easy Moment, without my Pen in my Hand. My Time might have been improved to some Purpose, in mowing Grass, raking Hay, or hoeing Corn, weeding Carrotts, picking or shelling Peas. Much better should I have been employed in schooling my Children, in teaching them to write, cypher, Latin French, English and Greek.

I sometimes think I must come to this—to be the Foreman upon my own Farm, and the school Master to my own Children.

I confess myself to be full of Fears that the Ministry and their Friends and Instruments, will prevail, and crush the Cause and Friends of Liberty. The Minds of that Party are so filled with Prejudices, against me, that they will take all Advantages, and do me all the Damage they can. These Thoughts have their Turns in my Mind, but in general my Hopes are predominant.

In a Tryal of a Cause here to Day, some Facts were mentioned, which are worth writing to you. It was sworn, by Dr Lyman, Elder Bradbury and others, that there had been a Number of Instances in this Town of fatal Accidents, happening from sudden Noises striking the Ears of Babes and young Children. A Gun was fired near one Child, as likely as any; the Child fell immediately into fits, which impaired his Reason, and is still living an Ideot. Another Child was sitting on a Chamber floor: A Man rapped suddenly and violently on the Boards which made the floor under the Child. The Child was so startled, and frightened, that it fell into fits, which never were cured.

This may suggest a Caution to keep Children from sudden Frights and surprizes.

Dr Gardiner arrived here to day, from Boston brings us News of a Battle at the Town Meeting, bet. Whigs and Tories, in which the Whiggs after a Day and an Halfs obstinate Engagement were finally victorious by two to one. He says the Tories are preparing a flaming Protest.

I am determined to be cool, if I can; I have suffered such Torments in my Mind, heretofore, as have almost overpowered my Constitution, without any Advantage: and now I will laugh and be easy if I can, let the Conflict of Parties, terminate as it will—let my own Estate and Interest suffer what it will. Nay whether I stand high or low in the Estimation of the World, so long as I keep a Conscience void of offence towards God and Man. And thus I am determined by the Will of God, to do, let what will become of me or mine, my Country, or the World.

I shall arouse myself ere long I believe, and exert an Industry a Frugality, a hard Labour, that will serve my family, if I cant serve my Country. I will not lie down and die in Dispair. If I cannot serve my Children by the Law, I will serve them by Agriculture, by Trade, by some Way, or other. I thank God I have a Head, an Heart and Hands which if once fully exerted alltogether, will succeed in the World as well as those of the mean spirited, low minded, fawning obsequious scoundrells who have long hoped, that my Integrity would be an Obstacle in my Way, and enable them to out strip me in the Race.

But what I want in Comparison of them, of Villany and servility I will make up in Industry and Capacity. If I dont they shall laugh and tryumph.

I will not willingly see Blockheads, whom I have a Right to despise, elevated above me, and insolently triumphing over me. Nor shall Knavery, through any Negligence of mine, get the better of Honesty nor Ignorance of Knowledge, nor Folly of Wisdom nor Vice of Virtue.

I must intreat you, my dear Partner in all the Joys and sorrows, Prosperity and Adversity of my Life, to take a Part with me in the struggle. I pray God for your Health—intreat you to rouse your whole Attention to the Family, the stock the Farm, the Dairy. Let every Article of Expence which can possibly be spared be retrench'd. Keep the Hands attentive to their Business. And the most prudent Measures of every kind be adopted and pursued with Alacrity and spirit.

I am &c

John Adams

John Adams to Abigail Adams

Falmouth July 6th: 1774

Our J[*ustic*]e H[*utchinso*]n, is eternally giving his Political Hints. In a Cause, this Morning, somebody named Captn. Mackay as a Refferee. I said "an honest Man"! "Yes" says H[*utchinso*]n, "he's an honest Man, only *misled*." "He he he," blinking, and grinning. At Dinner, to day—somebody mentioned Determinations in the Lords House (the Ct sitts in the Meeting House). "I've known many very bad Determinations in the Lords House of late" says he, meaning a Fling upon the Clergy. He is perpetually flinging about the Fasts, and ironically talking about getting Home to the Fast. A Gentn. told me, that he had heard him say frequently, that the Fast was perfect Blasphemy. "Why dont they pay for the Tea? and refuse to pay for the Tea!" and go to fasting and praying for Direction! perfect Blasphemy!

This is the Moderation, Candor, Impartiality, Prudence, Patience Forbearance, and Condescention of our J[*ustic*]e.

S[*amuel*] Q[*uincy*] said Yesterday, as Josa. told me, that he was for staying at home and not going to Meeting as they i.e. the Meetings are now managed.

Such is the Bitterness and Rancour, the Malice and Revenge, the Pride and Vanity which prevails in these Men—And such Minds are possessed of all the Power of the Province.

S. makes no Fortune this Ct. There is very little Business here, it is true, but S. gets very little of that little—less than any Body.

Wyer retains his old good Nature and good Humour, his Wit, such as it is, and his Fancy, with its, wildness.

Bradbury retains his Anxiety and his plaintive angry Manner, David Sewal his softness, and conceited Modesty.

Bradbury and Sewall always roast Dr Gardiner, at these Courts, but they have done it more now than usual, as Gardiner had not me to protect him. See how I think of myself!

I believe it is Time to think a little about my Family and Farm. The fine Weather, we have had for 8 or 10 days past I hope has been carefully improved to get in my Hay. It is a great Mortification to me that I could not attend every step of their Progress in mowing, making and carting. I long to see what Burden—But I long more still to see to the procuring more Sea Weed and Marsh Mud and sand &c.

However my Prospect is interrupted again I shall have no Time. I must prepare for a Journey to Philadelphia, a long Journey indeed! But if the Length of the Journey was all, it would be no burden. But the Consideration of What, is to be done, is of great Weight. Great Things are wanted to be done, and little Things only I fear can be done. I dread the Thought of the Congress's falling short of the Expectations of the Continent, but especially of the People of this Province.

Vapours avaunt! I will do my Duty, and leave the Event. If I have the approbation of my own Mind, whether applauded or censured blessed or cursed, by the World, I will not be unhappy.

Certainly I shall enjoy good Company, good Conversation, and shall have a fine Ride, and see a little more of the World than I have seen before.

I think it will be necessary to make me up, a Couple of Pieces of new Linnen. I am told, they wash miserably, at N. York, the Jerseys and Philadelphia too in Comparison of Boston, and am advised to carry a great deal of Linnen.

Whether to make me a Suit of new Cloaths, at Boston or to make them at Phyladelphia, and what to make I know not, nor do I know how I shall go—whether on Horse back, in a Curricle, a Phaeton, or altogether in a Stage Coach I know not.

The Letters I have written or may write, my Dear, must be kept secret or at least shewn with great Caution.

Mr Fairservice goes tomorrow: by him I shall send a Packett.

Kiss my dear Babes for me. Your

John Adams

I believe I forgot to tell you one Anecdote: When I first came to this House it was late in the afternoon, and I had ridden 35 miles at least. "Madam" said I to Mrs Huston, "is it lawfull for a weary Traveller to refresh himself with a Dish of Tea provided it has been honestly Smuggled, or paid no Duties"?

"No sir, said she, we have renounced all Tea in this Place. I cant make Tea, but I'le make you Coffee." Accordingly I have drank Coffee every afternoon since, and have borne it very well. Tea must be universally renounced. I must be weaned, and the sooner, the better.

"The Decisive Day Is Come"

AUGUST 1774–DECEMBER 1775

*John set out from Boston for Philadelphia to attend the Continental Congress on
10 August, accompanied by three other Massachusetts delegates. Stopping along
the way at various towns in New England, New York, and New Jersey, the group
reached Philadelphia on 29 August. While there, John stayed at the home of Sarah Yard, whose lodgings he would occupy through the spring of 1777 whenever
he was in the city.*

*The First Continental Congress met until late October, then adjourned until
May 1775, when the Second Continental Congress opened. During the first session, the delegates agreed to a series of resolves declaring its opposition to the Coercive Acts and initiated a boycott of British goods. They also drafted a petition to
King George III asking for redress but stopped well short of declaring independence.*

*Abigail and John kept up a remarkably steady correspondence despite the haz-
ards of war and British attempts to intercept their letters. As part of their first extended separation—and one marked by the longest physical distance to date—
they had to adjust to the length of time it could take for letters to travel back and
forth and the difficulty of maintaining ongoing communications. Small wonder,
then, that both Abigail and John spoke often of the emotional significance of this
correspondence during such a troubled time.*

Abigail Adams to John Adams

Braintree August 19 1774

The great distance between us, makes the time appear very long to me. It seems already a month since you left me. The great anxiety I feel for my country for you and for our family renders the day tedious, and the Night unpleasent. The Rocks and quick Sands appear upon every Side. What course you can or will take is all wrapt in the Bosom of futurity. Uncertainty and expectation leave the mind great Scope. Did ever any Kingdom or State regain their Liberty, when once it was invaded without Blood Shed? I cannot think of it with out horror. Yet we are told that all the Misfortunes of Sparta were occasiond by their too great Sollicitude for present tranquility, and by an excessive love of peace they neglected the means of making it sure and lasting. They ought to have reflected says polibius that as there is nothing more desirable, or advantages than peace, when founded in justice and honour, so there is nothing more shameful and at the same time more pernicious when attained by bad measures, and purchased at the price of liberty.

I have received a most charming Letter from our Friend Mrs. W[arre]n. She desires me to tell you that her best wishes attend you thro your journey both as a Friend and patriot—hopes you will have no uncommon difficulties to surmount or Hostile Movements to impeade you—but if the Locrians should interrupt you, she hops you will beware that no future Annals may say, you chose an ambitious Philip for your Leader, who subverted the Noble order of the American Amphyctions, and built up a Monarchy on the Ruins of the happy institution.

I have taken a very great fondness for reading Rollin's ancient History since you left me. I am determined to go thro with it if posible in these my days of solitude. I find great pleasure and entertainment from it—and I have persuaided Johnny to read me a page or two every day—and hope he will from his desire to oblige me entertain a fondness for it. We have had a charming rain which lasted 12 hours and has greatly revived the dying fruits of the Earth.

I want much to hear from you. I long impatiently to have you upon the Stage of action. The first of September or the month of September, perhaps may be of as much importance to great Britan as the Ides of March were to ceaser. I wish you every Publick as well, as private blessing—and that wisdom which is profitable both for instruction and Edification to conduct you in this difficult Day. The little flock remember Pappa, and kindly wish to see him. So does your most affectionate

Abigail Adams

John Adams to Abigail Adams

My Dr   Prince Town New Jersey Aug. 28th. 1774

I received your kind Letter, at New York, and it is not easy for you to imagine the Pleasure it has given me. I have not found a single opportunity to write since I left Boston, excepting by the Post and I dont choose to write by that Conveyance, for fear of foul Play. But as We are now within forty two Miles of Philadelphia, I hope, there to find some private Hand by which I can convey this.

The Particulars of our Journey, I must reserve, to be communicated after my Return. It would take a Volume to describe the whole. It has been upon the whole an Agreable Jaunt, We have had Opportunities to see the World, and to form Acquaintances with the most eminent and famous Men, in the several Colonies we have passed through. We have been treated with unbounded Civility, Complaisance, and Respect.

We Yesterday visited Nassau Hall Colledge, and were politely treated by the Schollars, Tutors, Professors and President, whom We are, this Day to hear preach. Tomorrow We reach the Theatre of Action. God Almighty grant us Wisdom and Virtue Sufficient for the high Trust that is devolved upon Us. The spirit of the People wherever we have been seems to be very favourable. They universally consider our Cause as their own, and express the firmest Resolution, to abide the Determination of the Congress.

I am anxious for our perplexed, distressed Province—hope they will be directed into the right Path. Let me intreat you, my Dear, to make yourself as easy and quiet as possible. Resignation to the Will of Heaven is our only Resource in such dangerous Times. Prudence and Caution should be our Guides. I have the strongest Hopes, that We shall yet see, a clearer Sky, and better Times.

Remember my tender Love to my little Nabby. Tell her she must write me a Letter and inclose it in the next you send. I am charmed with your Amusement with our little Johnny. Tell him I am glad to hear he is so good a Boy as to read to his Mamma, for her Entertainment, and to keep himself out of the Company of rude Children. Tell him I hope to hear a good Account of his Accidence and Nomenclature, when I return. Kiss my little Charley and Tommy for me. Tell them I shall be at Home by November, but how much sooner I know not.

Remember me to all enquiring Friends—particularly to Uncle Quincy your Pappa and Family, and Dr Tufts and Family. Mr Thaxter, I hope, is a good Companion, in your Solitude. Tell him, if he devotes his Soul and Body to his Books, I hope, notwithstanding the Darkness of these Days, he will not find, them unprofitable Sacrifices in future.

I have received three very obliging Letters, from Tudor, Trumble, and Hill. They have cheared us, in our Wanderings, and done us much Service.

My Compliments to Mr Wibirt and Coll Quincy, when you see them.

Your Account of the Rain refreshed me. I hope our Husbandry is prudently and industriously managed. Frugality must be our support. Our Expences, in this Journey, will be very great—our only Reward will be the consolatory Reflection that We toil, spend our Time, and tempt Dangers for the public Good. Happy indeed, if we do any good!

The Education of our Children is never out of my Mind. Train them to Virtue habituate them to industry, activity, and Spirit. Make them consider every Vice, as shamefull and unmanly: fire them with Ambition to be usefull—make them disdain to be destitute of any usefull, or ornamental Knowledge or Accomplishment. Fix their Ambition upon great and solid Objects—and their Contempt upon little, frivolous, and useless ones. [It] is Time, my dear, for you to begin to teach them French. Every Decency Grace, and Honesty should be inculcated upon them.

I have keep a few Minutes by Way of Journal, which shall be your Entertainment when I come home. But We have had so many Persons and so various Characters to converse with, and so many Objects to view, that I have not been able to be so particular as I could wish. I am, with the tenderest Affection and Concern, your wandering

John Adams

Given the limits of communication at this time, the prevalence of exaggerated rumors is hardly surprising. The "dreadfull Catastrophy" John fears in the following letter was in reality merely the seizure of powder stored in the arsenal in Boston for transfer to Castle Island in Boston Harbor.

John Thaxter and Nathan Rice were two of John's law clerks, both left behind when John departed for Philadelphia. Thaxter, a cousin of Abigail's, eventually became John Quincy Adams's tutor in Europe, while Rice left the legal profession to enlist in the Continental Army in 1775.

John Adams to Abigail Adams

My Dear   Phyladelphia Septr. 8. 1774

When or where this Letter will find you, I know not. In what Scenes of Distress and Terror, I cannot foresee. We have received a confused Account from Boston, of a dreadfull Catastrophy. The Particulars, We have not heard. We are waiting with the Utmost Anxiety and Impatience, for further Intelligence.

The Effect of the News We have both upon the Congress and the Inhabitants of this City, was very great—great indeed! Every Gentleman seems to consider the Bombardment of Boston, as the Bombardment, of the Capital of his own Province. Our Deliberations are grave and serious indeed.

It is a great affliction to me that I cannot write to you oftener than I do. But there are so many Hindrances, that I cannot.

It would fill Volumes, to give you an Idea of the scenes I behold and the Characters I converse with.

We have so much Business, so much Ceremony, so much Company, so many Visits to recive and return, that I have not Time to write. And the Times are such, as render it imprudent to write freely.

We cannot depart from this Place, untill the Business of the Congress is compleated, and it is the general Disposition to proceed slowly. When I shall be at home I cant say. If there is Distress and Danger in Boston, pray invite our Friends, as many as possible, to take an Assylum with you. Mrs Cushing and Mrs Adams if you can.

There is in the Congress a Collection of the greatest Men upon this Continent, in Point of Abilities, Virtues and Fortunes. The Magnanimity, and public Spirit, which I see here, makes me blush for the sordid venal Herd, which I have seen in my own Province. The Addressers, and the new Councillors, are held in universal Contempt and Abhorrence, from one End of the Continent to the other.

Be not, under any Concern for me. There is little Danger from any Thing We shall do, at the Congress. There is such a spirit, thro the Colonies, and the Members of the Congress are such Characters, that no Danger can happen to Us, which will not involve the whole Continent, in Universal Desolation, and in that Case who would wish to live?

Make my Compliments to Mr Thaxter and Mr Rice—and to every other of my Friends. My Love to all my dear Children—tell them to be good, and to mind their Books. I shall come home and see them, I hope, the latter End of next Month.

Adieu.

John Adams

Abigail Adams to John Adams

Dearest Friend   Braintree Sepbr 14 1774

Five weeks have past and not one line have I received. I had rather give a dollar for a letter by the post, tho the consequence should be that I Eat but one meal a day for these 3 weeks to come. Every one I see is inquiring after you and when did I hear. All my intelligance is collected from the News paper and I can only reply that I saw by that, that you arrived such a day. I know your fondness for writing and your inclination to Let me hear from you by the first safe conveyance which makes me suspect that some Letter or other has miscaried, but I hope now you have arrived at Philidelphia you will find means to convey me some inteligance. We are all well here. I think I enjoy better Health than I have done these 2 years. I have not been to Town since I parted with you there. The Govenor is making all kinds of warlike preperations such as mounting cannon upon Beacon Hill, diging entrenchments upon the Neck placeing cannon there, encamping a regiment there throwing up Brest works &c &c. The People are much allarmed, and the select men have waited upon him in concequence of it. The county congress have also sent a committee—all which proceedings you will have a more particuliar account of than I am able to give you from the publick papers. But as to the Movements of this Town perhaps you may not hear them from any other person. In consequence of the Powders being taken from charlstown, a General alarm spread thro many Towns and was caught pretty soon here. The report took here a fryday, and a Sunday a Soldier was seen lurking about the common Supposed to be a Spy, but most likely a Deserter.

However inteligence of it was communicated to the other Parishes—
and about 8 oclock a sunday Evening there pass by here about 200
Men, preceeded by a horse cart, and marched down to the powder
house from whence they took the powder and carried into the other
parish and there Secreeted it. I opened the window upon there return.
They pass'd without any Noise, not a word among them till they came
against this house, when some of them perceiveing me, askd me if I
wanted any powder. I replied not since it was in so good hands. The
reason they gave for taking it, was that we had so many Tories here
they dare not trust us with it. They had taken Vinton in their Train,
and upon their return they stoped between Cleverlys and Etters—and
calld upon him to deliver two Warrents. Upon his producing them,
they put it to vote whether they should burn them and it pass'd in the
affirmitive. They then made a circle and burnt them. They then call'd
a vote whether they should huzza, but it being Sunday Evening it
passd in the Negative. They call'd upon Vinton to swear that he would
never be instrumental in carrying into execution any of these New
atcts. They were not satisfied with his answers however they let him
rest. A few Days after upon his making some foolish speaches, they assembled to the amount of 2 and 2 hundred, swore vengance upon him
unless he took a solemn oath. Accordingly, they chose a committee
and sent with him to Major Miller to see that he complied, and they
waited his return, which proving satisfactory they disperced. This
Town appear as high as you can well immagine—and if necessary
would soon be in arms. Not a Tory but hides his head. The church
parson thought they were comeing after him, and run up garret they
say, an other jumpt out of his window and hid among the corn whilst a
third crept under his bord fence, and told his Beads.

September 16 1774

I Dined to Day at Coll Quincys. They were so kind as to send me,
and Nabby and Betsy an in vitation to spend the Day with them—and
as I had not been to see them since I removed to Braintree, I accepted

the invitation. After I got there, came Mr Samll Quincys wife and mr Sumner mr Josiah and Wife—a little classing of parties you may be sure. Mr Sam's Wife said she thought it high time for her Husband to turn about, he had not done half so clever since he left her advice. Said they both greatly admired, the most Excellent and much admired speach of the Bishop of st Asaph which suppose you have seen. It meets, and most certainly merrits the greatest encomiums.

Upon my return at Night mr Thaxter met me at the door with your Letter Dated from Prince town new Jersy. It really gave me such a flow of Spirits that I was not composed eno to sleep till one oclock. You make no mention of one I wrote you previous to that you received by mr Breck and sent by mr Cunningham. I am rejoiced to hear you are well; I want to know many more pertiuliars than you wrote me, and hope soon to hear from you again. I dare not trust myself with the thought of how long you may perhaps be absent. I only count the weeks already past—and they amount to 5. I am not so lonely as I should have been, without my two Neighbours. We make a table full at meal times, all the rest of their time they spend in the office. Never were two persons who gave a family less trouble than they do. It is at last determined that mr Rice keep the School here. Indeed he has kept ever since he has been here, but not with any expectation that He should be continued, but the people finding no small difference between, him and his predecessor chose he should be continued. I have not sent Johnny. He goes very steadily to mr Thaxter who I believe takes very good care of him—and as they seem to have a likeing to each other believe it will be best to continue him with him. However when you return we can then consult what will be best. I am certain that if he does not get so much good, he gets less harm—and I have always thought it of very great importance that children should in the early part of life be unaccustomed to such examples as would tend to corrupt the purity of their Words and actions that they may chill with horrour at the sound of an oath, and bluss with indignation at an obscene expression. These first principal which grow with their growth and strengthen with their strength neither time nor custom can totally eradicate. You will perhaps be tired no let it serve by way of relaxation from the more important concerns of the Day, and be such an amusement as your little hermitage used to afford you here. You have before you to express myself in the words of the Bishop the greatest National concerns that ever came before any people—and if the Prayers and peti[*ti*]ons assend unto Heaven which are daily offered for you, wisdom will flow down as a streem and Rithousness as the mighty waters—and your deliberations will make glad the cities of our God.

I was very sorry I did not know of mr Cary's going. It would have been so good an opportunity to have sent this as I lament the loss of. You have heard no doubt of the peoples preventing the court from Setting in various counties, and last week in Taunton, Anger urged the courts opening, and calling out the action, but could not effect it.

I saw a Letter from Miss Eunice wherein she gives an account of it, and says there were 2000 men assembled round the court house and by a committee of Nine presented a petition requesting that they would not set—and with the uttmost order waited 2 hours for there answer—when they disperced.

Your family all desire to be remembered to you, as well as unkle Quincy who often visits me, to have an hour of sweet communion upon politicks with me. Coll Quincy desires his complements to you. Dr Tufts sends his Love and your Mother and Brothers also. I have lived a very recluse life since your absence, seldom going any where except to my Fathers who with My Mother and sister desire to be rememberd to you. My Mother has been exceeding low, but is a little better. How warm your climate may be I know not, but I have had my bed warmed these two nights. I must request you to procure me some watermellon Seads and Muskmellon, as I determine to be well stocked with them an other year. We have had some fine rains, but as soon as the corn is gatherd you must release me of my promise. The Drougth has renderd cutting a Second crop impracticable, feeding a little cannot hurt it. However I hope you will be at home to be convinced of the utility of the measure. You will burn all these Letters least they should fall from your pocket and thus Expose your most affectionate Friend

Abigail Adams

Abigail Adams to John Adams

Boston Garison Sepbr 22 1774

I have just returnd from a visit to my Brother, with my Father who carried me there the day before yesterday, and call'd here in my return to see this much injured Town. I view it with much the same sensations that I should the body of a departed Friend—only put of its present Glory, for to rise finally to a more happy state. I will not despair, but will believe that our cause being good we shall finally prevail. The Maxim in time of peace prepair for war, (if this may be call'd a time of peace) resounds throughout the Country. Next tweseday they are warned at Braintree all above 15 and under 60 to attend with their arms, and to train once a fort night from that time, is a scheme which lays much at heart with many.

Scot has arrived, and brings news that he expected to find all peace and Quietness here as he left them at home. You will have more particuliars than I am able to send you from much better hands. There has been in Town a conspiracy of the Negroes. At present it is kept pretty private and was discoverd by one who endeavourd to diswaid them from it—he being threatned with his life, applied to justice Quincy for protection. They conducted in this ways, got an Irishman to draw up a petition to the Govener telling him they would fight for him provided he would arm them and engage to liberate them if he conquerd, and it is said that he attended so much to it as to consult Pircy upon it—and one [Leit?] Small has been very buisy and active. There is but little said, and what Steps they will take in consequence of it I know not. I wish most Sincerely there was not a Slave in the province. It allways appeard a most iniquitious Scheme to me, fight ourselfs for what we are daily robbing and plundering from those who have as good a right to freedom as we have. You know my mind upon this Subject. I left all our little ones well, and shall return to them to Night. I hope to hear from you by the return of the bearer of this and by Revere. I long for the Day of your return, yet look upon you much safer where you are, but know it will not do for you. Not one action has been brought to this court, no buisness of any sort in your way. All Law ceases, and the Gosple will soon follow—for they are supporters of each other. Adieu. My Father hurries me. Yours most Sincerely

Abigail Adams

John Adams to Abigail Adams

My Dear   Phyladelphia Octr. 9. 1774

I am wearied to Death with the Life I lead. The Business of the Congress is tedious, beyond Expression. This Assembly is like no other that ever existed. Every Man in it is a great Man—an orator, a Critick, a statesman and therefore every Man upon every Question must shew his oratory, his Criticism and his Political Abilities.

The Consequence of this is, that Business is drawn and spun out to an immeasurable Length. I believe if it was moved and seconded that We should come to a Resolution that Three and two make five We should be entertained with Logick and Rhetorick Law, History, Politicks and Mathematicks, concerning the Subject for two whole Days, and then We should pass the Resolution unanimously in the Affirmative.

The perpetual Round of feasting too, which we are obliged to Submit to, make the Pilgrimage more tedious to me.

This Day I went to Dr Allisons Meeting in the Forenoon and heard the Dr—a good Discourse upon the Lords Supper. This is a Presbyterian Meeting. I confess I am not fond of the Presbyterian Meetings in this Town. I had rather go to Church. We have better Sermons, better Prayers, better Speakers, Softer, Sweeter Musick, and genteeler Company. And I must confess, that the Episcopal Chh is quite as agreable to my Taste as the Presbyterian. They are both Slaves to the Domination of the Priesthood. I like the Congregational Way best—next to that the Independant.

This afternoon, led by Curiosity and good Company I Strolled away to Mother Church, or rather Grandmother Church, I mean the Romish Chappell. Heard a good, Short, moral Essay upon the Duty of Parents to their Children, founded in Justice and Charity, to take care of their Interests temporal and spiritual. This afternoons Entertainment, was to me, most awfull and affecting. The poor Wretches, fingering their Beads—chanting Latin, not a Word of Which they understood—their Pater Nosters and Ave Maria's. Their holy Water—their Crossing themselves perpetually—their Bowing to the Name of Jesus, wherever they hear it—their Bowings, and Kneelings, and Genuflections before the Altar. The Dress of the Priest was rich with Lace—his Pulpit was Velvet and Gold. The Altar Pice was very rich—little Images and Crucifixes about—Wax Candles—lighted up. But how shall I describe, the Picture of our Saviour in a Frame of Marble over the Altar at full Length upon the Cross, in the Agonies, and the Blood dropping and Streaming from his Wounds.

The Musick consisting of an organ, and a Choir of singers, went all the afternoon, excepting sermon Time—and the assembly chanted—most sweetly and exquisitely. Here is every Thing which can lay hold of the Eye Ear, and Imagination. Every Thing which can charm and bewitch the simple and ignorant. I wonder how Luther ever broke the spell.

Adieu

John Adams

Abigail Adams to John Adams

My Much Loved Friend   Braintree october 16 1774

I dare not Express to you at 300 hundred miles distance how ardently I long for your return. I have some very miserly Wishes; and cannot consent to your spending one hour in Town till at least I have had you 12. The Idea plays about my Heart, unnerves my hand whilst I write, awakens all the tender Sentiments that years have encreased and Matured, and which when with me were every day dispensing to you. The whole collected stock of ten weeks absence knows not how to brook any Longer restraint, but will break forth and flow thro my pen. May the Like Sensations enter thy breast (, and in spite of all the weighty cares of state) Mingle themselves with those I wish to communicate—for in giving them utterance I have felt more sincere pleasure than I have known since the 10 of August. Many have been the anxious hours I have spent since that day—the threatening aspect of our publick affairs the complicated distress of this province, the Arduous and perplexed Buisness in which you are engaged, have all conspired to agitate my bosom, with fears and apprehensions to which I have heretofore been a stranger, and far from thinking the Scene closed, it looks as tho the curtain was but just drawn and only the first Scene of the infernal plot disclosed and whether the end will be tragical Heaven alone know's. You cannot be I know, nor do I wish to see you an inactive Spectator—but if the Sword be drawn I bid adieu to all domestick felicity, and look forward to that Country where there is neither wars nor rumors of War in a firm belief that thro the mercy of its King we shall both rejoice there together. I greatly fear that the arm of treachery and voilence is lifted over us as a Scourge and heavy punishment from heaven for our numerous offences, and for the misimprovement of our great advantages. If we expect to inherit the blessings of our Fathers, we should return a little more to their primitive Simplicity of Manners, and not Sink into inglorious ease. We have too many high sounding words, and too few actions that correspond with them. I have spent one Sabbeth in Town since you left me. I saw no difference in respect to ornaments, &c &c but in the Country you must look for that virtue, of which you find but small glimerings in the Metropolis. Indeed they have not the advantages, nor the resolution to encourage our own Manufactories which people in the country have. To the Mercantile part, tis considerd as throwing away their own

Bread; but they must retrench their expenses and be content with a small share of gain for they will find but few who will wear their Livery. As for me I will seek wool and flax and work willingly with my Hands, and indeed their is occasion for all our industry and Economy. You mention the removal of our Books &c from Boston. I believe they are safe there, and it would incommode the Gentlemen to remove them, as they would not then have a place to repair to for study. I suppose they would not chuse to be at the expence of bording out. Mr Williams I believe keeps pretty much with his mother. Mr Hills father had some thoughts of removing up to Braintree provided he could be accommodated with a house, which he finds very difficult.

Mr Cranch's last determination was to tarry in Town unless any thing new takes place. His Friends in Town oppose his Removal so much that he is determind to stay. The opinion you have entertaind of General Gage is I believe just, indeed he professes to act only upon the Defensive. The People in the Co[untry] begin to be very anxious for the congress to rise. They have no Idea of the weighty Buisness you have to transact, and their Blood boils with indignation at the Hostile prepairations they are constant witnesses of. Mr Quincys so secret departure is Matter of various Specc007lation—some say he is Deputed by the congress, others that he is gone to Holland, and the Tories says he is gone to be hanged.

I rejoice at the favourable account you give me of your Health; May it be continued to you. My Health is much better than it was last fall. Some folks say I grow very fat. I venture to write most any thing in this Letter, because I know the care of the Bearer. He will be most sadly dissapointed if you should be broke up before he arrives, as he is very desirous of being introduced by you to a Number of Gentlemen of respectable characters. I almost envy him, that he should see you, before I can.

Mr Thaxter and Rice present their Regards to you. Unkle Quincy too sends his Love to you. He is very good to call and see me, and so have Many other of my Friends been. Coll Warren and Lady were here a monday, and send their Love to you. The Coll promiss'd to write. Mrs

Warren will spend a day or two on her return with me. I told Betsy to write to you. She says she would if you were her *Husband*.

Your Mother sends her Love to you—and all your family too Numerous to Name desire to be rememberd. You will Receive Letters from two, who are as earnest to write to Pappa as if the welfare of a kingdom depended upon it. If you can give any guess within a month Let me know when you think of returning to your most Affectionate

Abigail Adams

The months between the first two meetings of the Continental Congress were lively ones for the revolutionary cause. John returned home to Abigail and Braintree, where he stayed for the duration. During that time, he attended sessions of the first Provincial Congress in Cambridge and wrote his "Novanglus" essays in Boston.

Meanwhile, events were quickly outpacing congressional action. The Battles of Lexington and Concord on 19 April 1775 and the beginning of the siege of Boston radicalized New Englanders. Accommodation with Britain seemed increasingly unlikely and talk of independence became more common. The siege also sent numerous refugees to towns like Braintree, a problem confronting Abigail and complicating her attempts to keep the farm running in John's absence. The war—still a theoretical problem for most congressional delegates—had become her day-to-day reality.

John Adams to Abigail Adams

My Dear   Hartford May 2d. 1775

Mr Eliot of Fairfield, is this Moment arrived in his Way to Boston. He read us a Letter from the Dr. his Father dated Yesterday Sennight being Sunday. The Drs Description of the Melancholly of the Town, is enough to melt a Stone. The Tryals of that unhappy and devoted People are likely to be severe indeed. God grant that the Furnace of

Affliction may refine them. God grant that they may be relieved from their present Distress.

It is Arrogance and Presumption in human Sagacity to pretend to penetrate far into the Designs of Heaven. The most perfect Reverence and Resignation becomes us. But, I cant help depending upon this, that the present dreadfull Calamity of that beloved Town is intended to bind the Colonies together in more indissoluble Bands, and to animate their Exertions, at this great Crisis in the Affairs of Man kind. It has this Effect, in a most remarkable Degree, as far as I have yet seen or heard. It will plead, with all America, with more irresistable Perswasion, than Angells trumpet tongued.

In a Cause which interests the whole Globe, at a Time, when my Friends and Country, are in such keen Distress, I am scarcely ever interrupted, in the least Degree, by Apprehensions for my Personal Safety. I am often concerned for you and our dear Babes, surrounded as you are by People who are too timorous and too much susceptible of allarms. Many Fears and Jealousies and imaginary Dangers, will be suggested to you, but I hope you will not be impressed by them.

In Case of real Danger, of which you cannot fail to have previous Intimations, fly to the Woods with our Children. Give my tenderest Love to them, and to all.

John Adams to Abigail Adams

New York May 8. 1775

I have an opportunity by Captn. Beale, to write you a Line. We all arrived last Night in this City. It would take many sheets of Paper, to give you a Description of the Reception, We found here. The Militia were all in Arms, and almost the whole City out to Meet us. The Tories, are put to Flight here, as effectually as the Mandamus Council at Boston. They have associated, to Stand by Continental and Provincial Congresses, &c &c. &c. Such a spirit was never seen in New York.

Jose Bass met with a Misfortune, in the Midst of some of the unnecessary Parade that was made about us. My Mare, being galled with an ugly Buckle in the Tackling suddenly flinched and started in turning short round a Rock, in a shocking bad Road, overset the sulky which frightened her still more. She ran, and dashed the Body of the sulky all to Pieces. I was obliged to leave my sulky, ship my Bagage on board Mr Cushings Carriage, buy me a Saddle and mount on Horse back. I am thankfull that Bass was not kill'd. He was in the utmost danger, but not materially hurt. I am sorry for this Accident, both on Account of the Trouble and Expence, occasioned by it. I must pay your Father for his sulky. But in Times like these, such little Accidents should not affect us.

Let me caution you my Dear, to be upon your Guard against that Multitude of Affrights, and Alarms, which I fear, will surround you. Yet I hope the People with you, will grow more composed than they were.

Our Prospect of a Union of the Colonies, is promising indeed. Never was there such a Spirit. Yet I feel anxious, because, there is always more Smoke than Fire—more Noise than Musick.

Our Province is nowhere blamed. The Accounts of the Battle are exaggerated in our favour. My Love to all. I pray for you all—and hope to be prayed for. Certainly, There is a Providence—certainly, We must depend upon Providence or We fail. Certainly the sincere Prayers of good Men, avail much. But Resignation, is our Duty in all Events. I have this Day heard Mr Livingston in the Morning and Dr Rogers this afternoon—excellent Men, and excellent Prayers and sermons.

My Love to Nabby, Johnny, Charly and Tommy. Tell them they must be good, and Pappa, will come home, before long.

Abigail Adams to John Adams

24 May B[*raintre*]e 1775

Suppose you have had a formidable account of the alarm we had last Sunday morning. When I rose about six oclock I was told that the Drums had been some time beating and that 3 allarm guns were fired, that weymouth Bell had been ringing and mr Welds was then ringing. I immediatly sent of an express to know the occasion, and found the whole Town in confusion. 3 Sloops and one cutter had come out, and droped anchor just below great Hill. It was difficult to tell their design, some supposed they were comeing to Germantown others to Weymouth. People women children from the Iron Works flocking down this way—every women and child drove of from below my Fathers. My Fathers family flying, the Drs in great distress, as you may well immagine for my Aunt had her Bed thrown into a cart, into which she got herself, and orderd the boy to drive her of to Bridgwater which he did. The report was to them, that 300 hundred had landed, and were upon their march up into Town. The allarm flw lightning, and men from all parts came flocking down till 2000 were collected, but it seems their Expidition was to Grape Island for *Levets* hay. There it was impossible to reach them for want of Boats, but the sight of so many persons, and the fireing at them prevented their getting more than 3 ton of Hay, tho they had carted much more down to the water. At last they musterd a Lighter, and a sloop from Hingham which had six port holes. Our men eagerly jumpt on board, and put of for the Island. As soon as they perceived it, they decamped. Our people landed upon Island, and in an instant set fire to the Hay which with the Barn was soon consumed, about 80 ton tis said. We Expect soon to be in continual alarms, till something decisive takes place. We wait with longing Expectation in hopes to hear the best accounts from you with regard to union and harmony &c. We rejoice greatly on the Arival of Doctor Franklin, as he must certainly be able to inform you very perticuliarly of the situation of affairs in England. I wish you would if you can get time; be as perticuliar as you *may,* when you write—every one here abouts come to me to hear what accounts I have. I was so unlucky as not to get the Letter you wrote at New York. Capn Beals forgot it, and left it behind. We have a flying report here with regard to New York, but cannot give any credit to, as yet, That they had been engaged with the Ships which Gage sent there and taken them with great looss upon both Sides.

Yesterday we have an account of 3 ships comeing in to Boston. I believe it is true, as there was a salute from the other ships, tho I have not been able to learn from whence they come. Suppose you have had an account of the fire which did much damage to the warehouses— and added greatly to the distresses of the inhabitants whilst it contin- ued. The bad conduct of General Gage was the means of its doing so much damage.

Tis a fine growing season having lately had a charming rain, which was much wanted as we had none before for a fortnight. Your meadow is almost fit to mow. Isaac talks of leaving you, and going into the Army. I believe he will. Mr Rice has a prospect of an *adjutant* place in the Army. I believe he will not be a very hardy soldier. He has been sick of a fever above this week, and has not been out of His chamber. He is upon the recovery now.

Our House has been upon this alarm in the same scene of confusion that it was upon the first—soldiers comeing in for lodging for Break- fast, for Supper, for Drink &c &c. Sometimes refugees from Boston tierd and fatigued, seek an assilum for a Day a Night—a week. You can hardly imagine how we live.

> "Yet to the Houseless child of want
> our Doors are open still.
> And tho our portions are but scant
> we give them with good will."

I want to know how you do? How are your Eyes? Is not the weather very hot where you are? The children are well and send Duty to Pappa. This day Month you set of. I have never once inquired when you think it posible to return; as I think you could not give me any satisfactory answer. I have according to your direction wrote to mr Dilly, and given it to the care of Capn Beals who will deliver it with his own hand; I got mr Thaxter to take a coppy for me, as I had not time amidst our confusions; I send it to you for your approbation. You will be careful of it as I have no other coppy. My best wishes attend you both for your Health and happiness—and that you may be directed into the wisest and best measures for our safety—and the security of our posterity. I wish you was nearer to us. We know not what a day will bring forth—nor what distress one hour may throw us into. Heitherto I have been able to mantain a calmness and presence of Mind, and hope I shall let the Exigency of the time be what they will.

Mrs W[arre]n desires to be rememberd to you with her sincere regards. Mr C[ranc]h and family send their Love. He poor man has a fit of his old disorder. I have not heard one syllable from providence sine I wrote you last. I wait to hear from you, then shall act accordingly. I dare not discharge any debts with what I have Except to Isaac, least you should be dissapointed of the remainder. Adieu Breakfast calls your affectionate

Portia

John Adams to Abigail Adams

My Dear   Phyladelphia May 29. 1775

Our amiable Friend Hancock, who by the Way is our President, is to send his Servant, tomorrow for Cambridge. I am to send a few Lines by him. If his Man should come to you to deliver this Letter, treat him very kindly—because he is a kind, humane clever Fellow.

My Friend Joseph Bass, very cleverly caught the Small Pox, in two days after we arrived here, by Inoculation and has walked about the streets, every day since, and has got quite over it and quite well. He had about a Dozen Pimples upon the whole. Let his Father and Friends know this.

We are distressed here for Want of Intelligence and Information from you and from Boston, Cambridge &c. &c. &c. We have no regular Advices. I recd one kind Letter from you, in one from Coll Warren. An excellent Letter, I had from him. It has done him great Honour, and me much good.

My Duty and Love to all. I have had, miserable Health and blind Eyes almost ever since I left you. But, I found Dr Young here, who after scolding at me, quantum sufficit for not taking his Advice, has pill'd and electuary'd me into pretty good, Order. My Eyes are better, my Head is better, and so are my Spirits.

Private

The Congress will support, the Massachusetts. There is a good Spirit here. But We have an amazing Field of Business, before us. When I shall have the Joy of Meeting you and our little ones, I know not.

The military Spirit which runs through the Continent is truly amazing. This City turns out 2000 Men every day. Mr Dickinson is a Coll. Mr Reed a Lt Coll. Mr Mifflin a Major. He ought to have been a Genl. for he has been the animating Soul of the whole.

Coll Washington appears at Congress in his Uniform and, by his great Experience and Abilities in military Matters, is of much service to Us.

Oh that I was a Soldier! I will be. I am reading military Books. Every Body, must and will, and shall be a soldier.

John Adams

John Adams to Abigail Adams

[*The letter begins on 11 June 1775.*]
Phyladelphia June 17 [*1775*]

I can now inform you that the Congress have made Choice of the modest and virtuous, the amiable, generous and brave George Washington Esqr, to be the General of the American Army, and that he is to repair as soon as possible to the Camp before Boston. This appointment will have a great Effect, in cementing and securing the Union of these Colonies. The Continent is really in earnest in defending the Country. They have voted Ten Companies of Rifle Men to be sent from Pensylvania, Maryland and Virginia, to join the Army before Boston. These are an excellent Species of Light Infantry. They use a peculiar Kind of [Firearm ca]ll'd a Rifle—it has circular or [. . .] Grooves within the Barrell, and carries a Ball, with great Exactness to great Distances. They are the most accurate Marksmen in the World.

I begin to hope We shall not sit all Summer.

I hope the People of our Province, will treat the General with all that Confidence and Affection that Politeness and Respect, which is due to one of the most important Characters in the World. The Liberties of America, depend upon him, in a great Degree.

I have never been able to obtain from our Province, any regular and particular Intelligence since I left it. Kent, Swift, Tudor, Dr Cooper, Dr Winthrop, and others wrote me often, last Fall—not a Line from them this Time.

I have found this Congress like the last. When We first came together, I found a Strong Jealousy of Us, from New England, and the Massachusetts in Particular. Suspicions were entertained of Designs of Independeny—an American Republic—Presbyterian Principles—and twenty other Things. Our Sentiments were heard in Congress, with great Caution—and seemed to make but little Impression: but the longer We sat, the more clearly they saw the Necessity of pursuing vigorous Measures. It has been so now. Every Day We sit, the more

We are convinced that the Designs against Us, are hostile and sanguinary, and that nothing but Fortitude, Vigour, and Perseverance can save Us.

But America is a great, unwieldy Body. Its Progress must be slow. It is like a large Fleet sailing under Convoy. The fleetest Sailors, must wait for the dullest and slowest. Like a Coach and six—the swiftest Horses, must be slackened and the slowest quickened, that all may keep an even Pace.

It is long since I heard from you. I fear you have been kept in continual Alarms. My Duty and Love to all. My dear Nabby, Johnny, Charly and Tommy come here and kiss me.

We have appointed a continental Fast. Millions will be upon their Knees at once before their great Creator, imploring his Forgiveness and Blessing, his Smiles on American Councils and Arms.

My Duty to your Uncle Quincy—your Papa, Mama and mine—my Brothers and sisters and yours.

Adieu.

Abigail Adams to John Adams

Weymouth June [16?] 1775

I set down to write to you a monday, but really could not compose my-self sufficently: the anxiety I sufferd from not hearing one syllable from you for more than five weeks; and the new distress ariseing from the arrival of Recruits agitated me more than I have been since the never to be forgotton 14 of April.

I have been much revived by receiving two Letters from you last Night, one by the servant of your Friend and the other by the Gentleman you mention, tho they both went to Cambridge, and I have not seen them. I hope to send this as a return to you.

I feard much for your Health when you went away. I must intreat you to be as careful as you can consistant with the Duty you owe your

Country. That consideration alone prevaild with me to consent to your departure, in a time so perilous and so hazardous to your family—and with a body so infirm as to require the tenderest care and Nursing. I wish you may be supported and devinely assisted in this most important crisis when the fate of Empires depend upon your wisdom, and conduct. I greatly rejoice to hear of your union, and determination to stand by us.

We cannot but consider the great distance you are from us as a very great misfortune, when our critical situation renders it necessary to hear from you every week, and will be more and more so, as difficulties arise. We now Expect our sea coasts ravaged. Perhaps, the very next Letter I write will inform you that I am driven away from our, yet quiet cottage. Necessity will oblige Gage to take some desperate steps. We are told for Truth, that he is now Eight thousand Strong. We live in continual Expectation of allarms. Courage I know we have in abundance, conduct I hope we shall not want—but powder—where shall we get a sufficient supply? I wish we may not fail there. Every Town is fill'd with the distressd inhabitants of Boston—our House among others is deserted, and by this time like enough made use of as a Barrack. Mr Bowdoin with his Lady, are at present in the house of Mrs Borland, and are a going to middlebouragh to the house of Judge Oliver. He poor Gentleman is so low, that I apprehend he is hastening to an house not made with Hands—looks like a mere skelliton, speaks faint and low, is racked with a voilent cough, and I think far advanced in a consumption. I went to see him last saturday. He is very inquisitive of every person with regard to the times—beged I would let him know of the first inteligence I had from you—is very unable to converse by reason of his cough. He rides every pleasent Day, and has been kind enough to call at the Door, (tho unable to get out) several times—says the very name of Hutchinson distresses him—speaking of him the other day he broke out "religious Rascal, how I abhor his Name."

We have had very dry weather not a rainy day since you left us. The english Grass will not yeald half so great a crop as Last year. Fruit promises well, but the Cattepillars have been innumerable.

I wrote you with regard to the money I had got from providence. I have since that obtain the rest. I have done as you directed with regard to the payment of some you mentiond, but it incroachd some upon your stock. You will write me with regard to what you have necessity for and how I shall convey to you. Mr Rice is dissapointed of his place in the Army but has hopes of joining a company much talked of here under mr Hancock when he returns. I came here with some of my cousin Kents who came to see me a day, or two ago, and have left company to write you this afternoon least I should fail of conveyance. Pray be perticuliar when you write as possible—every body wants to hear, and to know what is doing, and what may be communicated, do not fail to inform me. All our Friends desire to be kindly rememberd to you. Gage'es proclamation you will receive by this conveyance. All the records of time cannot produce a blacker page. Satan when driven from the regions of bliss, Exibeted not more malice. Surely the father of lies is superceded. Yet we think it the best proclamation he could have issued. I shall when ever I can, receive and entertain in the best manner I am capable the gentlemen who have so generously proferd their service in our Army. Goverment is wanted in the army, and Else where. We see the want of it more from so large a body being to gether, than when each individual was imployd in his own domestick circle. My best regards attend every Man you esteem. You will make my complements to Mr Miflin and Lady. I do not now wonder at the regard the Laidies Express for a soldier—every man who wears a cockade appears of double the importance he used to—and I feel a respect for the Lowest Subaltern in the Army. You tell me you know not when you shall see me. I never trust myself long with the terrors which sometimes intrude themselves upon me.

I hope we shall see Each other again and rejoice together in happier Days. The Little ones are well, and send Duty to Pappa. Dont fail of letting me hear from you by every opportunity, every line is like a precious Relict of the Saints. Pray dont Expose me by a communication of any of my Letters—a very bad soar upon the middle finger of my right hand has prevented my writing for 3 weeks. This is the 5 Letter I have wrote you. I hope they have all come to hand. I have a request to make you, something like the Barrel of sand suppose you will think it, but really of much more importance to me. It is that you would send out mr Bass and purchase me a bundle of pins and put in your trunk for me. The cry for pins is so great that what we used to Buy for 7.6 are now 20 Shillings and not to be had for that. A bundle contains 6 thousand for which I used to give a Dollor—but if you can procure them for 50 or 3 pound, pray Let me have them. Mr Welch who carries this to head Quarters waits which prevents my adding more than that I am with the tenderest Regard your

Portia

Abigail Adams to John Adams

Dearest Friend   Sunday June 18 1775

The Day, perhaps the decisive Day is come on which the fate of America depends. My bursting Heart must find vent at my pen. I have just heard that our Dear Friend Dr Warren is no more but fell gloriously fighting for his Country—saying better to die honourably in the field than ignominiously hang upon the Gallows. Great is our Loss. He has distinguished himself in every engagement, by his courage and fortitude, by animating the Soldiers and leading them on by his own Example. A particuliar account of these dreadful, but I hope Glorious Days will be transmitted you, no doubt in the exactest manner.

The race is not to the swift, nor the battle to the strong—but the God of Israel is he that giveth strength and power unto his people. Trust in him at all times ye people pour out your hearts before him. God is a refuge for us. Charlstown is laid in ashes. The Battle began upon our intrenchments upon Bunkers Hill, a Saturday morning about 3 oclock and has not ceased yet and tis now 3 o'clock Sabbeth afternoon.

Tis Expected they will come out over the Neck to night, and a

Dreadful Battle must ensue. Almighty God cover [the] heads of our Country men, and be a shield to our Dear Friends. How [many ha]ve fallen we know not. The constant roar of the cannon [is so] distressing that we cannot Eat Drink or sleep. May we be supported and sustaind in the dreadful conflict. I shall tarry here till tis thought unsafe by my Friends, and then I have secured myself a retreat at your Brothers who has kindly offerd me part of his house. I cannot compose myself to write any further at present. I will add more as I hear further.

Portia

John Adams to Abigail Adams

My Dear   Philadelphia June 23. 1775

I have this Morning been out of Town to accompany our Generals Washington, Lee, and Schuyler, at little Way, on their Journey to the American Camp before Boston.

The Three Generals were all mounted, on Horse back, accompanied by Major Mifflin who is gone in the Character of Aid de Camp. All the Delegates from the Massachusetts with their Servants, and Carriages attended—Many others of the Delegates, from the Congress— a large Troop of Light Horse, in their Uniforms—many officers of Militia besides in theirs—Musick playing &c &c. Such is the Pride and Pomp of War. I, poor Creature, worn out with scribbling, for my Bread and my Liberty, low in Spirits and weak in Health, must leave others to wear the Lawrells which I have sown; others, to eat the Bread which I have earned. A Common Case.

We had Yesterday, by the Way of N. York and N. London, a Report, which distresses us, almost as much as that We had last fall, of the Cannonade of Boston. A Battle at Bunkers Hill and Dorchester Point—three Colls. wounded, Gardiner mortally. We wait to hear more particulars. Our Hopes and our Fears are alternately very strong. If there is any Truth in this Acct. you must be in great Confusion. God Almightys Providence preserve, sustain, and comfort you.

June 27

This Moment recd two Letters from you. Courage, my dear! We shall be supported in Life, or comforted in Death. I rejoice that my Countrymen behaved so bravely, tho not so skillfully conducted as I could wish. I hope this defect will be remedied by, the new modelling of the Army.

My Love every where.

Abigail Adams to John Adams

Dearest Friend   June 25 1775 Braintree

My Father has been more affected with the distruction of charlstown than with any thing which has heretofore taken place. Why should not his countanance be sad, when the city, the place of his Fathers Sepulchers lieth waste, and the gates thereof are consumed with fire, scarcly one stone remaineth upon an other. But in the midst of sorrow we have abundant cause of thankfulness that so few of our Breathren are numberd with the slain, whilst our enemies were cut down like the Grass before the sythe. But one officer of all the welch fuzelers remains to tell his story. Many poor wretches dye for want of proper assistance and care of their wounds.

Every account agrees in 14 and 15 hundred slain and wounded upon their side nor can I learn that they dissemble the Number themselves. We had some Heroes that day who fought with amazing intrepidity, and courage.

> "Extremity is the trier of spirits—
> common chances common men will bear;
> And when the sea is calm, all boats alike

Shew mastership in floating, but fortunes blows
When most struck home, being bravely warded, crave
a noble cunning." *Shakespear.*

I hear that general *How* should say the Battle upon the plains of Abram was but a Bauble to this. When we consider all the circumstances attending this action we stand astonished that our people were not all cut of. They had but one hundred foot intrenched, the number who were engaged did not exceed 800, and they not half amunition enough. The reinforcements not able to get to them seasonably. The tide was up and high so that their floating batteries came upon each side of the causway and their row gallies keeping a continual fire added to this the fire from fort hill and from the ship. The Town in flames all round them and the heat from the flames so intence as scarcely to be borne; the day one of the hottest we have had this Season and the wind blowing the smoke in their faces—only figure to yourself all these circumstances, and then consider that we do not count 60 Men lost. My Heart overflows at the recollection.

We live in continual Expectation of Hostilities Scarcely a day that does not produce some, but like Good Nehemiah having made our prayer unto God, and set the people with their Swords, their Spears and their bows. We will say unto them, Be not affraid of them Remember the Lord who is great and terible, and fight for your Breathren your sons and your Daughters your wives and your houses.

I have just received yours of the 17 of june in 7 days only; every line from that far Country is precious. You do not tell me how you do, but I will hope better. Alass you little thought what distress we were in the day you wrote. They delight in molesting us upon the sabbeth. Two Sabbeths we have been in Such Alarms that we have had no meeting. This day we have Set under our own vine in quietness, have heard mr Taft, from psalms. The Lord is good to all and his tender mercies are over all his works. The good man was earnest and pathetick. I could forgive his weakness for the sake of his sincerity—

but I long for a *Cooper* and an *Elliot*. I want a person who has feeling and sensibility who can take one up with *him*.

> "And in his Duty prompt at every call
> can watch, and weep, and pray, and feel for all."

Mr Rice joins General Heaths regiment to morrow as adjutant. Your Brother is very desirous of being in the army, but your good Mother is really voilent against it. I cannot persuaid nor reason her into a consent. Neither he nor I dare let her know that he is trying for a place. My Brother has a captains commission, and is stationd at cambridge. I thought you had the best of inteligence or I should have taken pains to have been more perticuliar. As to Boston, there are many persons yet there who would be glad to get out if they could. Mr Boylstone and mr Gill the printer with his family are held upon the black list tis said. Tis certain they watch them so narrowly that they cannot Escape, nor your Brother Swift and family. Mr Mather got out a day or two before Charlstown was distroyed, and had lodged his papers and what else he got out at mr Carys, but they were all consumed. So were many other peoples, who thought they might trust their little there; till teams could be procured to remove them. The people from the Alms house and work house were sent to the lines last week, to make room for their wounded they say. Medford people are all removed. Every sea port seems in motion. O North! may the Groans and cryes of the injured and oppressed Harrow up thy Soul. We have a prodigious Armey, but we lack many accomadations which we need. I hope the apointment of these new Generals will give satisfaction. They must be proof against calumny. In a contest like this continual reports are circulated by our Enimies, and they catch with the unwary and the gaping croud who are ready to listen to the marvellous, without considering of consequences even tho there best Friends are injured. I have not venturd to inquire one word of you about your return. I do not know whether I ought to wish for it—it seems as if your sitting together was absolutely necessary whilst every day is big with Events.

Mr Bowdoin called a fryday and took his leave of me desiring I would present his affectionate regards to you. I have hopes that he will recover—he has mended a good deal. He wished he could have staid in Braintree, but his Lady was fearful.

I have often heard that fear makes people Loving. I never was so much noticied *by some people* as I have been since you went out of Town, or rather since the 19 of april. Mr W[*inslo*]ws family are determined to be sociable. Mr A———n are quite Friendly. Nabby Johny Charly Tommy all send duty. Tom says I wish I could see *par*. You would laugh to see them all run upon the Sight of a Letter—like chicks for a crum, when the Hen clucks. Charls says *mar* What is it any good news? and who is for us and who against us, is the continual inquiry. Brother and sister Cranch send their Love. He has been very well since he removed, for him, and has full employ in his Buisness. Unkel Quincy calls to hear most every day, and as for the Parson, he determines I shall not make the same complaint I did last time, for he comes every other day.

Tis Exceeding dry weather. We have not had any rain for a long time. Bracket has mowed the medow and over the way, but it will not be a last years crop. Pray Let me hear from you by every opportunity till I have the joy of once more meeting you. Yours ever more

Portia

John Adams to Abigail Adams

My Dear   Philadelphia July 7 1775

I have recd your very agreable Favours of June 22d. and 25th. They contain more particulars than any Letters I had before recd from any Body.

It is not at all surprizing to me that the wanton, cruel, and infamous Conflagration of Charlestown, the Place of your Fathers Nativity should afflict him. Let him know that I sincerely condole with him, on that melancholly Event. It is a Method of conducting War long since become disreputable among civilized Nations: But every Year brings us fresh Evidence, that We have nothing to hope for from our loving Mother Country, but Cruelties more abominable than those which are practiced by the Savage Indians.

The account you give me of the Numbers slain on the side of our Enemies, is affecting to Humanity, altho it is a glorious Proof of the Bravery of our Worthy Countrymen. Considering all the Disadvantages under which they fought, they really exhibited Prodigies of Valour.

Your Description of the Distresses of the worthy Inhabitants of Boston, and the other Sea Port Towns, is enough to melt an Heart of stone. Our Consolation must be this, my dear, that Cities may be rebuilt, and a People reduced to Poverty, may acquire fresh Property: But a Constitution of Government once changed from Freedom, can never be restored. Liberty once lost is lost forever. When the People once surrender their share in the Legislature, and their Right of defending the Limitations upon the Government, and of resisting every Encroachment upon them, they can never regain it.

The Loss of Mr Mathers Library, which was a Collection, of Books and Manuscripts made by himself, his Father, his grand father, and Great grand father and was really very curious and valuable, is irreparable.

The Family picture you draw is charming indeed. My dear Nabby, Johnny, Charly and Tommy, I long to see you—and to share with your Mamma the Pleasures of your Conversation.

I feel myself much obliged to Mr Bowdoin, Mr Wibirt, and the two Families you mention, for their Civilities to you. My Compliments to them. Does Mr Wibirt preach against oppression, and the other Cardinal Vices of the Times? Tell him the Clergy here, of every Denomination, not excepting the Episcopalian, thunder and lighten every sabbath. They pray for Boston and the Massachusetts—they thank God most explicitly and fervently for our remarkable Successes—they pray for the American Army. They seem to feel as if they were among you.

You ask if every Member feels for Us? Every Member says he

does—and most of them really do. But most of them feel more for themselves. In every Society of Men, in every Clubb, I ever yet saw, you find some who are timid, their Fears hurry them away upon every Alarm—some who are selfish and avaricious, on whose callous Hearts nothing but Interest and Money, can make Impression. There are some Persons in New York and Philadelphia, to whom a ship is dearer than a City, and a few Barrells of flower, than a thousand Lives—other Mens Lives I mean.

You ask, can they reallize what We suffer? I answer No. They cant they dont—and to excuse them as well as I can, I must confess I shd. not be able to do it, myself, if I was not more acquainted with it by Experience than they are.

I am grieved for Dr Tufts's ill Health: but rejoiced exceedingly at his virtuous Exertions in the Cause of his Country.

I am happy to hear that my Brothers were at Grape Island and behaved well. My Love to them, and Duty to my Mother.

It gives me more Pleasure than I can express to learn that you sustain with so much Fortitude, the Shocks and Terrors of the Times. You are really brave, my dear, you are an Heroine. And you have Reason to be. For the worst that can happen, can do you no Harm. A soul, as pure, as benevolent, as virtuous and pious as yours has nothing to fear, but every Thing to hope and expect from the last of human Evils.

Am glad you have secured an Assylum, tho I hope you will not have occasion for it.

Love to Brother Cranch and sister and the Children.

There is an amiable, ingenious Hussy, named Betcy Smith, for whom I have a very great Regard. Be pleased to make my Love acceptable to her, and let her know, that her elegant Pen cannot be more usefully employed than in Writing Letters to her Brother at Phyladelphia, tho it may more agreably in writing Billet doux to young Gentlemen.

The other Day, after I had recd a Letter of yours, with one or two others, Mr William Barrell desired to read them. I put them into his Hand, and the next Morning had them returned in a large Bundle packed up with two great Heaps of Pins, with a very polite Card requesting Portias Acceptance of them. I shall bring them with me [when] I return: But when that will be is uncertain. I hope not more than a Month hence.

I have really had a very disagreable Time of it. My Health and especialy my Eyes have been so very bad, that I have not been so fit for Business as I ought, and if I had been in perfect Health, I should have had in the present Condition of my Country and my Friends, no Taste for Pleasure. But Dr Young has made a kind of Cure of my Health and Dr Church of my Eyes.

Have recd. two kind Letters from your Unckle Smith—do thank him for them—I shall forever love him for them. I love every Body that writes to me.

I am forever yours—

The letter that follows is one of a number of John's that were intercepted by the British and subsequently published in Tory newspapers, much to his embarrassment and chagrin. This one is reprinted from the loyalist Massachusetts Gazette and Boston Weekly News-Letter, *17 August 1775; while it circulated widely at the time, the manuscript original has since been lost.*

John Adams to Abigail Adams

My Dear   Philadelphia, July 24th, 1775

It is now almost three Months since I left you, in every Part of which my Anxiety about you and the Children, as well as our Country, has been extreme.

The Business I have had upon my Mind has been as great and important as can be intrusted to Man, and the Difficulty and Intricacy of it is prodigious. When 50 or 60 Men have a Constitution to form for a great Empire, at the same time that they have a Country of fifteen hundred Miles extent to fortify, Millions to arm and train, a Naval Power to begin, an extensive Commerce to regulate, numerous Tribes of Indians to negotiate with, a standing Army of Twenty seven Thousand Men to raise, pay, victual and *officer*, I really shall pity those 50 or 60 Men.

I must see you e'er long. Rice, has wrote me a very good Letter, and so has Thaxter, for which I thank them both. Love to the Children.

J. A.

I wish I had given you a compleat History from the Beginning to the End of the Journey, of the Behaviour of my Compatriots. No Mortal Tale could equal it. I will tell you in Future, but you shall keep it secret. The Fidgets, the Whims, the Caprice, the Vanity, the Superstition, the Irritability of some of us is enough to ——

Abigail Adams to John Adams

Dearest Friend   Braintree August 10 1775

Tis with a sad Heart I take my pen to write to you because I must be the bearer of what will greatly afflict and distress you, yet I wish you to be prepaired for the Event. Your Brother Elihu lies very dangerously Sick with a Dysentery. He has been very bad for more than a week, his life is despaired of. Er'e I close this Letter I fear I shall write you that he is no more.

We are all in great distress. Your Mother is with him in great anguish. I hear this morning that he is sensible of his Danger, and calmly resigned to the Will of Heaven; which is a great Satisfaction to his mourning Friend's. I cannot write more at present than to assure you of the Health of your own family. Mr Elisha Niles lies very bad with the same disorder. Adieu.

August 11

I have this morning occasion to sing of Mercies and judgments. May I properly Notice each—a mixture of joy and Grief agitate my Bosom. The return of thee my dear partner after a four months absence is a pleasure I cannot express, but the joy is overclouded, and the Day is darkned by the Mixture of grief and the Sympathy I feel for the looss of your Brother—cut of in the pride of life and the bloom of Manhood! in the midst of his usefulness; Heaven santify this affliction to us—and make me properly thankful that it is not my Sad Lot, to mourn the loss of a Husband in the room of a Brother.

May thy life be Spaired and thy Health confirmed for the benefit of thy Country and the happiness of thy family is the constant supplication of thy Friend.

Between August and early September, the Second Continental Congress briefly stood in recess. During that time, John returned to Massachusetts but stayed in Watertown to attend sessions of the General Court. He and Abigail visited together on weekends only.

Abigail Adams to John Adams

Dearest Friend   Braintree Sepbr 8 1775

Since you left me I have passed thro great, distress both of Body and mind; and whether greater is to be my portion Heaven only knows. You may remember Isaac was unwell when you went from home. His Disorder increasd till a voilent Dysentery was the consequence of his complaints. There was no resting place in the House for his terible Groans. He continued in this State near a week when his Disorder abated, and we have now hopes of his recovery. Two Days after he was sick, I was seaz'd with the same disorder in a voilent manner. Had I known you was at Watertown I should have sent Bracket for you. I sufferd Greatly betwen my inclination to have you return, and my fear of Sending least you should be a partaker of the common calamity. After 3 day an abatement of my disease relieved me from that anxiety. The Next person in the same week was Susy. She we carried home, hope she will not be very bad. Our Little Tommy was the Next, and he lies very ill now—there is no abatement at present of his disorder. I hope he is not Dangerous. Yesterday Patty was seazd and took a puke. Our House is an hospital in every part—and what with my own weakness and distress of mind for my family I have been unhappy enough.

And such is the distress of the Neighbourhood that I can scarcly find a well person to assist me in looking after the sick. Mrs Randle has one child that is not expected to live out the Night Mrs Belcher has an other Joseph Bracket an other, Deacon Adams has lost one, but is upon the recovery himself, and so are the rest of his family. Mr Wibird lies bad Major Miller is dangerous. Revd Mr Gay is not expected to live.

So Sickly and so Mortal a time the oldest Man does not remember. I am anxious for you. Pray Let me hear from you soon. I thought you would have left me a Letter at Watertown as you staid so long there. I was dissapointed that you did not. As to politicks I know nothing about them. The distresses of my own family are so great that I have not thought about them. I have wrote as much as I am able to, being very week. I hope to add a more pleasing account er'er I close. Adieu.

Sunday Sepbr 10

Tis now two Days since I wrote. As to my own Health I mend but very slowly—have been fearful of a return of my disorder to day but feel rather better now. Hope it is only oweing to my having been fatigued with looking after Tommy, as he is unwilling any body but Mamma should do for him, and if he was I could not find any body that is worth having but what are taken up already with the sick.

Tommy I hope is mending, his fever has abated, his Bowels are better, but was you to look in upon him you would not know him, from a hearty hale corn fed Boy, he is become pale lean and wan. Isaac is getting better, but very slowly. Patty is very bad. We cannot keep any thing down that she takes, her situation is very dangerous. Mr Trot and one of his children are taken with the Disorder.

I shall write every Day if I am able. Pray let me hear from you often. Heaven preserve both your life and health and all my sufferings will be but small. By the first safe conveyance be kind eno to send me 1 oz of turky Rhubub, the root, and to procure me 1 Quarter lb of Nutmegs for which here I used to give 2.8 Lawful 1 oz cloves 2 of cinnamon. You may Send me only a few of the Nutmegs till Bass, returns. I should be glad of 1 oz of Indian root. So much Sickness has occasiond a scarcity of Medicine.

Distroy this such a Doleful tale it contains can give no pleasure to any one. Our other children are well and send Duty to pappa. Bracket has been complaining but has got better. The small pox in the Natural way was never more mortal than this Distemper has proved in this and many neighbouring Towns. 18 have been buried Since you left us in mr Welds parish. 4 3 and 2 funerals in a day for many Days. Heitherto our family has been greatly favourd. Heaven still preserve us. Tis a melancholy time with us. I hope you will not think me in the Dismals, but publick and private judgments ought to be noticed by every one. I am most affectionately yours,

Portia

John Adams to Abigail Adams

My Dear   Philadelphia Septr. 26. 1775

I have not written, the usual Compliment of Letters since I left Braintree; nor have I received one Scratch of a Pen from any Body, till the last Evening, when the Post brought me a Line from Mrs Warren, in which she informs me that you had been ill, but was better. I shall be unhappy till I hear farther from you, tho I hope for the best.

I have enjoyed better Health, this session than the last, and have suffered less from certain Fidgets, Pidlings, and Irritabilities which have become so famous. A more Serious Spirit prevails than heretofore. We shall soon be in Earnest. I begin to think We are so. Our Injunctions of secrecy are so much insisted on, that I must be excused from disclosing one Iota of any Thing that comes to my Knowledge as a Member of the Congress. Our journal of the last session however, I conjecture will be speedily printed and then I will inclose it to you.

I want to be informed from Hour to Hour, of every Thing which passes in Boston—whether our Friends come out—What Property they bring?—how they fare in Town? How the Tories subsist &c &c &c. Whether the Troops are healthy or sickly?

I also want to know every Thing which passes in our Army. The Feats and Exploits of our little Naval Armaments would be very agreable.

Tudor is made easy. He must keep a Clerk, or there will be Jealousies. Indeed it is his Duty for it is impossible he can do the Business himself and if that is not done, Injustice to the public will be done.

I have seen the Utility of Geometry, Geography, and the Art of drawing so much of late, that I must intreat you, my dear, to teach the Elements of those Sciences to my little Girl and Boys. It is as pretty an Amusement, as Dancing or Skaiting, or Fencing, after they have once acquired a Taste for them. No doubt you are well qualified for a school Mistress in these Studies, for Stephen Collins tells me the English Gentleman, in Company with him, when he visited Braintree, pronounced you the most accomplished Lady, he had seen since he left England. You see a Quaker can flatter, but dont you be proud.

My best Wishes and most fervent Prayers attend our little Family. I have been banished from them, the greatest Part of the last Eighteen Months but I hope to be with them more, in Time to come. I hope to be excused from attending at Philadelphia, after the Expiration of the Year. I hope that Dr Winthrop, Mr sever, Mr Greenleaf Coll Warren,

Mr Hawley, Mr Gerry, some or all of them will take their Turns, in the States—and suffer me, at least to share with my Family, a little more than I have done, the Pleasures and Pains of this Life, and that I may attend a little more to my private Affairs that I may not be involved in total Ruin, unless my Country should be so and then I should choose to share its Fate.

The dysentery epidemic affected thousands in the Boston area, including Abigail herself and several members of her family. The most devastating blow for Abigail, however, was the death of her mother.

Elizabeth Quincy, from the prominent and affluent Quincy family of Massachusetts, married the small-town minister William Smith in 1740. For thirty-five years, the Smiths had presided over the parsonage in Weymouth; as the minister's wife, Elizabeth was responsible for seeing to the well-being of the entire community while simultaneously caring for her own family and raising her children. She served as a role model for Abigail, training her not only in managing a household on limited means but also in the importance of offering charity to those in need.

Abigail Adams to John Adams

Weymouth octobr 1 1775

Have pitty upon me have pitty upon me o! thou my beloved for the Hand of God presseth me soar.

Yet will I be dumb and silent and not open my mouth becaus thou o Lord hast done it.

How can I tell you o my (bursting Heart) that my Dear Mother has Left me, this day about 5 oclock She left this world for an infinitely better.

After sustaining 16 days Severe conflict Nature fainted and she fell assleep. Blessed Spirit where art thou? At times I almost am ready to faint under this severe and heavy stroke, seperated from *thee* who used to be a comfortar towards me in affliction, but blessed be God, his Ear is not heavy that he cannot hear, but he has bid us call upon him in time of Trouble.

I know you are a sincere and hearty mourner with me and will pray for me in my affliction. My poor father like a firm Believer and a Good christian Sets before his children the best of Examples of patience and submission. My sisters send their Love to you and are greatly afflicted. You often Express'd your anxiety for me when you left me before, surrounded with Terrors, but my trouble then was as the small dust in the balance compaird to what I have since endured. I hope to be properly mindful of the correcting hand, that I may not be rebuked in anger. You will pardon and forgive all my wanderings of mind I cannot be correct.

Tis a Dreadful time with this whole province. Sickness and death are in almost every family. I have no more shocking and terible Idea of any Distemper except the Plague than this.

Almighty God restrain the pestilence which walketh in Darkness and wasteth at noon day and which has laid in the dust one of the Dearest of parents. May the Life of the other be lengthend out to his afflicted children and your Distressd

Portia

John Adams to Abigail Adams

My Dear   Philadelphia Octr. 1. 1775

This Morning, I received your two Letters of September 8th. and September 16th. What shall I say? The Intelligence they contain, came upon me by surprize, as I never had the least Intimation before, that any of my Family was ill, excepting in a Card from Mrs Warren recd a few days ago, in which she informed me that Mrs Adams had been unwell but was better.

You may easily conceive the State of Mind, in which I am at present. Uncertain and apprehensive, at first I suddenly thought of setting off, immediately, for Braintree, and I have not yet determined otherwise. Yet the State of public affairs is so critical, that I am half afraid to leave my Station, Altho my Presence here is of no great Consequence.

I feel—I tremble for You. Poor Tommy! I hope by this Time, however, he has recovered, his plump Cheeks and his fine Bloom. By your Account of Patty I fear—but still I will hope she has been supported, and is upon the Recovery.

I rejoice to learn that Nabby and her Brothers have hitherto escaped and pray God that his Goodness may be still continued to them. Your Description of the distressed State of the Neighbourhood is affecting indeed.

It is not uncommon for a Train of Calamities to come together. Fire, Sword, Pestilence, Famine, often keep Company, and visit a Country in a Flock.

At this Distance I can do no good to you nor yours. I pray God to support you—I hope our Friends and Neighbours are kind as usual. I feel for them, in the general Calamity.

I am so far from thinking you melancholly, that I am charmed with that Admirable Fortitude, and that divine Spirit of Resignation which appears in your Letters. I cannot express the Satisfaction it gives me, nor how much it contributes to support me.

You have alarmed me however, by mentioning Anxieties which you do not think it prudent to mention to any one. I am wholly at a Loss to conjecture what they can be. If they arise from the Letters, be assured that you may banish them forever. These Letters have reached Philadelphia, but have produced Effects very different from those which were expected from the Publication of them. These Effects I will explain to you sometime or other. As to the Versification of them, if there is Wit or Humour in it laugh—if ill Nature, sneer—if mere Dullness, why you may even yawn or nod. I have no Anger, at it, nay even scarcly contempt. It is impotent.

As to Politicks, We have nothing to expect but the whole Wrath and Force of G. Britain. But your Words are as true, as an oracle "God helps them, who help themselves, and if We obtain the divine Aid by our own Virtue Fortitude and Perseverance, We may be sure of Relief."

It may amuse you to hear a Story. A few days ago, in Company with Dr Zubly, somebody said, there was nobody on our side but the Almighty. The Dr. who is a Native of Switzerland, and speaks but broken English, quickly replied "Dat is enough." "Dat is enough," and turning to me, says he, it puts me in mind of a fellow who once said, The Catholicks have on their side the Pope, and the K. of France and the K. of Spain, and the K. of Sardinia, and the K. of Poland and the Emperor of Germany &c &c. &c. But as to them poor Devils the Protestants, they have nothing on their side but God Almighty.

Abigail Adams to John Adams

Braintree october 9 1775

I have not been composed enough to write you since Last Sabbeth when in the bitterness of my sould, I wrote a few confused lines, since which time it has pleased the Great disposer of all Events to add Breach to Breach—

"Rare are solitary woes, they Love a Train
And tread each others heal."

The day week that I was call'd to attend a dying parents Bed I was again call'd to mourn the loss of one of my own Family. I have just returnd from attending Patty to the Grave. No doubt long before this will reach you, you have received a melancholy train of Letters in some of which I mention her as Dangerously Sick. She has lain 5 weeks wanting a few days so bad as that we had little hopes of her Recovery; the Latter part of the Time she was the most shocking object my Eyes ever beheld, and so Loathsome that it was with the utmost difficulty we could bear the House. A mortification took place a week before she dyed, and renderd her a most pityable object. We have great sickness yet in the Town; she made the fourth corpse that was this day committed to the Ground. We have many others now so bad as to dispair of their lives. But Blessed be the Father of Mercies all our family are now well, tho I have my apprehensions least the malignincy of the air in the House may have infected some of them, we have fevers of various kinds, the Throat Distemper as well as the dysentery prevailing in this and the Neighbouring Towns.

How long o Lord shall the whole land say I am sick? O shew us wherefore it is that thou art thus contending with us? In a very perticuliar manner I have occasion to make this inquiry who have had Breach upon Breach, nor has one wound been permitted to be healed e'er it is made to Blead affresh. In six weeks I count 5 of my near connections laid in the grave. Your Aunt Simpson died at milton about ten days ago with the Dysentery.

But the heavy stroke which most of all distresses me is my dear Mother. I cannot overcome my too selfish sorrow, all her tenderness towards me, her care and anxiety for my welfare at all times, her watchfulness over my infant years, her advice and instruction in maturer age; all, all indear her memory to me, and highten my sorrow for her loss. At the same time I know a patient submission is my Duty. I will strive to obtain it! But the lenient hand of time alone can blunt the keen Edg of Sorrow. He who deignd to weep over a departed Friend, will surely forgive a sorrow which at all times desires to be bounded and restrained, by a firm Belief that a Being of infinite wisdom and unbounded Goodness, will carve out my portion in tender mercy towards me! Yea tho he slay me I will trust in him said holy Job. What tho his corrective Hand hath been streached against me; I will not murmer. Tho earthly comforts are taken away I will not repine, he who gave them has surely a right to limit their Duration, and has continued them to me much longer than I deserved. I might have been striped of my children as many others have been. I might o! forbid it Heaven, I might have been left a solitary widow.

Still I have many blessing left, many comforts to be thankfull for, and rejoice in. I am not left to mourn as one without hope.

My dear parent knew in whom she had Believed, and from the first attack of the distemper she was perswaded it would prove fatal to her. A Solemnity possess'd her soul, nor could you force a smile from her till she dyed. The voilence of her disease soon weakned her so that she was unable to converse, but whenever she could speak, she testified her willingness to leave the world and an intire resignation to the Divine Will. She retaind her Senses to the last moment of her Existance, and departed the world with an easy tranquility, trusting in the merrits of a Redeamer. Her passage to immortality was marked with a placid smile upon her countanance, nor was there to be seen scarcly a vestage of the king of Terrors—

> "The sweet remembrance of the just
> Shall flourish when they sleep in Dust"

Tis by soothing Grief that it can be healed, "give Sorrow words"

> "The Grief that cannot speak
> Whispers the o'er fraught heart and bids it Break"

Forgive me then; for thus dwelling upon a subject Sweet to me, but I fear painfull to you. O how I have long'd for your Bosom, to pour forth my sorrows there, and find a healing Balm, but perhaps that has been denied me that I might be led to a higher and a more permamant consolater who has bid us call upon him in the day of trouble.

As this is the first day since your absence that I could write you that we were all well, I desire to mark it with perticuliar gratitude, and humbly hope that all my warnings and corrections are not in vain.

I most thankfully Received your kind favour of the 26 yesterday. It gives me much pleasure to hear of your Health. I pray Heaven for the continuance of it. I hope for the future to be able to give you more intelegance with regard to what passess out of my own little circle, but such has been my distress that I knew nothing of the political world.

You have doubtless heard, of the viliny of one who has professd himself a patriot, but Let not that man be trusted who can voilate private faith, and cancel solem covanants, who can leap over moral law, and laugh at christianity. How is he to be bound whom neither honour nor conscience holds? We have here a Rumor that Rhodiland has shared the fate of Charlstown—is this the Day we read of when Satan was to be loosed?

I do not hear of any inhabitants getting out of Town. Tis said Gage is superceeded and How in his place, and that How released the prisoners from Gaoil. Tis also said tho not much credited that Burgoine is gone to Philadelphia.

I hope to hear from you soon. Adieu. Tis almost twelve oclock at Night. I have had so little Sleep Lately that I must bid you good Night. With hearty wishes for your return I am most Sincerely Your

Portia

John Adams to Abigail Adams

Octr. 13. 1775

I this day received yours of the 29 of September, and the 1st. of October.

Amidst all your afflictions, I am greatly rejoiced to find that you all along preserve so proper and so happy a Temper—that you are sensible "the Consolations of Religion are the only sure Comforters." It is the Constitution under which We are born that if We live long ourselves We must bury our Parents and all our Elder Relations and many of those who are younger. I have lost a Parent, a Child and a Brother, and each of them left a lasting Impression on my Mind: But, you and I have [many] more Relations, and very good Friends to follow to the House [app]ointed for all Flesh, or else We must be followed by them.

In your last you make no Mention of Patty, poor distress'd Girl! I fear the next News I shall hear will be of her Departure, yet I will hope, that Youth, and a strong Constitution which has lasted so long will finally survive. If not We must submit.

I bewail more than I can express, the Loss of your excellent Mother. I mourn the Loss of so much Purity, and unaffected Piety and Virtue to the World. I knew of no better Character left in it. I grieve for you, and your Brother, and sisters, I grieve for your Father, whose Age, will need the Succour of so excellent a Companion. But I grieve for nobody more than my Children, and Brothers Smiths and Mr Cranch's. Her most amiable, and discreet Example, as well as her Kind Skill and Care I have ever relyed upon in my own Mind, for the Education of these little Swarms. Not that I have not a proper Esteem for the Capacity and Disposition of the Mothers, but I know that the Efforts of the Grand mother, are of great Importance, when they second those of the Parent. And I am sure that my Children are the better for the forming Hand of their Grandmother.

It gives me great Joy to learn that ours are well—let us be thankfull for this and many other Blessings yet granted us. Pray my dear cherish in the Minds of my Nabby and Johnny and Charly and Tommy the Remembrance of their Grand mamma, and remind them of her Precepts and Example.

God almighty grant to you and to every Branch of the Family, all the Support that you want! You and I, my dear, have Reason, if ever Mortals had, to be thoughtfull—to look forward beyond the transitory Scene. Whatever is preparing for Us, let us be prepared to receive. It is Time for Us to subdue our Passions of every Kind. The Prospect before Us is an Ocean of Uncertainties—in which no pleasing objects appear. We have few Hopes, excepting that of preserving our Honour and our Consciences untainted and a free Constitution to our Country. Let me be sure of these, and amidst all my Weaknesses, I cannot be overcome. With these I can be happy, in extream Poverty, in humble Insignificance, nay I hope and believe, in Death: without them I should be miserable, with a Crown upon my Head, Millions in my

Coffers, and a gaping, idolizing Multitude at my Feet. My Heart is too full of Grief for you and our Friends to whom I wish you to present my Regards, to say any Thing of News or Politicks. Yet the Affair of the surgeon general is so strange, and important an Event that I cannot close this gloomy Letter, without adding a Sigh for this imprudent, unfortunate Man! I know not whether, the Evidence will Support the Word Treachery, but what may We not expect after Treachery to himself, his Wife and Children!

Abigail Adams to John Adams

Braintree october 22 1775

Mr Lorthorp call'd here this Evening and brought me yours of the 1 of october a day which will ever be rememberd by me, for it was the most distressing one I ever Experienced. That morning I rose and went into my Mothers room, not apprehending her so near her Exit, went to her Bed with a cup of tea in my hand, raised her head to give it to her. She swallowed a few Drops, gaspd and fell back upon her pillow—opend her Eyes with a look that pirced my Heart and which I never shall forget. It was the eagerness of a last look—"and o! the Last sad silence of a Friend."

Yet she lived till 5 oclock that day, but I could not be with her. My dear Father prayed twice beside her Bed that day. God Almighty was with him and suported him that day and enabled him to go thro the Services of it. It was his communion day. He had there a tender Scene to pass through a young Grandaughter Betsy Cranch joining herself to the church and a Beloved wife dying to pray for weeping children weeping and mourning parishoners all round him, for every Eye streamed, his own heart allmost bursting as he spoke. How painful is the recollection, yet how pleasing?

I know I wound your Heart. Why should I? Ought I to give relief to my own by paining yours?

"Yet the Grief that cannot speak
whispers the o'er fraught heart and bids it burst"

My pen is always freer than my tongue. I have wrote many things to you that I suppose I never could have talk'd.

My Heart is made tender by repeated affliction. It never was a hard Heart. The Death of Patty came very near me, having lived four years with me, under my care. I hope it will make me more continually mindful and watchfull of all those who are still committed to my charge.

Tis a great trust. I daily feel more and more of the weight and importance of it, and of my own inability. I wish I could have more of the assistance of my dearest Friend but these perilous times swallow him up.

Mr Lorthrope has given me this account of the demand upon Falmouth. A Man of war and two tenders went down and sent to the inhabitants to demand their Arms and require them to stand Nutur. They required time to consider. They gave them till Nine oclock the Next day, which time they imployed in removeing the women children and *the rest of their most valuable Effects* out of danger when they sent their answer in the Negative. Upon which they began a cannonade and were continuing it when the Express came away. Hitchbourn and an other Gentleman got out of Town in a small Boat, one of the fogy Nights we have had this week. I have not heard what intelegance he brings. An other person says that How enlarged all the prisoners but Lovel and he would not come out.

I have since seen the pharaphrase as tis call'd but tis as Low as the mock oration tho no reflection upon your private character further than immoderately whiping your Schollers when you kept School a crime any one will acquit you of who knows you. As a Specimen of the wit and humour it contain I will give you the title—a pharaphrase upon the Second Epistle of John the round Head to James the prolocutor of the Rump parliament. Dear Devil &c.

I had it, but it was when I was in so much distress that I cared nothing about it. I will mention when I see you the foolish conjectures of some who want always to be finding out something Extraordinary in what ever happens.

Mr Cranchs family are well and send Love to you. Your Mother too, is always anxious for you, and is so apprehensive least a fleet should be sent to Bombard Philadelphia that she has not much comfort. Brothers family are well Except young crosby who had the dysentery very bad, and has left him Bereaved of his reason. Isaac is so far recoverd as to return after six weeks and Susy is returnd to me again. Our Neighbours are now all getting well.

I hope to hear often from you which is all the alleviation I have of your absence, and is next to seeing you the greatest comfort of your

Portia

John Adams to Abigail Adams

Octr. 29. 1775

I cannot exclude from my Mind your melancholly Situation. The Griefs of your Father and Sisters, your Uncles and Aunts, as well as the remoter Connections, often croud in upon me, when my whole Attention ought to be directed to other Subjects.

Your Uncle Quincy, my Friend as well as Uncle, must regret the loss of a beloved Sister, Dr Tufts my other Friend I know bewails the loss of a Friend, as well as an Aunt and a sister, Mr Cranch the Friend of my youth as well as of my riper Years, whose tender Heart Sympathizes with his fellow Creatures in every Affliction and Distress, in this Case feels the Loss of a Friend, a fellow Christian, and a Mother.

But alas what avail these mournfull Reflections. The best Thing We can do, the greatest Respect We can show to the Memory of our departed Friend, is to copy into Our own Lives, those Virtues which in her Life time rendered her the object of our Esteem, Love and Admiration. I must confess I ever feelt a Veneration for her, which seems increased by the News of her Translation.

Above all Things my dear, let us inculcate these great Virtues and bright Excellencies upon our Children.

Your Mother, had a clear, and penetrating Understanding and a profound Judgment, as well as an honest and a friendly and a charitable Heart.

There is one Thing however, which you will forgive me if I hint to you. Let me ask you rather, if you are not of my opinion? Were not her Talents, and Virtues too much confined, to private, social and domestic Life. My Opinion of the Duties of Religion and Morality, comprehends a very extensive Connection with society at large, and the great Interest of the public. Does not natural Morality, and much more Christian Benevolence, make it our indispensible Duty to lay ourselves out, to serve our fellow Creatures to the Utmost of our Power, in promoting and supporting those great Political systems, and general Regulations upon which the Happiness of Multitudes depends. The Benevolence, Charity, Capacity and Industry which exerted in private Life, would make a family a Parish or a Town Happy, employed upon a larger Scale, in Support of the great Principles of Virtue and Freedom of political Regulations might seure whole Nations and Generations from Misery, Want and Contempt. Public Virtues, and political Qualities therefore should be incessantly cherished in our Children.

Abigail Adams to John Adams

November 27 1775

Tis a fortnight to Night since I wrote you a line during which, I have been confined with the Jaundice Rhumatism and a most voilent cold; I yesterday took a puke which has releived me and I feel much better to day. Many, very many people who have had the dysentery, are now aflicted both with the Jaundice and Rhumatisim, some it has left in Hecticks, some in Dropsies.

The great and incessant rains we have had this fall, (the like cannot be recollected) may have occasiond some of the present disorders. The Jaundice is very prevalent in the Camp. We have lately had a week of very cold weather, as cold as January, and a flight of snow, which I hope will purify the air of some of the Noxious vapours. It has spoild many hundreds of Bushels of Apples, which were designd for cider, and which the great rains had prevented people from making up. Suppose we have lost 5 Barrels by it.

Col Warren returnd last week to Plymouth, so that I shall not hear any thing from you till he goes Back again which will not be till the last of this month.

He Damp'd my spirits greatly by telling me that the Court had prolonged your stay an other month. I was pleasing myself with the thoughts that you would soon be upon your return. Tis in vain to repine. I hope the publick will reap what I sacrifice.

I wish I knew what mighty things were fabricating. If a form of Goverment is to be Established here what one will be assumed? Will it be left to our assemblies to chuse one? and will not many men have many minds? and shall we not run into Dissentions among ourselves?

I am more and more convinced that Man is a Dangerous creature, and that power whether vested in many or a few is ever grasping, and like the grave cries give, give, the great fish swallow up the small, and he who is most strenuous for the Rights of the people, when vested with power, is as eager after the perogatives of Goverment. You tell me of Degrees of perfection to which Humane Nature is capapble of arriving, and I believe it, but at the same time Lament that our admiration should arise from the scarcity of the instances.

The Building up a Great Empire, which was only hinted at by my correspondent may now I suppose be realized even by the unbelievers. Yet will not ten thousand Difficulties arise in the formation of it? The Reigns of Goverment have been so long slakned, that I fear the people will not Quietly submit to those restraints which are necessary for the peace, and security, of the community. If we seperate from Brittain what code of Laws will be Established, how shall we be govern'd so as to retain our Liberties? Can any goverment be free which is not adminstred by general stated Laws? Who shall frame these Laws? Who will give them force and energy? Tis true your Resolution as a Body have heithertoo had the force of Laws? But will they continue to have?

When I consider these things and the prejudices of people in favour of Ancient customs and Regulations, I feel anxious for the fate of our Monarchy or Democracy or what ever is to take place. I soon get lost in a Labyrinth of perplexities, but whatever occurs, may justice and righteousness be the Stability of our times—and order arise out of confusion. Great difficulties may be surmounted, by patience and perseverance.

I believe I have tired you with politicks. As to News we have not any at all. I shudder at the approach of winter when I think I am to remain Desolate. Suppose your weather is warm yet. Mr Mason and Thaxter live with me, and render some part of my time less disconsolate. Mr Mason is a youth who will please you, he has Spirit taste and sense. His application to his Studies is constant and I am much mistaken if he does not make a very good figure in his profession. I have with me now, the only Daughter of your Brother; I feel a tenderer affection for her as she has lost a kind parent, though too young to be sensible of her own loss, I can pitty her. She appears to be a child of a very good Disposition—only wants to be a little used to company.

Our Little ones send Duty to pappa and want much to see him. Tom says he wont come home till the Battle is over—some strange notion he has got into his head. He has got a political cread to say to him when he returns.

I must bid you good Night, tis late for me who am much of an invalide. I was dissapointed last week in receiving a packet by the post, and upon unsealing it found only four news papers. I think you are more cautious than you need be. All Letters I believe have come safe to hand. I have Sixteen from you, and wish I had as many more. Adieu yours.

John Adams to Abigail Adams

My best Friend   Decr 3. 1775

Yours of Novr. 12 is before me. I wish I could write you every day, more than once, for although I have a Number of Friends, and many Relations who are very dear to me, yet all the Friendship I have for others is far unequal to that which warms my Heart for you. The most agreable Time that I spend here is in writing to you, and conversing with you when I am alone. But the Calls of Friendship and of private Affection must give Place to those of Duty and Honour, even private Friendship and Affections require it.

I am obliged by the Nature of the service I am in to correspond with many Gentlemen both of the Army and the two Houses of Assembly which takes up much of my Time. How I find Time to write half the Letters I do, I know not, for my whole Time seems engrossed with Business. The whole Congress is taken up, almost in different Committees from seven to Ten in the Morning—from Ten to four or sometimes five, we are in Congress and from six to Ten in Committees again. I dont mention this to make you think me a Man of Importance because it is not I alone, but the whole Congress is thus employed, but to Apologise for not writing to you oftener.

Indeed I know not what to write that is worth your reading. I send you the Papers, which inform you of what is public. As to what passes in Congress I am tied fast by my Honour to communicate Nothing. I hope the Journal of the session will be published, soon and then you will see what We have been about in one View, excepting what ought to be excepted.

If I could visit the Coffee Houses, in the Evening and the Coffee

Tables of the Ladies in the Afternoon, I could entertain you with many smart Remarks upon Dress and Air, &c and give you many Sprightly Conversations, but my Fate you know is to be moping over Books and Papers, all the Leisure Time I have when I have any.

I hope I shall be excused from coming to Philadelphia again, at least untill other Gentlemen have taken their Turns. But I never will come here again without you, if I can perswade you to come with me. Whom God has joined together ought not to be put asunder so long with their own Consent. ~~We will get your Father and sister Betcy to keep House for Us.~~ We will bring Master Johnny with Us, you and he shall have the small Pox here, and We will be as happy, as Mr Hancock and his Lady. Thank Nabby and John for their Letters, and kiss Charles and Tom for me. John writes like an Hero glowing with Ardor for his Country and burning with Indignation against her Enemies. When I return I will get the sulky back to New Haven, and there leave it to be repaired, to be brought home by the first Post after it is done.

Independence

"Reconciliation if practicable and Peace if attainable, you very well
know would be as agreable to my Inclinations and as advantageous to
my Interest, as to any Man's. But I see no Prospect,
no Probability, no Possibility."

—*John Adams*

"We are told the most dissagreable things by use become less so.
I cannot say that I find the truth of the observation verified. I am
sure no seperation was ever so painfull to me as the last."

—*Abigail Adams*

"Is there no Way for two friendly Souls, to converse together, altho
the Bodies are 400 Miles off? Yes by Letter. But I want a better
Communication. I want to hear you think, or to see your Thoughts.
The Conclusion of your Letter makes my Heart throb, more than
a Cannonade would. You bid me burn your Letters.
But I must forget you first."

—*John Adams*

"There are perticuliar times when I feel such an uneasiness such a
rest less ness, as neither company Books family Cares or any other
thing will remove. My Pen is my only pleasure, and writing to
you the composure of my mind."

—*Abigail Adams*

"We Are Determined to
Foment a Rebelion"

JANUARY–OCTOBER 1776

After another brief interlude in Massachusetts from early December 1775 to late January 1776, John once again returned to Philadelphia and the Congress. In the subsequent months, the scene of war would shift from Boston, which the British evacuated in March, to New York. There, a series of battles took place that by the end of 1776 had driven the Continental Army south toward Philadelphia and reduced its size by half.

But at the same time, political changes were occurring rapidly that shifted the conflict from an internal rebellion to a war for independence. After several more months of debate—much to John's frustration—Congress finally voted to issue a formal declaration of independence in July 1776. Military circumstances spurred on this change in sentiment but so too did the publication of Thomas Paine's Common Sense, *which galvanized opinion against the British government, including the monarchy, and made independence palatable to more of the American population.*

For Abigail, the evacuation of the British Army from Boston greatly improved her immediate situation. No longer living in constant fear of attack and kept awake by cannon fire, she felt "we might sit under our own vine and Eat the good of the land." But circumstances remained difficult. Smallpox prevailed throughout the region, the economy struggled, the separation from John at times seemed endless, and worry over the fate of the nation continued to dominate the correspondence between her and John.

John Adams to Abigail Adams

My dear Nabby   Watertown Jan. 24. 1776

I am determined not to commit a fault which escaped me, the last Time I sat out for the southward.

I waited on General Thomas at Roxbury this Morning, and then went to Cambridge where I dined at Coll Mifflins with the General, and Lady, and a vast Collection of other Company, among whom were Six or Seven Sachems and Warriours, of the French Cagnawaga Indians, with several of their Wives and Children. A savage Feast they made of it, yet were very polite in the Indian style. One of these sachems is an Englishman a Native of this Colony whose Name was Williams, captivated in his Infancy with his Mother, and adopted by some kind Squaw—another I think is half french Blood.

I was introduced to them by the General as one of the grand Council Fire at Philadelphia which made them prick up their Ears, they came and shook Hands with me, and made me low Bows, and scrapes &c. In short I was much pleased with this Days entertainment.

The General is to make them presents in Cloaths and Trinketts, they have visited the Lines at Cambridge and are going to see those at Roxbury.

Tomorrow We mount, for the grand Council Fire—Where I shall think often of my little Brood at the Foot of Pens Hill. Remember me particularly to Nabby, Johnny Charly and Tommy. Tell them I charge them to be good, honest, active and industrious for their own sakes, as well as ours.

John Adams to Abigail Adams

My dearest Friend   February 18. 1776

I sent you from New York a Pamphlet intituled Common Sense, written in Vindication of Doctrines which, there is Reason to expect that the further Encroachments of Tyranny and Depredations of oppression, will soon make the common Faith: unless the cunning Ministry, by proposing Negociations and Terms of Reconciliation, should divert the present Current from its Channell.

Reconciliation if practicable and Peace if attainable, you very well know would be as agreable to my Inclinations and as advantageous to my Interest, as to any Man's. But I see no Prospect, no Probability, no Possibility. And I cannot but despise the Understanding, which sincerely expects an honourable Peace, for its Credulity, and detest the hypocritical Heart, which pretends to expect it, when in Truth it does not. The News Papers here are full of free Speculations, the Tendency, of which you will easily discover. The Writers reason from Topicks which have been long in Contemplation, and fully understood by the People at large in New England, but have been attended to in the southern Colonies only by Gentlemen of free Spirits and liberal Minds, who are very few. I shall endeavour to inclose to you as many of the Papers and Pamphlets as I can, as long as I stay here. Some will go by this Conveyance.

Dr Franklin, Mr Chase, and Mr Charles Carroll of Carrollton in Maryland, are chosen a Committee to go into Canada. The Characters of the two first you know. The last, is not a Member of Congress, but a Gentleman of independant Fortune, perhaps the largest in America, 150 or 200, thousand Pounds sterling educated in some University in France, tho a Native of America of great Abilities and Learning, compleat Master of French Language and a Professor of the Roman catholic Religion yet a warm, a firm, a zealous Supporter of the Rights of America, in whose Cause he has hazarded his all.

Mr John Carroll of Maryland, a Roman Catholic Priest and a Jesuit, is to go with the Committee. The Priests in Canada having refused Baptism and Absolution to our Friends there.

General Lee is to command in that Country, whose Address Experience, and Abilities added to his Fluency in the French Language, will give him great Advantages.

The Events of War are uncertain: We cannot insure Success, but

We can deserve it. I am happy in this Provision for that important Department, because I think it the best that could be made in our Circumstances. Your Prudence will direct you to communicate the Circumstances of the Priest, the Jesuit and the Romish Religion only to such Persons as can judge of the Measure upon large and generous Principles, and will not indiscreetly divulge it. The Step was necessary, for the Anathema's of the Church are very terrible to our Friends in Canada.

I wish I understood French as well as you. I would have gone to Canada, if I had. I feel the Want of Education every Day—particularly of that Language. I pray My dear, that you would not suffer your Sons or your Daughter, ever to feel a similar Pain. It is in your Power to teach them French, and I every day see more and more that it will become a necessary Accomplishment of an American Gentleman and Lady. Pray write me in your next the Name of the Author of your thin French Grammar, which gives you the Pronunciation of the French Words in English Letters, i.e. which shows you, how the same sounds would be signified by English Vowells and Consonants.

Write me as often as you can—tell me all the News. Desire the Children to write to me, and believe me to be theirs and yours.

Abigail Adams to John Adams

Saturday Evening March 2 [*1776*]

I was greatly rejoiced at the return of your Servant to find you had safely arrived, and that you were well. I had never heard a word from you after you left New york, and a most ridiciolous story had been industerously propagated in this and the Neighbouring Towns to injure the cause and blast your Reputation, viz that you and your President had gone on board a Man of War from N. y and saild for England. I should not mention so Idle a report, but that it had given uneasiness to some of your Friends, not that they in the least credited the report, but because the Gaping vulgar Swallowed the story. One man had deserted them and proved a traitor, an other might &c. I assure you such high Disputes took place in the publick house of this parish, that some men were collerd and draged out of the shop, with great Threats for reporting such scandelous lies, and an unkle of ours offerd his life as a forfeit for you if the report proved true.

However it has been a Nine days marvel and will now cease. I heartily wish every Tory was Extirpated America. They are continually by Secret means undermineing and injuring our cause.

I am Charmed with the Sentiments of Common Sense; and wonder how an honest Heart, one who wishes the welfare of their country, and the happiness of posterity can hesitate one moment at adopting them; I want to know how those sentiments are received in Congress? I dare say their would be no difficulty in procuring a vote and instructions from all the Assemblies in New England for independancy. I most sincerely wish that now in the Lucky Minuet it might be done.

I have been kept in a continual state of anxiety and Expectation ever since you left me. It has been said to morrow and to morrow for this month, but when the dreadfull to morrow will be I know not—but hark! The House this instant shakes with the Roar of Cannon. I have been to the Door and find tis a cannonade from our Army, orders I find are come for all the remaining Militia to repair to the lines a monday Night by twelve o clock. No sleep for me to Night, and if I cannot who have no guilt upon my soul with regard to this Cause, how shall the misirible wretches who have been the procurers of this Dreadfull Scene and those who are to be the actors, lie down with the load of guilt upon their souls.

Sunday Eve March 3

I went to Bed after 12 but got no rest, the Cannon continued firing and my Heart Beat pace with them all Night. We have had a pretty quiet day, but what to morrow will bring forth God only knows.

Monday Evening

Tolerable quiet to day the Militia have all musterd with 3 days provision and are all march'd by 3 o clock this afternoon tho their Notice was no longer than 8 oclock Saturday, and now we have scarcly a Man but our regular guards either in W[*eymouth*], H[*ingham*] or B[*raintree*], or M[*ilton*] and the Militia from the more remote towns are call'd in as Sea coast guards. Can you form to your self an Idea of our Sensations. P[*alme*]r is chief C[*olone*]l, B[*as*]s is Leit c[*olone*]l and S[*ope*]r Major and Hall Captain.

I have just returnd from P[*enn*]s Hill where I have been sitting to hear the amazing roar of cannon and from whence I could see every shell which was thrown. The Sound I think is one of the Grandest in Nature and is of the true Speicies of the Sublime. Tis now an incessant Roar. But o the fatal Ideas which are connected with the sound. How many of our dear country men must fall?

Twesday morning

I went to bed about 12 and rose again a Little after one I could no more sleep than if I had been in the ingagement. The ratling of the windows the jar of the house and the continual roar of 24 pounders the Bursting of shells give us such Ideas, and realize a Scene to us of which we could scarcly form any conception. About Six this morning, there was quiet; I rejoiced in a few hours calm. I hear we got possession of Dorchester Hill Last Night. 4000 thousand men upon it to day—lost but one Man. The ships are all drawn round the Town. To Night we shall realize a more terible scene still. I sometimes think I cannot stand it—I wish my self with you, out of hearing as I cannot assist them. I hope to give you joy of Boston, even if it is in ruins before I send this away. I am too much agitated to write as I ought, and Languid for want of rest.

Thursday Fast day

All my anxiety, and Distress, is at present at an End. I feel dissapointed. This day our Militia are all returning, without Effecting any
thing more than taking possession of Dorchester Hill. I hope it is wise
and just, but from all the Muster and stir I hoped and expected more
important and decisive scenes; I would not have sufferd all I have, for
two such Hills. Ever since the taking of that we have had a perfect
calm nor can I learn yet what Effect it has had in Boston. I do not hear
of one persons Escapeing since.

I was very much pleased with your choise of a committe for Canada. All those to whom I have venturd to shew that part of your Letter
approve the Scheme of the Priest as a master stroke of policy; I feel
sorry that G Lee has left us, but his presence at New york was no
doubt of great importance as we have reason to think it prevented
Clinton from landing and gathering together such a Nest of virmin as
would at least have distressd us greatly. But how can you spair him
from there? Can you make his place good—can you supply it with a
man Eaquelly qualified to save us? How do the virginians realish the
Troops said to be destined for them? Are they putting themselves into
a state of Defence? I inclose to you a Coppy of a Letter sent by Capt
Furnance who is in mr Ned churchs imploy and who came into the
Cape about 10 days ago. You will Learn the Sentiments of our Cousin
by it, some of which may be true, but I hope he is a much better divine
than politician.

I hear in one of his Letters he mentions certain intercepted Letters
which he says have made much Noise in England, and Laments that
you ever wrote them.

What will he and others say to common Sense? I cannot Bear to
thing of your continuing in a state of supineness this winter.

> "There is a tide in the affairs of Men
> which taken, at the flood leads on to fortune;
> omitted, all the voyage of their life
> is bound in shallows and in miseries.

On such a full sea are we now a float;
And we must take the current when it serves,
or lose our ventures."
Shakespear

Sunday Eve March 10

I had scarcly finished those lines when my Ears were again assaulted with the roar of Cannon. I could not write any further. My Hand and heart will tremble, at this Domestick fury, and firce civil strife, which cumber all our parts tho,

Blood and destruction are so much in use.

And Dreadfull objects so familiar, yet is not pitty chok'd, nor my Heart grown Callous. I feel for the unhappy wretches who know not where to fly for safety. I feel still more for my Bleading Countrymen who are hazarding their lives and their Limbs. A most Terible and incessant Cannonade from half after 8 till six this morning. I hear we lost four men killed and some wounded in attempting to take the Hill nearest the Town called Nook Hill. We did some work, but the fire from [the ships] Beat [off] our Men so that they did not [secure] it but retired to the fort upon the other Hill.

I have not got all the perticuliars I wish I had but, as I have an opportunity of sending this I shall endeavour to be more perticuliar in my Next.

All our Little ones send duty. Tommy has been very sick with what is call'd the Scarlet or purple fever, but has got about again.

If we have Reinforcements here, I believe we shall be driven from the sea coast, but in what so ever state I am I will endeavour to be there with content.

Man wants but Little here below
Nor wants that Little long.

You will excuse this very incorrect Letter. You see in what pur-
tubation it has been written and how many times I have left of. Adieu
pray write me every opportunity.
Yours

Tooks Grammer is the one you mention.

Abigail Adams to John Adams

B[*raintr*]ee March 16 1776

I last Evening Received yours of March 8. I must confess my self in
fault that I did not write sooner to you, but I was in continual Expectation that some important Event would take place and give me a subject
worth writing upon. Before this reaches you I immagine you will have
Received two Letters from me; the Last I closed this Day week; since
that time there has been some movements amongst the Ministerial
Troops as if they meant to Evacuate the Town of Boston. Between 70
and 80 vessels of various Sizes are gone down and lay in a row in fair
sight of this place, all of which appear to be loaded and by what can be
collected from our own observations and from deserters they have
been plundering the Town. I have been very faithless with regard to
their quitting Boston, and know not how to account for it, nor am I yet
satisfied that they will leave it, tho it seems to be the prevailing opinion
of most people; we are obliged to place the Militia upon gaurd every
Night upon the shoars thro fear of an invasion. There has been no
firing since Last twesday, till about 12 o clock last Night, when I was
waked out of my sleep with a smart Cannonade which continued till
Nine o clock this morning, and prevented any further repose for me;
the occasion I have not yet heard, but before I close this Letter I may
be able to give you some account of it.

By the accounts in the publick papers the plot thickens; and some
very important Crisis seems near at hand. Perhaps providence see's

it Necessary in order to answer important ends and designs that the seat of War should be changed from this to the Southeren colonies that each may have a proper sympathy for the other, and unite in a seperation. The Refuge of the Believer amidst all the afflictive dispensations of providence, is that, the Lord Reigneth, and that he can restrain the Arm of Man.

Orders are given to our Army to hold themselves in readiness to March at a moments warning. I'll meet you at Philippi said the Ghost of Caesar to Brutus.

Sunday Noon

Being quite sick with a voilent cold I have tarried at Home to day; I find the fireing was occasiond by our peoples taking possession of Nook Hill, which they kept in spite of the Cannonade, and which has really obliged our Enemy to decamp this morning on board the Transports; as I hear by a mesenger just come from Head Quarters. Some of the Select Men have been to the lines and inform that they have carried of [every] thing they could possibly take, and what they could not they have [burnt, broke, or hove into the water. This] is I [believe fact,] many articles of good Household furniture having in the course of the week come on shore at Great Hill, both upon this and weymouth side, Lids of Desks mahogona chairs tables &c. Our People I hear will have Liberty to enter Boston, those who have had the small pox. The Enemy have not yet come under sail. I cannot help suspecting some design which we do not yet comprehend; to what quarter of the World they are bound is wholy unknown, but tis generally Thought to New york. Many people are Elated with their quitting Boston. I confess I do not feel so, tis only lifting the burden from one shoulder to the other which perhaps is less able or less willing to support it. To what a contemptable situation are the Troops of Britain reduced! I feel glad however that Boston is not Distroyed. I hope it will be so secured and guarded as to baffel all future attemps against it. I hear that general How said upon going upon some Eminence in Town to view our

Troops who had taken Dorchester Hill unperceived by them till sun rise, "By God these fellows have done more work in one night than I could make my Army do in three months" and he might well say so for in one Night two forts and long Breast works were sprung up besides several Barracks. 300 and 70 teems were imployed most of which went 3 load in the Night, beside 4000 men who worked with good Hearts.

From pens Hill we have a view of the largest Fleet ever seen in America. You may count upwards of 100 and 70 sail. They look like a Forrest. It was very lucky for us that we got possession of Nook Hill. They had placed their cannon so as to fire upon the Top of the Hill where they had observed our people marking out the Ground, but it was only to Elude them for they began lower upon the Hill and nearer the Town. It was a very foggy dark Evening and they had possession of the Hill six hours before a gun was fired, and when they did fire they over shot our people so that they were coverd before morning and not one man lost, which the Enemy no sooner discoverd than Bunker Hill was abandoned and every Man decamp'd as soon as he could for they found they should not be able to get away if we once got our cannon mounted. Our General may say with Ceasar veni vidi et vici.

What Effect does the Expectation of commisioners have with you? Are they held in disdain as they are here. It is come to that pass now that the longest sword must deside the contest—and the sword is less Dreaded here than the commisioners.

You mention Threats upon B[*raintre*]e. I know of none, nor ever heard of any till you mentiond them. The Tories look a little crest fallen; as for Cleverly he looks like the knight of the woful countanance. I hear all the Mongrel Breed are left in Boston—and our people who were prisoners are put into Irons and carried of.

As to all your own private affair I generally avoid mentioning them to you; I take the best care I am capable of them. I have found some difficulty attending the only Man I have upon the place being so often taking of. John and Jonathan have taken all the care in his absence, and performed very well. Bass got home very well. My Fathers horse came home in fine order and much to his satisfaction. Your own very poor. Cannot you hire a Sevant where you are. I am sorry you are put to so much difficulty for want of one. I suppose you do not think one word about comeing home, and how you will get home I know not.

I made a mistake in the Name of the Grammer—tis Tandons, instead of Took. I wish you could purchase Lord Chesterfields Letters—I have lately heard them very highly spoken of. I smiled at your couplet of Lattin, your Daughter may be able in time to conster it, as she has already made some considerable proficiency in her accidents, but her Mamma was obliged to get it translated.

Pray write Lord sterlings character. I want to know whether you live in any harmony with —— and how you setled matters. I think he seems in better humour.

I think I do not admire the speach from the Rostrum, tis a heavy unelegant, verbose performance and did not strike my fancy at all. I am very sausy suppose you will say—tis a Liberty I take with you; indulgance is apt to spoil one. Adieu—yours most sincerely.

PS Pray convey me a little paper I have but enough for one Letter more.

John Adams to Abigail Adams

March 19. 1776

Yesterday I had the long expected and much wish'd Pleasure of a Letter from you, of various Dates from the 2d to the 10 March. This is the first Line I have recd since I left you. I wrote you from, Watertown I believe, relating my Feast at the Qr Mr. Gen. with the Coghnawaga Indians and from Framingham, an Account of the ordnance there, and from New York I sent you a Pamphlet—hope you recd these. Since my arrival here, I have written to you as often as I could.

I am much pleased with your Caution, in your Letter in avoiding Names both of Persons and Places, or any other Circumstances, which might designate to Strangers, the Writer, or the Person written to, or the Persons mentioned. Characters and Descriptions will do as well.

The Lye, which you say occasioned such Disputes at the Tavern was curious enough. Who could make and spread it? Am much obliged to an Unkle, for his Friendship: my worthy fellow Citizens may be easy about me. I never can forsake what I take to be their Interests. My own have never been considered by me, in Competition with theirs. My Ease, my domestic Happiness, my rural Pleasures my Little Property, my personal Liberty, my Reputation my Life, have little Weight and ever had, in my own Estimation, in Comparison of the great object of my Country. I can say of it with great sincerity, as Horace says of Virtue—to America only and her Friends a Friend.

You ask, what is thought of Common sense. Sensible Men think there are some Whims, some sophisms some artfull Addresses to superstitious Notions, some keen attempts upon the Passions, in this Pamphlet. But all agree there is a great deal of good sense, delivered in a clear, simple, concise and nervous Style.

His sentiments of the Abilities of America, and of the Difficulty of a Reconciliation with G.B. are generally approved. But his Notions, and Plans of Continental Government are not much applauded. Indeed this Writer has a better Hand at pulling down than building.

It has been very generally propagated through the Continent that I wrote this Pamphlet. But altho I could not have written any Thing in so manly and striking a style, I flatter myself I should have made a more respectable Figure as an Architect, if I had undertaken such a Work. This Writer seems to have very inadequate Ideas of what is proper and necessary to be done, in order to form Constitutions for single Colonies, as well as a great Model of Union for the whole.

Yours Distresses which you have painted in such lively Colours, I feel in every Line as I read. I dare not write, all that I think upon this Occasion. I wish our People had taken Possession of Nook Hill, at the same Time when they got the other Heights, and before the Militia were dismissed.

Poor Cousin! I pitty him. How much soever he may lament, certain Letters, I dont lament. I never repent of what was no sin. Misfortunes may be born without Whining. But if I can believe Mr Dana those Letters, were much admired in England. I cant help laughing when I write it, because they were really such hasty crude Scraps. If I could have foreseen their Fate, they should have been fit to be seen and worth all the Noise they have made. Mr Dana says they were considered in England as containing a comprehensive Idea of what was necessary to be done, and as shewing Resolution enough to do it. Wretched Stuff as they really were, (according to him) they have contributed somewhat towards making certain Persons to be thought the greatest Statesmen in the World. So much for Vanity.

My Love, Duty, Respects, and Compliments, wherever they belong.

Virginia will be well defended, so will N.Y. so will S. Car. America will eer long, raise her Voice aloud—and assume a bolder Air.

Abigail's most famous expression—"Remember the Ladies"—comes from the letter to John immediately below. As is typical of most of her correspondence, it contains a mixture of military, political, and domestic news before she makes her argument for greater rights for women. Despite her somewhat lighthearted tone, Abigail expressed here and in numerous other letters a genuine concern that women receive greater opportunities for education and greater respect within their own households.

John's flippant reply regarding Abigail's "extraordinary Code of Laws" did not please Abigail. Writing to her friend Mercy Otis Warren, she recounted the exchange and noted sarcastically about John, "So I have help'd the Sex abundantly, but I will tell him I have only been making trial of the disintressedness of his Virtue, and when weigh'd in the balance have found it wanting."

Abigail Adams to John Adams

Braintree March 31 1776

I wish you would ever write me a Letter half as long as I write you; and tell me if you may where your Fleet are gone? What sort of Defence Virgina can make against our common Enemy? Whether it is so situated as to make an able Defence? Are not the Gentery Lords and the common people vassals, are they not like the uncivilized Natives Brittain represents us to be? I hope their Riffel Men who have shewen themselves very savage and even Blood thirsty; are not a specimen of the Generality of the people.

I am willing to allow the Colony great merrit for having produced a Washington but they have been shamefully duped by a Dunmore.

I have sometimes been ready to think that the passion for Liberty cannot be Eaquelly Strong in the Breasts of those who have been accustomed to deprive their fellow Creatures of theirs. Of this I am certain that it is not founded upon that Generous and christian principal of doing to others as we would that others should do unto us.

Do not you want to see Boston; I am fearfull of the small pox, or I should have been in before this time. I got Mr Crane to go to our House and see what state it was in. I find it has been occupied by one of the Doctors of a Regiment, very dirty, but no other damage has been done to it. The few thing which were left in it are all gone. Cranch has the key which he never deliverd up. I have wrote to him for it and am determined to get it Cleand as soon as posible and shut it up. I look upon it a new acquisition of property, a property which one month ago I did not value at a single shilling, and could with pleasure have seen it in flames.

The Town in General is left in a better state than we expected, more oweing to a percipitate flight than any Regard to the inhabitants, tho some individuals Discoverd a sense of honour and justice and have left the rent of the Houses in which they were, for the owners and the furniture unhurt, or if damaged sufficent to make it good.

Others have committed abominable Ravages. The Mansion House of your President is safe and the furniture unhurt whilst both the House and Furniture of the Solisiter General have fallen a prey to their own merciless party. Surely the very Fiends feel a Reverential awe for virtue and patriotism, whilst they Detest the paricide and traitor.

I feel very differently at the approach of spring to what I did a month ago. We knew not then whether we could plant or sow with safety, whether when we had toild we could reap the fruits of our own industery, whether we could rest in our own Cottages, or whether we should not be driven from the sea coasts to seek shelter in the wilderness but now we feel as if we might sit under our own vine and Eat the good of the land.

I feel a gaieti de Coar to which before I was a stranger. I think the sun looks brighter the Birds sing more melodiously, and Nature puts on a more chearfull countanance. We feel a temporary peace, and the poor fugitives are returning to their deserted habitations.

Tho we felicitate ourselves, we sympathize with those who are trembling least the Lot of Boston should be theirs. But they cannot be in similar circumstances unless pusilanimity and cowardise should take possession of them. They have time and warning given them to see the Evil and shun it. I long to hear that you have declared an independancy—and by the way in the New Code of Laws which I suppose it will be necessary for you to make I desire you would Remember the Ladies, and be more generous and favourable to them than your ancestors. Do not put such unlimited power into the hands of the Husbands. Remember all Men would be tyrants if they could. If perticuliar care and attention is not paid to the Laidies we are determined to foment a Rebelion, and will not hold ourselves bound by any Laws in which we have no voice, or Representation.

That your Sex are Naturally Tyrannical is a Truth so throughly established as to admit of no dispute, but such of you as wish to be happy willingly give up the harsh title of Master for the more tender and endearing one of Friend. Why then, not put it out of the power of the vicious and the Lawless to use us with cruelty and indignity with impunity. Men of sense in all Ages abhor those customs which treat us only as the vassals of your Sex. Regard us then as Beings placed by providence under your protection and in immitation of the Supreem Being make use of that power only for our happiness.

John Adams to Abigail Adams

Ap. 14. 1776

You justly complain of my short Letters, but the critical State of Things and the Multiplicity of Avocations must plead my Excuse. You ask where the Fleet is. The inclosed Papers will inform you. You ask what sort of Defence Virginia can make? I believe they will make an able Defence. Their Militia and minute Men, have been some time employed in training them selves, and they have Nine Battallions of regulars as they call them maintained, among them, under good officers, at the Continental Expence. They have set up a Number of Manufactories of Fire Arms, which are busily employed. They are tolerably supplied with Powder, and are successfull and assiduous, in making salt Petre. Their neighbouring Sister or rather Daughter Colony of North Carolina, which is a warlike Colony, and has several Battallions at the Continental Expence, as well as a pretty good Militia, are ready to assist them, and they are in very good spirits, and seem determined to make a brave Resistance. The Gentry are very rich, and the common People very poor. This Inequality of Property, gives an Aristocratical Turn to all their Proceedings, and occasions a strong Aversion in their Patricians, to Common Sense. But the Spirit of these Barons, is coming down, and it must submit.

It is very true, as you observe they have been duped by Dunmore. But this is a Common Case. All the Colonies are duped, more or less, at one Time and another. A more egregious Bubble, was never blown up, than the Story of Commissioners coming to treat with the Congress. Yet it has gained Credit like a Charm, not only without but against the clearest Evidence. I never shall forget the Delusion, which seized our best and most sagacious Friends the dear Inhabitants of Boston, the Winter before last. Credulity and the Want of Foresight, are Imperfections in the human Character, that no Politician can sufficiently guard against.

You have given me some Pleasure, by your Account of a certain House in Queen Street. I had burned it, long ago, in Imagination. It rises new to my View like a Phœnix. What shall I say of the Solicitor General? I pity his pretty Children, I pity his Father, and his sisters. I wish I could be clear that it is no moral Evil to pity him and his Lady. Upon Repentance they will certainly have a large Share in the Compassions of many. But let Us take Warning and give it to our Children. Whenever Vanity, and Gaiety, a Love of Pomp and Dress, Furniture, Equipage, Buildings, great Company expensive Diversions, and elegant Entertainments gets the better of the Principles and Judgments of Men or Women there is no knowing where they will stop, nor into what Evils, natural, moral, or political, they will lead us.

Your Description of your own Gaiety de Coeur, charms me. Thanks be to God you have just Cause to rejoice—and may the bright Prospect, be obscured by no Cloud.

As to Declarations of Independency, be patient. Read our Privateering Laws, and our Commercial Laws. What signifies a Word.

As to your extraordinary Code of Laws, I cannot but laugh. We have been told that our Struggle has loosened the bands of Government every Where. That Children and Apprentices were disobedient—that schools and Colledges were grown turbulent—that Indians Slighted their Guardians and Negroes grew insolent to their Masters. But your Letter was the first Intimation that another Tribe more numerous and powerfull than all the rest were grown discontented. This is rather too coarse a Compliment but you are so saucy, I wont blot it out.

Depend upon it, We know better than to repeal our Masculine systems. Altho they are in full Force, you know they are little more than

Theory. We dare not exert our Power in its full Latitude. We are obliged to go fair, and softly, and in Practice you know We are the subjects. We have only the Name of Masters, and rather than give up this, which would compleatly subject Us to the Despotism of the Peticoat, I hope General Washington, and all our brave Heroes would fight. I am sure every good Politician would plot, as long as he would against Despotism, Empire, Monarchy, Aristocracy, Oligarchy, or Ochlocracy. A fine Story indeed. I begin to think the Ministry as deep as they are wicked. After Stirring up Tories, Landjobbers, Trimmers, Bigots, Canadians Indians, Negroes, Hanoverians, Hessians, Russians, Irish Roman Catholicks, Scotch Renegadoes, at last they have stimulated the   to demand new Priviledges and threaten to rebell.

John Adams to Abigail Adams

April 15. 1776

I send you every News Paper, that comes out, and I send you now and then a few sheets of Paper but this Article is as scarce here, as with you. I would send a Quire, if I could get a Conveyance. I write you, now and then a Line, as often as I can, but I can tell you no News, but what I send in the public Papers.

We are Waiting it is said for Commissioners, a Messiah that will never come. This Story of Commissioners is as arrant an Illusion as ever was hatched in the Brain of an Enthusiast, a Politician, or a Maniac. I have laugh'd at it—scolded at it—griev'd at it—and I dont know but I may at an unguarded Moment have rip'd at it—but it is vain to Reason against such Delusions. I was very sorry to see in a Letter from the General that he had been bubbled with it, and still more to see in a Letter from my sagacious Friend at Plymouth, that he was taken in too.

My opinion is that the Commissioners and the Commission have been here I mean in America these two Months. The Governors Mandamus Councillors, Collectors and Comptrollers, and Commanders of the Army and Navy, I conjecture compose the List and their Power is to receive Submissions. But We are not in a very submissive Mood. They will get no Advantage of Us.

We shall go on, to Perfection I believe. I have been very busy for some time—have written about Ten sheets of Paper with my own Hand, about some trifling Affairs, which I may mention some time or other—not now for fear of Accidents.

What will come of this Labour Time will discover. I shall get nothing by it, I believe, because I never get any Thing by any Thing that I do. I am sure the Public or Posterity ought to get Something. I believe my Children will think I might as well have thought and laboured, a little, night and Day for their Benefit. But I will not bear the Reproaches of my Children. I will tell them that I studied and laboured to procure a free Constitution of Government for them to solace themselves under, and if they do not prefer this to ample Fortune, to Ease and Elegance, they are not my Children, and I care not what becomes of them. They shall live upon thin Diet, wear mean Cloaths, and work hard, with Chearfull Hearts and free Spirits or they may be the Children of the Earth or of no one, for me.

John has Genius and so has Charles. Take Care that they dont go astray. Cultivate their Minds inspire their little Hearts, raise their Wishes—Fix their Attention upon great and glorious Objects root out every little Thing—weed out every Meanness, make them great and manly. Teach them to scorn Injustice, Ingratitude, Cowardice, and Falshood. Let them revere nothing but Religion, Morality and Liberty.

Nabby and Tommy are not forgotten by me altho I did not mention them before. The first by Reason of her sex, requires a Different Education from the two I have mentioned. Of this you are the only judge. I want to send each of my little pretty flock, some present or other. I have walked over this City twenty Times and gaped at every shop like a Country man to find something, but could not. Ask every one of them what they would choose to have and write it to me in your next Letter. From this I shall judge of their Taste and Fancy and Discretion.

Abigail Adams to John Adams

B[*raintre*]e May 7 1776

How many are the solitary hours I spend, ruminating upon the past, and anticipating the future, whilst you overwhelmd with the cares of state, have but few moments you can devote to any individual. All domestick pleasures and injoyments are absorbed in the Great and importantt duty you owe your Country "for our Country is as it were a secondary God, and the First and greatest parent. It is to be preferred to Parents Wives Children, Friends and all things the Gods only Excepted. For if our Country perishes it is as imposible to save an Individual, as to preserve one of the fingers of a Mortified Hand." Thus do I supress every wish, and silence every Murmer, acquiesceing in a painfull seperation from the companion of my youth, and the Friend of my Heart.

I believe tis near ten days since I wrote you a line. I have not felt in a humour to entertain you. If I had taken up my pen perhaps some unbecomeing invective might have fallen from it; the Eyes of our Rulers have been closed and a Lethargy has seazd almost every Member. I fear a fatal Security has taken possession of them. Whilst the Building is on flame they tremble at the expence of water to quench it. In short two months has Elapsed since the Evacuation of Boston, and very Little has been done in that time to secure it, or the Harbour from future invasion till the people are all in a flame; and no one among us that I have heard of even mentions expence. They think universally that there has been an amaizing neglect some where. Many have turnd out as volunteers to work upon Nodles Island, and many more would go upon Nantaskit if it was once set on foot. "Tis a Maxim of state That power and Liberty are like Heat and moisture; where they are well mixt every thing prospers, where they are single, they are Destructive."

A Goverment of more stability is much wanted in this colony, and they are ready to receive it from the Hands of the Congress, and since

I have begun with Maxims of state I will add an other viz that a people may let a king fall, yet still remain a people, but if a king Let his people slip from him, he is no longer a king. And as this is most certainly our case, why not proclaim to the world in decisive terms your own importance?

Shall we not be dispiced by foreign powers for hesitateing so long at a word?

I can not say that I think you very generous to the Ladies, for whilst you are proclaiming peace and good will to Men, Emancipating all Nations, you insist upon retaining an absolute power over wives. But you must remember that Arbitary power, is like most other things which are very hard, very liable to be broken—and notwithstanding all your wise Laws and Maxims we have it in our power not only to free ourselves but to subdue our Masters, and without voilence throw both your natural and legal authority at our feet.

"Charm by accepting, by submitting sway
Yet have our Humour most when we obey."

I thank you for several Letters which I have received since I wrote Last. They alleviate a tedious absence, and I long earnestly for a saturday Evening, and Experience a similar pleasure to that which I used to find in the return of my Friend upon that day after a weeks absence. The Idea of a year dissolves all my Phylosophy.

Our Little ones whom you so often recommend to my care and instruction shall not be deficient in virtue or probity if the precepts of a Mother have their desired Effect, but they would be doubly inforced could they be indulged with the example of a Father constantly before them; I often point them to their Sire

"engaged in a corrupted state
Wrestling with vice and faction."

Portia

Abigail Adams to John Adams

May 14 1776

I set down to write you a Letter wholy Domestick with out one word of politicks or any thing of the Kind, and tho you may have matters of infinately more importance before you, yet let it come as a relaxation to you. Know then that we have had a very cold backward Spring, till about ten days past when every thing looks finely. We have had fine Spring rains which makes the Husbandary promise fair—but the great difficulty has been to procure Labourers. There is such a demand of men from the publick and such a price given that the farmer who Hires must be greatly out of pocket. A man will not talk with you who is worth hireing under 24 pounds pr year. Col. Quincy and Thayer give that price, and some give more. Isaac insisted upon my giving him 20 pounds or he would leave me. He is no mower and I found very unfit to take the lead upon the Farm, having no forethought or any contrivance to plan his Buisness, tho in the Execution faithfull. I found I wanted somebody of spirit who was wiser than myself, to Conduct my Buisness. I went about and my Friends inquired but every Labourer who was active was gone and going into the Service. I asked advice of my Friends and Neighbours they all adviced me to Let Isaac go, rather than give that price. I setled with him and we parted. Mr Belcher is now with me and has undertaken to conduct the Buisness, which he has hitherto done with spirit and activity. I know his virtues I know his faults. Hithertoo I give him 2 shillings pr day, and Daniel Nightingale works with him at the same lay. I would have hired him for the season but he was engaged to look after a place or two for people who are gone into the Army. I am still in quest of a Man by the year, but whether I shall effect it, I know not. I have done the best I could. We are just now ready to plant, the barly look charmingly. I shall be quite a Farmeriss an other year.

You made no perticulir agreement with Isaac so he insisted upon my paying him 13. 6 8. I paid him 12 pounds 18 and 8 pence, and thought it Sufficient.

When Bass returnd he brought me some Money from you. After the deduction of his account and the horse hire there remaind 15 pounds. I have Received 12 from mr Thaxter which with one Note of 20 pounds which I exchanged and some small matters of interest which I received and a Little Hay &c I have discharged the following debts—To my Father for his Horse twice 12 pounds (he would not have any thing for the last time). To Bracket, £13. 6s. 8d. To Isaac 12. 18. 8. To mr Hunt for the House 26. 15. 4. and the Rates of two years 1774. £4 14s 8d. and for 1775: £7. 11s. 11d. Besides this have supported the family which is no small one you know and paid all Little charges which have occurd in the farming way. I hardly know how I have got thro these things, but it gives me great pleasure to say they are done because I know it will be an Ease to your mind which amid all other cares which surround you will sometimes advert to your own Little Farm and to your Family. There remains due to mr Hunt about 42 pounds. I determine if it lays in my power to discharge the bond—and I have some prospect of it.

Our Little Flock send duty. I call them seperately and told them Pappa wanted to send them something and requested of them what they would have. A Book was the answer of them all only Tom wanted a picture Book and charlss the History of king and Queen. It was natural for them to think of a Book as that is the only present Pappa has been used to make them.

Adieu. Yours

Hermitta

John Adams to Abigail Adams

May 22d. 1776

When a Man is seated, in the Midst of forty People some of whom are talking, and others whispering, it is not easy to think, what is proper to write. I shall send you the News-Papers, which will inform you, of public affairs, and the particular Flickerings of Parties in this Colony.

I am happy to learn from your Letter, that a Flame is at last raised among the People, for the Fortification of the Harbour. Whether Nantaskett, or Point Alderton would be proper Posts to be taken I cant say. But I would fortify every Place, which is proper, and which Cannon could be obtained for.

Generals Gates and Mifflin are now here. Gen. Washington will be here tomorrow—When We shall consult and deliberate, concerning the Operations of the ensuing Campain.

We have dismal Accounts from Europe, of the Preparations against Us. This Summer will be very important to us. We shall have a severe Tryal of our Patience, Fortitude and Perseverance. But I hope We shall do valiantly and tread down our Enemies.

I have some Thoughts of petitioning the General Court for Leave to bring my Family, here. I am a lonely, forlorn, Creature here. It used to be some Comfort to me, that I had a servant, and some Horses—they composed a sort of Family for me. But now, there is not one Creature here, that I seem to have any Kind of Relation to.

It is a cruel Reflection, which very often comes across me, that I should be seperated so far, from those Babes, whose Education And Welfare lies so near my Heart. But greater Misfortunes than these, must not divert Us from superiour Duties.

Your Sentiments of the Duties We owe to our Country, are such as become the best of Women, and the best of Men. Among all the Disappointments, and Perplexities, which have fallen to my share in Life, nothing has contributed so much to support my Mind, as the choice

Blessing of a Wife, whose Capacity, enabled her to comprehend, and whose pure Virtue obliged her to approve the Views of her Husband. This has been the cheering Consolation of my Heart, in my most solitary gloomy and disconsolate Hours. In this remote situation, I am deprived in a great Measure of this Comfort. Yet I read, and read again your charming Letters, and they serve me, in some faint degree as a substitute for the Company and Conversation of the Writer.

I want to take a Walk with you in the Garden—to go over to the Common—the Plain—the Meadow. I want to take Charles in one Hand and Tom in the other, and Walk with you, Nabby on your Right Hand and John upon my left—to view the Corn Fields, the orchards, &c.

Alass poor Imagination! how faintly and imperfectly do you supply the Want of original and Reality!

But instead of these pleasing Scænes of domestic Life, I hope you will not be disturbed with the Alarms of War. I hope yet I fear.

John Adams to Abigail Adams

June 2. 1776

Yesterday I dined with Captain Richards, the Gentleman who made me the present of the brass Pistolls. We had Cherries Strawberries and Green Peas in Plenty. The Fruits are three Weeks earlier here than with you, in deed they are a fort night earlier on the East, than on the West side of Delaware River. We have had green Peas, this Week past, but they were brought over the River from New Jersey, to this Markett. There are none grown in the City, or on the West side of the River yet. The Reason is, the Soil of New Jersey is a warm Sand, that of Pensilvania, a cold Clay. So much for Peas and Berries.

Now for some thing of more Importance. In all the Correspondencies I have maintained, during a Course of twenty Years at least that I have been a Writer of Letters I never kept a Single Copy. This

Negligence and Inaccuracy, has been a great Misfortune to me, on many Occasions. I have now purchased a Folio Book, in the first Page of which, excepting one blank Leaff, I am writing this Letter, and intend to write all my Letters to you in it from this Time forward. This will be an Advantage to me in several Respects. In the first Place, I shall write more deliberately. In the second Place, I shall be able at all times to review what I have written. 3. I shall know how often I write. 4. I shall discover by this Means, whether any of my Letters to you, miscarry.

If it were possible for me to find a Conveyance, I would send you such another blank Book, as a Present, that you might begin the Practice at the same Time, for I really think that your Letters are much better worth preserving than mine. Your Daughter and sons will very soon write so good Hands that they will copy the Letters for you from your Book, which will improve them at the same Time that it relieves you.

On 2 July, Congress finally adopted a resolution in favor of independence, and on 4 July approved the Declaration of Independence. John sat on the committee appointed to draft the document and had himself encouraged Thomas Jefferson to write the original draft, which was accepted with some modifications. As is typical of John, he recognized the historical significance of the event but was just slightly off in his analysis of how it would be remembered—he was convinced Americans would always celebrate 2 July as "the most memorable Epocha, in the History of America."

John Adams to Abigail Adams

Philadelphia July 3. 1776

Your Favour of June 17. dated at Plymouth, was handed me, by yesterdays Post. I was much pleased to find that you had taken a Journey to Plymouth, to see your Friends in the long Absence of one whom you may wish to see. The Excursion will be an Amusement, and will serve your Heath. How happy would it have made me to have taken this Journey with you?

I was informed, a day or two before the Receipt of your Letter, that you was gone to Plymouth, by Mrs Polly Palmer, who was obliging enough in your Absence, to inform me, of the Particulars of the Expedition to the lower Harbour against the Men of War. Her Narration is executed, with a Precision and Perspicuity, which would have become the Pen of an accomplished Historian.

I am very glad you had so good an opportunity of seeing, one of our little American Men of War. Many Ideas, new to you, must have presented themselves in such a Scene; and you will in future, better understand the Relations of Sea Engagements.

I rejoice extreamly at Dr Bulfinches Petition to open an Hospital. But I hope, the Business will be done upon a larger Scale. I hope, that one Hospital will be licensed in every County, if not in every Town. I am happy to find you resolved, to be with the Children, in the first Class. Mr Whitney and Mrs Katy Quincy, are cleverly through Innoculation, in this City.

I have one favour to ask, and that is, that in your future Letters, you would acknowledge the Receipt of all those you may receive from me, and mention their Dates. By this Means I shall know if any of mine miscarry.

The Information you give me of our Friends refusing his Appointment, has given me much Pain, Grief and Anxiety. I believe I shall be obliged to follow his Example. I have not Fortune enough to support my Family, and what is of more Importance, to support the Dignity of that exalted Station. It is too high and lifted up, for me; who delight in nothing so much as Retreat, Solitude, Silence, and Obscurity. In private Life, no one has a Right to censure me for following my own Inclinations, in Retirement, Simplicity, and Frugality: in public Life, every Man has a Right to remark as he pleases, at least he thinks so.

Yesterday the greatest Question was decided, which ever was debated in America, and a greater perhaps, never was or will be decided among Men. A Resolution was passed without one dissenting Colony "that these united Colonies, are, and of right ought to be free and independent States, and as such, they have, and of Right ought to have full Power to make War, conclude Peace, establish Commerce, and to do all other Acts and Things, which other States may rightfully do." You will see in a few days a Declaration setting forth the Causes, which have impell'd Us to this mighty Revolution, and the Reasons which will justify it, in the Sight of God and Man. A Plan of Confederation will be taken up in a few days.

When I look back to the Year 1761, and recollect the Argument concerning Writs of Assistance, in the Superiour Court, which I have hitherto considered as the Commencement of the Controversy, between Great Britain and America, and run through the whole Period from that Time to this, and recollect the series of political Events the Chain of Causes and Effects, I am Surprized at the Suddenness, as well as Greatness of this Revolution. Britain has been fill'd with Folly, and America with Wisdom, at least this is my Judgment. Time must determine. It is the Will of Heaven, that the two Countries should be sundered forever. It may be the Will of Heaven that America shall suffer, Calamities still more wasting and Distresses yet more dreadfull. If this is to be the Case, it will have this good Effect, at least: it will inspire Us with many Virtues, which We have not, and correct many Errors, Follies, and Vices, which threaten to disturb, dishonour, and destroy us. The Furnace of Affliction produces Refinement, in states as well as Individuals. And the new Governments we are assuming, in every Part, will require a Purification from our Vices, and an Augmentation of our Virtues or they will be no Blessings. The People will have unbounded Power. And the People are extreamly addicted to Corruption and Venality, as well as the Great. I am not without Apprehensions from this Quarter. But I must submit, all my Hopes and Fears, to an overruling Providence, in which, unfashionable as the Faith may be, I firmly believe.

John Adams to Abigail Adams

Philadelphia July 3d. 1776

Had a Declaration of Independency been made seven Months ago, it would have been attended with many great and glorious Effects. We might before this Hour, have formed Alliances with foreign States. We should have mastered Quebec and been in Possession of Canada. You will perhaps wonder, how such a Declaration would have influenced our Affairs, in Canada, but if I could write with Freedom I could easily convince you, that it would, and explain to you the manner how. Many Gentleman in high stations and of great Influence have been duped, by the ministerial Bubble of Commissioners to treat. And in real, sincere Expectation of this Event, which they so fondly wished, they have been slow and languid, in promoting Measures for the Reduction of that Province. Others there are in the Colonies who really wished that our Enterprise in Canada would be defeated, that the Colonies might be brought into Danger and Distress between two Fires, and be thus induced to submit. Others, really wished to defeat the Expedition to Canada, lest the Conquest of it, should elevate the Minds of the People too much to hearken to those Terms of Reconciliation which they believed would be offered Us. These jarring Views Wishes and Designs, occasioned an opposition to many Salutary Measures, which were proposed for the support of that Expedition, and caused Obstructions, Embarrassments and studied Delays, which have finally, lost Us the Province.

All these Causes however in Conjunction would not have disappointed Us, if it had not been for a Misfortune, which could not be foreseen, and perhaps could not have been prevented, I mean the Prevalence of the small Pox among our Troops. This fatal Pestilence, compleated our Destruction. It is a Frown of Providence upon Us, which We ought to lay to heart.

But on the other Hand, the Delay of this Declaration to this Time, has many great Advantages attending it. The Hopes of Reconciliation, which were fondly entertained by Multitudes of honest and well meaning tho weak and mistaken People, have been gradually and at last totally extinguished. Time has been given for the whole People, maturely to consider, the great Question of Independence and to ripen their Judgments, dissipate their Fears, and allure their Hopes, by discussing it in News Papers and Pamphletts, by debating it, in Assemblies Conventions, Committees of safety and Inspection in Town and County Meetings, as well as in private Conversations, so that the whole People in every Colony of the 13, have now adopted it, as their own Act. This will cement the Union, and avoid those Heats and perhaps Convulsions which might have been occasioned, by such a Declaration Six Months ago.

But the Day is past. The Second Day of July 1776, will be the most memorable Epocha, in the History of America. I am apt to believe that it will be celebrated, by succeeding Generations, as the great anniversary Festival. It ought to be commemorated, as the Day of Deliverance by solemn Acts of Devotion to God Almighty. It ought to be solemnized with Pomp and Parade with shews, Games, Sports, Guns, Bells, Bonfires and Illuminations from one End of this Continent to the other from this Time forward forever more.

You will think me transported with Enthusiasm but I am not. I am well aware of the Toil and Blood and Treasure, that it will cost Us to maintain this Declaration, and support and defend these states. Yet through all the Gloom I can see the Rays of ravishing Light and Glory. I can see that the End is more than worth all the Means. And that Posterity will tryumph in that Days Transaction, even altho We should rue it, which I trust in God We shall not.

John Adams to Abigail Adams

Philadelphia July 7. 1776

It is worth the while of a Person, obliged to write as much as I do, to consider the Varieties of Style. The Epistolary, is essentially different from the oratorical, and the Historical Style. Oratory abounds with Figures. History, is Simple, but grave, majestic and formal. Letters, like Conversation, should be free, easy, and familiar. Simplicity and Familiarity, are the Characteristicks of this Kind of Writing. Affectation, is as disagreable, in a Letter, as in Conversation, and therefore, studied Language, premeditated Method, and Sublime Sentiments are not expected in a Letter. Notwithstanding which, the Sublime, as well as the beautifull, and the Novel, may naturally enough, appear, in familiar Letters among Friends. Among the ancients there are two illustrious Examples of the Epistolary Style Cicero and Pliny, whose Letters present you with Modells of fine Writing, which *has* borne the Criticism of almost two thousand Years. In these, you see, the Sublime, the beautifull, the Novell, and the Pathetick, conveyed in as much Simplicity Ease, Freedom, and Familiarity, as Language is capable of.

Let me request you, to turn over the Leaves of the Præceptor, to a Letter of Pliny the Younger, in which he has transmitted, to these days the History of his Uncles Philosophical Curiosity, his Heroic Courage and his melancholly Catastrophe. Read it, and say, whether it is possible to write a Narrative of Facts, in a better Manner. It is copious and particular, in selecting the Circumstances, most natural, remarkable and affecting. There is not an incident omitted, which ought to have been remembered, nor one insisted that is not worth Remembrance.

It gives you, an Idea of the Scæne, as distinct and perfect, as if a Painter had drawn it to the Life, before your Eyes. It interests your Passions, as much as if you had been an Eye Witness of the whole Transaction. Yet there are no Figures, or Art used. All is as simple, natural, easy, and familiar, as if the Story, had been told in Conversation, without a Moments Premeditation.

Pope and Swift have given the World a Collection of their Letters; but I think in general, they fall short, in the Epistolary Way, of their own Emminence in Poetry and other Branches of Literature. Very few of their Letters, have ever engaged much of my Attention. Gays Letter, concerning the Pair of Lovers kill'd by Lightning, is worth more than the whole Collection, in Point of Simplicity, and Elegance of Composition, and as a genuine Model of the epistolary Style. There is a Book, which I wish you owned, I mean Rollins Belles Letters, in which the Variations of Style are explained.

Early Youth is the Time, to learn the Arts and Sciences, and especially to correct the Ear, and the Imagination, by forming a Style. I wish you would think of forming the Taste, and Judgment of your Children, now before any unchaste Sounds have fastened on their Ears, and before any Affectation, or Vanity, is settled on their Minds, upon the pure Principles of Nature. Musick, is a great Advantage, for Style depends in Part upon a delicate Ear.

The Faculty of Writing is attainable, by Art, Practice, and Habit only. The sooner, therefore the Practice begins, the more likely it will be to succeed. Have no Mercy upon an affected Phrase, any more than an affected, Air, Gate, Dress, or Manners.

Your Children have Capacities equal to any Thing. There is a Vigour in the Understanding, and a Spirit and Fire in the Temper of every one of them, which is capable of ascending the Heights of Art, science Trade, War, or Politicks.

They should be set to compose Descriptions of Scænes and Objects, and Narrations of Facts and Events, Declamations upon Topicks, and other Exercises of various sorts, should be prescribed to them.

Set a Child to form a Description of a Battle, a Storm, a seige, a Cloud, a Mountain, a Lake, a City, an Harbour, a Country seat a Meadow, a Forrest, or almost any Thing, that may occur to your Thoughts.

Set him to compose a Narration of all the little Incidents and Events of a Day, a Journey, a Ride, or a Walk. In this Way, a Taste will be formed, and a Facility of Writing acquired.

For myself, as I never had a regular Tutor, I never studied any Thing methodically, and consequently never was compleatly accomplished in any Thing. But as I am conscious of my own Deficiency, in these Respects, I should be the less pardonable, if I neglected the Education of my Children.

In Grammar, Rhetoric, Logic, my Education was imperfect, because immethodical. Yet I have perhaps read more upon these Arts, and considered them in a more extensive View than some others.

Smallpox remained a virulent threat and as soon as possible after the evacuation of Boston, many people went to the city to receive inoculation. Abigail brought her four children, along with various members of her extended family, to town in July to undergo the same procedure John had endured in the spring of 1764.

Abigail Adams to John Adams

Boston July 13 1776

I must begin with apoligising to you for not writing Since the 17 of June. I have really had so many cares upon my Hands and Mind, with a bad inflamation in my Eyes that I have not been able to write. I now date from Boston where I yesterday arrived and was with all 4 of our Little ones innoculated for the small pox. My unkle and Aunt were so kind as to send me an invitation with my family. Mr Cranch and wife and family, My sister Betsy and her Little Neice, Cotton Tufts and mr Thaxter a maid who has had the Distemper and my old Nurse compose our family a Boy too I should have added 17 in all. My unkles maid with his Little daughter and a Negro Man are here. We had our Bedding &c to bring. A cow we have driven down from B[raintre]e and some Hay I have had put into the stable wood &c and we have really commenced housekeepers here. The House was furnished with almost every article, (Except Beds) which we have free use of, and think ourselves much obliged by the fine accommodations and kind offer of our Friends. All our Necessary stoers we purchase jointly. Our Little ones stood the opperation Manfully. Dr Bulfinch is our Physician. Such a spirit of innoculation never before took place; the Town and every House in it, is are as full as they can hold. I believe there are not less than 50 persons from Braintree. Mrs Quincy mrs Lincoln miss Betsy and Nancy are our near Neighbours. God Grant that we may all go comfortably thro the Distemper. The Phisick part is bad enough I know. I knew your mind so perfectly upon the Subject that I thought nothing, but our recovery would give you eaquel pleasure, and as to safety there was none. The Soldiers innoculated privately, so did many of the inhabitants and the paper curency spread it everywhere. I immediately determined to set myself about it, and get ready with my children. I wish it was so you could have been with us, but I submit.

I received some Letters from you last Saturday Night 26 of June. You mention a Letter of the 16 which I have never Received, and I suppose must relate something to private affairs which I wrote about in May and sent by Harry.

As to News we have taken several fine prizes since I wrote you as you will see by the news papers. The present Report is of Lord's Hows comeing with unlimited powers. However suppose it is so, I believe he little thinks of treating with us as independant states. How can any person yet dreem of a settlement accommodations &c. They have neither the spirit nor feeling of Men, yet I see some who never were call'd Tories, gratified with the Idea of Lords Hows being upon his passage with such powers.

Sunday july 14

By yesterdays post I received two Letters dated 3 and 4 of July and tho your Letters never fail to give me pleasure, be the subject what it will, yet it was greatly heightned by the prospect of the future happiness and glory of our Country; nor am I a little Gratified when I reflect that a person so nearly connected with me has had the Honour of Being a principal actor, in laying a foundation for its future Greatness. May the foundation of our New constitution, be justice Truth and Righteousness. Like the wise Mans house may it be founded upon those Rocks and then neither storms or temptests will overthrow it.

I cannot but feel sorry that some of the most Manly Sentiments in the Declaration are Expunged from the printed coppy—perhaps wise reasons induced it.

Poor Canady I lament Canady but we ought to be in some measure sufferers for the past folly of our conduct. The fatal Effects of the small pox there, has led almost every person to consent to Hospitals in every Town. In many Towns, already arround Boston the Selectmen have granted Liberty for innoculation. I hope the Necessity is now fully seen.

I had many dissagreable sensations at the Thoughts of comeing myself, but to see my children thro it I thought my duty, and all those feelings vanished as soon as I was innoculated and I trust a kind providence will carry me safely thro. Our Friends from Plymouth came into Town yesterday. We have enough upon our hands in the morning. The Little folks are very sick then and puke every morning but after that they are comfortable. I shall write you now very often. Pray inform me constantly of every important transaction. Every expression of tenderness is a cordial to my Heart. Unimportant as they are to the rest of the world, to me they are *every Thing*.

We have had during all the month of June a most severe drougth which cut of all our promiseing hopes of english grain and the first crop of grass, but since july came in we have had a Plenty of rain and now every thing Looks well. There is one Misfortune in our family which I have never mentiond in hopes it would have been in my power to have remided it, but all hopes of that kind are at an end. It is the loss of your Grey Horse. About 2 months ago, I had occasion to send Jonathan of an errant to my unkle Quincys (the other Horse being a plowing). Upon his return a little below the church she trod upon a rolling stone and lamed herself to that degree that it was with great difficulty that she could be got home. I immediately sent for Tirrel and every thing was done for her by Baths ointments polticeing Bleeding &c that could be done. Still she continued extreem lame tho not so bad as at first. I then got her carried to Domet but he pronounces her incurable—as a callous is grown upon her footlock joint. You can hardly tell, not even by your own feelings how much I lament her. She was not with foal, as you immagined, but I hope she is Now as care has been taken in that Respect.

I suppose you have heard of a fleet which came up pretty near the Light and keept us all with our mouths open ready to catch them, but after staying near a week and makeing what observations they could set sail and went of to our great mortification who were [prepared?] for them in every respect. If our ship of 32 Guns which [was] Built at Portsmouth and waiting only for Guns and an other of [. . .] at Plimouth in the same state, had been in readiness we should in all probability been Masters of them. Where the blame lies in that respect I know not, tis laid upon Congress, and Congress is also blamed for not appointing us a General. But Rome was not Built in a day.

I hope the Multiplicity of cares and avocations which invellope you will not be too powerfull for you. I have many anxietyes upon that account. Nabby and Johnny send duty and desire Mamma to say that an inflamation in their Eyes which has been as much of a distemper as the small pox, has prevented their writing, but they hope soon to be able to acquaint Pappa of their happy recovery from the Distemper. Mr C[ranch], and wife sister B[etsy] and all our Friend desire to be rememberd to you and foremost in that Number Stands your

Portia

P S A Little India herb would have been mighty agreable now.

Abigail Adams to John Adams

july 21 1776 Boston

I have no doubt but that my dearest Friend is anxious to know how his Portia does, and his Little flock of children under the opperation of a Disease once so formidable.

I have the pleasure to tell him that they are all comfortable tho some of them complaining. Nabby has been very ill, but the Eruption begins to make its appearence upon her, and upon Johnny. Tommy is so well that the Dr innoculated him again to day fearing it had not taken. Charlly has no complaints yet, tho his arm has been very soar.

I have been out to meeting this forenoon, but have so many dissagreable sensations this afternoon that I thought it prudent to tarry at home. The Dr says they are very Good feelings. Mr Cranch has passd thro the preparation and the Eruption is comeing out cleverly upon him without any sickness at all. Mrs Cranch is cleverly and so are all her children. Those who are broke out are pretty full for the New method as tis call'd, The Suttonian they profess to practice upon. I hope to give you a Good account when I write Next, but our Eyes are very weak and the Dr is not fond of either writing or reading for his patients. But I must transgress a Little.

I Received a Letter from you by wedensday Post 7 of july and tho I think it a choise one in the Litterary way, containing many usefull hints and judicious observations which will greatly assist me in the future instruction of our Little ones, yet it Lacked some Essential engrediants to make it compleat. Not one word respecting yourself your Health or your present Situation. My anxiety for your welfare will never leave me but with my parting Breath, tis of more importance to me than all this world contains besides. The cruel Seperation to which I am necessatated cuts of half the enjoyments of life, the other half are comprised in the hope I have that what I do and what I suffer may be serviceable to you to our Little ones and our Country; I must beseach you therefore for the future never to omit what is so Essential to my happiness.

Last Thursday after hearing a very Good Sermon I went with the Multitude into Kings Street to hear the proclamation for independance read and proclamed. Some Field peices with the Train were brought there. The troops appeard under Arms and all the inhabitants assembled there (the small pox prevented many thousand from the Country). When Col Crafts read from the Belcona of the State House the Proclamation, great attention was given to every word. As soon as he ended, the cry from the Belcona, was God save our American States and then 3 cheers which rended the air. The Bells rang the privateers fired the forts and Batteries, the cannon were discharged the platoons followed and every face appeard joyfull. Mr Bowdoin then gave a Sentiment, Stability and perpetuity to American independance. After dinner the kings arms were taken down from the State House and every vestage of him from every place in which it appeard and burnt in king street. Thus ends royall Authority in this state, and all the people shall say Amen.

I have been a Little surprized that we collect no better accounts with regard to the horrid conspiricy at New york, and that so Little mention has been made of it here. It made a talk for a few days but now seems all hushed in silence. The Torries say that it was not a conspiricy but an association, and pretend that there was no plot to assasinate the General. Even their hardned Hearts ~~Blush~~ feel —— the discovery. We have in Gorge a match for a Borgia and a catiline, a wretch Callous to every Humane feeling. Our worthy preacher told us that he believed one of our Great Sins for which a righteouss God has come out in judgment against us, was our Biggoted attachment to so wicked a Man. May our repentance be Sincere.

John Adams to Abigail Adams

[*The letter begins on 3 August 1776.*]

Aug. 4. [*1776*]

Went this Morning to the Baptist Meeting, in Hopes of hearing Mr Stillman, but was dissappointed. He was there, but another Gentn. preached. His Action was violent to a degree bordering on fury. His Gestures, unnatural, and distorted. Not the least Idea of Grace in his Motions, or Elegance in his Style. His Voice was vociferous and boisterous, and his Composition almost wholly destitute of Ingenuity. I wonder extreamly at the Fondness of our People for schollars educated at the Southward and for southern Preachers. There is no one Thing, in which We excell them more, than in our University our schollars, and Preachers. Particular Gentlemen here, who, have improved upon their Education by Travel, shine. But in general, old Massachusetts, outshines her younger sisters, still. In several Particulars, they have more Wit, than We. They have Societies; the philosophical Society particularly, which excites a scientific Emulation, and propagates their Fame. If ever I get through this scene of Politicks and War, I will spend the Remainder of my days, in endeavouring to instruct my Countrymen in the Art of making the most of their abilities and Virtues an Art, which they have hitherto, too much neglected. A philosophical society shall be established at Boston, if I have Wit and Address enough to accomplish it, sometime or other. Pray set Brother Cranch's Philosophical Head to plodding upon this Project. Many of his Lucubrations would have been published and preserved, for the Benefit of Mankind, and for his Honour, if such a Clubb had existed.

My Countrymen want Art and Address. They want Knowledge of the World. They want the exteriour and superficial Accomplishments of Gentlemen, upon which the World has set so high a Value. In solid Abilities and real Virtues, they vastly excell in general, any People upon this Continent. Our N. England People are Aukward and bashfull; yet they are pert, ostentatious and vain, a Mixture which excites Ridicule and gives Disgust. They have not the faculty of shewing themselves to the best Advantage, nor the Art of concealing this faculty. An Art and Faculty which some People possess in the highest degree. Our Deficiencies in these Respects, are owing wholly to the little Intercourse We have with strangers, and to our Inexperience in the World. These Imperfections must be remedied for New England must produce the Heroes, the statesmen the Philosophers, or America, will make no great Figure for some Time.

Our Army is rather sickly at N. York, and We live in daily Expectation of hearing of some great Event. May God almighty grant it may be prosperous for America. Hope is an Anchor and a Cordial. Disappointment however will not disconcert me.

If you will come to Philadelphia in september, I will stay, as long as you please. I should be as proud and happy as a Bridegroom. Yours.

Abigail Adams to John Adams

Boston August 5 1776

I this Evening Received your two Letters of july 10 and 11. and last Evening the post brought me yours of july 23. I am really astonished at looking over the Number I have received during this month, more I believe than for 3 months before. I hope tis your amusement and relaxation from care to be thus imployed. It has been a feast to me during my absence from Home, and cheerd me in my most painfull Moments. At Last I Hear what I have long Expected, and have feard for some time. I was certain that your Nerves must bee new Braced, and your Constitution new moulded, to continue well, through such a load of Buisness. Such intense application, in such a climate through the burning Heats of the summer, tis too much for a constitution of steel, and ought not to be required.

I intreat you to return, and that speidily. Mr Gerry has recoverd his Health and Spirits by his journey. He call'd upon me a few moments. I knew Him by the Same instinct by which I first discoverd him, and ventured to call him by Name tho his person was never discribed to me. I cannot account for it but so it was. He appeard a modest Man, and has a fine inteligent Eye. I wanted to ask him many questions which I could not do as he was a stranger, and we had company. He has promised to call upon me again before he returns which he proposes to do in about ten days.

I have been trying all day to get time to write to you. I am now obliged to Rob my sleep. Mrs Cranch Billy and Lucy are very unwell, all of them with the Symptoms I suppose. Lucy I fear has taken the Distemper in the Natural way, as tis more than 3 weeks since she was innoculated, and her Arm being inflamed deceived us. I took the precaution of having all mine who had not the symptoms the 9th day innoculated a second time, and I hope they have all pass'd through Except Charlly, and what to do with him I know not. I cannot get the small pox to opperate upon him. His Arm both times has been very soar, and he lives freely, that is he Eats a small Quantity of meat, and I have given him wine but all will not do. Tommy is cleverly has about a dozen, and is very gay and happy.

I have abundant reason to be thankfull that we are so many of us carried comfortably through a Disease so formidable in its Natural opperation, and though our Symptoms have run high, yet they have been the worst, for the Eruption has been a triffel, really should have been glad to have had them in greater plenty. I hope to be able to return to Braintree the Latter end of Next week which will compleat me 5 weeks. I have been unlucky in a Maid, who has not one qualification to recommend her but that she has had the small pox. She has been twice Sick since she has been with us, and put us to much difficulty. I have attended publick worship constantly, Except one day and a half ever since I have been in Town. I rejoice in a preacher who has some warmth some energy some feeling. Deliver me from your cold phlegmatick Preachers Politicians Friends Lovers and Husbands. I thank Heaven I am not so constituted my-self and so connected.

How destitute are they of all those Sensations which sweeteen as well as embitter our probationary state! And How seldom do we find true Genious residing in such a constitution, but may I ask if the same temperament and the same Sensibility which constitutes a poet and a painter will not be apt to make a Lover and a Debauchee?

When I reflect upon Humane Nature, the various passions and appetites to which it is subject I am ready to cry out with the Psalmist Lord what is Man?

You ask me How you shall get Home. I know not. Is there any assistance you can think of that I can procure for you. Pray Let me know. Our Court do not set till the 28 of this month. No delegates can be chosen to releave you till then, but if you are so low in Health do not wait for that. Mr Bowdoin has the Gout in his stomack, is very ill. I do not think he could by any means bear close application. Mr Dana and mr Lowell are very good Men, I wish they would appoint them. Our Friend ~~Warren~~ has some family difficulties. I know not whether he could possibly leave it. A partner dear to him you know beyond description almost Heart broken, by the situation of one very dear to *her* whose great attention and care you well know has been to Train them up in the way in which they ought to go. Would to Heaven they did not depart from it. Impaired in Health impaird in mind impaird in Morrals, is a situation truly deplorable, but do not mention the Matter—not even to them by the slightest hint. Tis a wound which cannot be touched.

God grant we may never mourn a similiar situation, but I have some times the Heartake when I look upon the fire spirit and vivacity, joind to a comely person in the Eldest, soft tender and pathetick in the second Manly firm and intrepid in the third. I fear less for him, but alass we are short sighted mortals.

> O Blindness to the future kindly given
> that Each may fill the circle marked by Heaven.

Adieu dearest Best of Friend adieu.

John Adams to Abigail Adams

Aug. 10. 76

Yours of 30. and 31 July was brought, me, to day, by Captain Cazneau. I am happy to think that you, and my oldest son, are well through, the distemper, and have sufficient Receipts. Nabby, I believe is also through. The Inflammation in her Arm, and the single Eruption, are nearly as much Evidence, as I had to shew—and I have seen, small Pox enough since I had it, to have infected 100 Armies. Tommy, I shall hear by next Post, is happily recoverd of it, I think. Charley, my dear Charley! I am sorry, that it is still pretty clear, that you have not taken it. But never fear, you will have it.

This Suspence and Uncertainty must be very irksome to you. But Patience and Perseverance, will overcome this, as well as all other Difficulties. Dont think of Time, nor Expence. 1000 Guineas, is not worth so much as security to a Wife, a good one I mean, and four Children good ones, I mean, against the small Pox. It is an important Event in a Mans Life, to go thro that distemper. It is a very great Thing, for a whole Family, to get well over it.

At the same Time that I am in a State of suspence, Uncertainty and Anxiety about my best, dearest, worthyest, wisest Friend, in this World and all my Children, I am in a State of equal suspence, Uncertainty, and Anxiety about our Army at N. York and Ticonderoga, and consequently about our Country and Posterity. The Lives of Thousands, and the Liberties of Millions are as much in suspence, as the Health of my family. But I submit to the Governance of infinite Wisdom.

Had my Advice been followed, in Season, We should now have been in Safety, Liberty and Peace, or at least We should have had a clear and indisputable Superiority of Power. But my Advice was not regarded. It never was, and never will be, in this World. Had N.Y. N.J. and Pensilvania, only been in compleat Possession of the Powers of Government only 3 Months sooner, We should have had an Army, at

N.Y. and Amboy, able to cope with double the Number of our Enemies. But now We trust to Chance: to the Chapter of Accidents: a long Chapter, it is, as long as the 119 Psalm: and well it is for us that it is so. If We trusted to Providence, I should be easy, but We do not.

I have now come to a Resolution, upon another Subject, which has kept me in suspence for some Time. I must request of you, to interceed with your Father to procure for me, two Horses, and send them to Philadelphia, with a servant, as soon as possible. I shall wait for their Arrival, let it be sooner or later. The sooner they come, the more agreable to my Wishes, and the better for my Health. I can live no longer, without Riding. If Bass, is willing to take one more Ride with his old Friend, let him, come, if he declines, send somebody else. I shall wait for Horses. If the Congress should adjourn, I shall attend the Board of War, untill they come. The General Court, I think might do something. Whether they have ever thought of granting me, a farthing, for my Time, I know not. Mr A. had an Horse and a fine Chaise, furnished him, by the Committee of supplies. Perhaps They might furnish me with a Pair of Horses too. Pray mention this to Coll Warren or Coll Palmer. If nothing can be done by them, if I have Credit enough left, to hire two Horses and a servant, let it be employed. The Loss of my fine Mare, has disconcerted me. The Gen. Ct. will send some Gentleman here to take my Place. But if my Horses come I shall not wait for that.

Abigail Adams to John Adams

August 14 1776

I wrote you to day by mr smith but as I suppose this will reach you sooner, I omitted mentioning any thing of my family in it.

Nabby has enough of the small Pox for all the family beside. She is pretty well coverd, not a spot but what is so soar that she can neither walk sit stand or lay with any comfort. She is as patient as one can ex-

pect, but they are a very Soar sort. If it was a disorder to which we
could be subject more than once I would go as far as it was possible to
avoid it. She is Sweld a good deal. You will receive a perticuliar account before this reaches you of the uncommon manner in which the
small Pox acts. It bafels the skill of the most Experience'd here. Billy
Cranch is now out with about 40, and so well as not to be detaind at
Home an hour for it. Charlly remains in the Same state he did. Your
Letter of August 3 came by this days Post. I find it very conveniant to
be so handy. I can receive a Letter at Night, sit down and reply to it,
and send it of in the morning.

You remark upon the deficiency of Education in your Countrymen.
It never I believe was in a worse state, at least for many years. The
colledge is not in the state one could wish. The schollars complain that
their professer in Phiselophy is taken of by publick Buisness to their
great detriment. In this Town I never Saw so great a neglect of Education. The poorer sort of children are wholly neglected, and left to
range the streets with out schools without Buisness, given up to all
Evil. The Town is not as formerly divided into Wards. There is either
too much Buisness left upon the hands of a few, or too little care to do
it. We daily see the Necessity of a regular Goverment. You speak of
our worthy Brother. I often lament it that a Man so peculiarly formed
for the Education of youth, and so well qualified as he is in many
Branches of Litrature, excelling in Philosiphy and the Mathematicks,
should not be imployd in Some publick Station. I know not the person
who would make half so good a successor to dr Winthrope. He has a
peculiar easy manner of communicating his Ideas to youth, and the
goodness of his Heart, and the purity of his morrals without an affected austerity must have a happy Effect upon the minds of Pupils.

If you complain of neglect of Education in sons, what shall I say
with regard to daughters, who every day experience the want of
it. With regard to the Education of my own children, I find myself
soon out of my debth, and destitute and deficient in every part of Education.

I most sincerely wish that Some more liberal plan might be laid and

Excecuted for the Benefit of the rising generation, and that our New constitution may be distinguished for Learning and virtue. If we mean to have Heroes Statesmen and Philosophers, we should have learned women. The world perhaps would laugh at me, and accuse me of vanity, But you I know have a mind too enlarged and liberal to disregard the Sentiment. If much depends as is allowed upon the early Education of youth and the first principals which are instilld take the deepest root, great benifit must arrise from litirary accomplishments in women.

Excuse me my pen has run away with me. I have no thoughts of comeing to P[*hiladelphi*]a. The length of time I have and shall be detaind here would have prevented me, even if you had no thoughts of returning till December, but I live in daily Expectation of seeing you here. Your Health I think requires your immediate return. I expected mr Gerry would have set off before now, but he finds it perhaps very hard to leave his Mistress—I wont say harder than some do to leave their wives. Mr Gerry stood very high in my Esteem—what is meat for one is not for an other—no accounting for fancy. She is a queer dame and leads people wild dances.

But hush—Post dont betray your trust and loose my Letter.

Nabby is poorly this morning. The Pock are near the turn, 6. or 7 hundred boils are no agreable feeling. You and I know not what a feeling it is. Miss Katy can tell. I had but 3 they were very clever and fill'd nicely. The Town instead of being clear of this distemper are now in the height of it, hundreds having it in the Natural way through the deceitfulness of innoculation.

Adieu ever yours.

Portia

John Adams to Abigail Adams

Philadelphia August 18. 1776

My Letters to you are an odd Mixture. They would appear to a Stranger, like the Dish which is sometimes called Omnium Gatherum. This is the first Time, I believe that these two Words were ever put together in Writing. The litteral Interpretation of them, I take to be "A Collection of all Things." But as I said before, the Words having never before been written, it is not possible to be very learned in telling you what the Arabic, Syriac, chaldaic, Greek and Roman Commentators say upon the Subject.

Amidst all the Rubbish that constitutes the Heap, you will see a Proportion of Affection, for my Friends, my Family and Country, that gives a Complexion to the whole. I have a very tender feeling Heart. This Country knows not, and never can know the Torments, I have endured for its sake. I am glad they never can know, for it would give more Pain to the benevolent and humane, than I could wish, even the wicked and malicious to feel.

I have seen in this World, but a little of that pure flame of Patriotism, which certainly burns in some Breasts. There is much of the ostentation and Affectation of it. I have known a few who could not bear to entertain a Selfish design, nor to be suspected by others of such a Meanness. But these are not the most respected by the World. A Man must be selfish, even to acquire great Popularity. He must grasp for himself, under Specious Pretences, for the public Good, and he must attach himself to his Relations, Connections and Friends, by becoming a Champion for their Interests, in order to form a Phalanx, about him for his own defence; to make them Trumpeters of his Praise, and sticklers for his Fame, Fortune, and Honour.

My Friend Warren, the late Governor Ward, and Mr Gadsden, are three Characters in which I have seen the most generous disdain of every Spice and Species of such Meanness. The two last had not, great abilities but they had pure Hearts. Yet they had less Influence, than many others who had neither so considerable Parts, nor any share at all of their Purity of Intention. Warren has both Talents and Virtues beyond most Men in this World, yet his Character has never been in Proportion. Thus it always is, has been, and will be.

Nothing has ever given me, more Mortification, than a suspicion, that has been propagated of me, that I was actuated by private Views and have been aiming at high Places. The Office of C. J. has occasioned this Jealousy, and it never will be allayed, untill I resign it. Let me have my Farm, Family and Goose Quil, and all the Honours and offices this World has to bestow, may go to those who deserve them better, and desire them more. I covet them not.

There are very few People in this World, with whom I can bear to converse. I can treat all with Decency and Civility, and converse with them, when it is necessary, on Points of Business. But I am never happy in their Company. This has made me a Recluse, and will one day, make me an Hermit.

I had rather build stone Wall upon Penns Hill, than be the first Prince in Europe, the first General, or first senator in America. Our Expectations are *very* high of some great Affair at N. York.

John Adams to Abigail Adams

Philadelphia August 25. 1776

The day before Yesterday and Yesterday, We expected Letters and Papers by the Post, but by some Accident, or Mismanagement of the Riders, no Post is arrived yet, which has been a great Disappointment to me. I watch, with longing Eyes for the Post, because you have been very good of late in writing by every one. I long to hear, that Charles is in as fair a Way, thro the Distemper as the rest of you.

Poor Barrell is violently ill, in the next Chamber to mine, of an inflammatory Fever. I hear every Cough, Sigh, and Groan. His Fate hangs in a critical Suspence, the least Thing may turn the Scale against him. Miss Quincy, is here very humanely employed in nursing him. This Goodness does her Honour.

Mr Paine has recovered of his illness, and by present appearances, is in better Health than before. I hope it will not be my Fate to be sick here. Indeed I am not much afraid of these acute disorders, mine are more chronical, nervous, and slow. I must have a Ride: I cannot make it do without it.

We are now approaching rapidly to the autumnal Æquinox, and no great Blow has yet been struck, in the martial Way, by our Enemies nor by Us. If We should be blissed this year, with a few Storms as happy as those which fell out last Year, in the Beginning of september, they will do much for us. The British Fleet, where they now lie, have not an Harbour, so convenient, or safe, as they had last Year. Another Winter will do much for Us too. We shall have more and better Soldiers—We shall be better armed—We shall have a greater Force at Sea—We shall have more Trade—our Artillery will be greatly increased, our Officers will have more Experience, and our Soldiers more Discipline—our Politicians more Courage and Confidence, and our Enemies less Hopes. Our American Commonwealths will be all compleatly form'd and organised, and every Thing, I hope, will go on, with greater Vigour.

After I had written thus far the Post came in and brought me, your Favour of the 14 of August. Nabby, by this Time, I conclude is well, and Charles I hope is broke out. Dont you recollect upon this occasion, Dr Biles's Benediction to me, when I was innoculated? As you will see the Picquancy of it, now more than ever you could before, I will tell the Story.

After having been 10 or 11 days innoculated, I lay lolling on my Bed, in Major Cunninghams Chamber, under the Tree of Liberty, with half a Dozen young Fellows as lazy as my self, all waiting and wishing for Symptoms and Eruptions. All of a sudden, appeared at the Chamber Door, the reverend Doctor, with his rosy Face, many curled Wigg, and pontifical Air and Gate. "I have been thinking says he, that the Clergy of this Town, ought upon this Occasion, to adopt the Benediction of the Romish Clergy, and, when we enter the Apartments of the sick, to cry, in the foreign Pronunciation *'Pax tecum.'*" These Words are spoken by foreigners as the Dr pronounced them *Pox take 'em.* One would think that Sir Isaac Newton's Discovery of the system of Gravitation did not require, a deeper reach of Thought, than this frivolous Pun.

Your Plan of making our worthy Brother, Professor, would be very agreable to me.

Your Sentiments of the Importance of Education in Women, are exactly agreable to my own. Yet the Femmes Scavans, are contemptible Characters. So is that of a Pedant, universally, how much so ever of a male he may be. In reading History you will generally observe, when you light upon a great Character whether a General, a Statesman, or Philosopher, some female about him either in the Character of a Mother, Wife, or Sister, who has Knowledge and Ambition above the ordinary Level of Women, and that much of his Emminence is owing to her Precepts, Example, or Instigation, in some shape or other.

Let me mention an Example or two. Sempronius Gracchus, and Caius Gracchus, two great tho unfortunate Men, are said to have been instigated to their, great Actions, by their Mother, who, in order to stimulate their Ambition, told them, that she was known in Rome by the Title of the Mother in Law of Scipio, not the Mother of the Gracchi. Thus she excited their Emulation, and put them upon reviving the old Project of an equal Division of the conquered Lands, (a genuine republican Measure, tho it had been too long neglected to be then practicable,) in order to make their Names as illustrious as Scipios.

The great Duke, who first excited the Portuguese to revolt from the Spanish Monarchy, was spurred on, to his great Enterprize by a most artfull, and ambitious Wife. And thus indeed you will find it very generally.

What Tale have you heard of Gerry? What Mistress is he courting?

Abigail Adams to John Adams

Dearest Friend   Boston August 29 1776

I have spent the 3 days past almost intirely with you. The weather has been stormy, I have had little company, and I have amused myself in my closet reading over the Letters I have received from you since I have been here.

I have possession of my Aunts chamber in which you know is a very conveniant pretty closet with a window which looks into her flower Garden. In this closet are a Number of Book shelves, which are but poorly furnished, however I have a pretty little desk or cabinet here where I write all my Letters and keep my papers unmollested by any one. I do not covet my Neighbours Goods, but I should like to be the owner of such conveniances. I always had a fancy for a closet with a window which I could more peculiarly call my own.

Here I say I have amused myself in reading and thinking of my absent Friend, Sometimes with a mixture of paine, sometimes with Pleasure, Sometimes anticipating a joyfull and happy meeting, whilst my Heart would bound and palpitate with the pleasing Idea, and with the purest affection I have held you to my Bosom till my whole Soul has dissolved in Tenderness and my pen fallen from my Hand. How often do I reflect with pleasure that I hold in possession a Heart Eaqually warm with my own, and full as Susceptable of the Tenderest impressions, and Who even now whilst he is reading here, feel's all I discribe.

Forgive this Revere this Delusion, and since I am debared real, suffer me, to enjoy, and indulge In Ideal pleasures—and tell me they are not inconsistant with the stern virtue of a senator and a Patriot.

I must leave my pen to recover myself and write in an other strain. I feel anxious for a post day, and am full as solicitious for two Letters a week and as uneasy if I do not get them, as I used to be when I got but one in a month or 5 weeks. Thus do I presume upon indulgance, and this is Humane Nature, and brings to my mind a sentiment of one of your correspondents viz "That Man is the only animal who is hungery with His Belly full."

Last Evening dr Cooper came in and brought one your favour from the post office of August 18 and Coll Whipple arrived yesterday morning and deliverd me the two Bundles you sent, and a Letter of the 12 of August. They have already afforded me much amusement, and I Expect much more from them.

I am sorry to find from your last as well as from some others of your Letters that you feel so dissatisfied with the office to which you are chosen. Tho in your acceptance of it, I know you was actuated by the purest motives, and I know of no person here so well qualified to discharge the important Duties of it. Yet I will not urge you to it. In accepting of it you must be Excluded from all other employments. There never will be a salery addequate to the importance of the office or to support you and your family from penury. If you possess a fortune I would urge you to it, in Spight of all the flears and gibes of minds who themselves are incapable of acting a Disintrested part, and have no conception that others can.

I have never heard any Speaches about it, nor did I know that such insinuations had been Thrown out.

Pure and disintrested virtue must ever be its own reward. Mankind are too selfish and too depraved to discover the pure Gold from the baser mettle.

I wish for Peace and tranquility. All my desires and all my ambition is to be Esteemed and Loved by my partner to join with him in the Education and instruction of our Little ones, to set under our own vines in Peace Liberty and safety.

Adieu my Dearest Friend, soon, soon return to your most affectionate

Portia

P S Charlly is cleverly. A very odd report has been propagated in Braintree viz that you were poisond upon your return at N.Y. Bass sets of on monday.

John Adams to Abigail Adams

Philadelphia Septr. 5. 1776

Mr Bass arrived this Day, with the joyfull News, that you were all well. By this opportunity, I shall send you a Cannister of Green Tea, by Mr Hare.

Before Mr G[*erry*] went away from hence, I asked Mrs Yard to send a Pound of Green Tea to you. She readily agreed. When I came home at Night I was told Mr G. was gone. I asked Mrs Y. if she had sent the Cannister? She said Yes and that Mr G. undertook to deliver it, with a great deal of Pleasure. From that Time I flattered my self, you would have the poor Relief of a dish of good Tea under all your Fatigues with the Children, and under all the disagreabble Circumstances attending the small Pox, and I never conceived a single doubt, that you had received it untill Mr Gerrys Return. I asked him, accidentally, whether he delivered it, and he said Yes to Mr S. A's Lady. I was astonished. He misunderstood Mrs Y. entirely, for upon Inquiry she affirms she told him, it was for Mrs J. A.

I was so vexed at this, that I have ordered another Cannister, and Mr Hare has been kind enough to undertake to deliver it. How the Dispute will be settled I dont know. You must send a Card to Mrs S. A, and let her know that the Cannister was intended for You and she may send it you if she chooses, as it was charged to me. It is amazingly dear, nothing less than 40s lawfull Money, a Pound.

I am rejoiced that my Horses are come. I shall now be able to take a ride. But it is uncertain, when I shall set off, for home. I will not go, at present. Affairs are too delicate and critical. The Panic may seize whom it will, it shall not seize me. I will stay here, untill the public Countenance, is better, or much worse. It must and will be better. I think it is not now bad. Lyes by the Million will be told you. Dont believe any of them. There is no danger of the Communication being cutt off, between the northern and southern Colonies. I can go home, when I please, in spight of all the Fleet and Army of Great Britain.

John Adams to Abigail Adams

Fryday Septr. 6. 1776

This day, I think, has been the most remarkable of all. Sullivan came here from Lord Howe, five days ago with a Message that his Lordship desired a half an Hours Conversation with some of the Members of Congress, in their private Capacities. We have spent three or four days in debating whether We should take any Notice of it. I have, to the Utmost of my Abilities during the whole Time, opposed our taking any Notice of it. But at last it was determined by a Majority "that the Congress being the Representatives of the free and independent states of America, it was improper to appoint any of their Members to confer, in their private Characters with his Lordship. But they would appoint a Committee of their Body, to wait on him, to know whether he had Power, to treat with Congress upon Terms of Peace and to hear any Propositions, that his Lordship may think proper to make."

When the Committee came to be ballotted for, Dr Franklin and your humble servant, were unanimously chosen. Coll R. H. Lee and Mr [*Edward*] Rutledge, had an equal Number: but upon a second Vote Mr R. was chosen. I requested to be excused, but was desired to consider of it untill tomorrow. My Friends here Advise me to go. All the stanch and intrepid, are very earnest with me to go, and the timid and wavering, if any such there are, agree in the request. So I believe I shall under take the Journey. I doubt whether his Ldship will see Us, but the same Committee will be directed to enquire into the State of the Army, at New York, so that there will be Business enough, if his Lordship makes none. It would fill this Letter Book, to give you all the Arguments, for and against this Measure, if I had Liberty to attempt it. His Lordship seems to have been playing off a Number of Machiavillian Maneuvres, in order to throw upon Us the odium of continuing this War. Those who have been Advocates for the Appointment of this Committee, are for opposing Maneuvre to Maneuvre, and are confident that the Consequence will be, that the odium will fall upon him. However this may be, my Lesson is plain, to ask a few Questions, and take his answers.

I can think of but one Reason for their putting me upon this Embassy, and that is this. An Idea has crept into many Minds here that his Lordship is such another as Mr Hutchinson, and they may possibly think that a Man who has been accustomed to penetrate into the mazy Windings of Hutchinsons Heart, and the Serpentine Wiles of his Head, may be tolerably qualified to converse with his Lordship.

Sunday Septr. 8

Yesterdays Post brought me yours of Aug. 29. The Report you mention "that I was poisoned upon my Return at New York" I suppose will be thought to be a Prophecy, delivered by the oracle in mystic Language, and meant that I should be politically or morally poisoned by Lord Howe. But the Prophecy shall be false.

Abigail Adams to John Adams

Braintree Sepbr 7. 1776

Last monday I left the Town of Boston underwent the opperation of a smoaking at the lines and arrived at my Brother Cranchs where we go for purification; there I tarried till wednesday, and then came Home, which seem'd greatly endeard to me by my long absence. I think I never felt greater pleasure at comeing Home after an absence in my Life yet I felt a vacuum in my Breast and Sent a Sigh to P[*hiladelphi*]a. I long'd for a dear Friend to rejoice with me. Charlly is Banished yet, I keep him at his Aunt Cranch's out of the way of those who have not had the distemper, his Arm has many Scabs upon it which are yet very soar. He is very weak and sweats a nights prodigiously. I am now giving him the Bark. He recoverd very fast considering how ill he was. I pitty your anxiety and feel sorry that I wrote you when he was so Bad, but I knew not how it might turn with Him, had it been otherways than well, it might have proved a greater shock than to have known that he was ill.

This Night our good unkle came from Town and brought me yours of August 20, 21 25 27 and 28th for all of which I most sincerely thank you. I have felt uneasy to Hear from you. The Report of your being dead, has no doubt reach'd you by Bass who heard enough of it before he came away. It took its rise among the Tories who as Swift said of himself "By their fears betray their Hopes" but How they should ever take it into their Heads that you was Poisond at New York a fort night before that we heard any thing of that villans Zedwitz plan of poisoning the waters of the City, I cannot tell. I am sometimes ready to suspect that there is a communication between the Tories of every State, for they seem to know all news that is passing before tis known by the Whigs.

We Have had many stories concerning engagements upon Long Island this week, of our Lines being forced and of our Troops retreating to New york. Perticuliars we have not yet obtain. All we can learn is that we have been unsuccessfull there; having Lost Many Men as prisoners among whom is Lord Sterling and General Sullivan.

But if we should be defeated I think we shall not be conquered. A people fired like the Romans with Love of their Country and of Liberty a zeal for the publick Good, and a Noble Emulation of Glory, will not be disheartned or dispirited by a succession of unfortunate Events. But like them may we learn by Defeat the power of becomeing invincible.

I hope to Hear from you by every Post till you return. The Herbs you mention I never Received. I was upon a visit to Mrs S. Adams about a week after mr Gerry returnd, when She entertaind me with a very fine dish of Green Tea. The scarcity of the article made me ask her where she got it. She replied her *Sweet Heart* sent it to her by mr Gerry. I said nothing, but thought my sweet Heart might have been eaquelly kind considering the disease I was visited with, and that was recommended as a Bracer. A Little after you mention'd a couple of Bundles Sent. I supposed one of them might contain the article but found they were Letters. How mr Gerry should make such a mistake I know not. I shall take the Liberty of sending for what is left of it tho I suppose it is half gone as it was very freely used. If you had mentiond a single Word of it in your Letter I should have immediately found out the mistake.

Tis said that the Efforts of our Enemies will be to stop the communication between the colonies by taking possession of Hudsons Bay. Can it be Effected? The Milford frigate rides triumphant in our Bay, taking vessels every day, and no Colony nor Continental vessel has yet attempted to hinder her. She mounts but 28 Guns but is one of the finest sailors in the British Navy. They complain we have not weighty mettle enough and I suppose truly. The Rage for privateering is as Great here, as any where and I believe the Success has been as Great.

It will not be in my power to write you so regularly as when I was in Town. I shall not faill doing it once a week. If you come home the Post Road you must inquire for Letters where ever the Post sit out from.

Tis Here a very General time of Health. I think tis Near a twelve month Since the Pestilance raged here. I fear your being seazd with a fever, tis very prevalant I hear where you are. I pray God preserve you and return you in Health. The Court will not accept your Resignation, they will appoint Mr Dalton and Dana to releave you.

I am most affectionately Yours.

Abigail Adams to John Adams

Braintree Sepbr 20 1777 [*1776*]

I sit down this Evening to write you, but I hardly know what to think about your going to N.Y. The story has been told so many times, and with circumstances so perticuliar that I with others have given some heed it tho my not hearing any thing of it from you leaves me at a loss.

Yours of Sepbr 4 came to hand last Night, our worthy unkle is a constant attendant upon the Post office for me and brought it me.

Yours of Sepbr 5 came to Night to B[*raintre*]e and was left as directed with the Cannister. Am sorry you gave yourself so much trouble about them. I got about half you sent me by mr Gerry. Am much obliged to you and hope to have the pleasure of making the greater part of it for you. Your Letter damp't my spirits; when I had no expectation of your return till December I endeavourd to bring my mind to acquiess in the too painfull situation, but I have now been in a state of Hopefull expectation. I have recond the days since Bass went away an hundred times over, and every Letter expected to find the day set for your return.

But Now I fear it is far distant. I have frequently been told that the communication would be cut of and that you would not be ever able to return. Sometimes I have been told so by those who really wish'd it might be so, with Malicious pleasure. Sometimes your timid folks have apprehended that it would be so. I wish any thing would bring you nearer. If there is really any danger I should think you would remove. Tis a plan your Enemies would rejoice to see accomplished, and will Effect if it lies in their Power.

I am not apt to be intimidated you know. I have given as little heed to that and a thousand other Bug Bear reports as posible. I have slept as soundly since my return not with standing all the Ghosts and hobgoblings, as ever I did in my life. Tis true I never close my Eyes at night till I have been to P[*hiladelphi*]a, and my first visit in the morning is there.

How unfealing are the world! They tell me they Heard you was dead with as little sensibility as a stock or a stone, and I have now got to be provoked at it, and can hardly help snubing the person who tells me so.

The story of your being upon this conference at New york came in a Letter as I am told from R. T. P[*aine*] to his Brother in Law

G[*reenlea*]fe. Many very many have been the conjectures of the Multitude upon it. Some have supposed the War concluded, the Nation setled, others an exchange of prisoners, others a reconsiliation with Britain &c &c. I cannot consent to your tarrying much longer. I know your Health must greatly suffer from so constant application to Buisness and so little excercise. Besides I shall send you word by and by as Regulus'es steward did, that whilst you are engaged in the senate your own domestick affairs require your presence at Home, and that your wife and children are in Danger of wanting Bread. If the Senate of America will take care of us, as the Senate of Rome *did* of the family of Regulus, you may serve them again, but unless you return what Little property you possess will be lost. In the first place the House at Boston is going to ruin. When I was there I hired a Girl to clean it, it had a cart load of dirt in it. I speak within Bounds. One of the chambers was used to keep poultry in, an other Sea coal, and an other salt. You may conceive How it look'd. The House is so exceeding damp being shut up, that the floors are mildewd the sealing falling down, and the paper mouldy and falling from the walls. I took care to have it often opened and aird whilst I tarried in Town. I put it into the best state I could.

In the Next place, the Lighter of which you are or should be part owner is lying rotting at the wharf. One year more without any care and she is worth nothing. You have no Bill of Sale no right to convey any part of her should any person appear to purchase her. The Pew I Let, after having paid a tax for the repairs of the meeting House.

As to what is here under my more immediate inspection I do the best I can with it, but it will not at the high price Labour is, pay its way.

I know the weight of publick cares lye so heavy upon you that I have been loth to mention your own private ones.

The Best accounts we can collect from new york assure us that our Men fought valiantly. We are no ways dispiritted here. We possess a spirit that will not be conquerd. If our Men are all drawn of and we should be attacked, you would find a Race of Amazons in America.

But I trust we shall yet tread down our Enemies.

I must intreet you to remember me often. I never think your Letters half long enough. I do not complain. I have no reason to, no one can boast of more Letters than your

Portia

John Adams to Abigail Adams

22 Sept. 1776

We have at last agreed upon a Plan, for forming a regular Army. We have offered 20 dollars, and 100 Acres of Land to every Man, who will inlist, during the War. And a new sett of Articles of War are agreed on. I will send you, if I can a Copy of these Resolutions and Regulations.

I am at a Loss what to write. News We have not. Congress seems to be forgotten by the Armies. We are most unfaithfully served in the Post Office, as well as many other Offices, civil and military. Unfaithfullness in public Stations, is deeply criminal. But there is no Encouragement to be faithfull. Neither Profit, nor Honour nor Applause is acquired by faithfullness. But I know by what. There is too much Corruption, even in this infant Age of our Republic. Virtue is not in Fashion. Vice is not infamous.

October 1. 1776

Since I wrote the foregoing Lines, I have not been able to find Time to write you a Line. Altho I cannot write you, so often as I wish, you are never out of my Thoughts. I am repining at my hard Lot, in being torn from you, much oftener than I ought. I have often mentioned to you, the Multiplicity of my Engagements, and have been once exposed to the Ridicule and Censure of the World for mentioning, the great Importance of the Business which lay upon me, and if this Letter should ever see the Light, it would be again imputed to Vanity, that I mention to you, how busy I am. But I must repeat it by Way of Apology for not writing you oftener. From four O Clock in the Morning untill ten at Night, I have not a single Moment, which I can call my own. I will not say that I expect to run distracted, to grow mellancholly, to drop in an Apoplexy, or fall into a Consumption. But I do say, it is little less than a Miracle, that one or other of these Misfortunes has not befallen me before now.

Your Favours of September 15, 20, and 23d are now before me. Every Line from you gives me inexpressible Pleasure. But it is a great Grief to me, that I can write no oftener to you.

There is one Thing which excites my utmost Indignation and Contempt, I mean the Brutality, with which People talk to you, of my Death. I beg you would openly affront every Man, Woman or Child, for the future who mentions any such Thing to you, except your Relations, and Friends whose Affections you cannot doubt. I expect it of all my Friends, that they resent, as Affronts to me, every Repetition of such Reports.

I shall inclose to you, Governor Livingstons Speech, the most elegant and masterly, ever made in America.

Depend upon it, the Enemy cannot cutt off the Communication. I can come home when I will. They have N. York—and this is their Ne Plus Ultra.

Abigail Adams to John Adams

Sepbr 23 1776

There are perticuliar times when I feel such an uneasiness such a rest less ness, as neither company Books family Cares or any other thing will remove. My Pen is my only pleasure, and writing to you the composure of my mind.

I feel that agitation this Evening, a degree of Melancholy has seazd my mind, owing to the anxiety I feel for the fate of our Arms at New york, and the apprehinsions I have for your Health and safety.

We Have so many rumours and Reports that tis imposible to know what to Credit. We are this Evening assurd that there has been a field Battle between a detachment of our Army commanded by General Miflin and a detachment of British Troops in which the Latter were defeated. An other report says that we have been obliged to Evacuate the city and leave our cannon Baggage &c &c. This we cannot credit, we will not Believe it.

Tis a most critical day with us. Heaven Crown our arms with Success.

Did you ever expect that we should hold long Island? And if that could not be held, the city of New york must lie at their mercy. If they command New york can they cut of the communication between the Colonies?

Tho I sufferd much last winter yet I had rather be in a situation where I can collect the Truth, than at a distance where I am distressd by a thousand vague reports.

> War is our Buisness, but to whom is give'n
> To die, or triumph, that determine Heav'n!

I write you an abundance, do you read it all? Your last Letters have been very short. Have you buried stifled or exausted all the ——— I wont ask the question you must find out my meaning if you can.

I cannot help smileing at your caution in Never subscribeing a Letter, yet frank it upon the outside where you are obliged to write your Name.

I hope I have a Letter by Saturdays Post. You say you are sometimes dissapointed, you can tell then How I feel. I endeavour to write once a week.

Poor Barrel I see by the paper is dead, so is our Neighbour Feild.

John Adams to Abigail Adams

Philadelphia Octr. 11. 1776

I suppose your Ladyship has been in the Twitters, for some Time past, because you have not received a Letter by every Post, as you used to do. But I am coming to make my Apology in Person. I, Yesterday asked and obtained Leave of Absence. It will take me till next Monday, to get ready, to finish off, a few Remnants of public Business, and to put my private Affairs in proper order. On the 14th. day of October, I shall get away, perhaps. But I dont expect to reach Home, in less than a fortnight, perhaps not in three Weeks, as I shall be obliged to make stops by the Way.

"Kind Providence Has Preserved to Me a Life"

JANUARY–NOVEMBER 1777

When John departed once again to attend Congress in January *1777*, he had to make his way around British-occupied New York City and on to Baltimore. Congress had adjourned there when the British Army, under Gen. William Howe, pressed into New Jersey and threatened Philadelphia. While life had become somewhat easier in New England, the war continued on as fiercely as ever in the middle colonies and to the south. Rather than escaping from danger, as John had done when he left the Boston area for Philadelphia in *1775* and *1776*, he was now riding toward it.

Another circumstance made this separation particularly difficult: Abigail was pregnant. In keeping with eighteenth-century norms that disapproved of explicit mentions of pregnancy in letters (the polite euphemisms were "in circumstances" or "stately"), neither Abigail nor John directly mentioned the situation until Abigail came close to "her time." But the correspondence below makes clear that it was rarely far from their minds and that John's concern for Abigail's well-being was particularly acute.

John Adams to Abigail Adams

My dear   Dedham January 9. 1777

The irresistable Hospitality of Dr Sprague and his Lady has prevailed upon me, and my worthy Fellow Traveller, to put up at his
happy Seat. We had an agreable Ride to this Place, and tomorrow
Morning We sett off, for Providence, or some other Rout.

Present, my affection, in the tenderest Manner to my little deserving
Daughter and my amiable sons. It was cruel Parting this Morning. My
Heart was most deeply affected, altho, I had the Presence of Mind, to
appear composed.

May God almightys Providence protect you, my dear, and all our
little ones. My good Genius my Guardian Angell whispers me, that We
shall see happier Days, and that I shall live to enjoy the Felicities of
domestic Life, with her whom my Heart esteems above all earthly
Blessings.

Abigail Adams to John Adams

Janry 26 1777

Tis a great grief to me that I know not how to write nor where to
send to you. I know not of any conveyance. I risk this by Major R[ic]e
who promisses to take what care he can to get it to you.

I have Received 3 Letters from you since you left me 2 from
H[artfor]d and one from D[edha]m. Tis a satisfaction to hear tho only
by a line.

We are told the most dissagreable things by use become less so. I
cannot say that I find the truth of the observation verified. I am sure
no seperation was ever so painfull to me as the last. Many circumstances concur to make it so—the distance and the difficulty of communication, the Hazards which if not real, my immagination repre-

sents so, all conspire [to] make me anxious, as well as what I need not mention.

I wish to Hear often from you and when a conveniant opportunity offers Let me know how you like your waiter. Many reports have been circulated since you went away concerning him none of which I regard as I find no proof to support them. One is that he is a deserted Regular, a Spy &c. I find tis all suspicion or Else told with a design to make me uneasy, but it has not that Effect.

The family are all well, and desire Pappa would write to them. I rejoice in our Late successes. Heaven Grant us a continuation of them.

Your M[othe]r desires to be rememberd to you.

I long to hear of your arrival and to get one Letter from B[altimor]e. The Situation will be New and afford me entertainment by an account of it. At all times remember in the tenderest manner her whose happiness depends upon your welfare.

Portia

John Adams to Abigail Adams

Baltimore Feby. 2. 1777

Last Evening We arrived safe in this Town after the longest Journey, and through the worst Roads and the worst Weather, that I have ever experienced. My Horses performed, extreamly well.

Baltimore is a very pretty Town, situated on Petapsco River, which empties itself into the great Bay of Cheasapeak. The Inhabitants are all good Whiggs, having sometime ago banished all the Tories from among them. The Streets are very dirty and miry, but every Thing else is agreable except the monstrous Prices of Things. We cannot get an Horse kept under a Guinea a Week. Our Friends are well.

The continental Army is filling up fast, here and in Virginia. I pray that the Massachusetts, may not fail of its Quota, in Season.

In this Journey, We have crossed four mighty Rivers Connecticutt,

Hudson, Delaware, and Susquehannah. The two first We crossed upon the Ice—the two last in Boats—the last We crossed, a little above the Place where it empties into Cheasapeak Bay.

I think I have never been better pleased with any of our American States than with Maryland. We saw most excellent Farms all along the Road, and what was very striking to me, I saw more sheep and more flax in Maryland than I ever saw in riding a like Distance in any other State. We scarce passed a Farm without seeing a fine flock of sheep, and scarce an House without seeing Men or Women, dressing Flax. Several Times We saw Women, breaking and swingling, this necessary Article.

I have been to Meeting, and heard my old Acquaintance Mr Allison, a worthy Clergyman of this Town whom I have often seen in Philadelphia.

John Adams to Abigail Adams

Baltimore Feby. 10. 1777

Fells Point, which I mentioned in a Letter this Morning, has a considerable Number of Houses upon it. The Shipping all lies now at this Point. You have from it on one side a compleat View of the Harbour, and on the other a fine Prospect of the Town of Baltimore. You see the Hill, in full View and the Court House, the Church and Meeting House, upon it. The Court House makes an haughty Appearance, from this Point. There is a Fortification erected, on this Point with a Number of Embrasures for Cannon facing the Narrows which make the Entrance into the Harbour. At the Narrows they have a Fort, with a Garrison in it.

It is now a Month and a few days, since I left you. I have heard nothing from you, nor received a Letter from the Massachusetts. I hope the Post office, will perform better than it has done.

I am anxious to hear how you do. I have in my Mind a Source of

Anxiety, which I never had before, since I became such a Wanderer. You know what it is. Cant you convey to me, in Hieroglyphicks, which no other Person can comprehend Information which will relieve me. Tell me you are as well as can be expected.

My Duty to your Papa and my Mamma. Love to Brothers, and Sisters. Tell Betcy I hope She is married. Tho I want to throw the Stocking. My Respects to Mr S[*haw*]. Tell him he may be a Calvinist if he will, provided always that he preserves his Candour Charity and Moderation.

What shall I say of or to my N. J. C. and T.? What will they say to me for leaving them, their Education and Fortune so much to the Disposal of Chance? May almighty and all gracious Providence, protect, and bless them.

I have this Day sent my Resignation of a certain mighty office. It has relieved me from a Burden, which has a long Time oppress'd me. But I am determined, that, while I am ruining my Constitution of Mind and Body, and running dayly Risques of my Life and Fortune in Defence of the Independency of my Country, I will not knowingly resign my own.

Relations between Abigail and her younger sister Elizabeth were strained over Betsy's decision to marry the Rev. John Shaw. Abigail disapproved of the marriage, possibly due to Shaw's religious beliefs but also possibly because Betsy had denied any relationship with Shaw for several years prior to their finally becoming engaged. Abigail here exaggerates Betsy's age—she was twenty-seven years old.

Abigail Adams to John Adams

[*The letter begins on 8 March 1777.*]
March 9 [*1777*]

I have this day Received a most agreable packet favourd by mr Hall, for which I return you my most hearty thanks, and which contains much amusement, and gave me much pleasure. Rejoice with you in your agreable situation, tho I cannot help wishing you nearer. Shall I tell you how near? You have not given me any politicks tho, have you so much of them that you are sick of them?

I have some thoughts of opening a political correspondence with your Namesake. He is much more communicative than you are, but I must agree with him to consider me as part of one of the Members of Congress. You must know that since your absence a Letter designd for you from him fell into my Hands.

You make some inquiries which tenderly affect me. I think upon the whole I have enjoyed as much Health as I ever did in the like situation—a situation I do not repine at tis a constant remembrancer of an absent Friend, and excites sensations of tenderness which are better felt than expressd.

Our Little ones are well and often talk and wish for ——. Master T. desires I would write a Letter for him which I have promised to do. Your Mamma tenderly inquires after you. I cannot do your message to B[*ets*]y sine the mortification I endure at the mention of it is so great that I have never changd a word with her upon the subject, alltho preparations are making for house keeping the ordination is the 12th of this month. I would not make an exchange with her for the mountains of mexico and Peru. She has forfeited all her character with me and the world for taste &c. All her acquaintance stand amazd. An Idea of 30 years and unmarried is sufficent to make people do very unacountable things. Thank Heaven my Heart was early fix'd and never deviated. The early impression has for succeeding years been

gathering strength, and will out last the Brittle frame that contains it—
tis a spark of Celestial fire and will burn with Eternal vigor.

Heaven preserve and return in safety the dearest of Friends to His

Portia

John Adams to Abigail Adams

Philadelphia March 16. 1777

The Spring advances, very rapidly, and all Nature will soon be
cloathed in her gayest Robes. The green Grass, which begins to shew
itself, here, and there, revives in my longing Imagination my little
Farm, and its dear Inhabitants. What Pleasures has not this vile War,
deprived me of? I want to wander, in my Meadows, to ramble over my
Mountains, and to sit in Solitude, or with her who has all my Heart, by
the side of the Brooks. These beautifull Scænes, would contribute
more to my Happiness, than the sublime ones which surround me.

I begin to suspect that I have not much of the Grand in my Compo-
sition. The Pride and Pomp of War, the continual Sound of Drums
and Fifes as well played, as any in the World, the Prancings and
Tramplings of the Light Horse numbers of whom are paraded in the
Streets every day, have no Charms for me. I long for rural and domestic scænes, for the warbling of Birds and the Prattle of my Children.
Dont you think I am somewhat poetical this morning, for one of my
Years, and considering the Gravity, and Insipidity of my Employment.
As much as I converse with Sages and Heroes, they have very little of
my Love or Admiration. I should prefer the Delights of a Garden to
the Dominion of a World. I have nothing of Cæsars Greatness in my
soul. Power, has not my Wishes in her Train. The Gods, by granting
me Health, and Peace and Competence, the Society of my Family and
Friends, the Perusal of my Books, and the Enjoyment of my Farm and
Garden, would make me as happy as my Nature and State will bear.

Of that Ambition which has Power for its object, I dont believe I have a Spark in my Heart. There other Kinds of Ambition of which I have a great deal.

I am now situated, in a pleasant Part of the Town, in Walnutt Street, on the south side of it, between second and third Streets, at the House of Mr Duncan, a Gentleman from Boston, who has a Wife and three Children. It is an agreable Family. General Wolcott of Connecticutt, and Coll Whipple of Portsmouth, are with me in the same House. Mr Adams, has removed to Mrs Cheasmans, in fourth Street near the Corner of Markett Street, where he has a curious Group of Company consisting of Characters as opposite, as North and South. Ingersol, the Stamp man and Judge of Admiralty, Sherman, an old Puritan, as honest as an Angell and as firm in the Cause of American Independence, as Mount Atlass, and Coll Thornton, as droll and funny as Tristram Shandy. Between the Fun of Thornton, the Gravity of Sherman, and the formal Toryism of Ingersol, Adams will have a curious Life of it. The Landlady too who has buried four Husbands, one Tailor, two shoemakers and Gilbert Tenant, and still is ready for a fifth, and well deserves him too, will add to the Entertainment. Gerry and Lovell are yet at Miss Leonards, under the Auspices of Mrs Yard.

Mr Hancock has taken an House in Chesnutt Street, near the Corner of fourth Street near the State House.

March 17.

We this day recd Letters from Dr Franklin and Mr Deane. I am not at Liberty to mention particulars. But in general the Intelligence is very agreable. I am now convinced, there will be a general War.

John's concern for "Toryism" in the letter below reflects an important facet of the American Revolution—that the nation remained substantially divided over the

drive for independence. While many people rallied to the patriot cause, equal or greater numbers were either indifferent or faithful to Britain. Likewise, individuals' loyalties shifted with the changing fortunes of the Continental Army.

John Adams to Abigail Adams

Philadelphia March 31. 1777

I know not the Time, when I have omitted to write you, so long. I have recd but three Letters from you, since We parted, and these were short ones. Do you write by the Post? If you do there must have been some Legerdemain. The Post comes now constantly once a Week, and brings me News Papers, but no Letters. I have ventured to write by the Post, but whether my Letters are received or not, I dont know. If you distrust the Post, the Speaker or your Unkle Smith will find frequent opportunities of conveying Letters.

I never was more desirous of hearing from Home, and never before heard so seldom. We have Reports here, not very favourable to the Town of Boston. It is said that Dissipation prevails and that Toryism abounds, and is openly avowed at the Coffee Houses. I hope the Reports are false. Apostacies in Boston are more abominable than in any other Place. Toryism finds worse Quarter here. A poor fellow, detected here as a Spy, employed as he confesses by Lord Howe and Mr Galloway to procure Pilots for Delaware River, and for other Purposes was this day at Noon, executed on the Gallows in the Presence of an immense Crowd of Spectators. His Name was James Molesworth. He has been Mayors Clerk to three or four Mayors.

I believe you will think my Letters, very trifling. Indeed they are. I write in Trammells. Accidents have thrown so many Letters into the Hands of the Enemy, and they take such a malicious Pleasure, in exposing them, that I choose they should have nothing but Trifles from me to expose. For this Reason I never write any Thing of Consequence from Europe, from Philadelphia from Camp, or any where else. If I could write freely I would lay open to you, the whole system of Politicks and War and would delineate all the Characters in Either Drama, as minutely, altho I could not do it, so elegantly, as Tully did in his Letters to Atticus.

We have Letters however from France by a Vessell in at Portsmouth—of her important Cargo you have heard. There is News of very great Importance in the Letters, but I am not at Liberty. The News, however, is very agreable.

Abigail Adams to John Adams

April 17. 1777

Your obliging favours of March 14, 16 and 22. have received, and most Sincerely thank you for them. I know not How I should support an absence already tedious, and many times attended with melancholy reflections, if it was not for so frequently hearing from you. That is a consolation to me, tho a cold comfort in a winters Night. As the Summer advances I have many anxieties, some of which I should not feel or at least should find them greatly alleviated if you could be with me. But as that is a satisfaction I know I must not look for, (tho I have a good mind to hold You to your promise since some perticuliar circumstances were really upon that condition.) I must summon all the Phylosophy I am mistress of since what cannot be help'd must be endured.

Mrs Howard a Lady for whom I know you had a great respect died yesterday to the inexpressible Grief of her Friends. She was deliverd of a son or daughter I know not which yesterday week, a mortification in her Bowels occasiond her death. Every thing of this kind Naturally shocks a person in similar circumstances. How great the mind that can overcome the fear of Death! How anxious the Heart of a parent who looks round upon a family of young and helpless children and thinks of leaving them to a world full of snares and temptations which they have neither discretion to foresee, nor prudence to avoid.

But I will quit a subject least it should excite painfull sensations in a Heart that I would not willingly wound.

You give me an account in one of your Letters of the removal of your Lodgings. The extravagance of Board is greater there than here tho here every thing is at such prices as was not ever before known. Many articles are not to be had tho at ever so great a price. Sugar Molasses Rum cotton wool Coffe chocolate, cannot all be consumed. Yet there are none, or next to none to be sold, perhaps you may procure a pound at a time, but no more. I have sometimes stoped 15 or 20 Butchers in a day with plenty of meat but not a mouthfull to be had unless I would give 4 pence pr pound and 2 pence pr pound for bringing. I have never yet indulged them and am determined I will not whilst I have a mouthfull of salt meat, to Eat, but the act is no more regarded now than if it had never been made and has only this Effect I think, that it makes people worse than they would have been without it. As to cloathing of any sort for myself or family I think no more of purchaseing any than if they were to live like Adam and Eve in innocence.

I seek wool and flax and can work willingly with my Hands, and tho my Household are not cloathed with fine linnen nor Scarlet, they are cloathed with what is perhaps full as Honorary, the plain and Decent manufactory of my own family, and tho I do not abound, I am not in want. I have neither poverty nor Riches but food which is conveniant for me, and a Heart to be thankfull and content that in such perilous times so large a share of the comforts of life are allotted to me.

I have a large share of Health to be thankfull for, not only for myself but for my family.

I have enjoyed as much Health Since the small pox, as I have known in any year not with standing a paleness which has very near resembled a whited wall, but which for about 3 weeks past I have got the Better of. Coulour and a clumsy figure make their appearence in so much that master John says, Mar, I never saw any body grow so fat as you do.

I really think this Letter would make a curious figure if it should fall into the Hands of any person but yourself—and pray if it comes safe to you, burn it.

But ever remember with the tenderest Sentiments her who knows no earthly happiness eaquel to that of being tenderly beloved by her dearest Friend.

John Adams to Abigail Adams

Saturday Evening 26 April 1777

I have been lately more remiss, than usual in Writing to you. There has been a great Dearth of News. Nothing from England nothing from France, Spain, or any other Part of Europe. Nothing from the West Indies. Nothing from Howe, and his Banditti nothing from General Washington.

There are various Conjectures that Lord How is dead, sick, or gone to England, as the Proclamations run in the Name of Will. Howe only, and nobody, from New York can tell any Thing of his Lordship.

I am wearied out, with Expectations that the Massachusetts Troops would have arrived, e'er now, at Head Quarters. Do our People intend to leave the Continent in the Lurch? Do they mean to submit? Or what Fatality attends them? With the noblest Prize in View, that ever Mortals contended for, and with the fairest Prospect of obtaining it upon easy Terms, The People of the Massachusetts Bay, are dead.

Does our State intend to send only half, or a third of their Quota? Do they wish to see another, crippled, disastrous and disgracefull Campaign for Want of an Army? I am, more sick and more ashamed of, my own Countrymen, than ever I was before. The Spleen, the Vapours, the Dismals, the Horrors, seem to have Seized, our whole State.

More Wrath than Terror, has seized me. I am very mad. The gloomy Cowardice of the Times, is intollerable in N. England.

Indeed I feel, not a little out of Humour, from Indisposition of Body. You know, I cannot pass a Spring, or fall, without an ill Turn— and I have had one these four or five Weeks—a Cold, as usual. Warm Weather, and a little Exercise, with a little Medicine, I suppose will cure me as usual. I am not confined—but moap about and drudge as usual, like a Gally Slave. I am, a Fool if ever there was one to be such a Slave. I wont be much longer. I will be more free, in some World or other.

Is it not intollerable, that the opening Spring, which I should enjoy with my Wife and Children upon, my little Farm should pass away, and laugh at me, for labouring, Day after Day, and Month after Month, in a Conclave, Where neither Taste, nor Fancy, nor Reason, nor Passion nor Appetite can be gratified?

Posterity! You will never know, how much it cost the present Generation, to preserve your Freedom! I hope you will make a good Use of it. If you do not, I shall repent in Heaven, that I ever took half the Pains to preserve it.

Abigail Adams to John Adams

[*April 1777*]

The young folks desire Mamma to return thanks for their Letters which they will properly notice soon. It would have grieved you if you had seen your youngest son stand by his Mamma and when she deliverd out to the others their Letters, he inquired for one, but none appearing he stood in silent grief with the Tears running down his face, nor could he be pacified till I gave him one of mine. Pappa does not Love him he says so well as he does Brothers, and many comparisons were made to see whose Letters were the longest.

Abigail Adams to John Adams

May 6 1777

Tis ten days I believe since I wrote you a Line, yet not ten minuts passes without thinking of you. Tis four Months wanting 3 days since we parted, every day of ye time I have mournd the absence of my Friend, and felt a vacancy in my Heart which nothing, nothing can supply. In vain the Spring Blooms or the Birds sing, their Musick has not its formour melody, nor the spring its usual pleasures. I look round with a melancholy delight and sigh for my absent partner. I fancy I see you worn down with Cares fatigued with Buisness, and solitary amidst a multitude.

And I think it probabal before this reaches you that you may be driven from the city by our Barbarous and Hostile foes, and the City shareing the fate of Charlestown and Falmouth, Norfolk and Daunbury. So vague and uncertain are the accounts with regard to the Latter that I shall not pretend to mention them. Tis more than a week since the Event, yet we have no accounts which can be depended upon. I wish it may serve the valuable purpose of arousing our degenerated Country Men from that state of security and torpitude into which they seem to be sunk.

John Adams to Abigail Adams

May 15. 1777

Gen. Warren writes me, that my Farm never looked better, than when he last saw it, and that Mrs —— was like to outshine all the Farmers. I wish I could see it—But I can make Allowances. He knows the Weakness of his Friends Heart and that nothing flatters it more than praises bestowed upon a certain Lady.

I am suffering every day for Want of my farm to ramble in. I have been now for near Ten Weeks in a drooping disagreable Way, loaded constantly with a Cold. In the Midst of infinite Noise, Hurry, and Bustle, I lead a lonely melancholly Life, mourning the Loss of all the Charms of Life, which are my family, and all the Amusement that I ever had in life which is my farm.

If the warm Weather, which is now coming on, should not cure my Cold, and make me better I must come home. If it should and I should get tolerably comfortable, I shall stay, and reconcile my self to the Misery I here suffer as well as I can.

I expect, that I shall be chained to this Oar, untill my Constitution both of Mind and Body are totally destroyed, and rendered wholly useless to my self, and Family for the Remainder of my Days.

However, now We have got over, the dreary, dismall, torpid Winter, when We had no Army, not even Three Thousand Men to protect Us against, all our Enemies foreign and domestic; and now We have got together a pretty respectable Army, which renders Us tolerably secure against both, I doubt not, We shall be able to perswade some Gentleman or other, in the Massachusetts, to vouch safe, to Undertake the dangerous Office of Delegate to Congress.

However, I will neither, whine, nor croak. The Moment our Affairs, are in a prosperous Way and a little more Out of Doubt—that Moment I become a private Gentleman, the respectfull Husband of the amiable Mrs A. of B. and the affectionate Father of her Children, two Characters, which I have scarcly supported for these three Years past, having done the Duties of neither.

Abigail Adams to John Adams

Sunday. May 18 1777

I think myself very happy that not a week passes but what I receive a Letter or two, some times more from you; and tho they are longer in comeing than formerly oweing I suppose to the posts being obliged to travel farther round, yet I believe they all faithfully reach me, even the curious conversation between mr Burn and your Honour arrived safe and made me laugh very Heartily.

Your Last which I believe came by a private Hand and was dated the 30 of April came to hand in about 12 days which is sooner than any other has reachd me since you came to Philadelphia. Two others accompanied it one of April 26 and 27. In one of them you mention your having been unwell, I hope nothing more than a cold. I feel more anxious than ever for your Health, and must intreat of you if you find it fail in any great measure that you would return during the summer Months; should I hear you were sick the imposibility of my comeing to you would render me misirable indeed.

I think before this time Many of our Troops must have arrived at Head Quarters, for tho we Have been dilatory in this and the Neighbouring Towns, others I hear have done their duty better. Not an Hour in the day but what we see soldiers marching. The sure way to prevent their distressing us Here would be to have a strong Army with the General. Their are a Number not more than half I believe tho, of this Towns proportion inlisted. The rest were to be drawn at our May meeting, but nothing was done in that way. They concluded to try a little longer to inlist them. The Town Send but one Rep, this year and that is mr N[ile]s of the middle parish. Give him His pipe and Let him laugh, He will not trouble any body. Philalutheris I suppose will be chosen into the Counsel since He finds that His plan for making them Lackies and Tools to the House was not so acceptable as he expected.

"Then let me Have the Highest post,
Suppose it but an inch at most."

I should feel more unhappy and anxious than ever if I realizd our being again invaded by the wickedest and cruelest of Enemies. I should not dare to tarry here in my present situation, nor yet know where to flee for safety; the recital of the inhumane and Brutal Treatment of those poor creatures who have fallen into thir Hands, Freazes me with Horrour. My apprehensions are greatly increasd; should they come this way again I know what course I should take.

Tis an observation of Bishop Butlers that they who have lost all tenderness and Fellow-feeling for others, Have with all contracted a certain Callousness of Heart, which renders them insensible to all other satisfactions, but those of the grossest kind.

Our Enemies Have proved the Truth of the observation in every instance of their conduct. Is it not astonishing what Men may at last bring themselves to, by suppressing passions and affections of the best kind, and suffering the worst to rule over them in their full strength.

Infidelity has been a growing part of the British character for many years. It is not so much to be wonderd at that those who pay no regard to a Supreeme Being Should throw of all regard to their fellow creatures and to those precepts and doctrines which require peace and good will to Men; and in a perticuliar manner distinguish the followers of him who hath said by this shall all men know that ye are my deciples if ye have love one towards an other.

Let them reproach us ever so much for our kindness and tenderness to those who have fallen into our Hands. I hope it will never provoke us to retaliate their cruelties; let us put it as much as posible out of their power to injure us, but let us keep in mind the precepts of him who hath commanded us to Love our Enemies; and to excercise towards them acts of Humanity Benevolence and kindness, even when they despitefully use us.

And here suffer me to quote an Authority which you greatly Esteem, Dr Tillotson. It is commonly said that revenge is sweet, but to a calm and considerate mind, patience and forgiveness are sweeter, and do afford a much more rational, and solid and durable pleasure than revenge. The monuments of our Mercy and goodness are a far more pleasing and delightfull Spectacle than of our rage and cruelty, and no sort of thought does usually haunt men with more Terror, than the reflexion upon what they have done in the way of Revenge.

If our cause is just, it will be best supported by justice and righteousness. Tho we have many other crimes to answer for, that of cruelty to our Enemies is not chargable upon Americans, and I hope never will be—if we have err'd it is upon the side of Mercy and have excercised so much lenity to our Enemies as to endanger our Friends—but their Malice and wicked designs against us, has and will oblige every state to proceed against them with more Rigor. Justice and self preservation are duties as much incumbant upon christians, as forgiveness and Love of Enemies.

Adieu. I have devoted an Hour this Day to you. I dare say you are not in debt.

Ever remember with the tenderest affection one whose greatest felicity consists in the firm belief of an unabated Love either by years or absence.

Portia

John Adams to Abigail Adams

May 22 [*1777*]. 4 O Clock in the Morning

After a Series of the Souerest, and harshest Weather that ever I felt in this Climate, We are at last, blessed, with a bright Sun and a soft Air. The Weather here has been like, our old Easterly Winds to me, and southerly Winds to you.

The Charms of the Morning, at this Hour are irresistable. The Streakes of Glory dawning in the East: the freshness and Purity in the Air, the bright blue of the sky, the sweet Warblings of a great Variety of Birds intermingling with the martial Clarions of an hundred Cocks now within my Hearing, all conspire to chear the Spirits.

This kind of puerile Description is a very pretty Employment for an old Fellow whose Brow is furrowed with the Cares of Politicks and War.

I shall be on Horseback in a few Minutes, and then I shall enjoy the Morning, in more Perfection.

I spent last Evening at the War-office, with General Arnold. He has been basely slandered and libelled. The Regulars say, "he fought like Julius Cæsar."

I am wearied to Death, with the Wrangles, between military officers, high, and low. They Quarrell like Cats and Dogs. The worry one another like Mastiffs. Scrambling for Rank and Pay like Apes for Nutts.

I believe there is no one Principle, which predominates in human Nature so much in every stage of Life, from the Cradle to the Grave, in Males and females old and young, black and white, rich and poor, high and low, as this Passion for Superiority. Every human Being, compares itself in its own Imagination, with every other round about it, and will find some Superiority over every other real or imaginary, or it will die of Grief and Vexation. I have seen, it among Boys and Girls at school, among Lads at Colledge, among Practicers at the Bar, among the Clergy in their Associations, among Clubbs of Friends, among the People in Town Meetings, among the Members of an House of Reps. among the Grave Councillors, on the more solemn Bench of Justice, and in that awfully August Body the Congress, and on many of its Committees—and among Ladies every Where—But I never saw it operate with such Keenness Ferocity and Fury, as among military Officers. They will go terrible Lengths, in their Emulations, their Envy and Revenge, in Consequence of it.

So much for Philosophy. I hope my five or six Babes are all well. My Duty to my Mother and your Father and Love to sisters and Brothers Aunts and Uncles.

Pray how does your Asparagus perform? &c.

I would give Three Guineas for a Barrell of your Cyder—not one drop is to be had here for Gold. And wine, is not to be had under, Six or Eight Dollars a Gallon and that very bad. I would give a Guinea for a Barrell of your Beer. The small beer here is wretchedly bad. In short I can get nothing that I can drink, and I believe I shall be sick from this Cause alone. Rum at forty shillings a Gallon and bad Water, will never do, in this hot Climate in summer where Acid Liquors, are necessary against Putrefaction.

John Adams to Abigail Adams

Monday June 2. 1777

Artillery Election! I wish I was at it, or near it.

Yours of the 18th. reached me this Morning. The Cause that Letters are so long in travelling, is that there is but one Post, in a Week who goes from hence to Peeks Kill, altho there are two that go from thence to Boston.

Riding every day, has made me better, than I was altho I am not yet quite well. I am determined to continue this Practice, which is very necessary for me.

I rejoice to find, that the Town have had the Wisdom to send but one Rep. The House last Year was too numerous and unwieldy. The Expence was too great. I suppose you will have a Constitution formed this Year. Who will be the Moses, the Lycurgus, the Solon? Or have you a score or two of such? Whoever they may be and whatever Form may be adopted, I am perswaded there is among the Mass of our People a Fund of Wisdom, Integrity and Humanity, which will preserve their Happiness, in a tolerable Measure.

If the Enemy come to Boston again, fly with your little ones all of them to Philadelphia. But they will scarcely get to Boston, this Campaign.

I admire your Sentiments concerning Revenge.

Revenge, in ancient Days, you will see it through the whole Roman History, was esteemed a generous, and an heroic Passion. Nothing was too good for a Friend or too bad for an Enemy. Hatred and Malice, without Limits against an Enemy, was indulged, was justified, and no Cruelty was thought unwarrantable.

Our Saviour, taught the Immorality of Revenge, and the moral Duty of forgiving Injuries, and even the Duty of loving Enemies. Nothing can shew the amiable, the moral, the divine Excellency of these Christian Doctrines in a stronger Point of Light, than the Characters and Conduct of Marius and Sylla, Cæsar, Pompey, Anthony and Augustus, among innumerable others.

Retaliation, we must practice, in some Instances, in order to make our barbarous Foes respect in some degree the Rights of Humanity. But this will never be done without the most palpable Necessity.

The Apprehension of Retaliation alone, will restrain them from Cruelties which would disgrace, Savages.

To omit it then would be cruelty to ourselves our Officers and Men.

We are amused here with Reports of Troops removing from R. Island, N. York, Staten Island &c—Waggons Boats, Bridges &c prepared—two old Indiamen cutt down into floating Batteries mounting 32 Guns sent round into Delaware R. &c &c. But I heed it no more, than the whistling of the Zephyrs. In short I had rather they should come to Philadelphia than not. It would purify this City of its Dross. Either the Furnace of Affliction would refine it of its Impurities, or it would be purged yet so as by fire.

This Town has been a dead Weight, upon Us—it would be a dead Weight also upon the Enemy. The Mules here wd plague them more than all their Money.

John Adams to Abigail Adams

June 4. 1777

I wish I could know, whether your season is cold or warm wet or dry, fruitfull or barren. Whether you had late Frosts. Whether those Frosts have hurt the Fruit, the Flax the Corn or Vines, &c. We have a fine season here and a bright Prospect of Abundance.

You will see by the inclosed Papers, in a Letter from my Friend Parsons, a very handsome Narration of one of the prettiest Exploits of this War—a fine Retaliation for the Danbury Mischief. Meigs who was before esteemed a good Officer has acquired by this Expedition a splendid Reputation.

You will see by the same Papers too, that the Writers here in opposition to the Constitution of Pensilvania, are making a factious Use of my Name and Lucubrations. Much against my Will, I assure you, for altho I am no Admirer of the Form of this Government, yet I think it is agreable to the Body of the People, and if they please themselves they will please me. And I would not choose to be impressed into the service of one Party, or the other—and I am determined I will not inlist.

Besides it is not very genteel in these Writers, to put my Name to a Letter, from which I cautiously withheld it myself.

However, let them take their own Way. I shant trouble myself about it.

I am, growing better, by Exercise and Air.

I must write a Letter, in Behalf of Mr Thaxter to the Bar and Bench in Boston, in order to get him sworn, at July Court.

Will my Brother, when the Time comes, officiate for his Brother at a Christening?

If it is a young Gentleman call him William after your Father—if a young Lady, call her Elizabeth after your Mother, and sister.

Abigail Adams to John Adams

june 8. 1777

I generally endeavour to write you once a week, if my Letters do not reach you, tis oweing to the Neglect of the post. I generally get Letters from you once a week, but seldom in a fortnight after they are wrote. I am sorry to find that your Health fails. I should greatly rejoice to see you. I know of no earthly blessing which would make me happier, but I cannot wish it upon the terms of ill Health. No seperation was ever more painfull to me than the last. May the joy of meeting again be eaquel to the pain of seperation; I regret that I am in a Situation to wish away one of the most precious Blessings of life, yet as the months pass of; I count them up with pleasure and reckon upon tomorrow as the 5th which has passd since your absence. I have some times melancholly reflections, and immagine these seperations as preparatory to a still more painfull one in which even hope the anchor of the Soul is lost, but whilst that remains no Temporary absence can ever wean or abate the ardor of my affection. Bound together by many tender ties, there scarcly wanted an addition, yet I feel that there soon will be an additionall one. Many many are the tender sentiments I have felt for the parent on this occasion. I doubt not they are reciprocal, but I often fell the want of his presence and the soothing tenderness of his affection. Is this weakness or is it not?

I am happy in a daughter who is both a companion and an assistant in my Family affairs and who I think has a prudence and steadiness beyond her years.

You express a longing after the enjoyments of your little Farm. I do not wonder at it, that also wants the care and attention of its master—all that the mistress can do is to see that it does not go to ruin. She would take pleasure in improvements, and study them with assiduity if she was possessd with a sufficency to accomplish them. The season promisses plenty at present and the english Grass never lookd better.

You inquire after the Asparagrass. It performs very well this year and produces us a great plenty. I long to send you a Barrell of cider, but find it impracticable, as no vessels can pass from this state to yours. I rejoice at the good way our affairs seem to be in and Hope your Herculian Labours will be crownd with more success this year than the last. Every thing wears a better aspect. We Have already taken two Transports of theirs with Hessians on board, and this week a prize was carried into Salem taken by the Tyranicide with 4000 Blankets and other valuable articles on board.

I do not feel very apprehensive of an attack upon Boston. I hope we shall be quiet. I should make a misirable hand of running now. Boston is not what it once was. It has no Head, no Men of distinguishd abilities, they behave like children.

Col Holland the infamous Hampshire counterfeiter was taken last week in Boston and is committed to Jail in Irons. I hope they will now keep a strong Guard upon him.

We are not like to get our *now* unpopular act repeald I fear. I own I was in favour of it, but I have seen it fail and the ill consequences arising from it have made me wish it had never been made. Yet the House are nearly divided about it. Genell W[*arre*]n will write you I suppose. He and his Lady have spent part of the week with me.

I wish you would be so good as to mention the dates of the Letters you receive from me. The last date of yours was May 22—5 dated in may since this day week. I wonder How you get time to write so much. I feel very thankfull to you for every line. You will I know remember me often when I cannot write to you.

Good Night tis so dark that I cannot see to add more than that I am with the utmost tenderness yours ever yours.

John Adams to Abigail Adams

Philadelphia June 16 1777

I had a most charming Packett from you and my young Correspondents, to day.

I am very happy, to learn that you have done such great Things in the Way of paying Debts. I know not what would become of me, and mine, if I had not such a Friend to take Care of my Interests in my absence.

You will have Patience with me this Time, I hope, for this Time will be the last. I shall stay out this year, if I can preserve my Health, and then come home, and bid farewell, to great Affairs. I have a Right to spend the Remainder of my days in small ones.

Abigail Adams to John Adams

june 23 1777

I Have just retird to my Chamber, but an impulce seazes me to write you a few lines before I close my Eye's. Here I often come and sit myself down alone to think of my absent Friend, to ruminate over past scenes, to read over Letters, journals &c.

Tis a melancholy kind of pleasure I find in this amusement, whilst the weighty cares of state scarcly leave room for a tender recollection or sentiment to steal into the Bosome of my Friend.

In my last I expressd some fears least the Enemy should soon invade us here. My apprehensions are in a great measure abated by late accounts received from the General.

We Have a very fine Season here, rather cold for a fort night, but nothing like a drought. You would smile to see what a Farmer our Brother C[ranc]h makes. His whole attention is as much engaged in it, as it ever was in Spermaciaty works watch work, or Prophesies. You must know he has purchased, (in spight of the C[olone]ls Threats) that Farm he talkd of. He gave a large price for it tis True, but tis a neat, profitable place, 300 sterling, but money is lookd upon of very little value, and you can scarcly purchase any article now but by Barter. You shall Have wool for flax or flax for wool, you shall Have, veal Beaf or pork for salt for sugar for Rum, &c but mony we will not take, is the daily language. I will work for you for Corn for flax or wool, but if I work for money you must give a cart load of it be Sure.

What can be done, and which way shall we help ourselves? Every article and necessary of life is rising daily. Gold dear Gold would soon lessen the Evils. I was offerd an article the other day for two dollors in silver for which they askd me six in paper.

I have no more to purchase with than if every dollor was a silver one every paper Dollor cost a silver one. Why then cannot it be eaquelly valuable? You will refer me to Lord Kames I know, who solves the matter. I hope in favour you will not Emit any more paper, till what we Have at least becomes more valuable.

Nothing remarkable has occurd since I wrote you last. You do not in your last Letters mention how you do—I will hope better. I want a companion a Nights, many of them are wakefull and Lonesome, and "tierd Natures sweet restorer, Balmy Sleep," flies me. How hard it is to reconcile myself to six months longer absence? Do you feel it urksome? Do you Sigh for Home? And would you willingly share with me what I have to pass through? Perhaps before this reaches you and meets with a Return. I wish the day passd, yet dread its arrival. Adieu most sincerely most affectionately Yours.

John Adams to Abigail Adams

My dearest Friend   Philadelphia June 29 1777

The enclosed Newspapers will communicate to you, all the News I know.

The Weather, here begins to be very hot. Poor Mortals pant and sweat, under the burning Skies. Faint and feeble as children, We seem as if We were dissolving away. Yet We live along.

The two Armies are now, playing off their Arts. Each acts with great Caution. Howe is as much afraid of putting any Thing to Hazard as Washington. What would Britain do, surrounded with formidable Powers in Europe just ready to strike her if Howes Army should meet a Disaster? Where would she find another Army?

How are you? I hope very well. Let Mr Thaxter write let the Children write, when you cannot. I am very anxious, but Anxiety at 400 Miles distance can do you no more good, than me. I long to hear, a certain Piece of News from Home, which will give me great Joy. Thank, Mr John for his kind Letter. I will answer him and all my little Correspondents as soon as I can.

Tell Mr John, that I am under no Apprehensions about his Proficiency in Learning. With his Capacity, and opportunities, he can not fail to acquire Knowledge. But let him know, that the moral Sentiments of his Heart, are more important than the Furniture of his Head. Let him be sure that he possesses the great Virtues of Temperance, Justice, Magnanimity, Honour and Generosity, and with these, added to his Parts he cannot fail to become a wise and great Man.

Does he read the Newspapers? The Events of this War, should not pass unobserved by him at his years.

As he reads History you should ask him, what Events strike him most? What Characters he esteems and admires? Which he hates and abhors? Which he despises?

No doubt he makes some observations, young as he is.

Treachery, Perfidy, Cruelty, Hypocrisy, Avarice, &c &c should be pointed out to him for his, Contempt as well as Detestation.

My dear Daughters Education is near my Heart. She will suffer by this War as well as her Brothers. But she is a modest, and discreet Child. Has an excellent Disposition, as well as Understanding. Yet I wish, it was in my Power, to give her, the Advantages of several Accomplishments, which it is not.

Childbirth was both a familiar process and a dangerous one. By 1777, at age 32, Abigail had successfully given birth five times before and largely knew what to expect, but that would not protect her if problems developed. Medical intervention was limited and could offer only modest assistance in dealing with any complications. A midwife usually oversaw the delivery, assisted by a variety of female friends and relatives, though some women might also consult with a doctor, as Abigail did with her uncle, Dr. Cotton Tufts.

Always indefatigable, Abigail was not kept even by labor from her correspondence. Writing to John on 10 July, she breaks off briefly to ride out her labor pains and "bear what I cannot fly from," then continues on with her letter as if nothing was amiss.

Abigail Adams to John Adams

july 9 1777

I sit down to write you this post, and from my present feelings tis the last I shall be able to write for some time if I should do well. I have been very unwell for this week past, with some complaints that have been new to me, tho I hope not dangerous.

I was last night taken with a shaking fit, and am very apprehensive that a life was lost, as I have no reason to day to think otherways; what may be the consequences to me, Heaven only knows. I know not of any injury to myself, nor any thing which could occasion what I fear.

I would not Have you too much allarmd. I keep up some spirits yet, tho I would have you prepaird for any Event that may happen.

I can add no more than that I am in every situation unfeignedly yours, yours.

Abigail Adams to John Adams

july 10 [*1777*] 9 o clock Evening

About an Hour ago I received a Letter from my Friend dated June 21: begining in this manner "my dearest Friend." It gave me a most agreable Sensation, it was a cordial to my Heart. That one single expression dwelt upon my mind and playd about my Heart, and was more valuable to me than any part of the Letter, except the close of it. It was because my Heart was softned and my mind enervated by my sufferings, and I wanted the personal and tender soothings of my dearest Friend, that [ren]derd it so valuable to me at this time. I Have [no] doubt of the tenderest affection or sincerest regard of my absent Friend, yet an expression of that kind will sooth my Heart to rest amidst a thousand anxietyes.

Tis now 48 Hours since I can say I really enjoyed any Ease, nor am

I ill enough to summons any attendance unless my sisters. Slow lingering and troublesome is the present situation. The dr encourages me to Hope that my apprehensions are groundless respecting what I wrote you yesterday, tho I cannot say I have had any reason to allter my mind. My spirits However are better than they were yesterday, and I almost wish I had not let that Letter go. If there should be agreable News to tell you, you shall know it as soon as the post can convey it. I pray Heaven that it may be Soon or it seems to me I shall be worn out. I must lay my pen down this moment, to bear what I cannot fly from—and now I have endured it I reassume my pen and will lay by all my own feelings and thank you for your obligeing Letters. A prize arrived this week at Marble Head with 400 Hogsheads of rum a board sent in by Manly. Every article and necessary of life rises here daily. Sugar has got to [8?] pounds pr hundred Lamb to 1 shilling pr pound and all ot[her] things in proportion. We have the finest Season here that I have known for many years. The fruit was injured by the cold East winds and falls of. The Corn looks well. Hay will be plenty, but your Farm wants manure. I shall endeavour to Have Sea weed carted every Leasure moment that can be had. That will not be many. Help is so scarce and so expensive I can not Hire a days mowing under 6 shillings.

How has done himself no honour by his late retreat. We fear most now for Tycon. Tis reported to day that tis takeen. We Have a vast many men who look like officers continually riding about. I wonder what they can be after, why they do not repair to the army.

We wonder too what Congress are a doing? We Have not Heard of late.

How do you do? Are you glad you are out of the way of sour faces. I could look pleasent upon you in the midst of sufferings—allmighty God carry me safely through them. I would hope I have a Friend ever nigh and ready to assist me, unto whom I commit my self. This is thursday Evening. It cannot go till monday, and then I hope will be accompanied with more agreable inteligance.

Most sincerely yours.

july 11

I got more rest last night than I expected, this morning am rather more ill than I was yesterday. This day ten years ago master John came into this world. May I have reason again to recollect it with peculiar gratitude. Adieu.

John Adams to Abigail Adams

Philadelphia July 10. 1777. Thursday

My Mind is again Anxious, and my Heart in Pain for my dearest Friend.

Three Times, have I felt, the most distressing Sympathy with my Partner, without being able to afford her any Kind of Solace, or Assistance.

When, the Family was sick of the Dissentery, and so many of our Friends died of it.

When you all had the small Pox.

And now I think I feel as anxious as ever. Oh that I could, be near, to say a few kind Words or shew a few Kind Looks, or do a few kind Actions. Oh that I could take from my dearest, a share of her Distress, or relieve her of the whole.

Before this shall reach you I hope you will be happy in the Embraces of a Daughter, as fair, and good, and wise, and virtuous as the Mother, or if it is a son I hope it will still resemble the Mother in Person Mind and Heart.

Abigail Adams to John Adams

july 16 1777

Join with me my dearest Friend in gratitude to Heaven, that a life I know you value, has been spaired and carried thro Distress and danger altho the dear Infant is numberd with its ancestors.

My apprehensions with regard to it were well founded. Tho my Friends would have fain perswaded me that the splen the vapours had taken hold of me I was as perfectly sensible of its discease as I ever before was of its existance. I was also aware of the danger which awaited me; and which tho my suffering were great thanks be to Heaven I have been Supported through, and would silently submit to its dispensations in the loss of a sweet daughter; it appeard to be a very fine Babe, and as it never opened its Eyes in this world it lookd as tho they were only closed for sleep. The circumstance which put an end to its Existance, was Evident upon its birth, but at this distance and in a Letter which may possibly fall into the Hands of some unfealing Ruffian I must omit particuliars. Suffice it to say that it was not oweing to any injury which I had sustain, nor could any care of mine have prevented it.

My Heart was much set upon a daughter. I had had a strong perswasion that my desire would be granted me. It was—but to shew me the uncertanty of all sublinary enjoyments cut of e'er I could call it mine. No one was so much affected with the loss of it as its sister who mournd in tears for Hours. I have so much cause for thankfullness amidst my sorrow, that I would not entertain a repiening thought. So short sighted and so little a way can we look into futurity that we ought patiently to submit to the dispensation of Heaven.

I am so comfortable that I am amaizd at myself, after what I have sufferd I did not expect to rise from my Bed for many days. This is but the 5th day and I have set up some Hours.

I However feel myself weakend by this exertion, yet I could not refrain the temptation of writing with my own Hand to you.

Adieu dearest of Friends adieu—yours most affectionately.

John Adams to Abigail Adams

My dearest Friend   Philadelphia July 28. 1777

Never in my whole Life, was my Heart affected with such Emotions and Sensations, as were this Day occasioned by your Letters of the 9. 10. 11. and 16 of July. Devoutly do I return Thanks to God, whose kind Providence has preserved to me a Life that is dearer to me than all other Blessings in this World. Most fervently do I pray, for a Continuance of his Goodness in the compleat Restoration of my, best Friend to perfect Health.

Is it not unaccountable, that one should feel so strong an Affection for an Infant, that one has never seen, nor shall see? Yet I must confess to you, the Loss of this sweet little Girl, has most tenderly and sensibly affected me. I feel a Grief and Mortification, that is heightened tho it is not wholly occasioned, by my Sympathy with the Mother. My dear little Nabbys Tears, are sweetly becoming her generous, Tenderness and sensibility of Nature. They are Arguments too of her good sense and Discretion.

Gen. William Howe's departure from New York City with an enormous fleet of over 250 ships frightened people up and down the East Coast, who were uncertain where the British would press their next attack. Rather than return to Boston, however, Howe sailed south and began his attack on Philadelphia. The fall of that city in late September forced Congress to relocate once again, to York, Pennsylvania.

Meanwhile, Gen. John Burgoyne, who had successfully captured Fort Ticonderoga in northern New York State, was unable to press his advantage. He and his army were defeated by Gen. Horatio Gates at Saratoga and he was eventually brought to Cambridge as a prisoner of war.

Abigail Adams to John Adams

August 5. [*1777*]

If allarming half a dozen places at the same time is an act of Generalship *How* may boast of his late conduct. We Have never since the Evacuation of Boston been under apprehensions of an invasion from them eaquel to what we sufferd last week. All Boston was in confusion, packing up and carting out of Town, Household furniture military stores, goods &c. Not less than a thousand Teams were imployd a fryday and Saturday—and to their shame be it told, not a small trunk would they carry under 8 dollors and many of them I am told askd a hundred dollors a load, for carting a Hogshead of Molasses 8 miles 30 dollors. O! Humane Nature, or rather o! inhumane nature what art thou? The report of the Fleets being seen of, of cape Ann a fryday Night, gave me the allarm, and tho pretty weak, I set about packing up my things and a Saturday removed a load. When I lookd around me and beheld the bounties of Heaven so liberally bestowed in fine Feilds of corn grass flax and english grain, and thought it might soon become a prey to these merciless ravagers, our habitations laid waste, and if our flight preserved our lives, we must return to barren Feilds, empty barns and desolated habitations if any we found, perhaps not where to lay our Heads my Heart was too full to bear the weight of alfliction which I thought just ready to overtake us, and my body too weak almost to bear the shock unsupported by my better Half.

But thanks be to Heaven we are at present releaved from our Fears, respecting ourselves. I now feel anxious for your safety but hope prudence will direct to a proper care and attention to yourselves.

May this second attempt of Hows prove his utter ruin. May destruction overtake him as a whirl wind.

We Have a report of an engagement at the Northward in which our troops behaved well, drove the Enemy into their lines killd and took 300 and 50 prisoners. The account came in last Night. I have not perticuliars. We are under apprehensions that the Hancock is taken.

Your obligeing Letters of the 8th 10th and 13th came to hand, last week. I hope before this time you are releaved from the anxiety you express for your Bosom Friend. I feel my sufferings amply rewarded in the tenderness you express for me, but in one of your Letters you have drawn a picture which drew a flood of tears from my Eyes, and rung my Heart with anguish inexpressible. I pray Heaven I may not live to realize it.

Tis almost 14 years since we were united, but not more than half that time have we had the happiness of living together.

The unfealing world may consider it in what light they please. I consider it as a sacrifice to my Country and one of my greatest misfortunes to be seperated from my children at a time of life when the joint instructions and admonition of parents sink deeper than in maturer years.

The Hopes of the smiles and approbation of my Friend sweetens all my toil and Labours.

John Adams to Abigail Adams

My dearest Friend   Phila. Aug. 11. 1777

I think I have sometimes observed to you in Conversation, that upon examining the Biography of illustrious Men, you will generally find some Female about them in the Relation of Mother or Wife, or Sister to whose Instigation, a great Part of their Merit is to be ascribed.

You will find a curious Example, of this, in the Case of Aspasia, the Wife of Pericles. She was a Woman of the greatest Beauty and the first Genius. She taught him, it is said, his refined Maxims of Policy, his lofty imperial Eloquence; nay, even composed the Speeches, on which so great a share of his Reputation was founded. The best Men in Athens, frequented her House, and brought their Wives to receive Lessons from her of Œconomy and right Deportment. Socrates himself was her Pupil in Eloquence and gives her the Honour of that funeral oration which he delivers in the Menexenus of Plato. Aristophanes indeed abuses this famous Lady but Socrates does her Honour.

I wish some of our great Men, had such Wives. By the Account in your last Letter, it seems the Women in Boston begin to think themselves able to serve their Country. What a Pity it is that our Generals in the Northern District had not Aspasias to their Wives!

I believe, the two Howes have not very great Women for Wives. If they had We should suffer more from their Exertions than We do. This is our good Fortune. A Woman of good Sense would not let her Husband spend five Weeks at Sea, in such a season of the year. A smart Wife would have put Howe in Possn. of Philadelphia, a long Time ago.

Abigail Adams to John Adams

August 12. [*1777*]

A few lines by way of remembrance every week tho I have nothing new to write you if I may judge you by myself are very acceptable. I long for a wednesday which to me is the happiest day of the week. I never fail of a pacquet, tis soon read, and then the next wednesday is thought of with the same solisitude.

"Man never is but always to be blest."

The last post brought me yours of july 16 18 and 20th.

You have often of late mentiond a daughter with much tenderness and affection, but before this time you must know of our Bereavement. I felt it last Sunday with all its poignancy. It was the first time of my going out. Your Brother held up a daughter and calld it by the Name of Susana. I wishd to have call'd ours had it lived after my own Dear Mother, and was much gratified by your mentioning it and requesting it—but tis now of no importance either the Name or the Relation. Do you feel in your own Breast any sentiments of tenderness for one you never knew, for one who could scarcly be said ever to Have had an existance? The loss occasions very different Sensation from those I once before experienced, but still I found I Had a tenderness and an affection greater than I immagined could have possess'd my Heart for one who was not endeard to me by its smiles and its graces. But the Parent is dear to me, dear to me beyond the power of words to discribe. I always feel a perticuliar regard for the young fellow who has attended upon him in the capacity of a servant. Nay even the sight of a Garment belonging to him will raise a mixture both of pleasure and pain in my Bosome.

Can it then be strange that I should feel a fondness and a tender affection for a pledg of unabated Love, a Love pure as the Gold without alloy.

> "I Glory in the sacred ties
> Which Modern Wits and fools dispise
> of Husband and of Wife."

John Adams to Abigail Adams

My best Friend   Philadelphia August 20th. 1777 Wednesday

This Day compleats three Years since I stepped into the Coach, at Mr Cushings Door, in Boston, to go to Philadelphia in Quest of Adventures. And Adventures I have found.

I feel an Inclination sometimes, to write the History of the last Three Years, in Imitation of Thucidides. There is a striking Resemblance, in several Particulars, between the Peloponnesian and the American War. The real Motive to the former was a Jealousy of the growing Power of Athens, by Sea and Land. The genuine Motive to the latter, was a similar Jealousy of the growing Power of America. The true Causes which incite to War, are seldom, professed, or Acknowledged.

We are now afloat upon a full Sea: When We shall arrive at a safe Harbour, no Mariner has Skill and experience enough to foretell. But, by the Favour of Heaven, We shall make a prosperous Voyage, after all the Storms, and shoals are passed.

Abigail Adams to John Adams

My Dearest Friend   Sepbr 10 1777

The accounts you give of the Heat of the weather, gives me great
uneasiness upon account of your Health. I fear it will through you into
a fever, or relax you so as to ruin your Health. We Have had some
extreem Hot weather here when the glasses have been at 92. I have
slept many Nights this Summer with all my windows open which I do
not remember ever to have done before. Our Hot weather you know
never lasts more than 3 days at a time, and since Sepbr came in I have
been glad to sit at a fire morning and Evening; we had a small frost a
night or two ago, but I believe it did not hurt any thing.

Yesterday compleated Eight months since you left me. When shall I
see you. I often dream of you, but the other Night I was very unhappy. Methought you was returnd but met me so Coldly that my
Heart ackd half an hour after I waked. It would ake in earnest if I once
realizd Such a reception, and yet if I had a Friend whom I cared little
or nothing about, I should be saved many an anxious hour, yet I would
not be destitute of that tender Solisitude, notwithstanding all the pain
it costs me.

I have setled with Turner and paid him his account which amounted
to £10. 16s. 8d including what you paid him. He is not in so good
Bread as he was at Philadelphia, he cannot procure any Materials to
work up. Sheeps wool is 8 shillings a pound Cotton 12, other articles in
proportion. What can be done? Our money will soon be as useless as
blank paper. Tis True I have not much to be anxious about, but it will
soon take all I have to pay my day labourers, mowing 12 shillings a
day, and much obliged to them to come at that. Butter is 3 shillings
cheeses 2, Mutton 18 pence Beaf 18 pence Lamb 1 and 4 pence, corn at
no price, none to be had Barly 8 shillings a Bushel, Rye now sold only
by way of Barter Sugar 15 pounds pr hundred coffe 10 shillings pr
pound, Molasses 24 pr Gallon rum 28 ditto. What is to become of
sallery people? With Hard money not one article of the produce of

this Country but what I could purchase cheeper than ever it was sold, nor do they value offering 8 dollors for one.

Necessity is the Mother of invention. There is a Manufactory of Molasses Set up in several Towns. Green corn Storks ground and boild down to Molasses, tis said an acre will produce a Barrel. I have seen some of it, it both tastes and looks like sugar Bakers molasses.

Tis confidently reported that How has landed his Troops, between Philadel and Baltimore. We are anxious to hear. We Have not had any late News from our Army at the Northward. The papers will inform you of several valuable prizes which have been sent in—and with their contents.

Tis almost a fortnight since I wrote you before. I have had but one baulk from you. I mean a News paper without a Letter. Our good unkle to whom you wrote as he thought, was very eager to get his Letter. He heard of it and rode up in Town on purpose, but behold when he opend it a News paper presented itself. He wanted to know if you had not a House call'd a bettering House proper for persons who were out of their Senses.

Adieu. I have nothing worth writing I think, and my Eyes are very weak which unfits me for writing much in the Evening.

Believe me at all times yours ever yours

Portia

Abigail Adams to John Adams

Best of Friends   Sep 17. [*1777*]

I Have to acknowledge a feast of Letters from you since I wrote last, their dates from August 19 to Sepbr 1. It is a very great satisfaction to me to know from day to day the movements of How, and his Bantitti. We live in hourly expectation of important inteligance from both armies. Heaven Grant us victory and peace, two Blessing I fear we are very undeserving of.

Enclossed you will find a Letter to mr L[*ovel*]l who was so obliging as to send me a plan of that part of the Country which is like to be the present seat of war. He accompanied it with a very polite Letter, and I esteem my self much obliged to him, but there is no reward this side the Grave that would be a temptation to me to undergo the agitation and distress I was thrown into by receiving a Letter in his Hand writing frankd by him. It seems almost imposible that the Humane mind could take in, in so small a space of time, so many Ideas as rushd upon mine in the space of a moment. I cannot describe to you what I felt.

The sickness or death of the dearest of Friends with ten thousand horrours seazd my immagination. I took up the Letter then laid it down, then gave it out of my Hand unable to open it, then collected resolution enough to unseal it, but dared not read it, begun at the bottom read a line, then attempted to begin it, but could not. A paper was enclosed. I venturd upon that, and finding it a plan, recoverd enough to read the Letter—but I pray Heaven I may never realize such a nother moment of distress.

I designd to have wrote you a Long Letter for really I owe you one, but have been prevented by our worthy P[*lymout*]h Friends who are Here upon a visit in their way Home and tis now so late at Night just struck 12 that I will defer any thing further till the Next post. Good Night Friend of my Heart, companion of my youth—Husband and Lover—Angles watch thy Repose.

Abigail Adams to John Adams

Sepbr 21. [*1777*]

I immagine before this reaches you some very important Event must take place betwen the two Armies. Affairs on all Sides seem to be workd up to a crissis. *How* is putting his whole force in action and seems determined to drive or be driven.

I feel in a most painfull situation between hope and fear. There must be fighting, and very Bloody Battle too I apprehend. O! how my Heart Recoils at the Idea. Why is Man calld *Humane* when he delights so

much in Blood slaughter and devastation; even those who are stiled
civilizd Nations think this little spot worth contending for, even to Blood.

John Adams to Abigail Adams

My best Friend   York Town Pensylvania, Septr. 30. 1777 Tuesday

It is now a long Time, since I had an opportunity of writing to you,
and I fear you have suffered, unnecessary Anxiety on my Account. In
the Morning of the 19th. Inst, the Congress, were allarmed, in their
Beds, by a Letter from Mr Hamilton one of General Washingtons
Family, that the Enemy were in Possn. of the Ford over the Schuylkill,
and the Boats so that they had it in their Power to be in Philadelphia,
before Morning. The Papers of Congress, belonging to the Secretary's
office, the War office, the Treasury office, &c were before sent to Bris-
tol. The President, and all the other Gentlemen were gone that Road,
so I followed, with my Friend Mr Merchant of Rhode Island, to Trenton in the Jersies. We stayed at Trenton, untill the 21. when We set
off, to Easton upon the Forks of Delaware. From Easton We went to
Bethlehem from thence to Reading, from thence to Lancaster, and
from thence to this Town, which is about a dozen Miles over the
Susquehannah River. Here Congress is to sit. In order to convey the
Papers, with safety, which are of more Importance than all the Members, We were induced to take this Circuit, which is near 180 Miles,
whereas this Town by the directest Road is not more than 88 Miles
from Philadelphia. This Tour, has given me an opportunity of seeing,
many Parts of this Country, which I never saw before.

This Morning Major Throop, arrived here with a large Packett from
General Gates, containing very agreable Intelligence, which I need not
repeat, as you have, much earlier Intelligence from that Part than We have.
I wish Affairs here wore as pleasing an Aspect—But alass they do not.

I shall avoid, every Thing like History, and make no Reflections.

However, General Washington, is in a Condition tolerably respectable, and the Militia, are now turning out, from Virginia, Maryland

and Pensilvania, in small Numbers. All the Apology that can be made, for this Part of the World is that Mr Howes march from Elke to Philadelphia, was thro the very Regions of Passive obedience. The whole Country thro which he passed, is inhabited by Quakers. There is not such another Body of Quakers in all America, perhaps not in all the World.

I am still of opinion that Philadelphia will be no Loss to Us.

I am very comfortably, situated, here, in the House of General Roberdeau, whose Hospitality has taken in, Mr S[amuel] A[dams] Mr. G[erry] and me. My Health is as good as common, and I assure you my Spirits not the worse for the Loss of Philadelphia. Biddle in the Continental Frigate as S. Carolina has made a noble Cruise and taken four very valuable W.I. Prizes.

Continue to write me by the Post, and I shall pay my Debts.

Abigail Adams to John Adams

Boston october 25 1777

The joyfull News of the Surrender of General Burgoin and all his Army to our victorious Troops prompted me to take a ride this afternoon with my daughter to Town to join to morrow with my Friends in thanksgiving and praise to the supreem Being who hath so remarkably deliverd our Enimies into our Hands.

And hearing that an express is to go of tomorrow morning, I have retired to write you a few lines. I have received no letters from you since you left P[hiladelphi]a by the post, and but one by any private Hand. I have wrote you once before this. Do not fail writing by the return of this express and direct your Letters to the care of my unkle who has been a kind and faithfull hand to me through the whole season and a constant attendant upon the post office.

Burgoine is expected in by the middle of the week. I have read many Articles of Capitulation, but none which ever containd so generous Terms before. Many people find fault with them but perhaps do not consider sufficently the circumstances of general Gates, who by delaying and exacting more might have lost all. This must be said of him that he has followed the golden rule and done as he would wish himself in like circumstances to be dealt with. Must not the vapouring Burgoine who tis said possesses great sensibility, be humbled to the dust. He may now write the Blocade of Saratago. I have heard it proposed that he should take up his quarters in the old South, but believe he will not be permitted to come to this Town. Heaven grant us success at the Southard. That saying of king Richard often occurs to my mind "God helps those who help themselves" but if Men turn their backs and run from an Enemy they cannot surely expect to conquer them.

This day dearest of Friends compleats 13 years Sine we were solemly united in wedlock; 3 years of the time we have been cruelly seperated. I have patiently as I could endured it with the Belief that you were serving your Country, and rendering your fellow creatures Essential Benefits. May future Generations rise up and call you Blessed, and the present behave worthy of the blessings you are Labouring to secure to them, and I shall have less reason to regreat the deprivation of my own perticuliar felicity.

Adieu dearest of Friends adieu.

John Adams to Abigail Adams

Easton, at the Forks of Delaware in Pensylvania Novr. 14. 1777

Here I am. I am bound home. I suppose it will take me 14 days, perhaps 18 or 20, to reach Home. Mr S. A is with me. I am tolerably well.

The American Colours are still flying at Fort Mifflin. The News on the other Side, is from a Merchant to his Partner.

I am in great Haste, most affectionately yours.

The Years Abroad

"It seems to be the Intention of Heaven, that We should be taught the full Value of our Liberty by the dearness of the Purchase, and the Importance of public Virtue by the Necessity of it."

—John Adams

"Who shall give me back Time? Who shall compensate to me those *years* I cannot recall? How dearly have I paid for a titled Husband; should I wish you less wise, that I might enjoy more happiness? I cannot find that in my Heart."

—Abigail Adams

"The total Idleness, the perpetual Uncertainty We are in, is the most insipid and at the Same Time disgusting and provoking Situation imaginable. I had rather be employed in carting Street Dust and Marsh Mud."

—John Adams

"And now my dear Friend let me request you to go to London some time in july that if it please God to conduct me theither in safety I may have the happiness to meet you there."

—Abigail Adams

"I Cast My Thoughts
Across the Atlantick"

FEBRUARY 1778–APRIL 1782

In the fall of 1777, the Continental Congress replaced Silas Deane with John Adams as one of the joint commissioners to France. If Abigail had previously considered Philadelphia far away, the distance to Europe was almost unimaginable. Traveling across the ocean even in good weather and without the threat of British warships was dangerous; with the British Navy lurking and the seas still churned up by winter storms, the passage became positively treacherous. Nonetheless, John determined to set sail in February 1778 and to bring his eldest son, John Quincy, along with him for the educational opportunities such a trip would offer.

Once in France, John quickly began the work of bringing order to the chaotic commission, overseen by the much-beloved but organizationally challenged Benjamin Franklin. John's situation was made more difficult by ongoing tensions between Franklin and the third commissioner, Arthur Lee. Meanwhile, back in Massachusetts, Abigail continued to take responsibility for their home and farm and to raise the children as best she could in John's absence.

John Adams to Abigail Adams

On Board the Frigate Boston

5 O Clock in the Afternoon

dearest of Friends   Feb. 13. 1778

I am favoured with an unexpected opportunity, by Mr Woodward the lame Man who once lived at Mr Belchers, and who promises in a very kind manner to take great Care of the Letter, to inform you of our Safe Passage from the Moon head, on Board the ship. The seas ran very high, and the Spray of the seas would have wet Us, but Captn. Tucker, kindly brought great Coats on Purpose with which he covered Up me and John so that We came very dry. Tomorrow Morning We Sail. God bless you, and my Nabby my Charley, my Tommy and all my Friends.

Yours, ever, ever, ever yours

John Adams

Abigail Adams to John Adams

March 8 1778

Tis a little more than 3 week since the Dearest of Friends and tenderesst of Husbands left his Solitary partner, and quitted all the fond endearments of Domestick felicity for the dangers of the sea, exposed perhaps to the attack of a Hostile foe, and o good Heaven can I add to the dark assassin to the secret Murderer and the Bloody Emissary of as cruel a Tyrant as God in his Riteous judgments ever sufferd to Discrace the Throne of Britain.

I have travelled with you over the wide atlantick, and could have landed you safe with Humble confidence at your desired Haven, and then have set myself down to have enjoyed a Negative kind of happiness, in the painfull part which it has pleased Heaven to allot me, but this intelligance with Regard to that great Philosopher able statesman and unshaken Friend of his Country, has planted a Dagger in my Breast and I feel with a double Edge the weapon that pierced the Bosom of a Franklin—

"For Nought avails the Virtues of the Heart
Nor tow'ring Genious claims its due Reward
From Britains fury, as from deaths keen dart
No worth can save us and no Fame can guard."

The more distinguished the person the greater the inveteracy of these foes of Humane Nature. The Arguments of my Friends to alleviate my anxiety by perswading me that this shocking attempt will put you more upon your Gaurd and render your person more secure than if it had never taken place, is kind in them and has some weight, but my greatest comfort and consolation arrisses from the Belief of a Superintending providence to whom I can with confidence commit you since not a sparrow falls to the ground with out his Notice. Were it not for this I should be misirable and overwhelmed by my fears and apprehensions.

Freedom of sentiment the life and soul of Friendshp is in a great measure cut of by the Danger of Miscarrages, and the apprehension of Letters falling into the hands of our Enemies. Should this meet with that fate may they Blush for their connextion with a Nation who have renderd themselves infamous and abhorred by a long list of crimes which not their high atchivements nor the Lusture of former Deeds, nor the tender appellation of parent nor the fond connextion which once Subsisted, can ever blot from our remembrance or wipe out those indellible stains cruelty and baseness. They have engraven them with a pen of Iron and Led in a Rock forever.

To my dear son Remember me in the most affectionate terms. I would have wrote to him but my notice is so short that I have not time. Injoin it upon him Never to Disgrace his Mother, and to behave worthy of his Father. Tender as Maternal affection is, it was swallowed up in what I found a stronger, or so intermingld that I felt it not in its full force till after he had left me. I console myself with the hopes of his

Reaping advantages under the carefull Eye of a tender parent which it was not in my power to bestow upon him.

There is nothing material taken place in the politicall world Since you left us. This Letter will go by a vessel for Bilboa from whence you may perhaps get better opportunities of conveyance than from any other place. The Letter you deliverd to the pilot came safe to hand. All the little folks are anxious for the safety of their Pappa and Brother to whom they desire to be rememberd—to which is added the tenderest Sentiments of affection and the fervent prayer for your happiness and Safty of your

Portia

John Adams to Abigail Adams

My dearest Friend   Passi Ap. 25. 1778

Monsieur Chaumont has just informed me of a Vessell bound to Boston: but I am reduced to such a Moment of Time, that I can only inform you that I am well, and inclose a few Lines from, Johnny to let you know that he is so. I have ordered the Things you desired, to be sent you. But I will not yet say by what Conveyance, for fear of Accidents.

If human Nature could be made happy by any Thing that can please the Eye, the Ear, the Taste or any other sense, or Passion or Fancy this Country would be the Region for Happiness: But, if my Country were at Peace, I should be happier, among the Rocks and shades of Pens hill: and would chearfully exchange, all the Elegance, Magnificence and sublimity of Europe, for the Simplicity of Braintree and Weymouth.

To tell you the Truth, I admire the Ladies here. Dont be jealous. They are handsome, and very well educated. Their Accomplishments, are exceedingly brilliant. And their Knowledge of Letters and Arts, exceeds that of the English Ladies much, I believe.

Tell Mrs W[*arren*] that I shall write her a Letter, as she desired, and let her know some of my Reflections in this Country.

My venerable Colleague, enjoys a Priviledge here, that is much to be envyd. Being seventy Years of Age, the Ladies not only allow him to ~~buss them as often as he~~ embrace them as often as he pleases, but they are perpetually embracing him. I told him Yesterday, I would, write this to America.

The pace of transatlantic mail was inevitably slow. If all went well, it could easily take six to eight weeks simply to cross the ocean, not including travel time on either end. But too often all did not go well. Ships were delayed in port; ships sank or were blown off course by bad weather. And some American ships, threatened with capture by the enemy, destroyed the letters they carried lest they contain confidential information that should not fall into British hands. All told, the months-long delays Abigail and John experienced in their correspondence, while difficult and frustrating, were not unprecedented.

Abigail Adams to John Adams

Dearest of Friends   june 30. [*1778*]

Shall I tell my dearest that tears of joy filld my Eyes this morning at the sight of his well known hand the first line which has bless my Sight since his four months absence during which time I have never been able to Learn a word from him, or my dear son till about ten days ago an english paper taken in a prize and brought into Salem contain an account under the paris News of your arrival at the abode of Dr Franklin, and last week a Carteel from Halifax brought Capt Welch of the Boston who informd that he left you well the Eleventh of March, that he had Letters for me but distroyed them, when he was taken, and this is all the information I have ever been able to obtain. Our Enemies have told us the vessel was taken and Named the frigate which took her and that she was carried into plimouth. I have lived a life of fear and anxiety ever since you left me. Not more than a week after your absence the Horrid story of Doctor Franklins assassination was received from France and sent by mr Purveyance of Baltimore to Congress and to Boston—near two months before that was contradicted. Then we could not hear a word from the Boston, and most people gave her up as taken or lost, thus has my mind been agitated like a troubled sea. You will easily conceive how gratefull to me your favour of April 25 and those of our Son were to me and mine, tho I regret your short warning and the little time you had to write, by which means I know not how you fared upon your voiage, what reception you have met with, (not even from the Ladies, tho you profess yourself an admirer of them,) and a thousand circumstances which I wish to know, and which are always perticuliarly interesting to Near connextion. I must request you always to be minute and to write me by every conveyance. Some perhaps which may appear unlikely to reach will be the first to arrive. I own I was mortified at so Short a Letter, but I quiet my Heart with thinking there are many more upon their passage to me. I Have wrote Seven before this and some of them very long. Now I know you are Safe I wish myself with you. Whenever you entertain such a wish recollect that I would have willingly hazarded all dangers to have been your companion, but as that was not permitted you must console me in your absence by a Recital of all your adventures, tho methinks I would not have them in all respects too similar to those related of your venerable Colleigue, whose Mentor like appearence age and philosiphy most certainly lead the polite scientifick Ladies of France to suppose they are embraceing the God of wisdom, in a Humane Form, but I who own that I never yet wish'd an Angle whom I loved a Man, shall be full as content if those divine Honours are omitted. The whole Heart of my Friend is in the Bosom of his partner, more than half a score of years has so riveted there that the fabrick which contains it must crumble into Dust e'er the particles can be seperated. I can hear of the Brilliant accomplishment of any of my sex with pleasure and rejoice in that Liberality of Sentiment which acknowledges them. At the same time I regret the trifling Narrow contracted Education of the Females of my own country. I have entertaind a Superiour opinion of the accomplishments of the French Ladies ever since I read the Letters of Dr Sherbear, who professes that he had rather take the opinion of an accomplished Lady in matters of polite writing than the first wits of Itally and should think himself Safer with her approbation than of a long List of Literati, and he give this reason for it that women have in general more delicate Sensations than Men. What touches them is for the most part true in Nature, whereas men warpt by Education, judge amiss from previous prejudice and refering all things to the model of the ancients, condemn that by comparison where no true Similitud ought to be expected.

But in this country you need not be told how much female Education is neglected, nor how fashonable it has been to ridicule Female learning, tho I acknowled it my happiness to be connected with a person of a more generous mind and liberal sentiments. I cannot forbear transcribing a few generous sentiments which I lately met with upon this subject. If women says the writer are to be Esteemed our Enemies, methinks it is an Ignoble Cowardice thus to disarm them and not allow them the same weapons we use ourselves, but if they deserve the titles of our Friend tis an inhumane Tyranny to Debar them of priviliges of ingenious Education which would also render their Friendship so much the more delightfull to themselves and us. Nature is seldom observed to be niggardly of her choisest Gifts to the sex. Their senses are Generally as quick as ours their Reason as Nervious their judgment as mature and solid. Add but to these natural perfections the advantages of acquired learning what polite and charming creatures would they prove whilst their external Beauty does the office of a Crystal to the Lamp not shrowding but discloseing their Brighter intellects. Nor need we fear to loose our Empire over them by thus improveing their Native abilities since where there is most Learning sence and knowledge there is always observed to be the most modesty and Rectitude of manners.

John Adams to Abigail Adams

My dearest Friend   Passi July 26. 1778

Yours of the Tenth of June by Captain Barnes was brought to me Yesterday, which is only the second that I have yet recd from you. The other is of 25 March. I have written to you, several Times, as often as I could, and hope they will arrive. I have put on board one ship, all the Articles in your Minute. By Captain Niles I have sent you a smal Present of Tea. By Captain Barnes, I will send some few Things.

You enquire how you shall pay Taxes? I will tell you. Ask the favour of your Uncle Smith or Some other Friend to let you have Silver, and draw your Bills upon me. The Money shall be paid, in the instant of the sight of your Bill, but let it be drawn in your own Hand Writing. Any body who wants to remit Cash to France, Spain, Holland or England, will let you have the Money. You may draw with Confidence, for the Cash shall be paid here. I suppose however, that one hundred Pounds, a Year, sterling will be as much as you will have occasion for. With silver, you may get your Father, or your Uncle or Brother Cranch to pay your Taxes.

You have made your Son very happy by your Letter to him—he is writing a long Answer. He begins to read and speak French, pretty well. He behaves well, and is much esteemed here, which gives me constant Pleasure. His Sister is to blame for not writing to him as well as to me. He has been very good, is almost constantly writing to her, and his Brothers, and to his Cousins and his Friend Joshua Green, and many other Correspondents. He wrote a french Letter the other Day to his Grand Pa. He will write to his Grand ma, to whom present his and my most affectionate and dutiful Respects.

As to Politicks, The Emperor and K of Prussia are at War. France and England are the same altho there is yet no formal Manifesto. America, I think has nothing to fear from Europe. Let her chase away the broken Remnants of her Ennemies, now within her Limits, and lay on Taxes, with a manly Resolution, in order to raise the Credit of her Currency and she will do very well.

This is a delicious Country. Every Thing that can sooth, charm and bewitch is here. But these are no Enchantments for me. My Time is employed in the public Business, in studying French like a school Boy, and in fervent Wishes, that the happy Time may arrive soon, when I may exchange the Elegances and Magnificence of Europe for the Simplicity of Pens Hill, and the Glory of War, for the Obscurity of private Contemplation. Farewell.

Abigail Adams to John Adams

[*Braintree, 21 October 1778*]

How dear to me was the Signature of my Friend this Evening received by the Boston a ship more valued to me than all the American Navy besides valuable for conveying safely my choisest comfort my dearest Blessings. "I Love the place where Helen was but born."

You write me that you have by several vessels convey'd me tokens of your Friendship. The only Letters I have received from you or my dear Son were dated last April and contain only a few lines— judge then what my Heart has sufferd. You could not have sufferd more upon your Voyage than I have felt cut of from all communication with you. My Harp has been hung upon the willows, and I have scarcly ever taken my pen to write but the tears have flowed faster than the Ink. I have wrote often to you but was unfortunate enough to have my last and largest packets distroyd the vessel being taken and carried into Halifax. Mr Ingraham of Boston will convey this to you with his own hand. You will I know rejoice to see him as a Bostonian an American and a Man of Merit. I need not ask you to Notice him. I apprehend that this will never reach you yet this apprehension shall not prevent my writing by every opportunity. The French Ships are still in the Harbour of Boston. I have received great civility and every mark of Respect that it has been in the power of their officers to shew me.

Count dEstaing has been exceeding polite to me. He took perticulir care to see me, sending an officer to request I would meet him at Col Q[*uinc*]ys as it was inconvenient to be at a greater Distance from his ship. I according waited upon his Excellency who very politely received me, insisted upon my Dineing on board his ship appointed his day and sent his Barge requested I would bring any of my Friends with me. We made up a company of 13 and waited upon him. An entertainment fit for a princiss was prepared, we spent a most agreable day. The Count is a most agreable Man Sedate polite affible with a dignity that is lost in Ease yet his brow at times would be overclouded with cares and anxieties so like a dear absent Friends that I was pained for him. But I determine to write you more perticuliarly by an other opportunity. I Lament the loss of my last packet. I hate to write duplicates. Our Friend here are all well. Let me intreat you to write me more Letters at a time sure you can not want subjects. They are my food by day and my Rest by night. Do not deal them so spairingly to your own

Portia

John Adams to Abigail Adams

My dearest Friend   Passy Novr 6 1778

We have received Information that so many of our Letters have been thrown overboard, that I fear you will not have heard so often from me, as both of us wish.

I have written often. But my Letters have not been worth so much as other Things which I have sent you. I sent you a small Present by Captain Niles. But he is taken by a Jersey Privateer. I sent you also, some other Things by Captain Barnes, and what affects me quite as much, I sent the Things that my dear Brother Cranch requested me to send, by the same Vessells. These Vessells were chosen because they were fast Sailers, and so small as to be able to see Danger before they could be seen, but all is taken and sent into Guernsy and Jersy.

By Captain Tucker I sent you the whole of the List you gave me of Articles for the Family. These I hope have arrived safe. But I have been so unlucky, that I feel averse to meddling in this Way. The whole Loss, is a Trifle if is true: but to you, in the Convenience of the Family, and to Mr Cranch in his Business they would have been of Value. If the Boston arrives, the little Chest she carries to you will be of service.

My Anxiety for, you and for the public is not diminished by Time or Distance. The great Number of accidental Dissappointments in the Course of the last summer are, afflicting. But We hope for better Luck another Year.

It seems to be the Intention of Heaven, that We should be taught the full Value of our Liberty by the dearness of the Purchase, and the Importance of public Virtue by the Necessity of it. There seems to be also a further Design, that of eradicating forever from the Heart of every American, every tender Sentiment towards Great Britain, that We may sometime or other know how to make the full Advantage of our Independence by more extensive Connections with other Countries.

Whatever Syren songs of Peace may be sung in your Ears, you may depend upon it from me, (who unhappily have been seldom mistaken in my Guesses of the Intentions of the British Government for fourteen Years,) that every malevolent Passion, and every insidious Art, will predominate in the British Cabinet against Us.

Their Threats of Russians, and of great Reinforcements, are false and impracticable and they know them to be so: But their Threats of doing Mischief with the Forces they have, will be verified as far as their Power.

It is by no means pleasant to me, to be forever imputing malicious Policy to a Nation, that I have ever wished and still wish I could esteem: But Truth must be attended to: and almost all Europe the Dutch especially, are at this day talking of G. Britain in the style of American sons of Liberty.

I hope the unfortunate Events at Rhode Island will produce no Heart Burnings, between our Countrymen and the Comte D'Estaing, who is allowed by all Europe to be a great and worthy officer, and by all that know him to be a zealous friend of America.

I have enjoyed uncommon Health, since my Arrival in this Country and if it was Peace, and my family here, I could be happy. But never never shall I enjoy, happy days, without either.

My little son, gives me great Pleasure, both by his Assiduity to his Books and his discreet Behaviour. The Lessons of his Mamma are a constant Law to him, and the Reflexion that they are so to his sister and Brothers, are a never failing Consolation to me at Times when I feel more tenderness for them, than Words can express, or than I should choose to express if I had Power.

Remember me, in the most affectionate Manner to our Parents Brothers sisters Unkles Aunts, and what shall I say—Children.

My Respects where they are due, which is in so many Places that I cannot name them.

With Regard to my Connections with the Public Business here, which you will be naturally inquisitive to know something of, I can only say that We have many Disagreable Circumstances here, many Difficulties to accomplish the Wishes of our Constituents, and to give Satisfaction to certain half anglified Americains, and what is more serious and affecting to real and deserving Americans who are suffering in England and escaping from thence: But from this Court, this City, and Nation I have experienced nothing, but uninterupted Politeness.

It is not possible for me to express more Tenderness and Affection to you than will be suggested by the Name of

John Adams

Abigail Adams to John Adams

[*Braintree, 12–23 November 1778*]

I Have taken up my pen again to relieve the anxiety of a Heart too susceptable for its own repose, nor can I help complaining to my dearest Friend that his painfull absence is not as formerly alleiviated by the tender tokens of his Friendship, 3 very short Letters only have reachd my Hands during 9 months absence.

I cannot be so unjust to his affection as to suppose he has not wrote much oftener and more perticularly, but must sit down to the score of misfortune that so few have reachd me.

I cannot charge myself with any Deficiency in this perticular as I have never let an opportunity Slip without writing to you since we parted, tho you make no mention of having received a line from me; if they are become of so little importance as not to be worth noticeing with your own Hand, be so kind as to direct your secretary.

I will not finish the sentance, my Heart denies the justice of the acquisition, nor does it believe your affection in the least diminished by distance or absence, but my Soul is wounded at a Seperation from you, and my fortitude all Dissolved in frailty and weakness. When I cast my thoughts across the atlantick and view the distance the dangers and Hazards which you have already passd through, and to which you must probably be again exposed, e'er we shall meet, the time of your absence unlimitted, all all conspire to cast a Gloom over my solitary hours, and bereave me of all domestick felicity. In vain do I strive to through of in the company of my Friends some of the anxiety of my Heart. It increases in proportion to my endeavours to conceal it; the only alleiviation I know of would be a ferequent intercourse by Letters unrestrained by the apprehension of their becomeing food for our Enemies. The affection I feel for my Friend is of the tenderest kind, Matured by years Santified by choise and approved by Heaven. Angles can witness to its purity, what care I then for the Ridicule of Britains should this testimony of it fall into their Hands, nor can I endure that so much caution and circumspection on your part should deprive me of the only consolor of your absence—a consolation that our Enemies enjoy in a much higher degree than I do Many of them having received 3 or 4 Letters from their Friend in england to one that I have received from France.

Thus far I wrote more than ten day ago, my mind as you will easily see far from tranquil, and my Heart so wounded by the Idea of inattention that the very Name of my Dearest Friend would draw tears from me. Forgive me for harbouring an Idea so unjust, to your affection. Were you not dearer to me than all this universe contains beside, I could not have sufferd as I have done. But yours Letters of April 12 of June 3 and June 16 calmd my Soul to peace. I cannot discribe the Effect they had upon me, cheerfullness and tranquility took place of greif and anxiety. I placed them Next my Heart and soothed myself to rest with the tender assurances of a Heart all my own.

I was not a little mortified to find that the few Lins wrote by way of Holland were the only ones you had received from me, when I had wrote many sheets of paper long before that time and sent by so many different hands that I thought you must have heard often from me.

But this circumstance will make me more cautions how I suffer such cruel Ideas to haras me again. Tis the 23 of November now. Count Estaing has saild near a fort night Biron with 15 sail Lay upon the watch for him, but a very terrible Storm prevented the count from sailing, and shatterd Birons Fleet 11 Sail only have arrived at Newport, the Somerset was lost upon Nantucket shoals. I fed many of the prisoners upon their march to Boston, about 40 were drowned the rest deliverd themselves as prisoners. The two other ships which are missing were supposed to be Lost there, as the Hulks appear and a 50 Gun ship which came out with Biron from england has not been heard of since. Thus they have made a fine voyage of watching destaing Lost 3 capital ships never saw the French Fleet, returnd into port with one Ship dismasted and the rest much damaged.

Heaven continue to be propitious to our Friends and allies for whom I have contracted a most sincere regard. If chastity temperance industery frugality sobriety and purity of morals, added to politeness and complasance can entitele any people to Friendship and respect, the Behaviour of this whole Fleet whilst they lay in this harbour which was more than two months, demand from every unprejudiced person an acknowledgment of their merrit. If I ever had any national prejudicees they are done away and I am ashamed to own I was ever possessd of so narrow a spirit, and I Blush to find so many of my country men possessd with such low vulgar prejudices and capable of such mean reflections as I have heard thrown out against the Nation of our allies though the unblamable conduct of this Fleet left them not one personal reflexion to cast.

Let me Imitate and instill it into my children the Liberal spirit of that great Man who declared he had no Local attachments. It is indifferent to me say he whether a man is rocked in his cradle on this side of the Tweed, or on that, I seek for merrit whereever it is to be found. Detested be national reflexions they are unjust.

In September 1778, Congress dissolved the joint commission to France and named Franklin as sole minister. Official word of that decision, however, did not reach John until February 1779, and in the interim, he heard conflicting reports regarding his status. Once he finally received notification, he began preparations to return home immediately. Still, from the time he took leave of the French court until he and John Quincy finally reached Boston, nearly six more months elapsed.

John Adams to Abigail Adams

My dearest Friend   Passy Decr 3 1778

Your two Letters of the [*29th*] of Sept. and [*10th*] of Oct. gave me more Concern that I can express. I will not say a Fit of the Spleen. But last night I got a Letter from Mr Vernon, in wh he acquaints me with the Arrival of the Boston, at Portsmouth. There were Letters from me on Boad, of the Boston Providence or Ranger, and there was all the Things mentioned in the Memorandum, you gave me, this News has given me great Pleasure. I have sent other Things, on Boad other Vessells since, with more Letters, which are all taken by the Ennemy, and among others all Mr Cranchs Watch Materials.

You must not expect to hear from me so often as you used: it is impossible. It is impossible for me to write so often. I have so much to do here, and so much Ceremony to submit to, and so much Company to see, so many Visits to make and receive, that, altho I avoid as many of them as I possibly can with Decency and some People think, more, it is impossible for me to write to you so often as my Inclination wd lead me.

I have been informed that Congress, on the 14 of September took up foreign Affairs and determined to have but one Minister, in France. By a Letter from Mr Lovel we learn that Congress had foreign Affairs on the 12 of October, still under Consideration, but gives no Hint of wt is done or intended. This keeps me in a State of Uncertainty that is very disagreable. I have applied every Moment of my Time when Awake, and not necessarily engaged otherwise in learning the Language, and the Laws the Manners and Usages of this Nation, an occupation indisspensable in my situation. In order to avoid Expence, as much as possible, I have kept no Clerk altho every other Gentleman has constantly had, two. In order to save Expences, and that I might be under the less Temptation to spend my Time unusefully, I have kept no Carriage, altho every other Gentn, has kept one Constantly and some Gentn two, and I am told I am the first public Minister that ever lived without a Carriage. By All these Causes together added to another Motive, viz a Fear of Trusting our Books and Papers without a Keeper I have been almost constantly at home. Here are a Thousand Things to do, and no Body else to do them. The extensive Correspondence We have with Congress, with the Court, with our Frigates, our Agents, and with Prisoners, and a thousand others, employs a vast deal of my Time in Writing. You must therefore excuse me, if I dont write so often as I would. Yet I have written very often, but my Letters have miscarried.

By your Letter, and another, I suspect that Parties are forming among you. I expect also by, some Letters I have seen from the Weathersfield Family, that a certain fine Gentleman, will join another fine Gentleman, and these some other fine Gentlemen, to obtain some Arragement that shall dishonnour me. And by Hints that are given out here, I should not wonder if I should be recalled, or sent to Vienna which would be worse.

I am extreamly unhappy to see such Symptoms of Selfishness, Vanity and Ambition as manifest themselves in various Quarters, but I will neither indulge these Passions myself, nor be made the Instrument of them in others. Observing as I have a long Time the Characters of several Persons, I have long foreseen, that Parties must arise and this foresight has been the most forcible Motive with me to refuse a certain elevated office. Because I knew, that my public Conduct, to which I was necessitated by the clearest Dictates of my Judgment, in the various intricate and hazardous Contingences of our Affairs, had exposed me to the Angry Passions of some Gentlemen of Consequence, who, altho obliged to cooperate with me had often differed from me in opinion. These I knew would render me, unhappy if not useless, in some situations, which determined me, to preserve my Independence, at the Expence of my Ambition, a Resolution in which I rejoice and ever shall rejoice.

The Conflicts of these Passions, I expect, will very soon relieve me from the Duties of this station, and enable me to return to my Family and my Garden, the Ultimate Object of all my Hopes, Wishes and Expectations, for myself. And happy indeed shall I be if by the favour of Heaven I can escape the danger of the Seas and of Ennemies, and return to the charming office of Preceptor to my Children.

John Adams to Abigail Adams

Passy Decr 18 1778

This Moment I had, what shall I say? The Pleasure or the pain of your Letter of 25 of Octr. As a Letter from my dearest Freind it gave me a pleasure that it would be in vain to attempt to describe: but the Complaints in it gave me more pain than I can express—this is the third Letter I have recd in this complaining style. The former two I have not answer'd. I had Endeavour'd to answer them. I have wrote several answers, but upon a review, they appear'd to be such I could not send. One was angry—another was full of Greif—and the third with Melancholy, so that I burnt them all. If you write me in this style I shall leave of writing intirely. It kills me. Can Professions of Esteem be Wanting from me to you? Can Protestation of affection be necessary? Can tokens of Remembrance be desir'd? The very Idea of this sickens me. Am I not wretched Enough, in this Banishment, without this. What Course shall I take to convince you that my Heart is warm? You doubt, it seems. Shall I declare it? Shall I swear to it? Would you doubt it the less? And is it possible you should doubt it? I know it is not? If I could once believe it possible, I cannot answer for the Consequences. But I beg you would never more write to me in such a strain for it really makes me unhappy.

Be assured that no time nor place, can change my heart: but that I think so often and so much, of the Blessings from which I am seperated as to be too unmindful of those who accompany me, and that I write to you so often as my Duty will permit.

I am extremely obliged to the Comte D'Estaing and his officers for their Politeness to you, and am very Glad you have had an opportunity, of seing so much of the french Nation. The accounts from all hands agree that there was an agreable intercourse, and happy harmony upon the whole between the inhabitants and the Fleet. The more this Nation is known, and the more their Language is understood, the more narrow Prejudices will wear away. British Fleet and Armys, are very different from theirs, in Point of Temperance and Politeness there is no Comparison.

This is not a correct Copy, but you will pardon it, because it is done by an Hand as dear to you as to your

John Adams

Abigail Adams to John Adams

Sunday Evening December 27 1778

How lonely are my days? How solitary are my Nights? Secluded from all society but my two Little Boys, and my domesticks by the Mountains of snow which surround me I could almost fancy myself in Greenland. We Have had four of the coldest Days I ever knew, and they were followed by the severest snow storm I ever remember, the wind blowing like a Hurricane for 15 or 20 hours renderd it imposible for Man, or Beast to live abroad, and has blocked up the roads so that they are impassible.

A week ago I parted with my Daughter at the request of our P[lymout]h Friends to spend a month with them, so that I am solitary indeed.

Can the best of Friends recollect that for 14 years past, I have not spent a whole winter alone. Some part of the Dismal season has here-tofore been Mitigated and softned by the social converse and participation of the Friend of my youth.

How insupportable the Idea that 3000 leigues, and the vast ocean now devide us—but devide only our persons for the Heart of my Friend is in the Bosom of his partner more than half a score years has so rivetted there, that the Fabrick which contains it must crumble into Dust, e'er the particles can be seperated.

> "For in one fate, our Hearts our fortunes
> And our Beings blend."

I cannot discribe to you How much I was affected the other day with a Scotch song which was sung to me by a young Lady in order to divert a melancholy hour, but it had a quite different Effect, and the Native Simplicity of it, had all the power of a well wrought Tradidy. When I could conquer my Sensibility I beg'd the song, and master charles has learnt it and consoles his Mamma by singing it to her. I will enclose it to you. It has Beauties in it to me, which an indifferent person would not feel perhaps.

> His very foot has musick in't,
> As he comes up the stairs.

How oft has my Heart danced to the sound of that Musick?

> And shall I see his face again?
> And shall I hear him speak?

Gracious Heaven hear and answer my daily petition, "by banishing all my Grief."

I am sometimes quite discouraged from writing. So many vessels are taken, that there is Little chance of a Letters reaching your Hands. That I meet with so few returns is a circumstance that lies heavy at my Heart. If this finds its way to you, it will go by the Alliance. By her I have wrote before. She has not yet saild, and I love to amuse myself with my pen, and pour out some of the tender sentiments of a Heart over flowing with affection, not for the Eye of a cruel Enemy who no doubt would ridicule every Humane and social sentiment long ago grown Callous to the finer sensibilities—but for the sympathetick Heart that Beats in unison with

Portias

John Adams to Abigail Adams

Passy Jany 1. 1779

I wish you an happy new Year, and many happy Years—and all the Blessings of Life. Who knows but this Year may be more prosperous for our Country than any We have seen. For my own Part I have hopes that it will. Great Blessings are in store for it, and they may come this Year as well as another. You and I however must prepare our Minds to enjoy the Prosperity of others not our own. In Poverty and Symplicity, We shall be happy, whenever our Country is so. Johnny sends Duty. Mr Williams waits—I knew of his going but this Moment. I think I shall see you this Year, in spight of British Men of War. If it should be otherwise ordered, however, we must submit.

Abigail Adams to John Adams

My Dearest Friend   *Febry 13.* 1779

This is the Anniversary of a very melancholy Day to me, it rose upon me this morning with the recollection of Scenes too tender to Name. Your own Sensibility will supply your Memory and Dictate to your pen a kind remembrance of those dear connections to whom you waved an adeiu, whilst the full Heart and weeping Eye followed your foot steps till intervening objects obstructed the Sight.

This Anniversary shall ever be more particularly Devoted to my Friend till the happy Day arrives that shall give him back to me again. Heaven Grant that it may not be far distant, and that the blessings which he has so unweariedly and constantly sought after may crown his Labours and bless his country.

It is with double pleasure that I hold my pen this day to acquaint my Friend that I have had a rich feast indeed—by the Miflin privateer, which arrived here the 8th of this month and brought his Letters of 9 of Sepbr 23 of october 2d of November 2d of December all together making more than I have received since your absence at one time. The Hankerchiefs in which the were tied felt to me like the return of an absent Friend. Tis Natural to feel an affection for every thing which belongs to those we Love, and most so when the object is far—far distant from us.

You chide me for my complaints, when in reality I had so little occasion for them. I must intreat you to attribute it to the real cause—an over anxious Solicitude to hear of your welfare—and an ill grounded fear least multiplicity of publick cares, and avocations might render you less attentive to your pen than I could wish. But bury my dear Sir, in oblivion every expression of complaint. Erase them from the Letters which contain them, as I have from my mind every Idea so contrary to that regard and affection you have ever manifested towards me. Have you a coppy of your Letter December the 2d. Some dissagreable circumstances had agitated your mind News from Rhoad Island—or what? Why was I not by to sooth my Friend to placidness—but I unhappily had contributed to it. With this consideration I read those passages, which would have been omited had the Letter been coppied.

And does my Friend think that there are no hopes of peace? Must we still endure the Desolations of war with all the direfull consequences attending it. I fear we must and that America is less and less worthy of the blessings of peace.

Luxery that bainfull poison has unstrung and enfeabled her sons. The soft penetrating plague has insinuated itself into the freeborn mind, blasting that noble ardor that impatient Scorn of base subjection which formerly distinguished your Native Land, and the Benevolent wish of general good is swallowed up by a Narrow selfish Spirit—by a spirit of oppression and extortion.

Nourished and supported by the flood of paper which has nearly overwhelmed us, and which Depreciates in proportion to the exertions to save it, and tho so necessary to us is of less value than any commodity whatever yet the demand for it is beyond conception, and those to whom great sums of it have fallen, or been acquired, vest it in Luxerys dissapate it in Extravagance—realize it at any rate. But I hope the time is not far distant when we shall in some measure be extricated from our present difficulties and a more virtuous spirit succeed the unfealing dissapation which at present prevails—And America shine with virtuous citizens as much as she now deplores her Degenerate sons.

Enclosed you will find a Letter wrote at your request, and if rewarded by your approbation it will abundantly gratify your

Portia

John Adams to Abigail Adams

My dearest Friend   Passy Feb. 13 1779

Yours of 15 Decr. was sent me Yesterday by the Marquiss whose Praises are celebrated in all the Letters from Americas. You must be content to receive a short Letter, because I have not Time now to write a long one. I have lost, many of your Letters, which are invaluable to me, and you have lost a vast Number of mine. Barns, Niles, and many other Vessells are lost.

I have received Intelligence much more agreable, than that of a removal to Holland, I mean that of being reduced to a private Citizen which gives me more Pleasure, than you can imagine. I shall therefore soon present before you, your own good Man. Happy—happy indeed shall I be, once more to see our Fireside.

I have written before to Mrs Warren and shall write again now.

Dr J. is transcribing your scotch song, which is a charming one. Oh my leaping Heart.

I must not write a Word to you about Politicks, because you are a Woman.

What an offence have I committed! a Woman!

I shall soon make it up. I think Women better than Men in General, and I know that you can keep a Secret as well as any Man whatever. But the World dont know this. Therefore if I were to write any Secrets to you and the letter should be caught, and hitched into a Newspaper, the World would say, I was not to be trusted with a Secret.

I never had so much Trouble in my Life, as here, yet I grow fat. The Climate and soil agree with me—so do, the Cookery and even the Manners of the People, of those of them at least that I converse with Churlish Republican, as some of you, on your side the Water call me. The English have got at me in their News Papers. They make fine Work of me—fanatic Bigot—perfect Cypher—not one Word of the Language awkward Figure—uncouth dress—no Address—No Character—cunning hard headed Attorney. But the falsest of it all is, that I am disgusted with the Parisians—Whereas I declare I admire the Parisians prodigiously. They are the happiest People in the World, I believe, and have the best Disposition to make others so.

If I had your Ladyship and our little folks here, and no Politicks to plague me and an hundred Thousand Lires a Year Rent, I should be the happiest Being on Earth—nay I believe I could make it do, with twenty Thousand.

One Word of Politicks—The English reproach the French with Gasconade, but I dont believe their whole History could produce so much of it as the English have practised this War.

The Commissioners Proclamation, with its sanction from the Ministry and Ratification by both Houses, I suppose is hereafter to be interpreted like Burgoines—Speaking Daggers, but using none. They cannot send any considerable Reinforcement, nor get an Ally in Europe—this I think you may depend upon. Their Artifice in throwing out such extravagant Threats, was so gross, that I presume it has not imposed on any. Yet a Nation that regarded its Character never could have threatned in that manner.

Adieu.

John Adams to Abigail Adams

Feb. 28. 1779

This Day, the Chevalier D'Arcy, his Lady, and Niece Mr Le Roy and his Lady, dined here. These Gentlemen are two Members of the Academy of Sciences.

Now are you the wiser for all this? Shall I enter into a Description of their Dress—of the Compliments—of the Turns of Conversation—and all that.

For mercy sake dont exact of me that I should be a Boy, till I am Seventy years of Age. This Kind of Correspondance will do for young Gentlemen and Ladies under 20, and might possibly be pardonable till 25—provided all was Peace and Prosperity. But old Men, born down with Years and Cares can no more amuse themselves with such Things than with Toys, Marbles and Whirligigs.

If I ever had any Wit it is all evaporated—if I ever had any Imagination it is all quenched.

Pray consider your Age, and the Gravity of your Character, the Mother of Six Children—one of them grown up, who ought never to be out of your sight, nor ever to have an Example of Indiscretion set before her.

I believe I am grown more austere, severe, rigid, and miserable than ever I was. I have seen more Occasion perhaps.

John Adams to Abigail Adams

My dearest Friend   L'orient May 14. 1779

When I left Paris, the 8 March, I expected to have been at Home before this Day and have done my Utmost to get to sea but the Embarrassements and Disappointments I have met with, have been many very many. I have however in the Course of them had a fine

Opportunity of seeing Nantes, L'orient and Brest, as well as the inter-mediate Country.

By the gracious Invitation of the King, I am now to take Passage in his Frigate the Sensible, with his new Ambassador to America the Chevalier De la Luzerne.

I hope to see you in six or seven Weeks. Never was any Man in such a state of Uncertainty and suspense as I have been from last October, entirely uninformed of the Intentions of Congress concerning me.

This would not have been very painfull to me if I could have got home, for Your Conversation is a Compensation to me, for all other Things.

My Son, has had a great Opportunity to see this Country: but this has unavoidably retarded his Education in some other Things.

He has enjoyed perfect Health from first to last and is respected wherever he goes for his Vigour and Vivacity both of Mind and Body, for his constant good Humour and for his rapid Progress in French, as well as his general Knowledge wh for his Age is uncommon. I long to see his Sister and Brothers—I need not Add.

John and John Quincy finally arrived home in August 1779. During the next four months, John represented the town of Braintree in a convention to frame a new constitution for the state of Massachusetts. He took the lead role in drafting the document, and the convention eventually adopted his draft with only minor amendments. Still in effect today—making it the oldest constitution continuously in use—and a model for other states, it is one of John's most important and last-ing contributions to American political life.

Meanwhile, in September 1779, Congress once again elected John to a ministe-rial post, this time to negotiate treaties of peace and commerce with Great Britain. Consequently, he was forced to return once again to Europe, this time taking both John Quincy and Charles with him. John Thaxter, John's former law student, also accompanied them to serve as John's secretary and tutor to the boys.

John Adams to Abigail Adams

My dearest Friend   Boston Novr. 13. 1779

I have just sent Mr Thaxter, Johnny and Stephens with the Things on Board. I shall go with Charles at four O Clock. It is now three. Have seen the Captain, and the Navy Board &c.

It is proposed to sail tomorrow. Perhaps however, it may not be till next day. Mr Dana will come on board at Nine tomorrow.

Mr Hancock, has sent me a Card, to invite me to go on board with him in the Castle Barge. Dont make many Words of this.

Your Aunt has given me a Barrell of Cramberries. I shall make a good Use of them, I hope.

Let me intreat you, to keep up your Spirits and throw off, Cares as much as possible. Love to Nabby and Thommy. We shall yet be happy, I hope and pray, and I dont doubt it. I shall have Vexations enough, as usual. You will have Anxiety and Tenderness enough as usual. Pray strive, not to have too much. I will write, by every Opportunity I can get.

Yours, ever, ever yours

John Adams

Abigail Adams to John Adams

Dearest of Friends   November 14 1779

My habitation, how disconsolate it looks! My table I set down to it but cannot swallow my food. O Why was I born with so much sensibility and why possessing it have I so often been call'd to struggle with it? I wish to see you again, was I sure you would not be gone, I could not withstand the temptation of comeing to town, tho my Heart would suffer over again the cruel torture of Seperation.

What a cordial to my dejected Spirits were the few lines last night received—and does your Heart forebode that we shall again be happy. My hopes and fears rise alternately. I cannot resign more than I do, unless life itself was called for. My dear sons I can not think of them without a tear, little do they know the feelings of a Mothers Heart! May they be good and usefull as their Father then will they in some measure reward the anxiety of a Mother. My tenderest Love to them. Remember me also to mr Thaxter whose civilities and kindness I shall miss.

God almighty bless and protect my dearest Friend and in his own time restore him to the affectionate Bosom of

Portia

John Adams to Abigail Adams

At sea, not far from the grand Bank of N.F.L.

My dearest Friend
Novr. 29 [20]. 1779

A brave fellow from Boston Captn. Carr, gives me an Oppty. of writing one Line, to let you know that We are all very well thus far. Charles behaves quite as well as John, and lies in my Bosom a nights. Mr Dana has been very sea sick but is now pretty well. We are now out of all Danger of the Romulus and Virginia, and I hope have little to fear, from the Ennemy. We have had one storm which made Us all sea sick, but brought Us on well in our Course. I wish I could write to you these two Hours, but Time fails. Ships cannot wait for each other at sea. My Love to Nabby and Thommy. Tell them, to mind their studies.

Tell Nabby, tho she has lost her french Master for some time, I hope, she will persevere, and perhaps a french Mistress in her Mamma may do better. Duty to your father, my Mother, Brothers, sisters &c &c &c. Dont fail to let me know how Constitution goes on.

God bless you.

John Adams

I write on my Knees, and the ship rolls so that I write worse than common.

Abigail Adams to John Adams

My Dearest Friend   December 10. 1779

I will not omit any opportunity of writing tho ever so great an uncertainty whether it will ever reach your Hand. My unkle Smith has a vessel bound to Calis. He advises me to write, and I most willingly comply tho my Faith in the conveyance is but poor—indeed I have lost my Faith with my spirits.

My Friends assure me from their observations that you must have had a good passage. God grant it I say, but my fears and anxieties are many—very many. I had a Faith and reliance before that supported me, but now my Heart so misgives me that I cannot find that confidence which I wish for. Your Letter from cape Ann arrived and cheered my drooping Spirits. Could I hear of your safe arrival, I would try to compose my agitated mind which has horrours both day and Night. My dear sons, Little do they know how many veins of their Mothers Heart bled when she parted from them. My delicate charles, how has he endured the fatigues of his voyage? John is a hardy Sailor, seasoned before I do not feel so much for him. Your fellow Travellers too I do not forget to think of them. I will not wish myself with you because you say a Lady cannot help being an odious creature at sea, and I will not wish myself in any situation that should make me so to you.

Nothing New in the political way but the raising the seige of Savannah, and being unfortunate.

You will have perticulars no doubt.

Our Friends are all well.

Enclosed are some papers and journals. Mr Lawrance is appointed to Holland—has not yet given his answer.

Adieu—ever ever yours

Portia

La Sensible, *the ship on which John and his sons had sailed, barely made it across the ocean, and was forced to land in Spain when it began rapidly taking on water. John had the choice of remaining in Spain until the ship could be repaired and sail on to France or attempting an overland trip through the Pyrenees mountains in midwinter. He chose the latter, which may have been the faster route but proved an ordeal for all involved. Bad weather, hard roads, and inadequate accommodations made the journey long and tedious. They finally arrived in Paris in February 1780.*

John Adams to Abigail Adams

My dearest Friend   Paris February 12. 1780

On Wednesday, the 9th. of this Month, We all arrived in tolerable Health at the Hotel De Valois, in Paris where We now are. On Thursday the 10th We waited on Dr F[*ranklin*] and dined with him at Passy. On Fryday the 11, the Dr accompanied Us to Versailles, where We waited on Mr De Vergennes Mr De Sartine and Comte Maurepas, from all of whom We had a polite Reception. To day We stay at home.

I put my three Children to Mr Pichini's Accademy the next day after my Arrival, where they are all well pleased.

We had a tedious Journey by Land, from Ferrol in Spain of not much short of four hundred Leagues. My dear Charles bears travelling by Land and Sea as well as his Brother. He is much beloved wherever he goes.

Since my Arrival here I had the Joy to find a Letter from you which came by your Unkles ship to Cadiz. It gives me more Pain than I can express to see your Anxiety, but I hope your fears will be happily disappointed.

I wrote you, from Cape Anne, from the Banks of Newfoundland from Corrunna and from Bilbao, from whence I orderd you some

Things by a Vessell to Mr Corbet, of Beverly and another to Mr Tracy of Newbury Port. These are a few necessaries for the Family. I will send Mr W. and Mr S. Things and my Brothers and Dr T.s and his Sons, by the first Safe Conveyance that I can hear of.

Yours, Yours Yours, ever, ever, ever yours.

Abigail Adams to John Adams

My dearest Friend   March 1 1780

I had scarcly closed my packet to you when I received your Letters dated Ferrol and Corruna. I am happy indeed in your safe arrival and Escape from the danger which threatned you.

> "Alas how more than lost were I,
> who in the thought already die."

I feel glad that you have determined to proceed by land tho so tedious and expensive a journey. I grow more and more apprehensive of the dangers of the sea, tho I have really no Right to Quarrel with old Neptune, since he has 3 times safely transported my Friend. Tho he has grumbled and growld, he has not shewn the extent of his power.

I hope you will meet with so much pleasure and entertainment in your journey, as will be some compensation for the fatigues of it, and the Recital amuse me whenever you can find opportunity to communicate it.

The sailors you relieved at Corruna passt through this Town, and told their story at Brackets, where a Number of persons collected 40 dollors for them. I wished they had called upon me, I should have been glad to have assisted them.

Enclosed are a few journals received yesterday. Am rejoiced to hear my charles behaves so well, but he always had the faculty of gaining

Hearts, and is more mournd for in this Neighbourhood than I could have believed if I had not heard it. Adieu most affectionately your

Portia

John Adams to Abigail Adams

My dear Portia   Paris 16 March 1780

I have not particularly answered your amiable Letter of 10 Decr. Your tender Anxiety distresses me, much: I hope your Faith however, has returned before now with your Spirits. If Captain Trash arrived safe from Corunna you have heard from me, or if Babson from Bilboa.

Your delicate Charles is as hardy as a flynt. He sustains every thing better than any of Us, even than the hardy Sailor his Brother. He is a delightful little fellow. I love him too much. My fellow Travellers too are very well. Mr D[ana]s head ack is perfectly cured—not a groan nor a wry look.

There are some ladys, one at least that can never be odious, by Sea nor Land yet she wd have been miserable in both if she had been with me. The Governor of Gallicia told me I risqued a great deal to bring my two with me, but I should have risqued my All if I had brought you.

We have a calm at present: no News from America—nor from any other Qtr since the long Roll of Rodneys successes, which have made the English very saucy for the Moment, but this will not last long.

Captain Carpenter of the Cartel ship has been here from London and dined with me yesterday. They took his ship from him, and refused the Exchange of Prisoners. Thus ill natured are they. The Refugees, according to him are in bad Plight not having recd their Pensions these 18 Months, wh are detained on some Pretence of waiting for Funds from Quebec. Yet they console themselves with the Thought that America cannot hold out another six Months.

Thus Whally and Goffe, expected Deliverance, Glory and Tryumph every day by the Commencement of the Millenium, but died without seeing it. Governor Hutchinsons son Billy died in London about 3 Weeks ago.

Yours, ever and forever.

John Adams to Abigail Adams

My dear Portia   Paris May 17. 1780

This day I recd yours of the first of March from Bilbao, with the Journals &c—the Postage of this Packet, is prodigious. I would not advise to send, many Journals, or Newspapers, this Way, or by Holland, but cut out pieces of Newspapers, and give me an Account of any Thing particularly interesting in the Journals, in your Letters, by such Conveyances, and send large Packetts of Journals and Papers directly to France. Dont omit any opportunity of Writing however by Holland or Spain. The Communication this Way is more frequent than any other. Your two Sons, were at Table, with me, when your Letters arrived, and a feast We had of it indeed. Your Uncle writes me that Babson has arrived, who carried you, Letters and Linnen. The same Articles are repeated in Trash. The Alliance, if she ever sails, has all your Affairs and those of our friends on board. I wish them safe.

Your account of the brave Jacks that I saw at Corunna, moves me. I saw another such Crew at Bilbao, who belonged to Mary land, and had the sweet satisfaction do them a similar service. Amidst all my Pains and Heart Achs, I have now and then the Pleasure of doing a little good, and that is all the Pleasure I have. I wish however it was in my Power to do more for the Numbers of my unfortunate Countrymen, who fall in my Way. The Rogues however, committed a great fault in not calling upon you, to give you, an opportunity of having the same satisfaction. They ought too to have called to let you know, I was ashore, and well.

John Adams to Abigail Adams

My dear Portia   June 17. 1780

   I yesterday recd a Letter of 26 April from Brother Cranch, for which I thank him and will answer as soon as possible. He tells me you have drawn a little Bill upon me. I am sorry for it, because I have sent and should continue to send you, small Presents by which you would be enabled to do better than by drawing Bills. I would not have you draw any more. I will send you Things in the family Way which will defray your Expences better. The Machine is horribly dear. Mr C. desires to know if he may draw on me. I wish it was in my power to oblige him but it is not. I have no Remittances nor any Thing to depend on, not a Line from Congress nor any member since I left you. My Expences thro Spain, were beyond all Imagination, and my Expences here are so exorbitant, that I cant answer any Bill from any body not even from you, excepting the one you have drawn. I must beg you, to be as prudent as possible. Depend upon it, your Children will have occasion for all your Œconomy. Mr Johonnot must send me some Bills. Every farthing is expended and more. You can have no Idea of my unavoidable Expences. I know not what to do.

   Your little affairs and those of all our Frds Mr Wibert &c are on Board the Alliance and have been so these 4 months, or ready to be. Pray write me by the Way of Spain and Holland as well as France. We are all well. My Duty to your father my Mother, and affections and Respects where due.

   My affections I fear got the better of my Judgment in bringing my Boys. They behave very well however.

   London is in the Horrors. Governor Hutchinson fell down dead at the first appearance of Mobs. They have been terrible. A Spirit of Bigotry and Fanaticism mixing with the universal discontents of the nation, has broke out into Violences of the most dreadful Nature—burnt Ld Mansfields House Books Manuscripts—burnd the Kings Bench Prison, and all the other Prisons—let loose all the Debtors and

John was born in the left-hand house in 1735. He and Abigail moved into the right-hand house—an inheritance from John's father—upon their marriage in 1764. Known as the John Adams and John Quincy Adams Birthplaces, respectively, both are now part of the Adams National Historical Park. (National Park Service, Adams National Historical Park)

The parsonage of William and Elizabeth Quincy Smith in Weymouth. Abigail Smith was born here in 1744. Twenty years later, William Smith presided at his daughter's wedding to John Adams in the same house on 25 October 1764. (Massachusetts Historical Society)

John and Abigail Adams
likely sat for these portraits
by Benjamin Blyth, a young
Salem artist, while visiting
Abigail's older sister Mary
and her husband Richard
Cranch in Salem in 1766.
(Massachusetts Historical
Society)

Miss Adorable

By the same Token that the Bearer hereof satt up with you last night I hereby order you to give him, as many Kisses, and as many Hours of your Company after 9 OClock as he shall please to Demand and charge them to my Account: This Order, or Requisition call it which you will is in Consideration of a similar order Upon Aurelia for the like favour, and I presume I have good Right to draw upon you for the Kisses as I have given two or three Millions at least, when one has been recd and of Consequence the account between us is immensely in favour of yours

octr 4th 1762

John Adams

The earliest extant letter from John to Abigail in October 1762, two years before their marriage, demonstrates the playful side of their relationship. Addressed to "Miss Adorable," this short note is John's "bill" to Abigail, requiring "as many Kisses, and as many Hours of your Company after 9 OClock as he shall please to Demand." (The Adams Papers)

"A Plan of the Town and Harbour of Boston" in 1775, this map shows the town of Braintree at the bottom center. Ten miles from Boston, Braintree was close enough that refugees from the occupied city took shelter in Braintree and Abigail and young John Quincy could clearly see the Battle of Bunker Hill from the top of Penn's Hill. Abigail found "the constant roar of the cannon" on 17 June 1775 so upsetting "that we cannot Eat Drink or sleep." (Library of Congress)

Abigail wrote in anguish to John on 18 June 1775: "My bursting Heart must find vent at my pen. I have just heard that our Dear Friend Dr Warren is no more but fell gloriously fighting for his Country—saying better to die honourably in the field than ignominiously hang upon the Gallows. Great is our Loss." Eleven years later, when Abigail had the opportunity in London to see John Trumbull's evocative *Death of General Warren at the Battle of Bunker's Hill*, her "Blood Shiverd" at the sight. (Yale University Art Gallery, Trumbull Collection)

"The Flight of the Congress," a British cartoon by William Hitchcock, portrays the departure of Congress from Philadelphia on 19 September 1777, following the American defeat at Brandywine Creek, as a mad dash of animals scurrying away from the British lion. John Adams and his cousin Samuel appear as foxes in the lower right-hand corner. (Boston Public Library, Prints Department)

July 9 1777

I sit down to write you this post, and from my present feelings tis the last I shall be able to write for some time if I should do well, I have been very unwell for this week past, with some complaints that have been new to me tho I hope not dangerous I was last night taken with a shaking fit, and am very apprehensive that a life was lost, as I have no reason to day to think otherways; what may be the consequences to me, Heaven only knows. I know not of any injury to myself, nor any thing which could occasion what I fear I would not Have you too much allarmd, I keep up some spirits yet, tho I would have you prepaid for any Event that may happen. I can add no more than that I am in every Situation unfeignedly yours, yours

John's absence in Philadelphia in the spring of 1777 was especially trying to Abigail, who was expecting her sixth child. While the pregnancy had proceeded smoothly, in the final days Abigail sensed a problem. On 9 July, she wrote to John about a "shaking fit" she had the night before and her apprehension that "a life was lost." She continued, "I would not Have you too much allarmd. I keep up some spirits yet, tho I would have you prepaird for any Event that may happen." Two days later, she gave birth to a stillborn child, a daughter they named Elizabeth. (The Adams Papers)

Abigail Adams 2d sat for this painting by Mather Brown in July 1785 in London. A year later, after his marriage to Nabby, Col. William Stephens Smith sat for a companion portrait. While John and Abigail were initially extremely pleased with the match, Smith's profligate ways and inability (or unwillingness) to support his family led to their ultimate disenchantment with him. (National Park Service, Adams National Historical Park)

Thomas Boylston Adams, John and Abigail's youngest son, appears in this miniature watercolor on ivory painted by a Mr. Parker of England in 1795. At the time, Thomas Boylston was serving as secretary to his brother John Quincy, then U.S. minister at The Hague. (Massachusetts Historical Society)

This published image of a miniature portrait of Charles Adams by an unknown artist is the only one extant of John and Abigail's second son. A lively youth known for his good looks and pleasing manners, he briefly had a successful legal career but succumbed to alcoholism. His downfall caused John to bemoan to Abigail: "I grieved, I mourned but could do no more. A Madman possessed of the Devil can alone express or represent. I renounce him."

(Massachusetts Historical Society)

John Quincy Adams sat for this portrait by John Singleton Copley while in London in 1796 exchanging the ratification of Jay's Treaty, shortly before his engagement to Louisa Catherine Johnson. Copley's wife, Susanna, presented it to Abigail as a gift in early 1797. (Museum of Fine Arts, Boston)

Six Months or sooner if possible to be c...

Sig...

In...

sign...

hav...

full...

the ...

and...

to be ...

Done at Paris, this third Day of September, In the Year of our Lord, one thousand seven hundred & Eighty three.

D Hartley   *John Adams*

Franklin

John Jay

Benjamin West never completed his group portrait of the American commissioners at the preliminary peace negotiations with Britain in Paris. He intended to include the British representative Richard Oswald but Oswald, who refused to sit for the portrait, died without leaving an appropriate image to copy. The signature and seals from the Definitive Treaty of Peace, signed on 3 September 1783, are from the copy of the treaty John Adams retained in his personal papers. (Winterthur Museum and The Adams Papers)

John considered Dutch recognition of the United States in April 1782 a "Signal Tryumph," the most important work of his diplomatic career to date. Even before recognition became official, John purchased a house on the Fluwelen Burgwal in The Hague to serve as the Hôtel des États-Unis, the first American foreign legation. A medal commemorating the event, designed by Jean George Holtzhey of Amsterdam, depicts the Netherlands as an armed woman and the United States as an Indian woman holding hands under the legend "Libera Soror" ("A Free Sister"). (The Adams Papers and Massachusetts Historical Society)

This crude political cartoon, dated 15 February 1798, depicts an infamous brawl on the floor of Congress between the cane-wielding Connecticut Federalist Roger Griswold and his Republican adversary Matthew Lyon of Vermont, shown defending himself with fireplace tongs. The event is symbolic of the intense partisanship seen in the United States following the passage of the Alien and Sedition Acts. (Library of Congress)

William Strickland's elegant painting (opposite) of the President's House in Philadelphia ca. 1820 belies John's opinion of the place when he moved into it in March 1797: "Last night for the first time I slept in our new House. But what a Scene! The Furniture belonging to the Publick is in the most deplorable Condition. There is not a Chair fit to sit in. The Beds and Bedding are in a woeful Pickle." (The Historical Society of Pennsylvania)

This house, located on the Hudson River in present-day Greenwich Village, served as the vice president's residence while the national capital remained in New York City. Abigail joined John there in June 1789. She soon became enamored of the rural setting and the house's imposing situation, from which she could see New Jersey across the Hudson, the city, and Long Island. This rendering by Cornelius Tiebout, which Abigail did not believe did the house justice, appeared in the *New York Magazine*, June 1790. (New-York Historical Society)

Presidents house Washington City, Nov. 2.1

My dearest friend

We arrived here last night, or rather yesterday one O Clock and here we dined and slept. The Building in a State to be habitable. And now we wish for yo Company. The account you give of the melancholy Sta of our dear Brother Mr Cranch and his family is rea distressing and must Severely afflict you. I most corde Sympathize with you and them.

I have Seen only Mr Marshall and Mr Stod General Wilkinson and the two Commissioners Mr Scott an Mr Thornton.

I Shall Say nothing of public affairs. I a very glad you consented to come on, for you would have be more anxious at Quincy than here, and I, to all my other Solicitudines Mordaces as Horace calls them i.e. "biting Cares" Should have added a great deal on your accoun Besides it is fit and proper that you and I Should m together and not one before the other

Before I end my Letter I pray Heaven to bestow the best of Blessings on this House and all that shall hereafter inhabit it. May none but honest and wise Men ever rule under this roof.

I shall not attempt a description of it. You will form the best Idea of it from Inspection.

Mr Brisler is very anxious for the arrival of the Man and Women and I am much more so for that of the Ladies. I am with unabated Confidence and affection your

John Adams

Wᵐ S Adams

This 1798 wash drawing by E. Malcom is the earliest depiction of John and Abigail's retirement home, later called the Old House, purchased by them in 1787 in anticipation of their return to Braintree from England. During John's vice presidency and presidency, he and Abigail spent as much time as they could manage in this house, a retreat from politics and the frustrations of public life. (National Park Service, Adams National Historical Park)

This 1822 rendering entitled a "View of the Seat of John Adams," by distant cousin Eliza Susan Quincy, shows the home with the 1798 addition that provided a parlor for Abigail and a library for John. The setting includes the surrounding farm with the bay and a distant Boston in the background. (Massachusetts Historical Society)

These portraits—of John by Gilbert Stuart Newton and of Abigail by an unknown artist, both after the originals by Gilbert Stuart—depict the Adamses at the time of their retirement and return to Massachusetts. After leaving Washington, D.C., John and Abigail had no need for further correspondence, as they spent their remaining years together in Quincy. (Massachusetts Historical Society)

Quincy November 10th 1818

My ever dear, ever affectionate, ever dutiful and deserving Son.
The bitterness of Death is past. The grim Spectre so terrible to human Nature has no Sting left for me.

My consolations are more than I can number. The Seperation cannot be so long as twenty Seperations heretofore. The Pangs and the Anguish have not been so great as when you and I embarked for France in 1778.

The Sympathy and Benevolence of all the World has been such as I shall not live long enough to discribe. I have not Strength to do Justice to Individuals. Louisa Susan Miss Harriet Welsh have been with us constantly. The Three Families of Greanleafs, Mrs John Greanleaf, has been (your Mother Said it to me, in her last moments "a Mother to me"). Mr Daniel Greanleaf has been really the good Samaritan.

Louisa Harriet and Mrs John Greanleaf have been above all praise, Mr and Mrs Quincy have been more like Sons and Daughters than like Neighbours, Mr Shaw and your Sons have been all you could desire.

Your Letter of the Second is all and no more than all that I expected. Never was a more dutifull Son. Never a more affectionate Mother. Love to your Wife. May you never experience her Loss. So prays your Aged and affected Father John Adams

J. Q. A.

Penned in the shaky handwriting characteristic of John's later years, this short letter from John to his son John Quincy clearly expresses his devastation at the death of his beloved Abigail. He took consolation, however, in the fact that "the Seperation cannot be so long as twenty Seperations heretofore"; he would look forward to being reunited with his dearest friend. (The Adams Papers)

Criminals. Tore to Pieces Sir G. Savilles House—insulted, all the Lords of Parliament &c &c—many have been killed—martial Law proclaimed—many hanged—Lord George Gordon committed to the Tower for high Treason—and where it will end God only knows. The Mobs all cryd Peace with America, and War with France—poor Wretches! as if this were possible.

In the English Papers they have inserted the Death of Mr Hutchinson with severity, in these words—Governor Hutchinson is no more. On Saturday last he dropped down dead. It is charity to hope that his sins will be buried with him in the Tomb, but they must be recorded in his Epitaph. His Misrepresentations have contributed to the Continuance of the War with America. Examples are necessary. It is to be hoped that all will not escape into the Grave, without a previous appearance, either on a Gibbet or a scaffold.

Govr Bernard I am told died last fall. I wish, that with these primary Instruments of the Calamities that now distress almost all the World the Evils themselves may come to an End. For although they will undoubtedly End, in the Welfare of Mankind, and accomplish the Benevolent designs of Providence, towards the two Worlds; Yet for the present they are not joyous but grievous.

May Heaven permit you and me to enjoy the cool Evening of Life, in Tranquility, undisturbed by the Cares of Politicks or War—and above all with the sweetest of all Reflections that neither Ambition nor Vanity, nor Avarice, nor Malice nor Envy nor Revenge, nor Fear nor any base Motive, or sordid Passion through the whole Course of this mighty Revolution, and the rapid impetuous Course of great and terrible Events that have attended it, have drawn Us aside from the Line of our Duty and the Dictates of our Consciences! Let Us have Ambition enough to keep our Simplicity, or Frugality and our Integrity and transmit these Virtues as the fairest of Inheritances to our Children.

Abigail Adams to John Adams

My dearest Love   july 24 1780

Your affectionate Letter by the Count de Noailles reachd me but yesterday, together with your present by Col. Fleury which was very nice and Good. Should you send any thing of the kind in the same way, be so good as to let it be blew white or red. Silk Gloves or mittins, black or white lace, Muslin or a Bandano hankerchief, and *even a few yd of Ribbon* might be conveyed in the same manner. I mention these things as they are small articles, and easily contained in a Letter, all of which by Resolve of congress are orderd to come Free. The Articles you orderd me from Bilboa are of great service to me. The great plenty of Barcelona hankerchiefs make them unsaleable at present, but Linnens are an article in great demand, and will exchange for any family necessary to good account, or sell for money, which is in greater demand at present than I have known it since paper was first Emitted. High prices high taxes, high bounties render such a Quantity of it necessary, that few people can procure sufficient to answer necessary demands. The usual Estimation is a dollor at a copper, yet exchange at the highest has been at 75 for one. Country produce exceeds foreign articles, Lamb at 10 dollors pr pound veal at 7, flower a hundred and 60 pound pr hundred Rye 100 and 10 dollors pr Bushel. I had determined not to have written you the account of prices &c have avoided it all along, chose you should learn it from inquiry of others but insensibly fell into it.

I have a request to you which I hope you will not dissapoint me of, a minature of Him I best Love. Indulge me the pleasing melancholy of contemplating a likeness. The attempt here faild, and was more the resemblance of a cloisterd Monk, than the Smileing Image of my Friend. I could not endure the sight of it. By Sampson will be a Good opportunity. Should he be taken none but a savage would rob a Lady, of what could be of no value, but to her. Let him put it into his chest, and it will come safe I dare say. Let it be set, it will be better done with you than here.

I mentioned sending Bill by this opportunity but as I have already sent 3 sets was advised to defer the others till I knew whether they had faild. If I have not been too extravagant already, I would mention one article more, as I do not expect an other opportunity from France for a twelve month. It is a Green umbrella.

You think you run great risks in taking our two sons—what then was mine? I could have accompanied you through any Dangers and fatigues, but whether I could have sustaind them I know not. An intimation that I could have renderd you more comfortable and happy, would have outweighd all my timidity. I should have had no other consideration. Yet the dangers of the sea of Enimies and the fatigues of a long journey are not objects that I wish to encounter. A small portion of my own Country will be all I shall ever visit, nor should I carry my wishes further, if they would not seperate what God joined together. Ever remember with tenderness and affection yours and yours only

Portia

In June 1780, Congress authorized John to open negotiations with the Netherlands for a loan. Even before he received word of this new appointment, frustrated with his lack of progress in Paris, he had gone to Amsterdam as a private citizen to see what he could accomplish there in promoting American interests. By winter, Congress had also elected him minister to the Netherlands, and he ended up remaining in Amsterdam and The Hague until the peace negotiations with the British finally began in the fall of 1782.

The goods John sent home to Abigail—and her explicit instructions about what she wanted—did not reflect some newfound vanity on Abigail's part. Rather, she sold these items as a way to supplement the family's income. Her natural business acumen made this a successful venture, despite the number of items that were lost or destroyed in transit.

John Adams to Abigail Adams

My dear Portia   Amsterdam Septr. 25. 1780

The new orders I have received from your side the Water, have determined me to stay, here untill further orders. Write to me, by every Vessell this Way, or to France or Spain. The Air of Amsterdam is not so clear and pure as that of France, but I hope to preserve my Health. My two Boys are at an excellent Latin School, or in the Language of this Country Den de Latynche School op de Cingel by de Munt. The Scholars here all speak French.

John has seen one of the Commencements when the young Gentlemen delivered their Orations and received their Premiums, and Promotions which set his Ambition all afire. Charles is the same amiable insinuating Creature. Wherever he goes he gets the Hearts of every Body especially the Ladies. One of these Boys is the sublime and the other the Beautifull.

You promised me a Description of the Castle you were building in the Air, but I have not recd it.

The English are revenging the Loss of their Power, upon those who have uniformly, endeavoured to save it. They are totally abandoned and lost. There is no Hope for them but in a civil War nor in that neither. Burke, Keppell, Sawbridge, Hartley are thrown out.

We are anxiously waiting for News from America and the Islands; but my Expectations are not very high. The Fleet is not strong enough in N. America. I sent the Things you wrote for by Captain Davis son of solomon, but they cost very dear.

I have written to Mr Thaxter to come here—Mr Dana is already here. I want to know how the season has been, with you—and who are your Governor and Lt Governor &c &c &c.

I shall loose all opportunity of being a man of Importance in the World by being away from home, as well as all the Pleasures of Life: for I never shall enjoy any, any where except at the Foot of Pens hill— When Oh When shall I see the Beauties of that rugged Mountain!

By your last Letters I fear my Brother is in Affliction. My Love to him and his family—and Duty and affection where due.

Abigail Adams to John Adams

My dearest Friend   october 18 1780

The vessel by which I mean to send this is bound for Amsterdam and had very nigh given me the slip.

I have been writing to you when ever I was able by other opportunities, and should have compleated Several Letters for this conveyance, but I have been very sick with a slow fever, and your Mother has been sick here of a fever, occasiond by great fatigue, the old gentleman dyeing about 3 weeks ago of a fever. Both of us are much better. I have got out, tho she has not yet left her chamber. The rest of our Friends are well.

I wish this Letter might find you in Holland. I think it not improbable if you have received a commission forwarded to you some months ago.

My Trunk about which you have been so anxious, and so often wished me safe, is not on board the Alliance to my no small mortification. You have found out the cause I dare say before this time. Party and cabal ran so high that the person to whose care it was intrusted, did not chuse to come in the ship—so that it may possibly lay in France till Sampson arrives. If it should I wish it may be put on Board of him and be so good as to get an invoice of mr Moylan and send the first opportunity. This I wish you to do. If it should come by the dr— it will be no damage to compare them.

Holland is so much improved in the way of Trade, that ten nay twenty opportunities offer for sending from there, to one from France.

Enclosed I send a set of Bills received from mr L[*ovel*]l. They do not amount to near the Balance reported in your favour but I suppose the rest to be connected with the other Gentlemens accounts, which they say can not be gone in to at present for want of a state of theirs. I have however written to mr L[*ovel*]l to know if it is really so.

As to politicks if I begin I shall not know where to end, yet I must tell you of a horrid plot, just ready to have been sprung, which would have given us a shock indeed. Arnold, you know him unprincipald as the —— he missirable wretch had concerted a plan to give up west point where he commanded with its dependancies, into the hands of the Enemy. He had made returns of every important matter to them; with a plan (but a little before concerted, between the general officers) and state of the Army. Major Andry was the person upon whom these papers were found, an officer in the British Army, sensible bold and enterprizing, universally beloved by them, and regreated with many tears. He was young and very accomplished, but taken in our Camp as a spy, he was tried comdemned and Executed. Arnold upon the first allarm that Andry was taken, conveyd himself on Board a ship of war and deserted to the Enemy. I have by two late papers sent you enclosed to you the whole of this Black transaction, so providentially Discoverd which must excite Gratitude in every Breast not wholy devoid of principal. It is now a long time since I heard from you, the 17 of June was the last date.

I have just sent Letters for mr T[*haxte*]r to Newport to go in a French Frigate. I shall write to him by a vessel soon to sail for France and to my dear Boys. Remember me tenderly to them. Oh! when shall I see them again, or their dear parent? I must bid you good Night tis late and I am yet feable and weak. Believe me with sentiments of tenderness and affection *ever yours.*

Abigail Adams to John Adams

My dearest Friend   November 13th 1780

How long is the space since I heard from my dear absent Friends? Most feelingly do I experience that sentiment of Rousseaus' "that one of the Greatest evils of absence, and the only one which reason cannot alleviate, is the inquietude we are under concerning the actual state of those we love, their health, their life their repose their affections. Nothing escapes the apprehension of those who have every thing to lose." Nor are we more certain of the present condition than of the future. How tormenting is absence? How fatally capricious is that situation in which we can only enjoy the past moment, for the present is not yet arrived. Stern Winter is making hasty strides towards me, and chills the warm fountain of my Blood by the Gloomy prospect of passing *it alone,* for what is the rest of the World to me?

"Its pomp its pleasures and its nonesence all?" The fond endearments of social and domestick life, is the happiness I sigh for, of that I am in a great measure deprived by a seperation from my dear partner and children, at the only season in life when it is probable we might have enjoyed them all to gether. In a year or two, the sons will be so far advanced in life as to make it necessary for their Benifit, to place them at the Seats of Learning and Science, indeed the period has already arrived, and whilst I still fondle over one, it is no small relief to my anxious mind, that those, who are seperated from me, are under your care and inspection. They have arrived at an age, when a Mothers care becomes less necessary and a Fathers more important. I long to embrace them. The Tears my dear Charles shed at parting, have melted my Heart a thousand times. Why does the mind Love to turn to those painfull scenes and to recollect them with pleasure?

I last week only received a Letter written last march, and sent by Monseiur John Baptiste Petry. Where he is I know not. After nameing a Number of persons, to whom I might apply for conveyance of Letters, you were pleased to add, they were your great delight when they did not censure, or complain. When they did, they were your greatest punishment.

I am wholy unconscious of giving you pain in this way since your late absence. If any thing of the kind formerly escaped my pen, had I not ample retaliation, and did we not Balance accounts tho the Sum was rather in your favour even after having distroyed some of the proof. In the most Intimate of Friendships, there must not be any recrimination. If I complain, it was from the ardour of affection which could not endure the least apprehension of neglect, and you who was conscious that I had no cause would not endure the supposition. We however wanted no mediating power to adjust the difference. We no sooner understood each other properly, but as the poet says, "The falling out of Lovers is the renewal of Love."

> "Be to my faults a little Blind
> Be to my virtues ever kind."

And you are sure of a Heart all your own, which no other Earthly object ever possessd; sure I am that not a syllable of complaint has ever stained my paper, in any Letter I have ever written since you left me. I should have been ungratefull indeed, when I have not had the shadow of a cause; but on the contrary, continual proofs of your attention to me. You well know I never doubted your Honour. Virtue and principal confirm the indissoluable Bond which affection first began and my security depends not upon passion, which other objects might more easily excite, but upon the sober and setled dictates of Religion and Honour. It is these that cement, at the same time that they ensure the affections.

> "Here Love his golden shafts employs; here lights
> His *constant* Lamp, and waves his purple wings."

John Adams to Abigail Adams

My dearest Portia   Amsterdam Decr 18. 1780

I have this morning sent Mr Thaxter, with my two Sons to Leyden, there to take up their Residence for some time, and there to pursue their Studies of Latin and Greek under the excellent Masters, and there to attend Lectures of the celebrated Professors in that University. It is much cheaper there than here: the Air is infinitely purer; and the Company and Conversation is better.

It is perhaps as learned an University as any in Europe.

I should not wish to have Children, educated in the common Schools in this Country, where a littleness of Soul is notorious. The Masters are mean Spirited Writches, pinching, kicking, and boxing the Children, upon every Turn.

Their is besides a general Littleness arising from the incessant Contemplation of Stivers and Doits, which pervades the whole People.

Frugality and Industry are virtues every where, but Avarice, and Stingyness are not Frugality.

The Dutch say that without an habit of thinking of every doit, before you spend it, no Man can be a good Merchant, or conduct Trade with Success. This I believe is a just Maxim in general. But I would never wish to see a Son of Mine govern himself by it. It is the sure and certain Way for an industrious Man to be rich. It is the only possible Way for a Merchant, to become the first Merchant, or the richest Man in the Place. But this is an Object that I hope none of my Children will ever aim at.

It is indeed true, every where, that those who attend to small Expences are always rich.

I would have my Children attend to Doits and Farthings as devoutly as the meerest Dutchman upon Earth, if such Attention was necessary to Support their Independence.

A Man who discovers a Disposition and a design to be independent seldom succeeds—a Jealousy arises against him. The Tyrants are alarmed on one side least he should oppose them. The slaves are allarmed on the other least he should expose their Servility. The Cry from all Quarters is, "He is the proudest Man in the World. He cant bear to be under Obligation."

I never in my Life observed any one, endeavouring to lay me under particular obligations to him, but I suspected he had a design to make me his dependant, and to have claims upon my Gratitude. This I should have no objection to—Because Gratitude is always in ones Power. But the Danger is that Men will expect and require more of Us, that Honour and Innocence and Rectitude will permit Us to perform.

In our Country however any Man with common Industry and Prudence may be independant.

But to put an End to this stuff. Adieu, most affectionately Adieu.

John Adams to Abigail Adams

My dearest Friend   Amsterdam April 28. 1781

Congress have been pleased to give me so much other Business to do, that I have not Time to write either to Congress, or to private Friends so often as I used.

Having lately recd Letters of Credence to their High mightinesses the states General of the United Provinces of the Low Countries and to his most serene Highness the Prince of orange, I am now fixed to this Country, untill I shall be called away to Conferences for Peace, or recalled by Congress. I have accordingly taken a House in Amsterdam upon the Keysers Gragt i.e. the Emperors Canal, near the Spiegel Straat i.e. the Looking Glass street, so you may Address your Letters to me, there.

I have hitherto preserved my Health in this damp Air better than I expected. So have all of Us, but Charles who has had a tertian fever but is better.

I hope this People will be in earnest, after the twentyeth of June. Americans are more Attended to and our Cause gains ground here every day. But all Motions are slow here—and much Patience is necessary. I shall now however be more settled in my own Mind having something like a Home. Alass how little like my real home. What would I give for my dear House keeper. But this is too great a felicity for me.

I dont expect to Stay long in Europe. I really hope I shall not. Things dont go to my Mind.

Pray get the Dissertation on the Cannon and feudal Law printed in a Pamphlet or in the Newspapers and send them to me by every opportunity untill you know that one has arrived. I have particular Reasons for this. My Nabby and Tommy, how do they do.

Abigail Adams to John Adams

My Dearest Friend   May 28 1781

I could not have conceived that a Letter written upon merely politi-cal subjects could have communicated so much pleasure to my Bosom as yours of the 28th of December to the president, of Congress, has given to mine.

This Letter was taken by the Enemy carried into New York, and published by them, and republished Edes. For what reason the Enemy published it I cannot tell, as it contains nothing which can possibly us or the writer. It has proved a cordial to my anxious Heart for by it I find you were then living, and in Amsterdam, two facts that I have not received under your own hand for 8 months. This Letter is 3 months later than any which has reachd me.

Dr Dexter by whom I have before written, has since, been polite enough to visit me, that he might, as he expresses it, have the pleasure to tell you, that he had seen me, and take from me any verbal message, that I would not chuse to write. But my pen must be the faithfull confident of my Heart. I could not say to a stranger, that which I could not write, nor dare I even trust to my pen the fullness of my Heart. You must measure it, by the contents of your own when softned by recollection.

Dr Dexter appears to be a sensible well bred Gentleman, and will give you much information respecting our state affairs which may not be so prudent to commit to paper. I have written to the House of de Neufvilla for a few articles by an other opportunity and have now inclosed a duplicate.

I intreat you my dearest Friend to forward Letters to the various ports in france as you have some acquaintance with many of them. I should then be able to hear oftner.

june 1

Our Friends from P[*lymout*]h have made me a visit upon their re-move to *Neponset Hill* which they have purchased of mr Broom. You

will congratulate me I know upon my acquisition in the Neighbourhood, it is a very agreable circumstance. By them I learnt that the late
vessels from France had brought them Letters from their son up to the
10 of March, in which he mentions being with my dear Friend my sons
and mr T[*haxte*]r. They have received five Letters, by different vessels
yet not a line has yet blest my hand. May I soon be made happy, and
the Number compensate for the delay.

I hope you do not think it necessary to continue in Holland through
the summer. I am very anxious for your Health—so flat a country will
never agree with you. Pray do not be negligent with regard to an article which so nearly concerns the happiness of your Ever affectionate

Portia

*After an initial unhappy experience with a Latin school in Amsterdam, John
Quincy and Charles had been attending the University of Leyden. But Charles's
ill-health and continuing homesickness led John to bring him back to Amsterdam
and shortly thereafter to arrange for him to return to the United States. Unfortunately, Charles's trip home proved nearly as lengthy and circuitous as his original
voyage to Europe, and he did not reach Massachusetts until January 1782.*

*At about this same time, Francis Dana convinced John to allow John Quincy to
accompany Dana on his mission to St. Petersburg, Russia, as a companion,
French interpreter, and private secretary.*

John Adams to Abigail Adams

My dear Portia   Paris July 11. 1781

I am called to this Place, in the Course of my Duty: but dont conceive from it any hopes of Peace. This desireable object is yet unhappily at a Distance, a long distance I fear.

My dear Charles will go home with Maj. Jackson. Put him to school and keep him steady. He is a delightfull Child, but has too exquisite sensibility for Europe.

John is gone, a long Journey with Mr Dana: he will serve as an Interpreter, and the Expence will be little more than at Leyden. He will be Satiated with travel in his Childhood, and care nothing about it, I hope in his riper Years.

I am distracted with more cares than ever, yet I grow fat. Anxiety is good for my Health I believe.

Oh that I had Wings, that I might fly and bury all my Cares at the Foot of Pens Hill.

Abigail Adams to John Adams

My dearest Friend   Sepbr 29 1781

Three days only did it want of a year from the date of your last Letter, when I received by Capt Newman in the Brig Gates your welcome favour of May 22d.

By various ways I had collected some little intelligence of you, but for six months past my Heart had known but little ease—not a line had reachd me from you not a syllable from my children—and whether living or dead I could not hear. That you have written many time, I doubted not, but such is the chance of war, and such the misfortune attending a communication between absent Friends.

I learn by mr Brush, that mr Dana is gone to Petersburgh, and with him master john. For this I am not sorry. Mr Danas care and attention to him, I shall be well satisfied in—and Russia is an Empire I should be very fond of his visiting. My dear Charles I hear is comeing home with Gillion.

I know not your motives for sending him but dare say you have weighty reasons. That of his Health is alone sufficient, if the low countries are as prejudicial to him, as I fear they are, and will be to his Father too. Why did you not write me about it? At first I learnt it, only by hearing of a list of passengers who were to come in the Indian—amongst which was a son of mr A[*dam*]s. This made me very uneasy—I had a thousand fear and apprehensions—nor shall I be much at ease, you may well suppose untill I hear of her arrival. I fear she will be an object, for the British to persue. The Event I must commit to the supreme Ruler of the universe. Our Friends here are all well. Your Mother has recoverd beyond my expectation. My Father too is in good Health for his years. Both our parents remember you with affection.

General Green, is making the Requisition you require, and setling the preliminarys for a Peace, by extirpating the British force from Carolina. We are from the present prospect of affairs in daily expectation that Cornwallis will meet the Fate of Burgoine. God Grant it, and that this winter may produce to America an *honorable Peace*. But my fears are well grounded when I add, that some of your colleagues are unfit for the Buisness and I really am in suspence whether you will hold your garbled commission, for reasons to which you will be no stranger before this reaches you. But if you resign, I am not the only persons by hundreds who dread the consequences, as it is probable you will find, from instructions, which I hear are to be sent, from several states to their delegates in Congress. You have a delicate part to act. You will do what you Esteem to be your duty, I doubt not; fearless of consequences—and futurity will discriminate the Honest Man from the knave tho the present Generation seem little disposed to.

I cannot write so freely as I wish. Your Memorial is in high Estimation here.

So you have set down at Amsterdam in the House keeping way. What if I should take a trip across the Atlantick? I tell mrs dana we should pass very well for Natives. I have received a very polite Letter from mr De Neufvilla. How did this Man discover, that extolling my Husband, was the sweetest musick in my ears? He has certainly touched the key which vibrates Harmony to me!

I think I have requested you to send me a chest of Bohea Tea, by any vessel of mr Tracys. Do not think me extravagant—I economize with the utmost Frugality I am capable of, but our Taxes are so high, and so numerous, that I know not which way to turn. I paied 60 hard dollors this week for a state and county Rate. I have 30 more to pay immediately for hireing a Man for 6 months in the service, and a very large town tax, now comeing out. Hard Money is our only currency. I have a sum of old and New paper which lies by me useless at present. Goods of the West India kind are low as ever they were. Bills sell greatly below par. Hard money is very scarce, but I hope never to see an other paper Medium. Difficult as the times are and, dull as Buisness is, we are in a better situation than we were before.

Where is my Friend mr Thaxter? That not a line has reachd me from him? His Friends are all well, but longing and impatient to hear from him. We see by the paper, that he was well enough to celebrate independance on the fourth of july. The Robinhood had Letters to all my Friends which I hope you have received. I send many to Bilboa, do you get any from thence, pray write to me by way of France and Bilboa.

This is to go by a Brig to France which I heard of but yesterday. You have I suppose received a commission for forming a Quardrupple alliance—such an one is made out. O my dear Friend, how far distant is the day when I may expect to receive you in your Native Land?

Haughty Britain sheath your sword in pitty to yourselves. Let not an other village be added to the long List of your depredations. The Nations arround you shudder at your crimes. Unhappy New London Named after your capital—may she close the devastation.

How many tender sentiments rise to mind when about to you bid you adieu. Shall I express them or comprise, them all in the assurance of being ever Ever Yours

Portia

John Adams to Abigail Adams

My dearest Friend   Amsterdam Decr 2 1781

Your favours of September 29 and Oct. 21. are before me. I avoided saying any Thing about Charles, to save you the Anxiety, which I fear you will now feel in its greatest severity a long time. I thought he would go directly home, in a short Passage, in the best opportunity which would probably ever present. But I am dissappointed. Charles is at Bilbao with Major Jackson and Coll Trumbull who take the best care of his Education as well as his Health and Behaviour. They are to go hence in Captain Hill in a good Vessell of 20 Guns. Charles's health was so much affected by this tainted Atmosphere, and he had set his heart so much upon going home in Gillon that it would have broken it, to have refused him. I desire I may never again have the Weakness to bring a Child to Europe. They are infinitely better at home. We have all been sick here, myself, Mr Thaxter Stephens and another servant, but are all better. Mr Thaxters Indisposition has been slight and short, mine and stevens's long and severe.

I beg you would not flatter yourself with hopes of Peace. There will be no such Thing for several Years.

Dont distress yourself neither about, any malicious Attempts to injure me in the Estimation of my Countrymen. Let them take their Course and go the Length of their Tether. They will never hurt your Husband whose Character is fortified with a shield of Innocence and Honour ten thousandfold stronger than brass or Iron. The contemptible Essays made by you know whom, will only tend to their own Confusion. My Letters have shewn them their own Ignorance a sight they could not bear. Say as little about it as I do. It has already brought them into the true system and that system is tryumphant. I laugh, and will laugh before all Posterity at their impotent, Rage and Envy. They could not help blushing themselves if they were to review their Conduct.

Dear Tom thy Letter does thee much honour. Thy Brother Charles shall teach thee french and Dutch, at home. I wish I could get time to correspond with thee and thy sister, more regularly but I cannot. I must trust Providence and thine excellent Mamma for the Education of my Children.

Mr Dana and our son are well, at P[*etersburg*].

Hayden has some things for you. Hope he is arrived. I am sorry to learn you have a sum of Paper—how could you be so imprudent? You must be frugal, I assure you. Your Children will be poorly off. I can but barely live in the manner that is indispensibly demanded of me by every Body. Living is dear indeed here.

My Children will not be so well left by their father as he was by his. They will be infected with the Examples and Habits and Tasts for Expensive Living, without the means. He was not.

My Children, shall never have, the smallest soil of dishonour or disgrace brought upon them by their father, no not to please Ministers Kings or Nations. At the Expence of a little of this my Children might perhaps ride at their Ease through Life, but dearly as I love them they shall, live in the service of their Country in her Navy her Army, or even out of either in the extreamest Degree of Poverty before I will depart in the Smallest Iota from my Sentiments of Honour and Delicacy, for I, even I have sentiments of Delicacy, as exquisite as the proudest Minister that ever served a Monarch. They may not be exactly like those of some Ministers.

I beg you would excuse me to my dear Friends, to whom I cannot write so often as I wish. I have indispensible Duties which take up all my time, and require more than I have.

General Washington has done me great Honour, and much public service by sending me, authentic Accounts of his own and Gen Greens, last great Actions. They are in the Way to negotiate Peace, it lies wholly with them. No other Ministers but they and their Colleagues in the Army can accomplish, the great Event.

I am keeping House, but I want an Housekeeper. What a fine Affair it would be if We could flit across the Atlantic as they say the Angels do from Planet to Planet. I would dart to Pens hill and bring you over on my Wings. But alass We must keep house seperately for some time.

But one thing I am determined on—If God should please to restore me once more to your fireside, I will never again leave it without your Ladyships Company. No not even to go to Congress at Philadelphia, and there I am determined to go if I can make Interest enough to get chosen, whenever I return.

I would give a Million sterling that you were here—and could Afford it as well as G. Britain can the thirty Millions she must spend the ensuing Year to compleat her own Ruin.

Farewell Farewell.

Abigail Adams to John Adams

My dearest Friend   April 10th. 1782

How great was my joy to see the well known signature of my Friend after a Melancholy solicitude of many months in which my hopes and fears alternately preponderated.

It was Janry when Charles arrived. By him I expected Letters, but found not a line; instead of which the heavy tidings of your illness reachd me. I then found my Friends had been No strangers of what they carefully conceald from me. Your Letter to Charles dated in November was the only consolation I had; by that I found that the most dangerous period of your illness was pass'd, and that you considerd yourself as recovering tho feeble. My anxiety and apprehensions from that day untill your Letters arrived, which was near 3 months, conspired to render me unhappy. Capt Trowbridge in the Fire Brand arrived with your favours of october and december and in some measure dispeld the Gloom which hung heavy at my heart. How did it leap for joy to find I was not the misirable Being I sometimes feared I was. I felt that Gratitude to Heaven which great deliverences both demand and inspire. I will not distrust the providential Care of the supreem disposer of events—from whose Hand I have so frequently received distinguished favours. Such I call the preservation of my dear Friend and children from the uncertain Element upon which they have frequently embarked; their preservation from the hands of their Enimies I have reason to consider in the same view, especially when I reflect upon the cruel and inhumane treatment experienced by a Gentleman of mr Laurences age and respectable character. The restoration of my dearest Friend from so dangerous a sickness, demands all my gratitude, whilst I fail not to supplicate Heaven for the continuance of a Life upon which my temporal happiness rests, and deprived of which my own existance would become a burden. Often has the Question which you say staggerd your philosophy occured to me, nor have I felt so misirable upon account of my own personal situation, when I considerd that according to the common course of Nature, more than half my days were allready passt, as for those in whom our days are renewed. Their hopes and prospects would vanish, their best prospects those of Education would be greatly diminished. But I will not anticipate those miseries which I would shun. Hope is my best Friend and kindest comforter; she assures me that the pure unabated affection, which neither time or absence can allay or abate, shall e'er long be crowned with the completion of its fondest wishes, in the safe return of the beloved object; the age of romance has long ago past—but the affection of almost Infant years has matured and strengthend untill it has become a vital principle nor has the world any thing to bestow which could in the smallest degree compensate for the loss. Desire and Sorrow were denounced upon our sex; as a punishment for the transgression of Eve. I have sometimes thought that we are formed to experience more exquisite Sensations than is the Lot of your sex. More tender and susceptable by Nature of those impression which create happiness or misiry, we suffer and enjoy in a higher degree. I never wonderd at the philosopher who thanked the Gods that he was created a Man rather than a woman.

I cannot say, but that I was dissapointed when I found that your return to your Native land was a still distant Idea. I think your situation cannot be so dissagreable as I feared it was, yet that dreadfull climate is my terror. You mortify me indeed when you talk of sending Charles to Colledge, who it is not probable will be fit under three or four years. Surely my dear Friend fleeting as time is I cannot reconcile myself to the Idea of living in this cruel state of seperation for [4?] or even three years to come. Eight years have already past, since you could call yourself an Inhabitant of this state. I shall assume the signature of Penelope for my dear Ulysses has already been a wanderer from me near half the term of years that, that Hero was encountering Neptune Calipso, the Circes and Syrens. In the poetical Language of penelope I shall address you

> "Oh! haste to me! A Little longer stay
> Will ev'ry grace, each fancy'd charm decay:
> Increasing cares, and times resistless rage
> Will waste my bloom, and wither it to age."

You will ask me I suppose what is become of my patriotick virtue? It is that which most ardently calls for your return. I greatly fear that the climate in which you now reside will prove fatal to your Life— whilst your Life and usefullness might be many years of Service to your Country in a more Healthy climate. If the Essentials of her political system are safe, as I would fain hope they are, yet the impositions and injuries, to which she is hourly liable, and daily suffering, call for the exertions of her wisest and ablest citizens. You know by many years experience what it is to struggle with difficulties—with wickedness in high places—from thence you are led to covet a private Station as the post of Honour, but should such an Idea generally prevail who would be left to stem the torrent?

Should we at this day possess those invaluable Blessings transmitted us by our venerable Ancestors, if they had not inforced by their example, what they taught by their precepts?

> "While pride oppression and injustice reign
> The world will still demand her Catos presence."

Why should I indulge an Idea, that whilst the active powers of my Friend remain they, will not be devoted to the service of his country?

Can I believe that the Man who fears neither poverty or dangers, who sees not charms sufficient either in Riches power or places to tempt him in the least to swerve from the purest sentiments of Honour and Delicacy; will retire, unnoticed, Fameless to a Rustick cottage there by dint of Labour to earn his Bread. I need not much examination of my Heart to say I would not willing consent to it.

Have not cincinnatus and Regulus been handed down to posterity, with immortal honour?

Without fortune it is more than probable we shall end our days, but let the well earned Fame, of having sacrificed those prospects, from a principal of universal Benevolence and good will to Man, descend as an inheritance to our ofspring. The Luxery of Foreign Nations may possibly infect them but they have not before them an example of it, so far as respects their domestick life. They are not Bred up with an Idea of possessing Hereditary Riches or Grandeur. Retired from the Capital, they see little of the extravagance or dissipation, which prevails there—and at the close of day, in lieu of the Card table, some usefull Book employs their leisure hours. These habits early fixed, and daily inculcated, will I hope render them usefull and ornamental Members of Society. But we cannot see into futurity. With Regard to politicks, it is rather a dull season for them, we are recruiting for the Army.

The Enemy make sad Havock with our Navigation. Mr Lovell is appointed continential Receiver of taxes and is on his way to this state.

It is difficult to get Gentlemen of abilities and integrity to serve in congress. Few very few are willing to Sacrifice their Interest as others have done before them.

Your favour of december 18th came by way of Philadelphia, but all those Letters sent By Capt Reeler were lost, thrown over Board. Our Friends are well and desire to be rememberd to you. Charles will write if he is able to, before the vessel sails, but he is sick at present, threatned I fear with a fever. I received one Letter from my young Russian to whom I shall write—and 2 from mr Thaxter. If the vessel gives me time I shall write. We wait impatiently for the result of your demand. These slow slugish wheels move not in unison with our feelings.

Adieu my dear Friend. How gladly would I visit you and partake of your Labours and cares, sooth you to rest, and alleviate your anxieties were it given me to visit you even by moon Light, as the faries are fabled to do. I cheer my Heart with the distant prospect. All that I can hope for at present, is to hear of your welfare which of all things lies nearest the Heart of your ever affectionate

Portia

"A Signal Tryumph"

JULY 1782–MARCH 1788

John's move to Amsterdam bore fruit in April 1782 when the Dutch govern-
ment finally acknowledged American independence and granted him full diplo-
matic status. Shortly thereafter, he was able to secure a much-needed loan from
Dutch bankers and by October 1782 he had successfully negotiated a commer-
cial treaty. These accomplishments rightly gave John great satisfaction, reflected
in the happier tones of his letters home. They also freed him to return to Paris
and turn to the resurgent peace negotiations, which carried on through the fall
of 1782.

The period from the winter of 1779, when John left for Europe for the second
time, and the summer of 1784, when Abigail finally arrived in London, marked
the longest separation the couple ever endured. The uncertainty of John's posi-
tion—caused substantially by Congress's indecisiveness—made the situation par-
ticularly irksome. Abigail and John were unable to decide whether John should
return home or Abigail should come and join him in Europe. Even after Abigail
declared her clear willingness to come to Paris—despite her fears that she would
seem uncouth and provincial in the face of European sophistication, "a scene
of Life so different from that in which I have been educated"—nearly two years
elapsed before they could put the plan into action.

John Adams to Abigail Adams

My dearest Friend   The Hague July 1. 1782

Your charming Letters of April 10 and 22d were brought me, Yesterday. That of 22d is upon Business. Mr Hill is paid, I hope. I will honour your Bill if you draw. But be cautious—dont trust Money to any Body. You will never have any to lose or to spare. Your Children will want, more than you and I shall have for them.

The Letter of the 10 I read over and over without End—and ardently long, to be at the blue Hills, there to pass the Remainder of my feeble days. You would be surprised to see your Friend—he is much altered. He is half a Century older and feebler than ever you knew him. The Horse, that he mounts every day is of service to his Health and the Air of the Hague is much better than that of Amsterdam, and besides he begins to be a Courtier, and Sups and Visits at Court among Princesses and Princes, Lords and Ladies, of various Nations. I assure you it is much wholesomer to be a complaisant, good humoured, contented Courtier, than a Grumbletonian Patriot, always whining and snarling.

However I believe my Courtierism will never go any great Lengths. I must be an independent Man, and how to reconcile this to the Character of Courtier is the Question.

A Line from Unkle Smith of 6. of May makes me tremble for my Friend and Brother Cranch! I must hope he is recoverd.

I can tell you no News about Peace. There will be no Seperate Peaces made, not even by Holland—and I cannot think that the present English Ministry are firm enough in their Seats to make a general Peace, as yet.

When shall I go home? If a Peace should be made, you would soon see me. I have had strong Conflicts within, about resigning all my Employments, as soon as I can send home a Treaty. But I know not, what is duty as our Saints say. It is not that my Pride or my Vanity is piqued by the Revocation of my envied Commission. But in such Cases, a

Man knows not what Construction to put. Whether it is not intended to make him resign. Heaven knows I never solicited to come to Europe. Haven knows too what Motive I can have, to banish my self from a Country, which has given me, unequivocal Marks of his affection, Confidence and Esteem, to encounter every Hardship and every danger by Sea and by Land, to ruin my Halth, and to suffer every Humiliation and Mortification that human Nature can endure.

What affects me most is the Tryumph given to Wrong against Right, to Vice against Virtue, to Folly vs Wisdom to Servility against Independance, to base and vile Intrigue against inflexible Honour and Integrity. This is saying a great deal, but it is saying little more than Congress have said upon their Records, in approving that very Conduct for which I was sacrificed. I am sometimes afraid that it is betraying the Cause of Independence and Integrity or at least the Dignity, which they ought to maintain to continue in the service. But on the other Hand I have thought, whether, it was not, more dangerously betraying this Dignity, to give its Ennemies, perhaps the compleat Tryumph which they wished for and sought but could not obtain.

You will see, the American Cause has had a signal Tryumph in this Country. If this had been the only Action of my Life, it would have been a Life well spent. I see with Smiles and Scorn, little despicable Efforts to deprive me of the Honour of any Merit, in this Negotiation, but I thank God, I have enough to shew. No Negotiation to this or any other Country was ever recorded in greater detail, as the World will one day see. The Letters I have written in this Country, are carefully preserved. The Conversations I have had are remembered. The Pamphlets, the Gazettes, in Dutch and French, will shew to Posterity, when it comes to be known what share I have had in them as it will be, it will be seen that the Spanish Ambassador expressed but the litteral Truth, when He said

"Monsieur, a frappé la plus grand Coup de tout L'Europe. Cette Reconnaisance fait un honneur infinie a Monsieur. C'est lui qui a effrayée et terrassee les Anglomanes. C'est lui qui a rempli cet nation d'Enthusiasm." &c.

Pardon, a Vanity, which however is conscious of the Truth, and which has a right to boast, since the most Sordid, Arts and the grossest Lies, are invented and propagated, by Means that would disgrace the Devil, to disguise the Truth from the sight of the World. I laugh at this, because I know it to be impossible.

Silence!

John Adams to Abigail Adams

Aug 31. 1782

All well. You will send these Papers to some Printer when you have done with them.

We have found that the only Way of guarding against Fevers is to ride. We accordingly mount our Horses every day. But the Weather through the whole Spring and most of the Summer has been very dull damp cold, very disagreable and dangerous. But shaking on Horseback guards pretty well against it.

I am going to Dinner with a Duke and a Dutchess and a Number Ambassadors and Senators, in all the Luxury of this luxurious World: but how much more luxurious it would be to me, to dine upon roast Beef with Parson Smith, Dr Tufts or Norton Q[uincy]—or upon rusticrat Potatoes with Portia—Oh! oh! hi ho hum!—and her Daughter and sons.

Abigail Adams to John Adams

My dearest Friend   Sepbr 5 1782

Your kind favours of May 14th and june 16th came to Hand last Evening; and tho I have only just time to acknowledge them; I would not omit a few lines; I have written before by this vessel; which is Bound to France. Mr Allen your old fellow traveller is a passenger on Board, and promises to be attentive to the Letters. In my other Letter I mention a serious proposal made in a former; but do not inform you of the Nature of it, fearing a rejection of my proposal and it is of so tender a Nature I could scarcly bear a refusal; yet should a refusal take place; I know it will be upon the best grounds and reasons. But your mention in your two kind favours, your wishes with more seariousness than you have ever before expresst them; leads me again to repeat my request; it is that I may come to you; with our daughter, in the spring, provided you are like to continue abroad. In my other Letter I have stated to you an arrangement of my affairs, and the person with whom I would chuse to come; I have slightly mentiond it to him; and he says he should like it exceedingly and I believe would adjust his affairs and come with me. Mr Smith is the person I mean. I mention him least my other Letter should fail.

I am the more desirious to come now I learn mr Thaxter is comeing home. I am sure you must feel a still greater want of my attention to you. I will endeavour to find out the disposition of Congress, but I have lost my intelligence from that Quarter by mr Lovels return to this state. I have very little acquaintance with any Gentleman there. Mr Jackson and mr osgood are the only two members there from this state. Mr Lowell has lately returnd. I will see him and make some inquiry; as to peace, you have my opinion in the Letter referd to by this vessel.

The acknowledgment of our Independance by the united provinces is considerd here as a most important Event, but the News papers do not anounce it to the world with that Eclat, which would have been rung from all Quarters had this Event been accomplished by a certain character. Indeed we have never received an official account of it untill now. Let me ask you Dear Friend, have you not been rather neglegent in writing to your Friends? Many difficulties you have had to encounter might have been laid open to them, and your character might have had justice done it. But Modest Merrit must be its own Reward. Bolingbrook in his political tracts observes, rather Ironically (but it is a certain fact,) that Ministers stand in as much need of publick writers, as they do of him. He adds, "in their prosperity they can no more subsist without daily praise, than the writers without daily Bread and the further the minister extends his views the more necessary are they to his support. Let him speak as contemptuously of them as he pleases, yet it will fare with his ambition; as with a lofty Tree, which cannot shoot its Branches into the Clouds unless its Root work into the dirt."

You make no mention of receiving Letters from me. You certainly must have had some by a vessel which arrived in France some time before the Fire Brand reachd Holland. She too had Letters for you.

Accept my acknowledgement for the articles sent. As the other arrived safe, I could have wished my little memorandom by the Fire Brand had reachd you before this vessel saild; but no Matter, I can dispose of them. My Luck is great I think. I know not that I have lost any adventure you have ever sent me. Nabby requests in one of her Letters a pr of paste Buckles. When your hand is in you may send a pr for me if you please. Adieu my dearest Friend. Remember that to render your situation more agreable I fear neither the Enemy or old Neptune but then you must give me full assureance of your intire approbation of my request. I cannot accept a half way invitation. To say I am happy here, I cannot but it is not and Idle curiosity that make me wish to hazard the watery Element. I much more sincerely wish your return. Could I hope for that during an other year I would endeavour to wait patiently the Event.

Once more adieu. The Messenger waits and hurrys me. Ever Ever yours

Portia

John Adams to Abigail Adams

My dearest Friend   Saturday 12 Oct. 1782 at the Hague

I believe I shall set off for Paris next Fryday. Mr Thaxter and Mr Storer will go with me.

The Treaty of Commerce and the Convention respecting recaptures were Signed on the 8 of this Month, and they go by this and Several other opportunities. I hope they will give Satisfaction.

Mr Jay writes me that on the 28 of Septr. that the Day before Mr Oswald recd a Commission to treat with the United States of America—and writes pressingly for me to come but I have not been able to dispatch the Treaty and the Loan before. I know not what to Say about Peace. It will be a troublesome Business.

Dr Franklin has been a long time much indisposed, as I lately learn with the Gout and Strangury.

Mr Dana is well and so is our son, who may perhaps return to me this Fall.

Charles minds his Book I hope. I wish John was with him, and his Father too.

I dont know whether in future Job should be reckoned "The patient Man." It Seems to me, that I have had rather more Tryals that he, and have got thro them. I am now going to Paris, to another Furnace of Affliction. Yet I am very gay, more so than usual. I fear nothing. Why should I. I had like to have Said nothing worse can happen. But this is too much. Heaven has hitherto preserved my Country and my Family.

I have Sent you an whole Piece of most excellent and beautiful Scarlet Cloth—it is very Saucy. 9 florins almost a Guinea a Dutch ell, much less than an English Yard. I have sent some blue too very good. Give your Boys a suit of Cloths if you Will or keep enough for it some Years hence and yourself and Daughter a Ridinghood in honour of the Manufactures of Haerlem. The Scarlet is "croisée" as they call it. You never saw such a Cloth. I send also a Suit of Curtains for Miss Nabby. As to her request it will be long Ad referendum. There is also a Remnant of Silk, Green. Make the best of all—but dont meddle any more with Vermont.

If We make Peace, you will see me next summer. But I have very little faith as yet. I am most inclind to think there will be another Campaign.

I am exceedingly honoured of late by the French and Spanish Ambassadors.

I never know how to close, because I can never express the Tenderness I feel.

John Adams to Abigail Adams

My dearest Friend   Paris November 8. 1782

The King of Great Britain, by a Commission under the great Seal of his Kingdom, has constituted Richard oswald Esqr his Commissioner to treat with the Ministers Plenipotentiary of the United States of America, and has given him full Powers which have been mutually exchanged. Thus G.B. has shifted suddenly about, and from persecuting Us with unrelenting Bowells, has unconditionally and unequivocally acknowledged Us a Sovereign State and independant Nation. It is surprizing that she should be the third Power to make this Acknowledgment. She has been negotiated into it, for Jay and I peremptorily refused to Speak or hear, before We were put upon an equal Foot. Franklin as usual would have taken the Advice of the C[*omte*] de V[*ergennes*] and treated, without, but nobody would join him.

As to your coming to Europe with Miss Nabby, I know not what to say. I am obliged, to differ in opinion so often from Dr Franklin and the C. de Vergennes, in Points that essentially affect the Honour Dignity and most prescious Interests of my Country, and these Personages are so little disposed to bear Contradiction, and Congress have gone so near enjoining upon me passive Obedience to them, that I do not expect to hold any Place in Europe longer than next Spring. Mr Jay is in the Same Predicament, and So will every honest Man be, that Congress can Send.

Write however to Mr Jackson in Congress and desire him candidly to tell you, whether he thinks Congress will continue me in Europe, upon Terms which I can Submitt to with honour, another Year. If he tells you as a Friend that I must Stay another Year come to me, in the Spring with your Daughter. Leave the Boys in good Hands and a good school. A Trip to Europe, for one Year may do no harm to you or your Daughter. The Artifices of the Devil will be used to get me out of the Commission for Peace. If they succeed I abandon Europe for ever, for the Blue Hills without one Instants Loss of Time or even waiting for Leave to return.

For whoever is Horse Jockeyed, I will not be. Congress means well, but is egregiously imposed upon and deceived.

Mrs Jay and Mrs Izard will be excellent Companions for you and the Miss Izards for Miss Nabby.

Abigail Adams to John Adams

My Dearest Friend   *November 13. 1782*

I have lived to see the close of the third year of our seperation. This is a Melancholy Anniversary to me; and many tender scenes arise in my Mind upon the recollecttion. I feel unable to sustain even the Idea, that it will be half that period e'er we meet again. Life is too short to have the dearest of its enjoyments curtaild. The Social feelings grow Callous by disuse and lose that pliancy of affection which Sweetens the cup of Life as we drink it. The Rational pleasures of Friendship and Society, and the still more refined Sensations to which delicate minds only are susceptable like the tender Blosom when the rude Nothern Blasts assail them shrink within, collect themselves together, deprived of the all chearing and Beamy influence of the sun. The Blosom falls, and the fruit withers and decays—but here the similitude fails—for tho lost for the present, the season returns; the Tree vegetates anew; and the Blossom again puts forth.

But alass with me; those days which are past, are gone forever: and time is hastning on that period, when I must fall, to rise no more; untill Mortality shall put on immortality, and we shall meet again, pure and unimbodied Spirits. Could we live to the age of the Antediluvians we might better support this seperation, but when three score years and ten circumscribe the Life of Man, how painfull is the Idea, that of that short space only a few years of social happiness are our allotted portion.

Perhaps I make you unhappy. No you will enter with a soothing tenderness into my feelings; I see in your Eyes the Emotions of your Heart, and hear the sigh that is wafted across the atlantick to the Bosom of portia. But the philosopher and the statesman stiffels these Emotions, and regains a firmness which arrests my pen from my Hand.

November 25

I last evening received a line from Boston, to hasten my Letter down or I should again lose an opportunity of conveyance. I was most unfortunate by the Fire Brands sailing and leaving all my Letters behind. A storm prevented my sending the day appointed, and she Saild by sun rise the Next morning. Tho my Letters were in town by nine oclock they missd. I know if she arrives how dissapointed you will feel. I received from France pr the Alxander yours bearing no date, but by the contents written about the same time, with those I received pr mr Guild. Shall I return the compliment, and tell you in a poeticall stile

> "Should at my feet the worlds great Master fall
> Himself, his world his Throne, I'd scorn them all."

No give me the Man I love. You are neither of an age or temper to be allured with the splendour of a Court—or the smiles of princessess. I never sufferd an uneasy sensation on that account. I know I have a

Right to your whole Heart, because my own never knew an other Lord—and such is my confidence in you that if you was not withheld by the strongest of all obligations those of a moral Nature, your Honour would not suffer you to abuse my confidence.

But whither am I rambling? We have not any thing in the political way worth noticeing. The Fleet of our Allies still remains with us.

Our Friend Genll W[arre]n is chosen Member of C[ongres]s. I should be loth he should for the 3d time refuse as it leaves impression upon the minds of our good citizens no ways to his advantage. But this good Man is some how or other embitterd—his *Lady* opposes if not by words, by that which has as strong an influence.

Who is there left that will sacrifice as others have done? Portia I think stands alone alone alass! in more senses than one. This vessel will convey to you the packets designd for the Fire Brand. I hope unimportant as they are, they will not be lost.

Shall I close here without a word of my voyage? I believe it is best to wait a reply before I say any thing further. Our Friends desire me to remember them to you. Your daughter your Image your Superscription desires to be affectionately rememberd to you. O! how many of the sweet domestick joys do you lose by this seperation from your Family. I have the satisfaction of seeing my children thus far in life behaveing with credit and honour. God Grant the pleasing prospect may never meet with an alloy and return to me the dear partner of my early years Rewarded for his past sacrifices by the consicousness of having been extensively usefull, not having lived to himself alone, and may the approveing voice of his Country crown his later days in peacefull retirement in the affectionate Bosom of

Portia

John Adams to Abigail Adams

My dearest Friend   Paris December 4. 1782

 Your Proposal of coming to Europe, has long and tenderly affected me. The Dangers and Inconveniences are such and an European Life would be so disagreable to you that I have suffered a great deal of Anxiety in reflecting upon it. And upon the whole, I think it will be most for the Happiness of my Family, and most for the Honour of our Country that I should come home. I have therefore this Day written to Congress a Resignation of all my Employments, and as soon as I shall receive their Acceptance of it, I will embark for America, which will be in the Spring or beginning of Summer. Our Son is now on his Journey from Petersbourg through Sweeden Denmark and Germany, and if it please God he come safe, he shall come with me, and I pray We may all meet once more, you and I never to Seperate again.
 Yours most tenderly

               J. Adams

Abigail Adams to John Adams

My dearest Friend   December 23. 1782

 I have omited writing by the last opportunity to Holland; because I had but small Faith in the designs of the owners or passengers. The vessel sails from Nantucket. Dr winship is a passenger a mr Gray and some others, and I had just written you so largely by a vessel bound to France, the General Galvaye that I had nothing New to say. There are few occurences in this Northen climate at this season of the year to divert or entertain you—and in the domestick way should I draw you the picture of my Heart, it would be what I hope you still would Love; tho it contain nothing New; the early possession you obtained there; and the absolute power you have ever mantaind over it; leaves not the smallest space unoccupied. I look back to the early days of our acquaintance; and Friendship, as to the days of Love and Innocence; and with an undiscribable pleasure I have seen near a score of years roll over our Heads, with an affection heightned and improved by time. Nor have the dreary years of absence in the smallest degree Effaced from my mind the Image of the dear untittled man to whom I gave my Heart. I cannot sometimes refrain considering the Honours with which he is invested as badges of my unhappiness. The unbounded confidence I have in your attachment to me, and the dear pledges of our affection, has soothed the solitary hour, and renderd your absence more supportable; for had I have loved you with the same affection it must have been misiry to have doubted. Yet a cruel world too often injures my feelings, by wondering how a person possesst of domestick attachments can sacrifice them by absenting himself *for years.*

If you had known said a person to me the other day; that mr A.s would have remained so long abroad; would you have consented that he should have gone? I recollected myself a moment, and then spoke the real dictates of my Heart. If I had known sir that mr A. could have affected what he has done; I would not only have submitted to the absence I have endured; painfull as it has been; but I would not have opposed it, even tho 3 years more should be added to the Number, which Heaven avert! I feel a pleasure in being able to sacrifice my selfish passions to the general good, and in imitating the example which has taught me to consider myself and family, but as the small dust of the balance when compaired with the great community.

Your daughter most sincerely regrets your absence. She sees me support it, yet thinks she could not imitate either parent in the disinterested motives which actuate them. She has had a strong desire to encounter the dangers of the sea to visit you. I however am not without a suspicion that she may loose her realish for a voyage by spring. The tranquility of mine and my dear sisters family is in a great measure restored to us, since the recovery of our worthy Friend and Brother. We had a most melancholy summer. The young folks of the two families together with those of col Q[*uinc*]ys and genll W[*arre*]n preserve a great Intimacy, and as they wish for but few connections in the Beau

Mond, it is not to be wonderd at that they are fond of each others company. We have an agreable young Gentleman by the Name of Robbins who keeps our little school, son to the Revd mr Robbins of plimouth. And we have in the little circle an other gentleman who has opend an office in Town, for about nine months past, and boarded in mr Cranch family. His Father you knew. His Name is Tyler. He studied Law upon his comeing out of colledge with mr dana, but when mr dana went to congress he finished his studies with mr Angers Loosing his Father young and having a very pretty patrimony left him, possessing a sprightly fancy a warm imagination and an agreable person, he was rather negligent in persueing his buisness in the way of his profession; and dissipated two or 3 years of his Life and too much of his fortune for to reflect upon with pleasure; all of which he now laments but cannot recall. At 23 the time when he took the resolution of comeing to B[osto]n, and withdrawing from a too numerous acquaintance; he resolved to persue his studies; and his Buisness; and save his remaining fortune which sufferd much more from the paper currency than any other cause; so that out of 17 thousand pounds which fell to his share; he cannot now realize more than half that sum; as he told me a few days past. His Mamma is in possession of a large Estate and he is a very favorite child. When he proposed comeing to settle here he met with but little encouragement, but he was determined upon the trial. He has succeeded beyond expectation. He has popular talants, and as his behaviour has been unexceptionable since his residence in Town; in concequence of which his Buisness daily increases—he cannot fail making a distinguished figure in his profession if he Steadily persues it. I am not acquainted with any young Gentleman whose attainments in literature are equal to his, who judges with greater accuracy or discovers a more Delicate and refined taste. I have frequently looked upon him with the Idea that you would have taken much pleasure in such a pupil. I wish I was as well assured that you would be equally pleased with him in an other character, for such I apprehend are his distant hopes. I early saw that he was possest with powerfull attractions—and as he obtain and deserved, I believe the character of a gay; tho not a criminal youth, I thought it prudent to keep as great a reserve as possible. In this I was seconded by the discreet conduct of a daughter, who is happy in not possessing all her Mothers sensibility. Yet I see a growing attachment in him stimulated by that very reserve. I feel the want of your presence and advise. I think I know your sentiments so well that the merit of a gentleman will be your first consideration, and I have made every inquiry which I could with decency; and without discloseing my motives. Even in his most dissipated state he always applied his mornings to Study; by which means he has stored his mind with a fund of usefull knowledge. I know not a young fellow upon the stage whose language is so pure—or whose natural disposition is more agreable. His days are devoted to his office, his Evenings of late to my fire side. His attachment is too obvious to escape notice. I do not think the Lady wholy indifferent; yet her reserve and apparent coldness is such that I know he is in misirable doubt. Some conversation one Evening of late took place which led me to write him a Billet and tell him, that at least it admitted a possibility that I might quit this country in the spring; that I never would go abroad without my daughter, and if I did go, I wished to carry her with a mind unattached, besides I could have but one voice; and for that I held myself accountable to you; that he was not yet Established in Buisness sufficient to think of a connection with any one; to which I received this answer.

Madam

I have made an exertion to answer your Billet. I can only say that the second impulse in my Breast is my Love and respect for you; and it is the foible of my nature to be the machine of those I Love and venerate. Do with me as seemeth good unto thee. I can safely trust my dearest fondest wishes and persuits in the hands of a Friend that can feel, that knows my situation and her designs. If reason pleads against me, you will do well to hestitate. If Friendship and reason unite I shall be happy—only say I shall be happy when *I deserve;* and it shall be my every exertion to augment my merit; and this you may be assured of, whether I am blessed in my wishes or not, I will endeavour to be a character that you shall not Blush once to have entertaind an Esteem for.

Yours respectfully &c.

What ought I to say? I feel too powerfull a pleader within my own heart and too well recollect the Love I bore to the object of my early affections to forbid him to hope. I feel a regard for him upon an account you will smile at. I fancy I see in him sentiments opinions and actions which endeared to me the best of Friends. Suffer me to draw you from the depths of politicks to endearing family scenes. I know you cannot fail being peculiarly interested in the present. I inclose you a little paper which tho trifling in itself, may serve to shew you the truth of my observations. The other day the gentleman I have been speaking of; had a difficult writ to draw. He requested the favour of looking into your Book of forms, which I readily granted; in the Evening when he returned me the key he put in to my hands a paper which I could not tell what to make of; untill he exclaimed "O! Madam Madam, I have new hopes that I shall one day become worthy your regard. What a picture have I caught of my own Heart, my resolutions my designs! I could not refrain breaking out into a Rhapsody. I found this coppy of a Letter in a pamphlet with observations upon the study of the Law and many excellent remarks; you will I hope forgive the theft, when I deliver the paper to you; and you find how much benifit I shall derive from it." I daily see that he will win the affections of a fine Majestick Girl who has as much dignity as a princess. She is handsome, but not Beautifull. No air of levity ever accompanies either her words or actions. Should she be caught by a tender passion, sufficient to remove a little of her natural reserve and soften her form and manners, she will be a still more pleasing character. Her mind is daily improveing, and she gathers new taste for literature perhaps for its appearing in a more pleasing form to her. If I can procure a little ode which accompanied an ice Heart I will inclose it to you.

It is now my dear Friend a long long time since I had a line from you. The Fate of Gibralter leads me to fear that a peace is far distant, and that I shall not see you—God only knows when; I shall say little about my former request, not that my desire is less, but before this can reach you tis probable I may receive your opinion. If in favour of my comeing to you; I shall have no occasion to urge it further. If against it, I would not embarrass you; by again requesting it. I will endeavour to set down, and consider it as the portion alloted me. My dear sons are well their application and improvements go hand in hand. Our Friends all desire to be rememberd. The Fleet of our allies expect to sail daily but where destined we know not; a great harmony has subsisted between them and the Americans ever since their residence here. I wish to write to mr T[*haxte*]r but fear I shall not have time. Mrs d[*an*]a and children are well. The judge has been very sick of a fever but I believe is better. This Letter is to go by the Iris which sails with the Fleet. I hope it will reach you in safety. If it should fall into the hands of an Enemy, I hope they will be kind enough to distroy it; as I would not wish to see such a family picture in print; adieu my dear Friend. Why is it that I hear so seldom from my dear John; but one Letter have I ever received from him since he arrived in petersburgh? I wrote him by the last opportunity. Ever remember me as I do you; with all the tenderness which it is possible for one object to feel for an other; which no time can obliterate no distance alter, but which is always the same in the Bosom of

Portia

John Adams to Abigail Adams

My dearest Friend   Paris Jan. 22. 1783

The Preliminaries of Peace and an Armistice, were Signed at Versailles on the 20 and on the 21. We went again to pay our Respects to the King and Royal Family upon the occasion. Mr Jay was gone upon a little Excursion to Normandie and Mr Laurens was gone to Bath, both for their health, so that the signature was made by Mr Franklin and me. I want an Excursion too.

Thus drops the Curtain upon this mighty Trajedy. It has unravelled itself happily for Us—and Heaven be praised. Some of our dearest Interests have been saved, thro many dangers. I have no News from my son, since the 8th. december, when he was at Stockholm, but hope every hour to hear of his Arrival at the Hague.

I hope to receive the Acceptance of my Resignation So as to come home in the Spring ships.

I had written thus far when yours of 23 decr was brought in. Its Contents have awakened all my sensibility, and shew in a stronger Light than ever the Necessity of my coming home. I confess I dont like the Subject at all. My Child is too young for such Thoughts, and I dont like your Word "Dissipation" at all. I dont know wt it means it may mean every Thing. There is not Modesty and Diffidence enough in the Traits you Send me. My Child is a Model, as you represent her and as I know her, and is not to be the Prise, I hope of any, even reformed Rake. A Lawyer would be my Choice, but it must be a Lawyer who spends his Midnights as well as Evenings at his Age over his Books not at any Ladys Fire side. I Should have thought you had seen enough to be more upon your Guard than to write Billets upon such a subject to such a youth. A Youth who has been giddy enough to Spend his Fortune or half his Fortune in Gaieties, is not the Youth for me, Let his Person Family, Connections and Taste for Poetry be what they will. I am not looking out for a Poet, nor a Professor of belle Letters.

In the Name of all that is tender dont criticise Your Daughter for those qualities which are her greatest Glory her Reserve, and her Prudence which I am amazed to hear you call Want of Sensibility. The more Silent She is in Company, the better for me in exact Proportion and I would have this observed as a Rule by the Mother as well as the Daughter.

You know moreover or ought to know my utter Inability to do any Thing for my Children, and you know the long dependence of young Gentlemen of the most promising Talents and obstinate Industry, at the Bar. My Children will have nothing but their Liberty and the Right to catch Fish, *on* the Banks of Newfoundland. This is all the Fortune that I have been able to make for myself or them.

I know not however, enough of this subject to decide any Thing. Is he a Speaker at the Bar? If not he will never be any Thing. But above all I positively forbid, any Connection between my Daughter and any Youth upon Earth, who does not totally eradicate every Taste for Gaiety and Expence. I never knew one who had it and indulged it, but what was made a Rascall by it, sooner or later.

This Youth has had a Brother in Europe, and a detestible Specimen he exhibited. Their Father had not all those nice sentiments which I wish, although an Honourable Man.

I think he and you have both advanced too fast, and I should advise both to retreat. Your Family as well as mine have had too much Cause to rue, the Qualities which by your own Account have been in him. And if they were ever in him they are not yet out.

This is too Serious a Subject, to equivocate about. I dont like this method of Courting Mothers. There is something too fantastical and affected in all this Business for me. It is not nature, modest virtuous noble nature. The Simplicity of Nature is the best Rule with me to judge of every Thing, in Love as well as state and War.

This is all between you and me.

I would give the World to be with you Tomorrow. But there is a vast Ocean—No Ennemies—But I have not yet Leave from my Masters. I dont love to go home in a Miff, Pet or Passion nor with an ill Grace, but I hope Soon to have leave. I can never Stay in Holland—the Air of that Country chills every drop of Blood in My Veins. If I were to stay in Europe another Year I would insist upon your coming with your daughter but this is not to be and I will come home to you.

Adieu ah ah Adieu.

John Adams to Abigail Adams

My dearest Friend   Paris March 28. 1783

On the 30 Nov. our Peace was Signed. On the 28. March We dont know that you have Yet heard of it. A Packet Should have been Sent off. I have not yet received the Ratification of my Dutch Treaty. I know not when I Shall be able to embark for home. If I receive the Acceptance of my Resignation, I Shall embark in the first ship, the first good ship I mean, for I love you too well, to venture myself in a bad one and I love my own Ease to well to go in a very Small one.

I am Sometimes half afraid, that those Persons who procured the Revocation of my Commission to King George, may be afraid I shall do them more harm in America, than in England, and therefore of two Evils to choose the least and manoeuvre to get me sent to London. By several Coaxing hints of that Kind, which have been written to me and given me in Conversation, from Persons who I know are employed to do it, I fancy that Something of that is in Contemplation. There is another Motive too—they begin to dread the Appointment of some others whom they like less than me. I tremble when I think of such a Thing as going to London. If I were to receive orders of that sort, it would be a dull day to me. No Swiss ever longed for home than I do. I Shall forever be a dull Man in Europe. I cannot bear the Thought of transporting my Family to Europe. It would be the Ruin of my Children forever. And I cannot bear the Thought of living longer Seperate from them. Our foreign Affairs, are like to be in future as they have been in times past an eternal Scæne of Faction. The fluctuation of Councils at Philadelphia have encouraged it, and even good Men Seem to be Seized with the Spirit of it.

The definitive Treaty is yet delayed, and will be for any Thing I can see till Mid Summer. It may however be signed in a few Weeks. If it should be signed I could go home with the Dutch Ambassador, in a Frigate which will sail from the Texel in June. But So many Points are uncertain, that I cannot determine on any thing. Dont think of coming to Europe however, unless you should receive a further desire from me, which is not at all probable. My present Expectations are to pay my Respects to you, at Braintree, before Mid summer.

My dear Daughters happiness employs my Thoughts night and Day. Dont let her form any Connections with any one, who is not devoted entirely to study and to Business—to honour and Virtue. If there is a Trait of Frivolity and Dissipation left, I pray that She may renounce it, forever. I ask not Fortune nor Favour for mine, but Prudence, Talents and Labour. She may go with my Consent whenever she can find enough of these.

My Son, has been another Source of Distress to me. The terrible Weather has made his Journey from Petersbourg very long. But I have a Letter from him at Hamborough the 14th. and hope he is at the Hague by this day. I am much relieved on his Account. My Charles and Thomas how are they? Fine Boys I dare Say? Let them take Care how they behave if they desire their Fathers approbation. My Mother and your Father enjoy I hope a good Share of Health and Spirits. Mr Cranch's Health is perfectly restored I hope, and Uncle Quincy and Dr Tufts as good and as happy as ever. Why should not my Lot in Life be as easy as theirs? So it would have been if I had been as wise as they and staid at home as they do. But where would have been our Cod and Haddock, our Bever skins Deer skins and Pine Trees? Alass all lost, perhaps. Indeed I firmly believe so, in a good Conscience. I cannot therefore repent of all my fatigues, Cares, Losses, Escapes, anxious Days and Sleepless nights.

Nothing in Life ever cost me so much Sleep, or made me so many grey Hairs, as the Anxiety, I have Suffered for these Three Years on the Score of these Objects. No body knows of it: Nobody cares for it. But I shall be rewarded for it, in Heaven I hope. Where Mayhew, and Thatcher and Warren are rewarded I hope, none of whom however were permitted to suffer so much. They were taken away from the Evil to come.

I have one favour for you to ask of Mr Adams the President of the senate. It is that he would make a compleat Collection of his Writings and publish them in Volumes. I know of no greater service that could be rendered to the Rights of Mankind. At least that he would give you a List of them. They comprize a Period of forty Years. And although they would not find so many Rakes for Purchasers, as the Writings of Voltaire they would do infinitely more good to mankind especially in our rising Empire. There Posterity will find a Mass of Principles, and Reasonings, Suitable for them and for all good Men. The Copy, I fancy would Sell to Advantage in Europe.

Yours most affectintly and eternally.

Abigail Adams to John Adams

My dearest Friend   April 28th 1783

At length an opportunity offers after a space of near five Months, of again writing to you. Not a vessel from any port in this state has sailed since Jan'ry, by which I could directly convey you a line. I have written twice by way of Virgina, but fear they will never reach you: from you I have lately received several Letters containing the most pleasing intelligence.

"Peace o'er the world her olive Branch extends. Hail! Goddess heavenly bright profuse of joy, and pregnant with delight." The Garb of this favorite of America, is woven of an admirable texture and proves the great skill, wisdom, and abilities, of the Master workmen. It was not fabricated in the Loom of France, nor are the materials english, but they are the product of our own American soil, raised and Nurtured, not by the gentle showers of Heaven, but by the hard Labour and indefatigable industery and firmness of her Sons, and waterd by the Blood of many of them. May its duration be in proportion to its value, and like the Mantle of the prophet descend with blessings to generations yet to come.

And may you my dearest Friend, return to your much loved solitude with the pleasing reflextion of having contributed to the happiness of Millions.

We have not yet received any account of the signing the definitive Treaty, so that no publick rejoiceings have taken place as yet. The 5th article in the Treaty has raised the old spirit against the Tories to such a height that it would be at the risk of their lives should they venture here: it may subside after a while, but I Question whether any state in the union will admit them even for 12 Months. What then would have been the concequence if compensation had been granted them?

Your journal has afforded me and your Friends much pleasure and amusement. You will learn, perhaps from Congress that the journal, you meant for mr Jackson; was by some mistake enclosed to the Minister for foreign affairs; and concequently came before Congress with other publick papers. The Massachussets Delegates applied for it, but were refused it. Mr Jackson was kind enough to wait upon me, and shew me your Letter to him, and the other papers inclosed, and I communicated the journal to him. Mr Higginson writes that it was moved in congress by Hamilton of Virginia and wilson of Pensilvana to censure their ministers, for Departing from their duty in not adhering to their instructions, and for *giving offence* to the Court of France, by *distrusting their Friendship;* they however could not carry their point. It was said the instruction alluded was founded upon Reciprocity, and that the C.V [*Comte de Vergennes*] had not acted upon that principal. When these Gentry found that it would not be considerd in the Light in which they wished, they gave out that if no more was said upon that subject, the other would drop. This is all I have been able to collect— my intelligence is very imperfect since mr L[*ovel*]l left congress mr G[*e*]r[*ry*] I believe is determined to go again. I shall then have a Friend and correspondent who will keep me informed. Upon receiving a Letter from you in which you desire me to come to you should you be longer detained abroad, I took the Liberty of writing to dr Lee, requesting him to give me the earliest intelligence respecting the acceptance of your resignation. I do not think it will be accepted, by what I have already learnt; if it should not; I shall still feel undetermined what to do. From many of your Letters I was led to suppose you would not return without permission; yet I do not imagine the bare renewal of a former commission would induce you to tarry. I shall not run the risk unless you are appointed minister at the Court of Britain. Mr Smith is waiting for me to hear from congress. He means to go whether I do or not, but if I do he will take Charge of every thing respecting my voyage. Our two sons together with mr Cranch's, are placed in the family of mr Shaw. He had one young gentleman before whom he offers this year for Colledg. I doubt not he will contribute every thing in his power towards their instruction and improvement. I last evening received Letters from them, and they appear to be very contented and happy. With Regard to some domestick affairs which I wrote you about last winter, certain reasons have prevented their proceeding any further—and perhaps it will never again be renewed. I wished to have told you so sooner, but it has not been in my power. Our Friends are all well and desire to be affectionately rememberd to you. Where is our son, I hear no more of him than if he was out of the world. You wrote me in yours of december 4th that he was upon his journey to you, but I have never heard of his arrival.

Need I add how earnestly I long for the day when Heaven will again bless us in the society of each other. Whether upon European or American ground is yet in the Book of uncertainty, but to feel intirely happy and easy, I believe it must be in our own Republican cottage; with the simplicity which has ever distinguished it—and your ever affectionate

Portia

My dearest Friend   29 April

I last Evening received yours of Febry 18th in which you are explicit with Regard to your return. I shall therefore let Congress renew or create what commission they please, at least wait your further direction tho you should be induced to tarry abroad. I have taken no step as yet with regard to comeing out, except writing to dr Lee as mentiond before. Heaven send you safe to your ever affectionate

Portia

John Adams to Abigail Adams

June 9. [*1783*]

What would I not give for an Arrival from America or for Advice from London what the Ministry intend to do? Mr Hartley is now here but We advance slowly to the definitive Treaty. I can now have no hopes of Seeing you before late in the Fall. If the Acceptance of my Resignation arrives, as I expect, and We finish the Peace, as soon as I can reasonably hope, I shall not now be able to embark before October. The affairs of the World have little Complaisance for my Happiness, or yours, but it is not worth our while to be impatient, because it will do us no good. I am astonished however that We have nothing from Congress nor from you.

If you and your Daughter were with me, I could keep up my Spirits, but idly and insipidly as I pass my time, I am weary worn and disgusted to death. I had rather chop Wood, dig Ditches, and make fence upon my poor little farm. Alass! poor Farm and poorer Family what have you lost, that your Country might be free and that others might catch fish and hunt Deers and Bevers at their Ease?

There will be as few of the "Tears of Gratitude" or "the Smiles of Admiration," or the "Sighs of Pity" for Us, as for the Army. But all this should not hinder me from going over the same Scænes again upon the same Occasion, Scænes which I would not encounter for all the Wealth Pomp and Powers of the World.

Boys! if you ever Say one Word, or utter one Complaint I will disinherit you. Work you Rogues and be free. You will never have so hard Work to do as Papa has had.

Daughter! Get you an honest Man for a Husband, and keep him honest. No matter whether he is rich, provided he be independent. Regard the Honour and moral Character of the Man more than all other Circumstances. Think of no other Greatness but that of the soul, no other Riches but those of the Heart. An honest, Sensible humane Man, above all the Littlenesses of Vanity, and Extravagances of Imagination, labouring to do good rather than be rich to be usefull rather than make a show, living in a modest Simplicity clearly within his Means and free from Debts or Obligations, is really the most respectable Man in Society, makes himself and all about him the most happy.

I long to see my dear John, as much as the Rest, but he is well at the Hague and I cannot go to him nor do I think it prudent to bring him to Paris.

I have accomplished a Correspondence between the Royal society of Medicine here, and the Rebublican one at Boston at the Desire of Dr Tufts but have not yet found a carefull Hand to send the Diploma. Adieu Adieu Adieu.

Through the spring and summer of 1783, John waited patiently to sign the definitive peace treaty with Britain. The preliminary peace treaty had already been signed and John had tendered his resignation to Congress—without receiving a response. By fall he believed he had a new responsibility to negotiate a commercial treaty with Great Britain, but Congress's exact determination on this point was unclear and the British were uninterested in any event. John made the best of his time, traveling with John Quincy and negotiating a new loan with the Dutch, but the uncertainty complicated Abigail's decision as to whether to join John in Europe.

Abigail Adams to John Adams

My Dearest Friend   Braintree June 20th 1783

If I was certain I should welcome you to your native Land in the course of the summer, I should not regret mr Smiths going abroad with out me. Should it be otherways, should you still be detained abroad—I must submit, satisfied that you judge best, and that you would not subject me to so heavy a dissapointment, or yourself to so severe a mortification as I flatter myself it would be, but for the general good; a European life would, you say, be the ruin of our Children. If so, I should be as loth as you, to hazard their embibeing sentiments and opinions which might make them unhappy in a sphere of Life which tis probable they must fill, not by indulging in Luxeries for which tis more than possible they might contract a taste and inclination, but in studious and Labourious persuits.

You have before this day, received the joint commission for forming a commercial treaty with Britain. I am at a loss to determine whether you will consider yourself so bound by it, as to tarry longer abroad. Perhaps there has been no juncture in the publick affairs of our country; not even in the hour, of our deepest distress, when able statesmen and wise Counsellors were more wanted than at the present day. Peace abroad leaves us at leisure to look into our own domestick affairs. Altho upon an Estimate of our National debt, it appears but as the small dust of the balance, when compared to the object we have obtained, and the benifits we have secured. Yet the Restless spirit of man will not be restrained; and we have reason to fear that Domestick Jars and confusions, will take place, of foreign contentions and devastations. Congress have Commuted with the Army by engageing to them 5 years pay, in lieu of half pay for Life. With Security for this they will disband contented. But our wise Legislators are about disputing the power of Congress to do either, without considering their hands in the mouth of the Lion, and if the just and necessary food is not supplied, the outragious animal may become so ferocious as to spread horrour, and devastation, or an other Theseus may arise who by his reputation, and exploits of valour, whose personal character and universal popularity, may distroy our Amphictionic system and subjugate our infant republick, to Monarchical domination.

Our House of Representitives is this year composed of more than a hundred New members, some of whom no doubt are good Men. Near all the able and skillfull Members who composed the last House have lost their seats, by voting for the return of mr Brattle; notwithstanding the strongest evidence in his favour, and the many proofs which were produced of his Friendly conduct towards America. For this crime, our worthy Friend mr Cranch was droped by this Town. The Senate is a loser this year by the resignation of some excellent Members. We have in this state an impost of 5 prcent, and an excise act, whilst the Neighbouring states have neither. Foreigners finding this the case, cary their Cargoes to other states. At this the Merchant grumbles, the Farmer groans with his taxes, and the Mechanick for want of employ. Heaven Avert that like the Greek Republicks we should by civil discension weaken our power, and crush our rising greatness; that the Blood of our citizens, should be shed in vain; and the labour, and toil, of our statesmen; be finally bafled; through niggardly parsimony; Lavish prodigality; or Ignorance of our real Interest. We want a soloman in wisdom, to guide and conduct this great people; at this critical acre, when the counsels which are taken, and the measures which are persued; will mark our future Character either with honour, and Fame, or disgrace, and infamy; in adversity, we have conducted with prudence and magninimity. Heaven forbid, that we should grow giddy with prosperity, or the height to which we have soared, render a fall conspicuously fatal.

Thus far I had written when your welcome favour of March 28th reached me; I was not dissapointed in finding you uncertain with regard to the time of your return; should the appointment which I fear; and you have hinted at; take place, it would indeed be a dull day to me. I have not a wish to join in a scene of Life so different from that in which I have been educated; and in which my early and I must suppose, happier days, have been spent; curiosity satisfied and I should sigh for tranquil scenes.

> "And wish that Heaven had left me still
> The whisp'ring zephyr, and the purling rill?"

Well orderd home is my chief delight, and the affectionate domestick wife with the Relative Duties which accompany that character my highest ambition. It was the disinterested wish of sacrificeing my personal feelings to the publick utility, which first led me to think of unprotectedly hazarding a voyage. I say unprotectedly for so I consider every lady who is not accompanied by her Husband. This objection could only be surmounted by the earnest wish I had to soften those toils which were not to be dispenced with, and if the publick welfare required your Labours and exertions abroad, I flatterd myself, that if I could be with you, it might be in my power to contribute to your happiness and pleasure, but the day is now arrived, when with honour and well earned Fame, you may return to your native land—when I cannot any longer consider it as my duty to submit to a further seperation, and when it appears necessary that those abilities which have crownd you with Laurels abroad, should be exerted at home for the publick safety. I do not wish you to accept an Embassy to england, should you be appointed. This little Cottage has more Heart felt satisfaction for you than the most Brilliant Court can afford, the pure and undiminished tenderness of weded Love, the filial affection of a daughter who will never act contrary to the advise of a Father, or give pain to the Maternal Heart. Be assured that she will never make a choice without your approbation which I know she considers as Essential to her happiness. That she has a partiality I know, and believe, but that she has submitted her opinion to the advise of her Friends, and relinquished the Idea of a connection upon principal, of prudence and duty, I can with equal truth assure you. Yet nothing unbecomeing the Character which I first entertaind has ever appeard in this young Gentleman since his residence in this Town, and he now visits in this family with the freedom of an acquaintance, tho not with the intimacy of a nearer connection. It was the request of Emelia who has conducted with the greatest prudence, that she might be permitted to see and treat this Gentleman as an acquaintance whom she valued. "Why said she should I treat a Gentleman who has done nothing to forfeit my Esteem, with neglect or contempt, merely because the word have said, that he entertained a preferable regard for me? If his foibles are to be treated with more severity than the vices of others, and I submit my judgment and opinion to the disapprobation of others in a point which so nearly concerns me, I wish to be left at liberty to act in other respects with becomeing decency." And she does and has conducted so as to meet with the approbation of all her Friends. She has conquerd herself. An extract from a little poetick peice which Some months ago fell into my Hands may give you some Idea of the situation of this matter. You will tell me you do not want a poet, but if there is a mind otherways well furnished, you would have no objection to its being a mere amusement. You ask me if this Gentleman is a speaker at the Bar. He attends plimouth Court and has spoke there. He is not yet sworn in to the superiour court, but is proposed to be sworn in the Next court with his cotemporaries. I cannot say what he will make, but those who most intimately know him, say he has talants to make what he pleases, and fluency to become a good Speaker. His buisness encreases here, and I know nothing but what he is well esteemed. His temper and disposition appear to be good. The family in which he boards find no fault with his conduct. He is Regular in his liveing, keeps no company with Gay companions, seeks no amusement but in the society of two or 3 families in Town, never goes to Boston but when Buisness calls him there. If he has been the Gay thoughtless young fellow which he is said to have been and which I believe he was, he has at least practised one year of reformation. Many more will be necessary to Establish him in the world, whether he will make the man of worth and steadiness time must determine.

Our two sons are placed under the care, and in the family of mr Shaw. They have been near 3 months absent from me. This week with my daughter and mr Smith to accompany us I go to see them. My dear John, where is he? I long to see him. I have been very anxious about him. Such a winter journey. I hope he is with you. I want to receive a Letter from him. If you should continue abroad untill fall I should be glad you would make me a small remittance, goods will not answer. We are glutted with them. I do not wish for any thing more, than I want for my family use. In this way few peices of Irish linnen and a peice of Russia sheeting together with 2 green silk umbrellas I should be glad of as soon as convenient. If you should have an opportunity from France to send me 3 Marsels cotton and silk quilts I should be very glad; they are like the Jacket patterns you sent me by charles. I want a white, a Blew and a pink. Mr dana sent 3 to mrs dana; I think she said mr Bonfeild procured them. I mentiond in a former Letter a few other articles. I am going to marry one of my family, to a young fellow whom you Liberated from jail, a son of capt Newcombs, to the Jane Glover who has lived 7 years with me and as she never would receive any wages from me I think myself obligated to find her necessaries for house keeping. I have been buying land, and my last adventure came to so poor a market, that I am quite broke. My Letter is an unreasonable long one, yet I may take an other sheet of paper—not to night however. I will bid you good by.

I seal this least mr Smith should sail before I return, mean to write more have a Letter for mr T[*haxter*].

John Adams to Abigail Adams

My dearest Friend   Paris July 17. 1783

No Letter from you, yet. I believe I shall Set off Tomorrow or next day, for the Hague, and Shall bring John with me back to Paris in about 3 Weeks. There will be an Interval, before the Signature of the definitive Treaty, and Several publick Concerns oblige me to go to the Hague for a Short time. When I get my Son with me, I shall be ready to go to any Place, where I may embark for home, as soon as I get Leave.

I am weary beyond all Expression of waiting in this State of Uncertainty about every Thing. It is at this Moment as uncertain as it was six months ago when the definitive Treaty will be signed. Mr Laurens and Mr Dana have leave to go home. Mr Danas is upon a Condition, however, which is not yet fullfilled so that he will not go home for some time. Dr Franklin Says he is determined to go home, and Mr Jay talks of going next Spring.

In Short it is a terrible Life We lead. It wearies out the Patience of Job, and affects the health of Us all.

Mr Smith writes me that Charles and Thomas are gone or were going to Haverhill, under the Care of Mr Shaw. I approve of this very much. They will learn no Evil there. With them at Haveril, yourself and Miss Nabby and Mr John with me, I could bear to live in Europe another Year or two. But I cannot live much longer without my Wife and Daughter and I will not. I want two Nurses at least: and I wont have any, at least female ones but my Wife and Daughter.

I tremble too, least a Voyage and change of Climate should alter your health. I dare not wish you in holland for there my Charles, Mr Thaxter, My servants and myself were forever Sick. I am half a Mind to come home with the definitive Treaty, and then if Congress dismiss me, well. If they send me back again I can take you and your Daughter with me. However I can determine upon nothing. I am now afraid We shall not meet till next Spring. I hear, by Word of Mouth that Congress will not determine upon my Resignation till they have recd the definitive Treaty. Heaven know when this will be. It will be a Mercy to Us all, if they let me come home: for if you and your Daughter come to Europe you will get into your female Imaginations, fantastical Ideas that will never wear out, and will Spoil you both.

The Question is whether it is possible for a Lady, to be once accustomed to the Dress, Shew &c of Europe, without having her head turned by it? This is an awfull Problem. If you cannot be Mistress enough of yourself, and be answerable for your Daughter, that you can put on and put off these Fooleries like real Philosophers, I advise you never to come to Europe, but order your husband home, for this you may depend on, your Residence in Europe will be as uncertain as the Wind. It cannot be depended on for one Year no nor for Six Months. You have Seen two or three very Striking Instances of the Precariousness, of Congress Commissions, in my first, second and third. The Bread that is earned on a Farm is simple but sure. That which depends upon Politicks is as uncertain as they.

You know your Man. He will never be a Slave. He will never cringe. He will never accommodate his Principles, sentiments or Systems, to keep a Place, or to get a Place, no nor to please his Daughter, or his Wife. He will never depart from his Honour, his Duty, no nor his honest Pride for Coaches, Tables, Gold Power or Glory. Take the Consequences then. Take a Voyage to Europe if the Case should so happen that I shall write to you to come live three Months. Let your Man See something in a different Light from his Masters, and give them offence, be recalled. You and he return back to the Blue Hills, to live upon a Farm. Very good. Let Lyars and slanderers without any of this, write Reports and nourish Factions behind his back, and the same Effect is produced. I repeat it. It will be a Blessing to Us all, if I am permitted to return. Be cautious my Friend, how you Speak upon these subjects. I know that Congress are bound, from regard to their own honour as well as mine, to send me to England, but it is the most difficult Mission in the Universe, and the most desperate, there is no Reputation to be got by it, but a great deal to be lost. It is the most expensive and extravagant Place in Europe, and all that would be allowed would not enable one to live, as a set of insolent Spenthrifts would demand. I am quite content to come home and go to Farming, be a select Man, and owe no Man any Thing but good Will. There I can get a little health and teach my Boys to be Lawyers.

I hope New York and Penobscot will be evacuated before this reaches you. That will be some Comfort. You must pray Mr Storer or your Unkle Smith to send your Letters to me, by Way of New York Philadelphia, London Bilbao, Holland France or any way. If they inclose them to any of their Friends in London they will get to me.

Farewell, my dearest Friend Farewell.

John Adams to Abigail Adams

My dearest Friend   Paris September 7. 1783

This Morning for the first Time, was delivered me the Resolution of Congress of the first of May, that a Commission and Instructions Should be made Out, to Me, Dr Franklin and Mr Jay to make a Treaty of Commerce with Great Britain. If this Intelligence had been Sent Us by Barney, who sailed from Philadelphia a Month after, the 1st of May, and has now been Sailed from hence on his return home above a Month it would have Saved me and others much Anxiety. I am now even at a Loss. It is of great Importance that such a Treaty Should be well made. The Loan in Holland must be attended to, and when the present one is full, another must be opened, which cannot be done but by me or my Successor. There are other Things too to be done in Europe of great Importance. Mr Laurens has Leave to go home, and Mr Dana is gone so that there remain in service only Mr Franklin Mr Jay and myself. In these Circumstances I must stay another Winter. I cannot justify going home. But what shall I do for Want of my Family. By what I hear, I think Congress will give us all Leave to come home in the Spring. Will you come to me this fall and go home with me in the Spring? If you will, come with my dear Nabby, leaving the two Boys at Mr Shaws, and the House and Place under the Care of your Father Uncle Quincy or Dr Tufts, or Mr Cranch. This Letter may reach you by the middle of October, and in November you may embark, and a Passage in November, or all December will be a good Season. You may embark for London, Amsterdam, or any Port in France. On your Arrival, you will find Friends enough. The Moment I hear of it, I will fly with Post Horses to receive you at least, and if the Ballon, Should be carried to such Perfection in the meantime as to give Mankind the safe navigation of the Air, I will fly in one of them at the Rate of thirty Knots an hour. This is my Sincere Wish, although the Expence will be considerable, the Trouble to you great and you will probably have to return with me in the Spring. I am so unhappy without you that I wish you would come at all Events. You must bring with you at least one Maid and one Man servant.

I must however leave it with your Judgment, you know better than I the real Intentions at Philadelphia, and can determine better than I whether it will be more prudent to wait untill the Spring. I am determind to be with you in America or have you with me in Europe, as soon as it can be accomplished consistent with private Prudence and the publick Good. I am told that Congress intend to recall Us all, as soon as a few affairs are finished. If this should be the Case, all will be well. I shall go home with infinite Pleasure. But it may be longer than you think of, before all their necessary affairs will be dispatched. The Treaty of Commerce with G. B. must take Time. A Treaty will be wanted with Portugal and Denmark if not with the Emperor and Empress. If you come to Europe this Fall, in my Opinion you will be glad to go home in the Spring. If you come in the Spring you will wish to return the next fall. I am sure I shall, but Six months of your Company is worth to me, all the Expences and Trouble of the Voyage.

This Resolution of Congress deserves my Gratitude; it is highly honourable to me, and restores me, my Feelings, which a former Proceeding had taken away. I am now perfectly content to be recalled whenever they think fit, or to stay in Europe, untill this Business is finished, provided you will come and live with me. We may spend our Time together in Paris London or the Hague, for 6 or 12 Months as the Public Business may call me and then return to our Cottage, with contented Minds. It would be more agreable to my Inclinations to get home and endeavour to get myself and Children into a Settled Way, but I think it is more necessary for the Publick that I should stay in Europe, untill this Piece of Business is finished. You dont probably know the Circumstances which attended this Proceeding of Congress. They are so honourable to me, that I cannot in Gratitude or Decency refuse.

I must Submit your Voyage to your Discretion and the Advice of your Friends, my most earnest Wishes are to see you but if the Uncertainties are such as to discourage you, I know it will be upon reasonable Considerations and must submit. But if you postpone the Voyage for this Fall, I shall insist on your coming in the Spring, unless there is a certainty of my going home to you. Congress are at such grievous Expences, that I shall have no other Secretary than my son. He however is a very good one. He writes a good hand very fast, and is very steady, to his Pen and his Books. Write me by every Ship to Spain France Holland or England, that I may know. You give me more public Intelligence than any body. The only hint in Europe of this Comn. was from you.

To yours forever

John Adams

Abigail Adams to John Adams

My dearest Friend   Braintree November 11. 1783

Col' Trumble has been so kind as to visit me, and request a Letter from me to you; I have promised him one. You direct me to write by every opportunity. I very seldom let one slip unimproved, but I find many more conveyances by way of england than any other. I have written twice to you since the recept of your last favour, which was dated july 17th.

I wish you to write by way of England but to send no letters to the southard.

I pleased myself with the Idea of seeing you here during the summer, but when I found how publick Buisness was delayed I endeavourd to banish the Idea, for one month of daily expectation, is more tedious than a year of certainty. I think it would be a releif to my mind if your next Letter was to assure me, that you had no intention of comeing out till next spring; yet think not, that I am more reconciled to your absence, or less ardently desire your return, but your Life and Health are too dear to me, to gratify my wishes at the expence of either.

I have but last evening returnd, from a visit to Haverhill, where I was led at this season, by the sickness of Master Tommy, who has a second time experienced a severe fit of the Rheumatism. It was an unfortunate bequest, but it is so similar to what at his age I was excersised with, that I think it must have descended to him. He lost the use of his Limbs for a fortnight. It was attended with a fever, and stricture across his Breast. I had the satisfaction to find him upon the recovery, and much better than my fears, for seazing him at this season and with so much voilence, I feard he would have been disabled all winter.

Both mr and Mrs Shaw, speak very well of our young Lads, who begin to think of a Colledge Life, as not more than a year and half distance. Charles is very desirious that he may be ready at 15, and master Tommy is determined that he shall not out strip him, in his learning, what ever he may do in his entrance at colledge for which purpose he requests that his lessons may be the same with his Brothers. He took great pains to overtake Charles, during his absence and sickness with the Measles, nor did he rest untill he accomplished it. Mr Shaw is I believe an excellent preceptor and takes great pains with them. Their Morals and manners are strickly attended to, and I have every satisfaction I can wish with respect to care and tenderness both in sickness and Health. I wanted for nothing but to see you Mamma, says master during my sickness. Mrs Shaw is the same amiable good woman you always knew her. She has one son and one daughter, but her Health is feeble and her frame exceedingly delicate and tender, her spirits lively her temper placid. The children Love her with a filial affection.

I longed for you to accompany me in this journey, and to have participated the pleasure of seeing our children attentive to their studies, and promiseing to be wise and good.

While your own Heart dilates, you will tell me, that the season for temptation is not yet arrived, that altho they are carefully Guarded against evil communications; and warned of the danger of bad examples, no humane foresight can effectually preserve them from the contagion of vice; True, but I have a great opinion of early impressions of virtue, and believe that they take such hold of the mind, as neither time, or temptations can wholy subdue. They recall the wanderer to a sense of his Duty, tho he has strayed many many times. Attend says the Good Ganganella, more to the Hearts, than the understanding of your pupils, if the Heart is good, all will go well.

I have a thousand fears for my dear Boys as they rise into Life, the most critical period of which is I conceive; at the university; there infidelity abounds, both in example and precepts. There they imbibe the speicious arguments of a Voltaire a Hume and Mandevill if not from the fountain, they receive them at second hand. These are well calculated to intice a youth, not yet capable of investigating their principals, or answering their arguments. Thus is a youth puzzeld in Mazes and perplexed with error, untill he is led to doubt, and from doubting to disbelief. Christianity gives not such a pleasing latitude to the passions. It is too pure, it teaches moderation humility and patience, which are incompatable, with the high Glow of Health, and the warm blood which riots in their veins. With them, "to enjoy, is to obey." I hope before either of our children are prepaird for colledge you will be able to return and assist by your example and advise, to direct and counsel them; that with undeviating feet they may keep the path of virtue.

I have heitherto been able to obtain their Love their confidence and obedience, but I feel unequal to the task of guiding them alone, encompassed as I know they must be with a thousand snares and temptations. I hope our dear son abroad will not imbibe any sentiments or principals which will not be agreable to the Laws the Goverment and Religion of our own Country. He has been less under your Eye than I could wish, but never I dare say without your advise and instruction. If he does not return this winter, I wish you to remind him, that he has forgotten to use his pen, to his Friends upon this side the water.

With Regard to what passes in the political world I hear little said upon the subject. We are anxious to receive official accounts of the Signing the definitive Treaty. The Merchants will Clamour if the commercial Treaty is not to their taste. The Peace necessitates many of them to a less extravagant mode of living, and they must retrench still more if ever they pay their debts abroad. Bills are now sold at par, if you continue abroad, I shall be under a necessity of drawing upon you for tho the War is ceased, taxes have not. Since I took my pen, and within this hour, I have been visited by the collector with 3 tax Bills; the amount of which is 29 pounds 6 and 8 pence, the continental tax state tax and town tax beside which, I have just paid a parish tax. I live with all the frugality in my power. I have but two domesticks, yet I find it as much as I can do to Muster cash enough to pay our sons Quarter Bills and Cloath them decently.

Of one thing you may rest assured, that I involve you in no debts, no go one Inch without seeing my way Clear; you laugh at me with regard to my Virmont purchase. I still value it, and do not doubt of its becomeing so. I have a right in about [2?] hundred acers of land some where in northburry which comes to me from my Mother; I will exchange with you. My Father left to me and Mrs shaw his Medford Farm stock buildings &c and his medow in Malden the value of which is Estimated at near 800. Now what I wish is to persuade my sister to sell you her part of the Farm, and make a purchase in the Town where she lives, but I do not chuse to say any thing upon the subject at present. I suppose it will sell for more than the apprizement, and as I hope you will return early in the spring, that will be as soon as any thing can be done about it. The estate is some cloged in concequence of a Numerous family but the personal estate will clear it and pay the Legacies which amount to about 300 pounds and some small debts.

Adieu my dearest Friend. Heaven preserve your Life and Health, and safely conduct you to your ever affectionate

Portia

Abigail Adams to John Adams

My Dearest Friend   November 20. 1783

Your favour dated at Amsterdam in july was last evening handed to me; and this evening your Letter of the 10th of sepbr by col. ogden reached me. I had for some time supposed that the delay of publick buisness would retard your return; hearing that the definitive treaty was not compleated untill september, and knowing that the commercial Treaty was still to form; I had little reason to expect you; unless your State of Health required an immediate resignation of all your publick employments. Your Letter therefore which informs me of your determination to pass an other winter abroad is by no means unexpected. That we must pass it with a vast ocean between us; is a painfull reflection to me, yet thus it must be. I am so much of a coward upon the water, that even a summers voyage had its terrors. A winter passage I cannot possibly think of encountering. If I was instantly to set about it, I could not adjust my affairs so as to leave them in any order under a month. Mr Temple and family sail this week. I do not know any person except mr Jackson of Newburry port, who is going abroad; with whom I should like to become a passenger, and he goes to Ireland.

But I have a stronger objection than even a winters voyage against comeing at present. It is the undetermined counsels of Congress. They have not yet made any appointment to the Court of Britain. Many are seeking for the place, with more splendid titles, if wealth can give them, and many more thousands to claim it with: I am informd that mr jay, has written pressingly to Congress in your favour, at the same time assureing them, that he would absolutely refuse the appointment, if it should be offerd him; but whether you will finally be the person, is left to futurity.

Of this I am sure, that I do not wish it. I should have liked very well, to have gone to France, and resided there a year, but to think of going to england in a publick Character, and resideing there; engageing at my time of life in scenes quite New, attended with dissipation parade and Nonsense; I am sure I should make an awkward figure. The retired Domestick circle "the feast of reason and the flow of soul" are my Ideas of happiness, and my most ardent wish is, to have you return and become Master of the Feast.

My Health is infirm. I am frequently distresst with a nervous pain in my Head, and a fatigue of any kind will produce it. Neither of us appear to be built for duration. Would to Heaven the few remaining days allotted us, might be enjoyed together. I have considerd it as my misfortune, that I could not attend to your Health, watch for your repose, alleviate your Hours of anxiety, and make you a home where ever you resided. More says a very skillfull Dr. depends upon the Nurse than the physician.

My present determination is to tarry at home this winter; lonely as it is without my children; and if I cannot prevail upon you to return to Me in the spring—you well know that I may be drawn to you; one strong tie which held me here is dissolved, my dear Parent; who used to say; I cannot consent to your going child, whilst I live. An other cord and almost the only one which binds me to this place, is like to be loosed, I mean mr Cranchs family who talk of removeing to Boston in the spring. Should this take place Braintree would indeed become a lonely spot to me.

Mr Thaxter will be able to give me when he arrives; the best intelligence upon the Subject.

I hope I shall not miss the French Brig which was to sail to day, but may possibly be detained. I knew not of her going untill last evening.

Adieu and believe me whether present or absent, most affectionately Yours

A Adams

John Adams to Abigail Adams

My dearest Friend   The Hague Jan. 25. 1784

I was much disappointed, on the Arrival of Mr Temple in London, at not finding a Letter from you, but last Week at Amsterdam, I had the Happiness to receive your kind favours of Sept. 20. and Oct. 19. Mr Trumbull is not arrived.

The Loss of my kind Father, has very tenderly affected me, but I hope, with full Confidence to meet him in a better World. My ever honoured Mother I still hope to see in this. I feel for you, as I know how justly dear to you, your father was.

You have Seen, before now Mr Thaxter and I hope Mr Dana. The Determinations of Congress, upon the Arrival of the definitive Treaty will be your best Guide for your own Conduct. You will juge best from thence whether it is worth your while to come to The Hague or to Europe. If Congress would determine to continue me in Europe, I must intreat you to come to me, for I assure you, my Happiness depends so much upon it, that I am determined, if you decline coming to me, to come to you. If Miss Nabby is attached, to Braintre, and you think, upon Advizing with your Friends, her Object worthy, marry her if you will and leave her with her Companion in your own House, Office, Furniture Farm and all. His Profession is, the very one, I wish. His Connections are respectable, and if he has Sown his will Oats and will Study, and mind his Business, he is all I want.

I must at present leave all to your Judgment. If you think it not advizeable to come to Europe, I will come to you although I should be Sorry, to break away and return, without Permission from Congress. I should not care, a Farthing my self whether it were in England or Holland, if I could preserve my Health, which I should hope to do with my Family in a settled Way of Life, for I am determined, not to venture in future upon Such Journies and Wanderings as have heretofore been necessary, and have done me so much harm. Somewhere or other, I am determined to have a regular Habitation and Settled Abode.

John is a great Comfort to me. He is every Thing you could wish him. Wholly devoted to his studies he has made a Progress, which gives me intire Satisfaction. Miss N[*abby'*]s Friend must rise very early or he will be soon overtaken by her worthy Brother. In the Course of two or three Years, John must go home, and go into some office, and if he should have a Brother in Law of sufficient Merit, why should he wish for any other Master? These Things are but Speculations. Miss hopes I shall approve of her Taste. I can Scarcely think it possible for me to disapprove, of her final Judgment formed with deliberation, upon any Thing which so deeply concerns her whole Happiness. But she will listen to the Advice of her Mother Grandmother, and her Aunts, in whose Wisdom I have great Confidence.

The next Dispatches from Congress, and from you, after Mr Thaxters Arrival will determine me and I shall write you more fully.

I have enjoyed better Health, Since my Fever last Septr. at Paris. I got poisoned at Amsterdam with the Steams of the Canals, and bad Water in the Cisterns, and my Constitution has been labouring, these two or three Years to throw it off. Two violent Fevers, have not been Sufficient, wholly to relieve me, but the last has made me better. I am cured of the Imprudence of living in a great City in hot Weather.

Adieu my dearest Friend. Adieu.

After months of debate back and forth, Abigail finally resolved to sail to Europe and join John. More than four years apart was simply long enough and she was no longer willing to wait for Congress to make a decision about John's position. Daughter Nabby would join her on this trip, leaving behind her fiancé, Royall Tyler. While John's letter formally granting approval of the match did not arrive until after Abigail and Nabby had departed, Nabby had gone ahead and reached an understanding with Tyler that they would marry after she returned from the trip abroad. Abigail and John's two youngest sons, Charles and Thomas Boylston, were already living with Abigail's sister, Elizabeth, and her husband, John Shaw, who was tutoring the boys in preparation for their eventual admittance to Harvard College.

Abigail chose to leave a former slave, Phoebe Abdee, in charge of the Adamses' home. Phoebe had belonged to Abigail's father, who had manumitted her in his will.

Abigail Adams to John Adams

Febry 11th 1784

Two days only are wanting to compleat six years since my dearest Friend first crost the atlantick. But three months of the Six years have been spent in America. The airy delusive phantom Hope, how has She eluded my prospects, and my expectations of your return from month to month, have vanished "like the baseless Fabrick of a vision."

You invite me to you, you call me to follow you. The most earnest wish of my soul is to be with you, but you can scarcly form an Idea of the conflict of my mind. It appears to me such an enterprize, the ocean so formidable, the quitting my habitation and my Country, leaving my Children, my Friends, with the Idea that prehaps I may never see them again, without my Husband to console and comfort me under these apprehensions—indeed my dear Friend there are hours when I feel unequal to the trial. But on the other hand I console myself with the Idea, of being joyfully and tenderly received by the best of Husbands and Friends, and of meeting a dear and long absent Son. But the difference is; my fears, and anxieties, are present; my hopes, and expectations, distant.

But avaunt ye Idle Specters the desires and requests of my Friend are a Law to me. I will sacrifice my present feelings and hope for a blessing in persuit of my duty.

I have already arranged all my family affairs in such a way that I hope nothing will suffer by my absence. I have determined to put into this House Pheby, to whom my Father gave freedom, by his will, and the income of a hundred a year during her Life. The Children furnished her to house keeping, and she has ever since lived by herself, untill a fortnight ago, she took unto her self a Husband in the person of mr Abdee whom you know. As there was no setled minister in weymouth I gave them the liberty of celebrating their nuptials here, which they did much to their satisfaction.

I proposed to her taking care of this House and furniture in my absence. The trust is very flattering to her, and both her Husband and she seem pleased with it. I have no doubt of their care and faithfullness, and prefer them to any other family. The Farm I continue to let to our old tennant, as no one thinks I shall supply myself better.

I am lucky too in being able to supply myself with an honest faithfull Man Servant. I do not know but you may recollect him, John

Brisler, who was brought up in the family of genll Palmer, has since lived with Col. Quincy and is recommended by both families as a virtuous Steady frugal fellow, with a mind much above the vulgar, very handy and attentive. For a maid servant I hope to have a Sister of his, who formerly lived with Mrs Trott, who gives her a good character. It gave me some pain to refuse the offerd service of an old servant who had lived 7 years with me, and who was married from here, as I wrote you sometime ago. Both she and her Husband solicited to go, but I could not think it convenient as Babies might be very inconvenient at Sea, tho they offerd to leave it at Nurse if I would consent to their going, but tho I felt gratified at their regard for me I could not think it would answer. On many accounts a Brother and sister are to be prefered. Thus far have I proceeded but I know not yet what Ship, or what month or what port I Shall embark for, I rather think for England.

I wrote you largely by Capt Love, who saild for England 3 weeks ago. By him I mentiond a set of Bills which I expected to draw in favour of uncle smith for 200 dollors. He did not send me the Bills untill yesterday. Instead of 60 pounds Lawfull, he requested me to sign a Bill for 60 sterling, as that was just the sum he wanted, and that it would oblige him. I have accordingly drawn for that; as I supposed it would not make any great odds with you; whether I drew now; or a month hence, as I suppose I shall have occasion before I embark. You will be so kind as to honour the Bill.

I have not heard from you since mr Robbins arrived. I long to hear how your Health is, heaven preserve and perfect it. Col Quincy lies very dangerously ill of the same disorder which proved fatal to my dear and honourd parent. The dr is apprehensive that it will put a period to his life in a few days.

Your Honourd Mother is as well as usual. The thoughts of my going away is a great grief to her, but I shall leave her with a particular request to my sister Cranch, to pay the same attention to her during her Life, which I have done and to supply my place to her in sickness and Health.

However kind sons may be disposed to be, they cannot be daughters to a Mother. I hope I shall not leave any thing undone which I ought to do. I would endeavour in the discharge of my duty towards her, to merit from her the same testimony which my own parent gave me, that I was a good kind considerate child as ever parent had. However undeserving I may have been of this testimony, it is a dear and valuable Legacy to me and will I hope prove a stimulous to me, to endeavour after those virtues which the affection and partiality of a parent assribed to me.

Our sons are well. I hope your young companion is so too. If I should not now be able to write to him please to tell him I am not unmindfull of him.

I have been to day to spend a few Hours with our good uncle Quincy, who keeps much confined a winters and says he misses my two Boys almost as much as I do; for they were very fond of visiting him, and used to go as often as once a week when they lived at home.

There is nothing stiring in the political world. The Cincinati makes a Bustle, and will I think be crushed in its Birth. Adieu my dearest Friend. Yours most affectionately

A. A

John Adams to Abigail Adams

My Dearest Friend   The Hague July 3. 1784

From the first of April to this time, I have been in constant and anxious Expectation of hearing of your Arrival in London. Your Letters encouraged me to hope and expect it, otherwise I should have been with you at Braintree before now. I still expect to hear of your arrival every moment, but as your last letters by Mr: Warren expressed a doubt, it is possible, even that this Letter may find you in America. If it does, I shall leave it to your discretion, to embark or not, if you embark, burn the inclosed. But notwithstanding that you will probably have to return again to America in the Spring with me, if you do not embark, send the enclosed on to the President of Congress, and I will be at home as soon as I can. But I fear it will not be before the Spring, perhaps not before June or July; if you conclude to come to me, you may marry your Daughter beforehand if you will and bring her Husband with her. If you do not come, you may still marry your Daughter if you think proper.

My own Opinion is, you had better Stay. I will come home, and make my Hill shine as bright as General Warren's, and leave Politicks to those who understand them better and delight in them more, Breed my Boys, to the Bar and to Business, and My Girls too, and live and die in primaeval simplicity and Innocence. You may depend upon it, I will not be jockied again.

Your's &c.

Abigail Adams to John Adams

London july 23. 1784.
Osbornes new family Hotel,
Adelphi at Mrs Shffields No. 6

My dearest Friend

At length Heaven be praised, I am with our daughter safely landed upon the British Shore after a passage of 30 days from Boston to the downs. We landed at deal the 20 instant, rejoiced at any rate to set our feet again upon the land. What is past, and what we sufferd by sickness and fatigue, I will think no more of. It is all done away in the joyfull hope of soon holding to my Bosom the dearest best of Friends.

We had 11 passenger. We travelled from Deal to London all in company, and tho thrown together by chance, we had a most agreeable set, 7 Gentlemen all except one, American, and marri'd men every one of whom strove to render the passage agreeable and pleasent to us. In a more particular manner I feel myself obliged to mr Foster who is a part owner of the ship, a modest kind obliging Man, who paid me every service in his power, and to a dr Clark who served his time with Dr Loyd and is now in partnership with him. He took a kind charge of Nabby in a most Friendly and Brotherly way shewed us every attention both as a Gentleman physician and sometimes Nurss, for we all stood in great want of both. My maid was unfortunately sick the whole passage, my manservant was so sometimes. In short for 2 or 3 days the Captain and dr who had frequently been to sea before, were the only persons who were not sea sick. Capt Lyde is a son of Neptune, rather rough in his manners, but a most excellent Sea man, never leaving his deck through the passage for one Night. He was very obligeing to me. As I had no particular direction to any Hotel when I first arrived a Gentleman passenger who had formerly been in London advised me to Lows Hotel in Covent Garden, where we stoped. My first inquiry was to find out mr Smith, who I presumed could inform me with respect to you. Mr Spear a passenger undertook this inquiry for me, and in less than half an hour, both he and mr Storer, were with me. They had kindly provided lodgings for me to which I removed in the morning after paying a Guiney and half for tea after I arrived and lodging and Breakfast a coach included to carry me to my lodgings. I am now at lodgings at 34 and 6 pence pr week for myself daughter and two servants. My Man servant I left on Board the ship to come up with it, but it has not yet got up. I drew upon you before I left America one Bill in favour of dr Tufts of an hundred pound Lawfull Money, 98 of which I paid for our passages. This Bill is to be paid to mr Elworthy. I drew for two hundred more in favour of Natll Austin to be paid in holland. One hundred and 80 pounds of this money I shall bring with me to the Hague as I cannot use it here without loss, it being partly Dollors partly french crowns and French Guineys. Mr Smith has advised me to this and tells me that what money I have occasion for he can procure me here. My expences in landing travelling and my first Nights entertainment have amounted to 8 Guineys. I had a few english Guineys with me. I shall wish to shelter myself under your wing immediately for the expences frighten me. We shall be dear to you in more senses than one. Mr Jefferson I left in Boston going to portsmouth where he designd spending a week and then to return to Newyork to take passage from thence to France. He urged me to wait his return and go with him to New York, but my passage was paid on Board capt Lyde, the Season of the year was the best I could wish for and I had no desire to take such a journey in the Heat of summer. I thanked him for his politeness, but having taken my measures, I was determined to abide by them. He said col Humphries the Secretary to the commercial commission had sailed before he left philadelphia, and that he did not doubt I should find you in France. I have a Letter from him which I inclose and several other Letter from your Friends. Mr Smith thinks Master John will be here to Night from the intelligence he forwarded to you before I arrived. I do not wish to tarry a day here without you, so that if he comes I shall immediately set out, provided I have not to wait for the Ship to come up. How often did I reflect during my voyage upon what I once heard you say, that no object in Nature was more dissagreeable than a Lady at sea. It realy reconciled me to the thought of being without you, for heaven be my witness, in no situation would I be willing to appear thus to you. I will add an observation of my own, that I think no inducement less than that of comeing to the tenderest of Friends could ever prevail with me to cross the ocean, nor do I ever wish to try it but once more. I was otherways very sick, beside sea sickness but you must not expect to see me pined, for nothing less than death will carry away my flesh, tho I do not think I eat more the whole passage than would have sufficed for one week. My fatigue is in some measure gone of and every hour I am impatient to be with you.

Heaven give us a happy meeting prays your ever affectionate

A Adams

John Adams to Abigail Adams

My dearest Friend   The Hague July 26. 1784

Your Letter of the 23d has made me the happiest Man upon Earth. I am twenty Years younger than I was Yesterday. It is a cruel Mortification to me that I cannot go to meet you in London, but there are a Variety of Reasons decisive against it, which I will communicate to you here. Meantime, I Send you a son who is the greatest Traveller, of his Age, and without Partiality, I think as promising and manly a Youth as is in the World.

He will purchase a Coach, in which We four must travel to Paris. Let it be large and Strong, with an Imperial, and Accommodations for travelling. I wish you to see the Hague before you go to France. The season is beautifull both here and in England. The Journey here will be pleasant excepting an Hour or two of Sea sickness between Harwich and Helvoet Sluis. You may come conveniently with your two Children and your Maid, in the Coach and your Man may ride on Horseback, or in the Stage Coach.

I can give you no Council, about Cloaths. Mr Puller will furnish the Money you want, upon your Order or Receipt. Expences I know will be high but they must be born, and as to Cloaths for yourself and Daughter, I beg you to do what is proper let the Expence be what it will.

Every Hour to me will be a Day, but dont you hurry, or fatigue or disquiet yourself upon the Journey. Be carefull of your Health.

After Spending a Week or two here, you will have to set out with me to France, but there are no Seas between, a good Road a fine season and We will make moderate Journeys and See the Curiosities of Several Cities in our Way—Utrecht, Breda, Antwerp Brussells &c &c.

It is the first Time in Europe that I looked forward to a Journey with Pleasure. Now, I promise myself a great deal. I think it lucky that I am to go to Paris where you will have an opportunity to see that

City, to acquire its Language &c. It will be more agreable to you to be there, than here perhaps for some time.

For my own Part I think myself made for this World. But this very Idea makes me feel for a young Pair who have lately seperated. If my Consent only is Wanting they shall be asunder no longer than they choose. But We must consult upon Plans about this. They have discovered a Prudence. Let this Prudence continue and All will be right by and by.

Yours with more Ardor than ever.

John Adams

John and Abigail spent the next four years together, first in Auteuil, France, then at Grosvenor Square in London, as John served as the United States' first ambassador to Great Britain. They exchanged only fifteen letters during those years, when one or the other went away for short trips, either for business or pleasure.

Abigail enjoyed Europe more than she had expected she would, revelling in the opportunity to travel and see the sights. She wrote long travelogues to her sisters and nieces recounting her activities. Still, she never lost her love of New England and also used her letters to compare American society favorably with that of the British.

John found his position as minister to Great Britain difficult at best. While he encountered a surprisingly cordial reception from King George III, the British had little interest in negotiating a commercial treaty with the United States. By early 1787, John had recognized the futility of his mission and submitted his resignation to Congress, though it would take John and Abigail another full year to make arrangements and actually depart.

Meanwhile, circumstances for John and Abigail's daughter Nabby changed substantially while she was abroad. After a year of silence from Royall Tyler and indications from her family back home of troubles with the relationship, she finally decided to break off her engagement with him. In the meantime, she had met William Stephens Smith, her father's secretary. The two fell in love and mar-

ried in June 1786. When the Adamses returned to Braintree, the Smiths moved to New York with their young son, William Steuben Smith.

Abigail Adams to John Adams

my dearest Friend   Bath Hotell March 23 1788

I received yours of the 14th and ever Since thursday have been in Hourly expectation of seeing you. I hope it is oweing to all the packets being detaind upon this Side, as is reported, and not to any indisposition that your return is delayed. That unpleasing detention is sufficiently mortifying particularly as we wish to proceed to Falmouth as soon as possible, tho I shall fear to go from hence untill the ship is gone, for from the best information I can get callihan has as yet scarcly any thing but our Bagage &c on Board, and even that has been several days delayd by him. I came last monday Evening to this Hotell, that the Beds and remaining furniture might be sent on Board and the House given up. This will be wholy accomplish'd on the morrow if the weather permits, and has been oweing to that, for several days that all has not been accomplished.

The packet arrived this week from Newyork and brings an account that seven states had accepted the Constitution. The Massachusetts convention consisted of 300 and 40 members. It was carried by a Majority of Nineteen. Georgia and South Carolina are the two other states of which we had not before any certain accounts. New Hamshire was sitting. Newyork are becomeing more National and mr Duer writes mr Smith, that he may consider the constitution as accepted, and begining to operate at the Commencment of an other Year. Newyork had agreed to call a convention. Thus my dear Friend I think we shall return to our Country at a very important period and with more pleasing prospects opening before her than the turbulent Scenes which massachusetts not long since presented. May wisdom Govern her counsels and justice direct her opperations.

Mr and Mrs Smith set off this week for Falmouth. She is now confined with a Soar throat, similar to the complaint which afficted me ten days ago. I write in hopes the Baron de Lynden will meet you on your return.

I shall be exceedingly anxious if I do not see, or hear from you soon.

Adieu and believe me ever yours

A Adams

A New Government

"I have as many difficulties here, as you can have; public and private. But my Life from my Cradle has been a Series of difficulties and that Series will continue to the Grave."

—*John Adams*

"I check every rising wish and suppress every anxious desire for your return, when I see how necessary you are to the welfare and protection of a Country which I love, and a people who will *one day* do justice to *your memory.*"

—*Abigail Adams*

"You Apologize for the length of your Letters and I ought to excuse the shortness and Emptiness of mine. Yours give me more entertainment than all the speeches I hear. There is more good Thoughts, fine strokes and Mother Wit in them than I hear in the whole Week."

—*John Adams*

"My days of anxiety have indeed been many and painfull in years past; when I had many terrors that encompassed me arround. I have happily Surmounted them, but I do not find that I am less solicitious to hear constantly from you than in times of more danger."

—*Abigail Adams*

"The Most Insignificant Office"

December 1788–January 1794

Abigail and John did not remain settled long after their June *1788* return to Braintree. In November Abigail traveled to Jamaica, New York, for three months, to assist Nabby after the birth of her second child, John Adams Smith. In April *1789*, newly elected vice president John Adams journeyed to New York City to assume his duties in the new government. Until Abigail joined him in June, he wrote frequently, imploring her to come soon but warning that New York's high prices and his modest salary would necessitate living in a "Style much below our Rank and station."

Despite John's anxieties over their living arrangements, Abigail found Richmond Hill, the house they rented about two miles north of New York City, much to her liking. And, as a bonus, Nabby and the grandchildren resided with them most of the time. Richmond Hill, however, remained their home only until late *1790*, when they moved to Philadelphia with the national government.

During the remainder of his terms in the executive department, John always returned to Braintree (later Quincy) in the summer. As the presiding officer of the Senate, he looked forward to the government's summer recess as an opportunity to escape to his farm, where he longed to reside permanently. Philadelphia had a well-earned reputation as an unhealthy place in the heat of the year, especially in the wake of the terrible *1793* yellow fever epidemic that ravaged the city. During the twelve years that John served in the national government, he and Abigail spent at least part of each summer together. After Abigail left Philadelphia in *1792* she did not return until *1797*.

Abigail Adams to John Adams

my dearest Friend   Jamaica December 3d 1788

This day three weeks I left Home, since which I have not heard a word from thence. I wrote you from Hartford and once from this place since my arrival. I cannot give you any account eitheir of Newyork or Jamaica as I got into the first at seven in the Evening and left it at Nine the next morning, and in this place my only excursion has been in the garden. The weather has been bad cloudy and rainy ever since I came untill within these two days, and now it is very cold and Blustering. When I think of the distance I am from Home, the Idea of winter and Snow has double terrors for me. I think every Seperation more painfull as I increase in Years. I hope you have found in the Learned and venerable Company you proposed keeping, an ample compensation for my absence. I imagine however if these cold Nights last a little vital Heat must be wanting. I would recommend to you the Green Baize Gown, and if that will not answer, you recollect the Bear skin. I hope you will gaurd with all possible precaution against the Riggors of winter. I wish to hear how mr John Q A stands this cold. I hope he rest well, and duly excercises. I learn nothing further in politicks for except when col Smith goes to Town which is but seldom, we hear no News and see nobody but the Family. Mrs Smith remains very well for the Time and young master grows, but he and William should change Names, as William bears not the least likness to His Father or Family and the Young one is very like. For myself I am tolerably a little Homeish, however, the more so perhaps through the fear of not being able to reach it, just when I wish. If our out of Door Family should increase in my absence, I hope proper attention will be paid to the preservation of the Young family. If it should be numerous it will be rather expensive, and I would offer to your consideration whether two of the young Females had not better be put in a condition for disposal, viz fatted. The Beaf I Suppose is by this time in the cellar. I wish you would mention to Brisler and to Esther, a constant attention to every thing about House to Gaurd against the incroachment of Rats and mice. The cider Should be drawn off, and my Pears and Apples picked over and repack'd. If I should not reach Home by christmass, would it not be best to purchase a pork for winter, and to secure a few legs of pork to Bacon? I wish amongst other things you would frequently caution them about the fires a Nights. I should be loth to trust any one in this Matter but Brisler.

Pray write me by the next post and tell me how you all do.

Mr and Mrs Smith present their duty. Pray do not forget to present mine to our venerable parent. Little william says Grandpa ha ha. I should certainly bring him home if it was not winter and such a distance.

Love to mrs Cranch and my Neices.

Yours most tenderly

A Adams

John Adams to Abigail Adams

My dearest Friend   Braintree Decr. 28. 1788

I have recd your favours of the 3 and 13th and have opened that to our Son, who has been absent from me these 3 Weeks at Newbury, where I Suppose he is very well. I am as anxious as you are about your coming home. There are but two Ways. 1. If Coll Smith can bring you and his Family with you, will be the more obliging and agreable. 2. If he cannot, I must send your eldest son, with a Coach from Boston, to wait on you. As soon as I can receive a Letter from you, informing me, of the Necessity of it, I will Send him off. I expect him every day from Newbury Port. All has gone very well at home, and all your Friends are in health. Your sisters Family are in affliction by the Death of Gen. Palmer. You will not expect from me, much upon Public affairs. I shall only Say that the federal or more properly national Spirit runs high and bids fair to defeat every insidious as well as open Attempt of its Adversaries. This gives us a comfortable Prospect of a good Government, which is all that will be necessary to our Happiness. Yet I fear that confused and ill digested Efforts at Amendments will perplex for sometime.

I am very Sensible of that Affection which has given the Name to my Grandson, but although I have twice sett the Example of it, I do not approve of the Practice of intermixing the Names of Families. I wish the Child every Blessing from other Motives, besides its name. My Love to Mr and Mrs Smith; the sight of them and their two Sons with you, will give me high Pleasure. I am with the tenderest Affection your

John Adams

John received a warm send-off when he left Boston on 13 April 1789 as the newly elected vice president. After a week-long procession, during which the communities en route honored him, he arrived in New York City with little fanfare. He assumed his duties as the presiding officer of the Senate the morning of 21 April with a brief speech and no ceremony. George Washington arrived the next day but his inauguration did not take place until 30 April.

Abigail Adams to John Adams

my dearest Friend   Braintree April 22d 1789

I received mr Bourn's Letter to day, dated this day week, and I was very happy to Learn by it that you had made so Rapid a progress. I hope you stoped at my old acquaintance Avery's, and that you met with as good entertainment as I had led you to expect. All your Friends rejoiced in the fine weather which attended you, and conceive it, a propitious omen. I enjoyed, the Triumph tho I did not partake the 'Gale, and perhaps my mind might have been a little Elated upon the Late occasion if I had not have lived Long enough in the world to have seen the fickleness of it, yet to give it, its due, it blew from the right point on that day.

Mr Allen was so polite as to come out to Braintree to day to know if I had any Letters or package that I wish'd to send forward to you, and that he would take them. I pomis'd to forward a Letter and News papers. Mr A. I presume has *buisness* of *importance* by his return so soon. I hope it is not an office that a Friend of yours now hold's, and who is in some little anxiety about his own Fate. I received a Letter from him this Evening. I will inclose it by *an other* opportunity, yet I promis'd to mention to you what I conceived almost, or quite needless, because I knew your sentiments with respect to him so well, that I was sure you would interest yourself for his continuance in office whatever the *System* might be. If I have written a little ambiguously you may the more easily guess at the person meant.

The Children are now at home. Charles tells me that the Class which take their degree leave colledge the 21 of June and that if you have occasion for him he can come on as soon after that day as you wish, that he can have his degree as well as if he was present. He seems to be fond of the thought of getting rid of the parade of commencment. If it would be no injury to him, I should be equally fond of getting rid of a trouble in which there is very little Satisfaction, a good deal of expence and generally many affronts given by omissions.

I mentiond it to the dr and he approves it. I wrote thus early that I might know your mind upon the subject. You will give me the earliest information respecting prospects. I hope you will be carefull of your Health, and be enabled to go through the arduous task in which you are engaged. I wish to hear from you as often as possible. My Love to mrs Smith and children. Let Brisler know that his wife and child are very cleverly, that She is able to Nurse it, and much better than she was before she was confin'd. Mr Bass moves tomorrow into our House. I have reserved a part of it for Esther if Brisler should continue at Newyork, and that will obviate the difficuly of being alone in a House. I had the misfortune of loosing one of the Young creatures a day or two after you left me by the Horn sickness. It faild of eating in the morning and before I could get any body to it, it was dead. The Horns were hollow upon inspection but I suppose your Farm is quite out of your head by this Time and you will only think of it as a departed Friend, and without the consolation of thinking its situation better'd, the 20 Trees are all set out, and came in good order.

I am my dearearst Friend most affectionatly yours

A Adams

John Adams to Abigail Adams

My dearest Friend   New York. April 22. 1789

This is the first Moment I have been able to Seize, in order to acquaint you of my Arrival and Situation. Governor Clinton The Mayor of New York, all the old officers of the Continental Government, and the Clergy, Magistrates and People, have Seemed to emulate the two houses of Congress, in shewing every respect to me and to my office. For Particulars I must refer you to the public Papers. Yesterday for the first time I attended the Senate. Tomorrow or next day, The President is expected. Mr Jay with his usual Friendship, has insisted on my taking Apartments in his noble house. No Provision No Arrangement, has been made for the President or Vice P. and I See, clearly enough, that Minds are not conformed to the Constitution, enough, as yet, to do any Thing, which will Support the Government in the Eyes of the People or of Foreigners. Our Countrymens Idea of the "L'Air imposant" is yet confined to volunteer Escorts, verbal Compliments &c.

You and I however, are the two People in the World the best qualified for this Situation. We can conform to our Circumstances. And if They determine that We must live on little, We will not Spend much. Every Body enquires respectfully for Mrs A. of her affectionate

J. A.

Abigail Adams to John Adams

my dearest Friend   Braintree May 1. 1789

I received your kind favours of the 19 and 22 of April. The print-
ers were very obliging in taking particular care to supply me daily
with the paper's by which I learnt the arrival and Reception of the
Pressident, and vice Pressident. If I thought I could compliment in so
courtly and masterly a stile, I would say that the address to the Senate
was exactly what it ought to be, neither giving too little, or too much.
It has been much admired, yet every one do not see the force of the
first part of it; when I read the debates of the House, I could not but
be surprized at their permitting them to be open, and thought it would
have been a happy circustance if they could have found a dr Johnson
for the Editor of them. I think there is much of the old leaven in the
New Loaf. "I dare not lay a duty upon salt, the people will not bear it,
I dread the concequences to the People" is a language to teach the people to rise up in opposition to Government. The people would bear a 5
pr ct duty upon every article imported, and expect as much, but will
grumble perhaps at the duty upon molasses. Be sure it is a little hard
for *us Yankees* who Love it so well and make such liberal use of it, it
has already raised the price of it here. I hope the Senate will never
consent to draw backs. It will be a constant source of knavery, will not
small duties operate best, be most productive and least atroxious?
Johnson, whom you know I have lately been reading with great attention, and have become his great admirer, more fully convinc'd than
ever, that he was a very accurate observer of Human Life and manners. Johnson in one of his papers proves that there is no such thing as
domestick Greatness. Such is the constitution of the world that much
of Life must be spent in the same manner by the wise and the Ignorant
the exalted and the low. Men however distinguish'd by external accidents or intrinsick qualities, have all the same wants, the same pains,
and as far as the senses are consulted the same pleasures. The Petty
cares and petty duties are the same in every station to every under-

standing, and every hour brings us some occasion on which we all sink to the Common level. We are all naked till we are dressed, and hungry till we are fed. The Generals Triumph and Sage's disputation, end like the Humble Labours of the smith or plowman in a dinner or a sleep. Let this plead my excuse when I frequently call of your attention from weighty National objects to the petty concerns of domestick Life. I have been trying to dispose of the stock on Hand, but no purchaser appears—immediate profit is what all seek, or credit, where little is to be given. The weather is cold the spring backward, and the stock expensive. You will not wonder that I am puzzeld what to do, because I am in a situation which I never was before. Yours I presume cannot be much better. The Bill is setled with 48£.18s damages. Vacancy is up and the children have returnd to Cambridge.

My best Respects attend mr Jay and his Lady whose health I hope is mended. You do not mention mrs Smith or the little Boys—nor have I heard from them since mr Bourn came. By the way I heard a Report yesterday that Marble Head and Salem had voted you an anual present of ten Quintals of fish. How well founded the Report is I cannot presume to say, time must determine it. I want to hear how you do and how you can bear the application and confinement of your office. I say nothing about comeing. You will know when it will be proper and give me timely notice. The Children desired me to present their duty. I am my dearest Friend with the tenderest affection ever yours

Abigail Adams

John Adams to Abigail Adams

My dearest Friend   New York May 1. 1789

It has been impossible to get time to write you. Morning, Noon, and Night, has been taken up with Business, or Visits. Yesterday the President was Sworn, amidst the Acclamations of the People. But I must refer you to Gazettes and Spectators. I write this abed. Mr Allen deld.

me, Yesterday your Letter. I like very much your Plan of coming on, with Charles and Thomas, before Commencement. But as yet I have no House, nor Furniture. When you come you must bring, Table and Chamber Linnen and the Plate, and I expect, some beds. But all is uncertain as yet. You may send by a Stage, or a Cart to Providence and there embark, many necessary Things in the Packett. The House of Representatives will I hope, soon determine something. But my Expectations are not raised. I fear We shall be Straightened, and put to difficulty to live decently. We must however live in Proportion to our means.

The President has received me with great Cordiality, of affection and Confidence, and every Thing has gone very agreably. His Lady is expected this Month.

My Duty to my Mother, Love to Brothers Adams Cranch &c and sisters and every friendly, grateful sentiment to our Honourable Dr, our Guardian Protector and Friend, and to Mr Quincy, whom I had not opportunity to see, before I came away, and to all other friends and Acquaintance &c.

I ought to thank Captn. Beal, Mr Allen Mr Black &c for their obliging Attention in accompanying me, on my Journey.

You will receive by Barnard, some more fruit Trees. The Ladies universally enquire very respectfully after Mrs Adams, when she will arrive &c.

The last Sunday, I Spent very agreably at Col Smiths. Nabby and the Children very well. William, had no Knowledge of me, but John knew me at first glance.

I long to take a Glance at my [farm?] but this cannot be. Write me as often as you can. Yours with the tenderest Affection.

John Adams

I have Sent the Horse. You may sell him or give him to my worthy son John, for his Health, if you think it possible to pay for his Keeping.

John Adams to Abigail Adams

My dearest Friend   New York May 14. 1789

    I have recd yours of the 5th. If you think it best, leave Thomas at Colledge: but I pray you to come on with Charles, as soon as possible. As to the Place let my Brother plough and plant if he will, as much as he will. He may Send me, my half of the Butter Cheese &c here. As to Money to bear your Expences you must if you can borrow of some Friend enough to bring you here. If you cannot borrow enough, you must Sell Horses Oxen Sheep Cowes, any Thing at any Rate rather than not come on. If, no one will take the Place leave it to the Birds of the Air and Beasts of the Field: but at all Events break up that Establishment and that Household. A great Part of the Furniture must be shipped for this Place. As to Daniel, he has a Wife and cannot leave her: besides he makes great wages where he is: but if you have a Mind to bring Daniel you may. We can do without him.

    I have as many difficulties here, as you can have; public and private. But my Life from my Cradle has been a Series of difficulties and that Series will continue to the Grave. I hope Brisler will come; but if he cannot We can do without him. I have taken Montiers House, on the North River, a mile out of Town. There is room enough and Accommodations of all sorts—but no furniture.

    I am &c, tenderly

John Adams

John Adams to Abigail Adams

My dearest Friend   New York May 30. 1789

    Your old Acquaintance Mr Harrison of Cadiz will deliver you this, if you should not, as I hope you will, be Sett off for this place before he can reach Braintree.

    I expect you, here indeed in a Week or ten days at farthest, from this date. Mrs Washington is arrived. My House and Garden want Us very much. We Shall be obliged to bring all our Furniture and most of our Books, except the Law books and the great Collections, such as the Byzantine History, Muratory, the Encyclopædia &c. But I hope you will come on, and send Beds and necessaries as soon as possible. Barnard has delivered here, some Trunks and Cases but no Keys nor Letter informing what is in them. We must make this place our home, and think no more of Braintree, for four years, not forgetting however our Friends there. And what is the most disagreable of all: We must live, as I apprehend, in a Style much below our Rank and station. I Said four years, upon the supposition that the Government should Support itself so long: but it must be supported by Providence if at all, against the Usual Course of Things, if the human Means of Supporting it, should not be soon better understood. You and I can live however as plainly as any of them.

Yours most tenderly

J. A.

Abigail Adams to John Adams

my dearest Friend   Sunday May 31. 1789

I received yesterday your Letter of May the 24th and shall begin tomorrow to get such things in readiness as will enable us to keep House. I feel a reluctance at striping this wholy at present, because I am well persuaded that we shall in some future period if our lives are prolonged return to it, and even supposing a summer recess, we might wish to come and spend a few months here. An other reason is, that I do not wish to bring all our own furniture, because congress are not, or do not possess Sufficient stability to be sure of continuing long in any one state. I am fully satisfied with the House you have taken and glad that it is a little removed from the city. The advantages will overbalance the inconvenience I doubt not. I suppose Barnard has arrived before this. Would it not be best to let him know that he will have a full freight ready, returns as soon as he will, and that I must look out for some other vessel if he delay's, tho I have not the least prospect of getting one, for mr Tufts's is yet at Newyork Barnard's is calculated for the Buisness, and I could get a small vessel to come here to mr Blacks and take in my things and carry them along side of Barnard, which will be less expence, and damage than carting them to Boston. In the mean time I will get the dr to look out, and see if any other vessel can be hired for the purpose provided Barnard should delay at Newyork. This you can advise me of by the next post. With the greatest expedition I do not think I can get them ready under a week. I must leave Brisler to come by water with them, if you think it best for me to come before my furniture is ship'd, but I do not see what advantage I can be of, to you situated as you are. An additional incunberence to mr Jays family would be still more indelicet than imposing the vice Pressident upon him for Several months, and rendering his situation so delicate that he could neither leave him with decency, or stay with decorum, and to be at Jamaica I could do no more than if I was at Braintree to assist in any thing. The Trunks which I sent contain Bed and table Linnen some Cloths and the cases contain carpets. I will however be directed wholy by your wishes and come next week if you think it best, and you have any place to put me. You must be sensible from the tenor of Your Letters that I have not known hetherto what to do, any more than you have from your situation, What to direct. You will be as patient as possible and rest assured that I will do my utmost with the means I have, to expidite every thing. As to insurence there will be no occasion for it by Barnard who is so well acquainted with the coast, and at this season of the Year.

The Pressident and Lady dinned with me yesterday. He has got permission for Charles's absence. Polly Tailor would cry a week if I did not bring her, for a House maid I know not where I could get her equal. Elijahs Mother thinks it is too far for her son to go, but if they consent mr Brisler can take him on Board Barnard when he comes, but

I shall not press it. Poor daniel has been sick with a soar which gatherd in his Throat and which nearly proved fatal to him. He expected from you some gratuity for himself. Oweing to the multiplicity of cares which on all sides surrounded you, at that time, it was omitted. As it was Customary and daniels expectations were dissapointed, he mentiond it to one or two persons, amongst whom woodard was one, who having just returnd from Newyork, clapt his hands into his pocket and taking out two crowns, gave them to him, telling him that you was so much engaged at the time, that it had slipt your mind but that he saw you at Newyork and that he had brought them for him. This came to my knowledge by the way of mr Wibird who insisted upon letting me know it. I immediatly repaid mr woodard and thank'd him for his kindness.

your Brother I believe will take care of the place when I leave it. The leave for Breaking up the Hill came too late for this season. The weather is remarkably cold and Backward, the pastures bare and vegetation very slow there is a fine blow upon the place, and if the frost last week which killd Beans, has not injured the Blossom, we shall have a large crop of fruit. I had yesterday a fine plate of fair Russets upon the table, sound as when they were taken from the Trees. My Garden looks charmingly, but it wants warmth. I have got some Large asparagrass Beds made, and my little grass plots before the door, pay well for the manure which I had put on in short I regreet leaving it. Your Mother is well as usual. Her Eyes are very troublesome to her. You will let me hear from you by the next post. I hope to be able to relieve you soon from [all] domestick, cares and anxieties. At least my best endeavours sh[all] not be wanting. I know you want your own Bed and pillows, your Hot coffe and your full portion of kian where habit has become Natural. How many of these little matters, make up a large portion of our happiness and content, and the more of publick cares and perplexities that you are surrounded with, the more necessary these alleviations. Our blessings are sometimes enhanced to us, by feeling the want of them. As one of that Number it is my highest ambition to be estimated, and shall be my constant endeavour to prove in all situations and circumstances affectionatly yours

A Adams

John Adams to Abigail Adams

My dearest Friend   New York June 6. 1789

I must now most Seriously request you to come on to me as soon as conveniently you can. Never did I want your assistance more than at present, as my Physician and my Nurse. My disorder of Eight years standing has encreased to such a degree as to be very troublesome and not a little alarming.

I have agreed to take Col Smith and his Family and Furniture into the House with us and they will be removed into it by next Wednesday. If Charles has a Mind to stay and deliver his French oration at Commencement, I am willing, and I think it will be greatly for his Reputation and Advantage. In that Case Charles and Tommy may both come to gether to New York after Commencement by the Way of Rhode Island, or by the Stage.

As to Louisa, our Family will be very great, and vastly expensive and House very full. If you think however you can find room and Beds &c I will not say any Thing against your bringing her.

You must leave the Furniture to be packed by others and sent after you. We must have it all removed and Sent here, as well as all the Liquers in the Cellar, and many of the Books, for here We must live, and I am determined not to be running backward and forward, till the 4 years are out, unless my Health should oblige me to resign my office of which at present there is some danger.

It has been a great dammage that you did not come on with me.
Yours affectionately

John Adams

After the first session of Congress adjourned on 29 September, John returned, this time without Abigail, to Massachusetts. George Washington made a tour of New England that fall and John participated in ceremonies with him in Boston. John returned to New York in late November.

Abigail Adams to John Adams

My dearest Friend   Richmond Hill october 20. 1789

I yesterday received your kind favour dated at Fairfield and am happy to find that you had advanced thus far with no greater inconvenience than Rocky Roads and a Blundering Servant. I will take better care of his Horses than he appears to have done of his master, for the old Proverb was never more verified, what is every bodys buisness, is nobodys buisness, than in Roberts going of without your Bagage, but he was still more culpable, to leave a part of it at Kings Bridge when it was sent on to him. Your shoes and Night cap were brought back by col Smith when he returnd Home. I presume the President will overtake you on the Road [as] he sat of on Thursday. He went in his chariot alone, and his two secretaries on horse back. You recollect what past the saturday Evening when you took leave of him. On Sunday he exprest himself anxious to mr Lear least he had not been sufficiently urgent with you to accompany him, and desired him to come out to you. Mr Lear in replie observed that if he came out, it was probable that you would think yourself not at liberty to refuse, and that it might break in upon your own arrangments. He will I fancy send you an invitation to accompany him to portsmouth which I hope you will find it convenient to accept. I went in to Town on saturday and brought out miss custos, and in the afternoon mrs Washington and mr Nelson and Lewis came out and drank Tea with me. This morning mrs W sent out her Servant to request that the Family would come in and dine with her to day and this being the last concert, that we should go together to it. This we comply with as you will readily suppose. Col smith Major Butler mr King Webb, Platt, Lawrence &c are all gone to long Island on a grousing Party.

Our Family are better than for a week past. Two days after you went away, George the footman was Seaized with a Plurisy Fever and that to so high a degree that I was obliged to have him bled Blisterd &c in the course of a few hours, but taking it immediatly, he is on the Recovery, but every person in the Family have had the Epidemick disorder which has so generally prevaild in a greater or lesser degree. As to small pox neither Louissa or John have had it, the dr says oweing to their being sick with this disorder, and that two disorders will not opperate at the Same time, but I fancy much more owing to the matters not being good.

The last Post brought you a Letter from our Friend mr Hollis dated in june. He makes many complaints and is much Grieved at not having heard oftner from you, Says he, but on 2d thought I will inclose you the Letter that you may write to him. There is also a Letter from the dr in which he request to know what Quantity of cheese we shall want. Perhaps you would like that made under your mothers care best. All the butter that can be procured from either place some of the Russet Apples the Pears—N york cannot shew the like—Hams &c.

Charls is very steady to the office in the day and to his own Room in the Evening. My duty to mother Love to Brothers and sisters Nephews and Neices. Let me hear from you as often as you possibly can. I rejoice in the fine weather you have and hope Your journey will prove highly benificial to your Health. I wish that a visit from the President may tend to conciliate the minds of our Nothern countrymen and that they will lay asside all sedition and evil speaking. A peice signed a centinal in Edds paper of last week dated Philadelphia, but I believe written in Boston is worthy Notice, might be call'd Treason against the Government. It is very seditious.

Adieu yours most affectionatly

A Adams

William says duty to Ganpa. Want him to come home and go see the cows.

John Adams to Abigail Adams

My dearest Friend   Braintree Nov. [1] Sunday 1789

I thank you for your kind Letter inclosing that from our Friend Hollis. The Influenza is here as general as it was at N. York. Your youngest Son has been laid up with it at Mr Cranche's; but is better. Mr Wibirt is confined with it, so that We had no Meeting. I have been to visit him: He is not very bad: but not fit to go out. My great Horse, had a Misfortune last night in the Stable, that he will not get over this fortnight. I am thankful that he is alive.

Mr Brisler is preparing his Goods to go by Bernard, who Sails on Wednesday, and will go with his Family next Week in the Stage.

I have Spent a Week in Boston which I have not done before these fifteen years. General Washington between Sam. Adams and John, The Fratrum dulce Par, mounted up to View in the Stone Chapell and in Concert Hall to be sure was a Spectacle for the Town of Boston. The Remarks were very Shrewd. Behold three Men, Said one, who can make a Revolution when they please. There, Said another are the three genuine Pivots of the Revolution. The first of these Observations is not I hope, so true as I fear the last is. Of all the Pictures that ever were or ever will be taken this ought to be done with the greatest Care, and preserved in the best Place. But H[ancock]'s Creatures will cast a Damper upon that.

The Presidents Behaviour was in Character, and consequently charming to all. I write no Particulars, because the News papers will give you the details. His Reception has been cordial and Splendid. His Journey will do much public good.

I Shall return, in the first Week in December, if not sooner, and bring Thomas with me. You must be very prudent and cautious, of my

Letters. Let them be seen by none, but the Family: for altho I shall write no harm there are Chemists who are very skilful in extracting evil out of Good. I have Seen the new Mrs Tufts, and admire the Drs Taste. She is in appearance, a fine Woman.

There is a three-year break in the correspondence at this point. After John com-pleted his two-month trip to Massachusetts in late 1789, he and Abigail were not separated again until John left Abigail in Braintree upon his return to Philadel-phia in late 1792. Other than the years in Europe, this is the longest period they spent together since John left for the First Continental Congress in 1774.

Abigail decided to remain in Braintree for a number of reasons beyond her preference for her native Massachusetts. The vice president's accommodations in Philadelphia were less appealing than those in New York and she did not have her daughter close at hand as she had at Richmond Hill. Most important, Philadel-phia's notoriously disease-ridden atmosphere remained a constant threat to her precarious health. The breaks that appear in the correspondence from this time un-til Abigail returned to the capital as First Lady in 1797 are the periods, usually summer and fall, when John returned to Braintree.

John Adams to Abigail Adams

My dearest Friend   Hartford Nov. 24. 1792

The Weather has been so disagreable and the Roads so bad, that I have not been able to advance farther on my Journey than to Bulls Tavern in this Town where I arrived last night after an unpleasant ride in the snow from Springfield. It Snowed all last night and has blocked up the roads so that I cannot move onwards till monday.

I have fallen into Several curious Conversations, on the road, which however would be too trifling to commit to Paper. A Gentleman of very respectable Appearance told me last Evening without knowing or Suspecting me, all the Politicks of New York and Philadelphia for and against the V. President. "The V. P. had been as all Acknowledged a great Friend to this Country, but had given Offence to his Fellow Citizens in Massachusetts, by writing something in favour of hereditary descent. That he had been long in Europe and got tainted." I told him laughing that it was hard if a Man could not go to Europe without being tainted, that if Mr Adams had been Sent to Europe upon their Business by the People, and had done it, and in doing it had necessarily got tainted I thought the People ought to pay him for the Damage the Taint had done him, or find some Means to wash it out and cleanse him.

Govr H[*ancock*] has been here and made a Dinner for the Gentlemen of this Town. One asked after the V. P. "The Governor had not Spoken to the V. P. this year; He was not one of the Well born." A Gentleman remarked upon it afterwards What would Mr H. have been if he had not been well born the Nephew of the rich Uncle Thomas? In short his Silly Envy of the V. P. is perceived and ridiculed by all the World out of Massachusetts. He is considered as a mere rich Man prodigal of his Wealth to obtain an empty Bubble of Popularity.

I am told that an unanimous Vote will be for me in Vermont New Hampshire, Connecticut and Rhode Island. This is generally expected, but I know full well the Uncertainty of Such Things, and am prepared to meet an Unanimous Vote against me. Mr P[*ierpont*] E[*dwards*] came off miserably. He gave such offence by mentioning his Nephew, that they would not appoint one Man who had any connection with him.

I would not entertain you with this political Title tattle, if I had any thing of more importance to say. One Thing of more importance to me, but no News to you is that I am yours with unabated Esteem and affection forever

J. A.

Abigail Adams to John Adams

my dearest Friend   Quincy Decbr 4th 1792

I was very happy to receive on thanksgiving day the 29 of Novbr. Your Letter dated Hartford. I feard that you had not reachd so far the weather was so dissagreable, but if the Roads have mended as much with you as they have this way, you have reachd Philadelphia by this time. I shall with impatience wait to hear of your arrival there. The snow remaind with us but one week Since which we have had pleasent weather. There has not anything occurd material that I know of since you left us. If you get Russels paper you will see a little deserved Burlesque upon the Govenours speach respecting the expressions made us of by Congress which gave him such umbrage. Tomorrow is a very important day to the united states, much more important to them, than it can possibly be to you or to me for think of it as they please tomorrow will determine whether their Government shall stand four years longer or Not. Mr Clinton seems to be the only competitor held up. I fancy he will receive no aid from N England. I hope you will order Fenno to continue his paper to me. We have had a Gang of Thieves infesting this Town since you left it. The thursday after you went away Shaw and James went into the woods and in the day time the best saddle was stolen out of the Barn closset. The same Night mr Cary had his best Horse stolen and mr Smith who lives on mrs Rows place had his taken the same night and last Sunday morning James came Running in to inform me that his Stables had been attempted, and his Lock broken, but being doubly secured the villan could not effect his purpose. He tried the Coach house door and split of a peice of the door, but could not get the Bar out. He went on to mr Adams's at Milton and stole his Horse. A Traveller lodged at Marshes Tavern on saturday night, who got up in the Night Rob'd the House of various articles of wearing Apparal and made of. We Suppose that he was the person who attempted our Stables and that he belongs to a Gang. They are in persuit of him.

Your Mother was well this day. She spent it with me. She and your Brother and family all dinned with me on thanksgiving day as well as our Son. Tis the first thanksgiving day that I have been at Home to commemorate for Nine years. Scatterd and dispersed as our Family is, God only knows whether we shall ever all meet together again. Much of the pleasure and happiness resulting from these N England Annual feltivals is the family circles and connections which are brought together at these times, but whether seperate or together I am Sensible that every year has been productive of many Blessings, and that I have great cause of thankfulness for preserving mercies both to myself and Family.

I inclose a Letter for Brisler. I wish him to inquire the price of Rye that I may know whether it would quit cost to send me a dozen Bushel. Tis five and six pence pr Bushel here. Superfine flower I want to know the price of. It has taken a rise here.

My Love to Thomas. Tell him to write me often. I hope the House of Reps will be in a little better humour after all Elections are over. I trust they will not follow the French example and Lop of Heads, even of Departments. They appear to have a great terror of them. I see a Lucius and a Marcus. I should like to know who they are. [Pray ma]ke many compliments and respects to all my good Friends in Philadelphia. I flatter myself I have some there, and be assured of the affectionate Regard of your

A Adams

John Adams to Abigail Adams

My dearest Friend   Philadelphia Decr 5. 1792

Last night I arrived at Philadelphia in tolerable Health and found our Friends all well. I have concluded to accept of the kind offer of Mr and Mrs Otis and taken a bed in their House. Thomas is charmingly accommodated and is very well. This Day decides whether I shall be a

Farmer or a Statesman after next March. They have been flickering in the Newspapers and caballing in Parties: but how the result will be I neither know nor care. I have met a very cordial and friendly reception from the Senate. All lament that Mrs Adams is not here: but none of them so much as her Friend forever

John Adams

The first American political parties began to take shape during this period. While John recognized that most of the Federalist electors would select him as their candidate for a second term as vice president, he remained highly critical of partisan divisions. The clear identification of Alexander Hamilton and Thomas Jefferson as the leaders of the contending Federalists and Democratic-Republicans fueled much of the Adamses' correspondence from this time forward.

John Adams to Abigail Adams

My dearest Friend   Philadelphia Decr. 28. 1792

Your Friends who are numerous enquire continually after your health and my Answer is that you have not informed me that it is worse, from which my conclusion is that I hope it is better.

The Noise of Election is over, and I have the Consolation to find that all the States which are fœderal have been unanimous for me, and all those in which the Antifœderalists were the predominant Party, unanimous against me: from whence my Vanity concludes that both Parties think me decidedly fœderal and of Some consequence. Four years more will be as long as I shall have a Taste for public Life or Journeys to Philadelphia. I am determined in the meantime to be no longer the Dupe, and run into Debt to Support a vain Post which has answered no other End than to make me unpopular.

The Southern States I find as bitter against Mr Jay as they are against me and I suppose for the same Reason. I am Surprized to find how little Popularity Mr Hancock has in any of the states out of Mass. Mr Pierpoint Edwards has been here: although he did not vouchsafe me the honour of a Visit or a Card, he was seen in close Consultation at his Lodgings with Mr Jefferson and Mr Baldwin. I am really astonished at the blind Spirit of Party which has Lived on the whole soul of this Jefferson: There is not a Jacobin in France more devoted to Faction. He is however Selling off his Furniture and his Horses: He has been I believe a greater fool than I have, and run farther into Debt by his French Dinners and Splendid Living. Farewell for me all that Folly forever. Jefferson may for what I know pursueing my Example and finding the Blanket too short taking up his feet. I am sure, all the officers of Government must hall in their horns as I have done.

Mr Ingersoll has wrote me for his Fee with Thomas and I must pay it, if the House make any Appropriation. My Love to all—My Duty to my Mother. I am as impatient to see you as I used to be twenty year ago.

J. A.

Abigail Adams to John Adams

my Dearest Friend   Quincy Janry 7th 1793

I received your Letters by mr Roberdeau who with our Son and young mr Quincy came out and dinned with me to day. I was pleased to see a son of your old Friend and acquaintance for whom you have so often expresd a Regard; as well as the agreeable Husband of miss Blair that was; we had much conversation about my acquaintances in Philadelphia, many of whom he could give me a particular account of. We past a very pleasent day. I once or twice last summer exprest an anxiety at not hearing from Thomas so often as I wishd; I recollect you askd me, if I was equally anxious about you when absent. My days of anxiety have indeed been many and painfull in years past; when I had many terrors that encompassed me arround. I have happily Surmounted them, but I do not find that I am less solicitious to hear constantly from you than in times of more danger, and I look for every Saturday as a day on which I am to receive a Boon. I have received a Letter every week since you left me, and by this days post two, one of the 28 and one of the 29th Decbr. for which receive my thanks, particularly that part in which you say you are not less anxious to see me than when seperated 20 years ago. Years Subdue the ardour of passion but in lieu thereof a Friendship and affection Deep Rooted subsists which defies the Ravages of Time, and will survive whilst the vital Flame exists. Our attachment to Character Reputation and Fame increase I believe with our years. I received the papers National Gazzet and all I see the dissapointed Electors wish to excuse their vote by Representations respecting you, that prove them to have been duped and deceived, while the Antis fly of assureing the publick that the Monarchy Men, and the Aristocracy have become quite harmless. If so it is to be hoped that their hue and cry will subside. Present me kindly to all the good Ladies who favour me by their inquiries after my Health. It is better than the last winter tho very few days pass in which I can say that I feel really well.

I have not heard any thing of the Chaise since you wrote me that it was left at Harford. I believe it will not reach Home till Spring. The Narrow Road to the water have been so blockd up with Snow that Shaw has not been able to get up any sea weed lately: he attempted it but could not succeed, and the ground has been bare in the Road. The Timber for the corn House is all cut and part of it got home, one day more will compleat it. Faxon was going this last week to the Ceadar Swamp it being now a fine time but very unfortunately a Man on the Road near it, broke out with the Small Pox and refused to be moved so that he cannot go. We have not had any sleding in the Road this winter yet the Ground has been pretty much coverd with a thin Snow and Ice, the weather in General very cold. Hay is fallen I am told to 4 and 6 pence pr hundred. Grain still holds its price, superfine flower 7 dollors pr Barrel oats 3 shillings pr Bushel. I have not had occasion yet to purchase. My Horses are so little used that they are high Spirited enough with 8 quarts a day. James takes very good care of them. I do not regreet your parting with the others. One pr are sufficient here, and a good able Farm Horse will do us more service and be much more prudent for us. I hope you live prudent enough now for the most Republican Spirit of them all. From the debates there appears a jealous carping ill naturd spirit subsisting and a great desire to crush the Secretary of the Treasury and the minister of war.

You was right. The chief Majestrate denies his having given permission to the Mobility to pull down the Theater. His Prime minister under the Signature of a Friend to Peace, has undertaken to defend his whole conduct, whilst a writer under the Signature of Menander defends his fellow citizens, to Say no more like an able counsel. These Peices you will find in the Centinal of December 19 and 22 and 26th. Those of the 19 and 22th are written in a masterly stile.

Your Friends here are all well excepting Brother Cranch who has had a very ill Turn. I fear he will not tarry long with us.

I am my Dear Husband with the tenderest Regard and attachment your affectionate

A Adams

John Adams to Abigail Adams

My dearest Friend   Philadelphia Feb. 17. 1793

We have had such falls of snow and rain that I Suppose the Mail has been retarded and I have no Letters; and you may be in the same Case. I have written however as regularly as usual. I have no Letters nor Message from our dear Family at N. York since their Arrival excepting a Line from Charles the next morning announcing it. Another fortnight and I shall sett out on my return home. I shall make a short stay at N. Y. for fear of worse roads as well as from a Zeal to get home. Indeed I have so little affection for that *southern state* as it has lately become, that the sooner I get thro it the better.

I have a great Mind to send home our furniture. My Salary has become ridiculous, sunk more than half in its Value and about to be reduced still lower by another Million of Paper to be emitted by a new Bank of Pensilvania. Before I was aware I got abominably involved in debt and I shall not easily get out. By I will be no longer a Dupe. The hospitality of Philadelphia would have kept me, the whole Winter at Dinner with one Family and at Tea and Cards with another: but I have made it a rule to decline all Invitations excepting such as came from Families where I had never dined before, and excepting once with the senators who have families here, once with our Ministers of State and once with foreign Ministers. It has been Employment enough to write Apologies in Answer to Invitations. I should have been down with the Ague long before now if I had accepted Invitations to Evening Parties. I never dine out without loosing the next nights Sleep, which shews that there is still a disposition to a fever.

I live in terror least the State of Europe should force the President to Call Congress together in summer. I am not without hopes however that the national Convention of France will give England Satisfaction about Holland, the Austrian Netherlands and the Seheld, that We may still be blessed with Peace: but if there should be war We shall be intrigued into it, if possible.

The Personal hatreds and Party Animosities which prevail here, have left me more in tranquility than any other Person. The Altercations between the humble Friends of the two or three Ministers have done no service to the Reputation of either. The S. of the Treasury has suffered as much as the Secretary of State. Ambition is imputed to both, and the Moral Character of both has Suffered in the S[. . .]ting. They have been Lifted by Satan like Wheat and all the Spots that have been discoverd have been circulated far and wide. I am afraid that Hamiltons Schemes will become unpopular, because the State Legislatures are undermining them and Congress will be obliged either to let them fall in the Publick opinion, or to support them by measures which will be unpopular. Hamilton has been intemperately puffed and this has excited green Eyed Jealousy and haggard Envy. Jays Friends have let Escape feelings of Jealousy as well as Jeffersons. And it is very natural. Poor me who have no Friends to be jealous, I am left out of the Question and pray I ever may. Yours tenderly

J. A.

Abigail Adams to John Adams

my dearest Friend   Quincy Febry 22 1793

My Last Letter was written to you in Bed. I write this from my chair, my fever is leaving me and I am mending So that I can set up the chief of the day. The Dr Says it was the unexpected News of mrs Smiths return that had so happy an effect upon me as to Break my fever. I am languid and weak but hope to be well by the Time you return. I shall forward my next Letter to you, to be left at N york as it might not reach you in Philadelphia if you set out as soon in March as you propose. I would mention to you your Coupons for the year least it should slip your mind. I believe I mentiond in my last all that I could think of respecting domestick concerns. Our weather is so changeable that it retards the kind of Buisness which I should be glad to have compleated. This week we have had floods of rain, which has carried of the chief of the heavy snow which fell the week before. O I forgot to mention to mr Brisler to cut me some of the weeping willows, and put on Board any of the vessels comeing this way, some of mr Morriss peach tree Grafts, we have some young plumb trees which will answer for stocks. Your Brother told me on monday Evening that the Senate had made choice of mr Strong; I presume the House will concur. Tis an ill wind which blows no good to any one. The late failures in Boston have thrown some buisness into the hands of our son. He is well and grows very fat.

Present me affectionatly to all my Friends particularly to Mrs Washington whom I both Love and respect. Remember me to Mrs otis and tell her that her sister Betsy complains that she does not write to her. A Kiss to Miss Harriot, tell her she must find out how I sent it. Your Mother desires to be rememberd to you. One day last week whilst I was the most Sick, the Severest N East snow storm came that we have had through the winter. We could not pass with a carriage, and I desired my People not to let her know how ill I was as she could not get to See me, but no sooner was there a foot tract than she put on stockings over her shoes, and I was astonishd to hear her voice below Stairs. She has had better health than for some years past.

Adieu all Friends send their Regards. Ever Yours

A Adams

John Adams to Abigail Adams

My dear   Philadelphia March 2. 1793

Your Letter from your Sick Chamber if not from your Sick bed, has made me so uneasy that I must get away as soon as possible. Monday Morning at Six, I am to Sett off in the Stage, but how many days it will take to get home will depend on the Roads, and/or the Winds. I dont believe Nabby will go with me. Her Adventurer of an Husband is so proud of his Wealth that he would not let her go I suppose without a Coach and four, and such Monarchical Trumpery I will in future have nothing to do with. I will never travel but by the Stage nor live at the seat of Government but at Lodgings, while they give me so despicable an Allowance. Shiver my Jibb and start my Planks if I do.

I will Stay but one night at New York. Smith says that my Books are upon the Table of every Member of the Committee for framing a Constitution of Government for France except Tom Paine, and he is so conceited as to disdain to have any Thing to do with Books.

Although I abused Smith, a little above he is very clever and agreable: but I have been obliged to caution him against his disposition to boasting. Tell not of your Prosperity because it will make two Men mad to one glad; nor of your Adversity for it will make two Men glad to one Sad. He boasts too much of having made his fortune, and placed himself at his ease; above all favours of Government. This is a weakness, and betrays too little knowledge of the World: too little Penetration; too little discretion. I wish however that my Boys had a little more of his Activity. I must soon treat them as The Pidgeons treat their Squabs—push them off the Limb and make them put out their Wings or fall. Young Pidgeons will never fly till this is done.

Smith has acquired the Confidence of the French Ministry and the better sort of the Members of the national Convention: but the Executive is too changeable in that Country to be depended on, without the Utmost caution.

Adieu, Adieu, tendrement

J. A.

John Adams to Abigail Adams

Col Smiths Cottage,

My Dearest Friend   near New York Nov. 28 1793

I arrived here Yesterday, and had the Pleasure to dine with our Children and The Baron: All are very well and send their Duty. Charles is well, fat and handsome, and persists in the Line of Conduct which We so much approved. His Business increases and he will do well.

Accounts from Philadelphia continue to be favourable. Mr Otis has written for his Family to come on, as Mrs Smith informs me. If so I shall be at no loss.

Mr Genet has made a curious Attack upon Mr Jay and Mr King which you will see in the Papers. My Duty to Mother, Love to Brothers Sisters Cousins, particularly Louisa. I go on towards Philadelphia to day. Yours

J. A.

John Quincy Adams, under the pen name "Columbus," wrote a series of articles questioning the conduct of "Citizen" Edmond Genêt, France's controversial minister to the United States. Genêt, who had foolishly challenged the president's authority, saw his popularity and influence plummet. Abigail and John, as their letters reveal, were immensely proud of their son.

John Adams to Abigail Adams

My dearest Friend   Philadelphia Decr. 26. 1793

I have enough to do to write Apologies in Answer to Invitations to dinner and to Tea Parties: but I have long since taken the Resolution that I will not again loose myself and all my time in a wild vagary of Dissipation. As it is not in my Power to live on equal terms with the Families and Personages who exhibit so much real Hospitality in this City, I would not lay myself under Obligations to them which I could not repay. But besides this I have other Motives. I have Occasion for some time to write Letters to my friends, and for more, that I may read something, and not be wholly ignorant of what is passing in the litterary World. There is more pleasure and Advantage to me, in this than is to be found in Parties at dinner or at Tea.

Columbus is republishing in New York, in a public Paper, of whose Title I am ignorant, whose Editor is Mr Noah Webster who is lately removed from Hartford to that City, and is said to conduct his Gazette with Judgment and Spirit upon good Principles. He has given a conspicuous Place and a large handsome Type, as I am told to the Speculations of the Bostonian. Here they are unknown, except to two or three, but I have heard they are to appear a Printer having heard Mr Ames Say they were *a very compleat Thing* and that there was but one Man in Boston that he knew of who could write them.

Our Friend Mr Cabot has bought a Farm in Brokelyne, adjoining to that of my Grandfathers, where he is to build an House next Summer. He delights in nothing more than in talking of it. The Searchers of Secret motives in the heart have their Conjectures that this Country Seat in the Vicinity of Boston was purchased with the same Views which some ascribed to Mr Gerry in purchasing his Pallace at Cambridge and to Gen. Warren in his allighting on Milton Hill. Whether these Shrewd Conjectures are right or not, I own I wish the State may never have worse Governors, than Gerry or Cabot, and I once thought the same of the other.

I am told Mr Jefferson is to resign tomorrow. I have so long been in an habit of thinking well of his Abilities and general good dispositions, that I cannot but feel some regret at this Event: but his Want of Candour, his obstinate Prejudices both of Aversion and Attachment: his real Partiality in Spite of all his Pretensions and his low notions about many Things have so nearly reconciled me to it, that I will not weep. Whether he will be chosen Governor of Virginia, or whether he is to go to France, in Place of Mr Morris I know not. But this I know that if he is neglected at Montecello he will soon see a Spectre like the disgraced Statesman in Gill Blass, and not long afterwards will die, for instead of being the ardent pursuer of science that some think him, I know he is indolent, and his soul is prisoned with Ambition. Perhaps the Plan is to retire, till his Reputation magnifies enough to force him into the Chair in Corse. So be it, if it is thus ordained. I like the Precedent very well because I expect I shall have occasion to follow it. I have been thirty years planning and preparing an Assylum for myself and a most admirable one it is, for it is so entirely out of order, that I might busy myself, to the End of my Life, in making Improvements. So that God willing I hope to conquer the fowl Fiend whenever I shall be obliged or inclined to retire. But of this prattle, (entre nous) enough.

Yours as ever.

Abigail Adams to John Adams

my dearest Friend   Quincy Dec'br 31 1793

Your two kind Letters of the 19 and 20th reachd me on the 28th. They are my Saturday evenings repast. You know my mind is much occupied with the affairs of our Country. If as a Female I may be calld an Idle, I never can be an uninterested Spectator of what is transacting upon the great Theater, when the welfare and happiness of my Children and the rising generation is involved in the present counsels and conduct of the Principal Actors who are now exhibiting upon the stage. That the Halcion days of America are past I fully believe, but I cannot agree with you in sentiment respecting the office you hold; altho it is so limited as to prevent your being so actively usefull as you have been accustomed to, Yet those former exertions and Services give a weight of Character which like the Heavenly orbs silently diffuse a benign influence. Suppose for Instance as things are often exemplified by their contraries, a Man, in that office, of unbridled Ambition, Subtile intriguing, warpd and biased by interested views, joining at this critical crisis, his Secret influence against the Measures of the President, how very soon would this Country be involved in all the Horrours of a civil war. I am happy to learn that the only fault in your political Character, and one which has always given me uneasiness, is wearing away, I mean a certain irritability which has some time thrown you of your Gaurd and shewn as is reported of Louis 14.th that a Man is not always a Hero. Partizans are so high, respecting English and French politicks, and argue so falsly and Reason so stupidly that one would suppose they could do no injury, but there are so many who read and hear without reflecting and judging for themselves and there is such a propensity in humane Nature to believe the worst, especially when their interest is like to be affected, that if we are preserved from the Calamities of war it will be more oweing to the superintending Providence of God than the virtue and wisdom of Man. How we are to avoid it with France supposing Genet should not be recall'd I know not. Must we Submit to such insults? Judging from the manner in which France has carried on the present war, I should not wonder if they feard a Partition of their Kingdom. A Frenchman reminding an Englishman of the Time when in the Reign of Henry the Sixth, the English were almost absolute Masters of France Said Sneerlingly to him "When do you think you will again become Lords of our kingdom?" to which the Englishman replied, "When your iniquities shall be greater than ours." How can any Nation expect to prosper who war against Heaven?

By this time you will have seen all the Numbers of Columbus. I should like to know the Presidents opinion of them, as well as some other Gentlemen who are judges. They assuredly are ably written, and do honour both to the Head and Heart of the writer, who deserves well of his fellow citizens for the information he has thrown upon a subject of so much importance at so critical a period. But their is a "barberous Noise of asses Apes and dogs" raisd by it in the Chronical. Nevertheless sound reason and cool Argument will prevail in the end.

Having spun my thread out with respect to politicks I will think a little of our own private affairs. Dr Tufts has paid two hundred pounds and become responsible himself for the remainder. I wrote to you his further intention. The 17 of Janry he proposes to discharge two hundreds pounds more. I have closed my account this day. I have kept an exact account of my expenditures and payments since you left me, which I inclose to you. Mr Cary offerd to bring me an other load of Hay at the same price. What he brought is agreed to be of the first quality, and it was all weighd, but I did not feel myself in a capacity to engage it absolutely. We have hitherto had so little snow that Buisness is dull. Mr Belcher has cleard of all the Sea weed untill Some high Tide brings more. He is now getting home the pine wood.

Our Friends desire to be rememberd to you. Mrs Brisler and family are well. You will present me affectionatly to mrs washington who I respect and Love.

My Love to Thomas. I hear he is for fighting the Algerines, but I am not sure that would be the best oconomy, tho it might give us a good pretence for Building a Navy that we need not be twichd by the Nose by every sausy Jack a Nips. He had better find Law for his countrymen and prevail upon them to take it.

I am as ever most affectionately yours

A Adams

John Adams to Abigail Adams

My dearest Friend　　　　　　　　　　Philadelphia January 6. 1794

The Door Keeper has just brought me your kind Letter of Decr 28.

Freneau's Paper is discontinued and Fenno's is become a daily advertising Paper and has not yet been worth Sending you. The State Papers will be reprinted in Russells Paper which you have and there has been nothing else worth Reading. I Send you the Negotiations with Genet, inclosed.

The Algerines will cost this Country very dear. We may curse them, as much as We please and fight them as long as We will and after all We must advance them the Cash. This has been long my Opinion but I could not be believed. We may rave against the English and Spaniards: but We had better learn better manners than wantonly to insult and provoke Nations who have Power to hurt Us.

Genet has not appeared at the Levee: but he made me a Visit in Ceremony, soon after he came to Town, which I returned the second day afterwards.

Jefferson went off Yesterday, and a good riddance of bad ware. I hope his Temper will be more cool and his Principles more reasonable in Retirement than they have been in office. I am almost tempted to wish he may be chosen Vice President at the next Election for there if he could do no good, he could do no harm. He has Talents I know, and Integrity I believe: but his mind is now poisoned with Passion Prejudice and Faction.

You have drawn an affecting Picture of Distress in the Family of

Dr Rhoads. How it is possible for People to marry and proceed to get-ting a Brood of Children without any means of support, I know not. A more imprudent Enterprize never was undertaken than the Removal of that Family to Braintree, and after they came there, they never took one Step, which common Sense would have dictated to get into Busi-ness. I hope however you will contribute as much as you can to allevi-ate her Distress. My Imagination has often painted to me exactly such a Picture in a Case of our Silly Charles, who was once in a fair Way to have raised as happy a family but who I hope is grown wiser. You ought to have written the history of Mrs Rhoads and her Children to him.

We have had a cold day or two: but the Weather is now as beautiful as it was last Winter. I think it is not quite so warm and therefore I hope will not lay a foundation for another Summer like the last. We have no News of Cheesman. Brisler wants his Cloaths more than I do, mine.

Columbus has been reprinted in Several Papers in New York but not yet in this City. Parties run high in South Carolina. A Mr S. Drayton has published a curious Narration of his own Sufferings but has not even denied the Fact of which he was charged. My News Mans Address has it

> At home dissentions Seem to rend
> Or threat, our Infant State
> 'Bout Treaties made; yet unexplain'd
> With Citizen Genet.

The People in general are wise, upright, firm and Steady: But There are little groups of Wrong heads in every principal Town.

I am with ardent Wishes and fervent Prayers for your health yours

J A

John Adams to Abigail Adams

My dearest Friend   Philadelphia January 21. 1794

We go slowly forward: so Slowly as to produce no Results, which is a better course than to run rapidly in a Career of Mischief.

I go to Senate every day, read the News papers before I go and the Public Papers afterwards, see a few Friends once a Week, go to Church on Sundays; write now and then a Line to you and to Nabby: and oftener to Charles than to his Brothers to see if I can fix his Attention and excite his Ambition: in which design I flatter myself I shall have Success.

John may pursue his Studies and Practice with Confidence as well as Patience. His Talents, his Virtues his Studies and his Writings are not unknown, nor will they go without their Recompence, if Trouble is a Recompence for Trouble. If the People neglect him the Government will not: if the Government neglect him the People will not, at least very long.

Thomas is reading Clarendon, in order to form a Judgment of the Duration of the French Republick; and all other such Democratical Republicks which may arise in the great Maritime and commercial, Avaricious and corrupted Nations of Europe.

Cheesman I hear is returned to Boston. Our Trunk had better be taken out. Thomas's Books and Boots should be Sent here: but the rest may be carried to Quincy. I want nothing and Brisler says having done without his Things so long, he had rather do without them now till We return.

The Senators and Reps. say that We must Sit here till May. Some hope to be up in April. I cannot flatter myself to be at home till the first of May. If the Yellow Fever should make its Appearance, We shall Seperate earlier, but the general opinion and universal hope is that it will not return at all: at least till after the extream Heats of summer.

Col. Smith Spent about a fortnight here and is now returned. He is tormented by his Ambition but has taken very unsagacious measures to remove his Pains. I know not what he is in Pursuit of.

I am affectionately Yours.

John Adams to Abigail Adams

My dearest Friend   Philadelphia January 22 1794

I am weary of this Scæne of Dulness. We have done nothing and shall do nothing this Session, which ought to be done, unless We should appropriate a sufficient sum of Money, for treating with the Algerines. We are afraid to go to War, though our Inclinations and Dispositions are strong enough to join the French Republicans. It is happy that our Fears are a Check to our Resentments: and our Understandings are better than our Hearts.

One Day spent at home would afford me more inward Delight and Comfort than a Week or a Winter in this Place.

We have frequent Rumours and Allarms about the yellow fever: but when they come to be traced to their Sources they have hitherto proved to be false. There is one at present in Circulation which is not quite cleared up, and the Weather is extreamly warm, muggy foggy and unfavourable for the Season.

The River is open and some say is never frozen over after this time. Others say there have been Instances in the last Week in January.

Thomas visits me of Evenings and We converse concerning Hampden and Faulkland, Charles and Oliver Essex and Rupert of whose Characters and Conduct he reads every day in Lord Clarendon. I fear he makes too many Visits in Families where there are young Ladies. Time is spent and nothing learn'd. Pardon me! Disciple of Woolstoncroft! I never relished Conversations with Ladies excepting with one at a time and alone rather than in Company. I liked not to loose my time.

I begin now to think All time lost, that is not employed in Farming. Innocent, healthy gay, elegant Amusement! Enchanting Employment! How my imagination roves over my rocky Mountains and through my brushy Meadows!

Yours &c.

"This Whirligig of a World"

February 1794–December 1795

John's frustration with his life in Philadelphia during these years filled his letters. The emergence of political parties, increasing sectional disputes, and the growing influence of Revolutionary France upon Americans, especially the Democratic-Republican opposition, troubled him. His second term as vice president became a grinding ordeal in which debate and conflict in Congress replaced action. He longed "for the Times when Old Sam. and Old John conducted with more Wisdom and more success." The insignificance of his office galled him, and he frequently mentioned retirement.

Abigail's letters inspired him to continue. She too feared that the pernicious French ideas might infect and ruin the new republic, and claimed much lost sleep worrying. Her letters became John's refuge as he isolated himself from much of the capital's society.

Despite all of the national and international issues that beset the government and kept John in a state of agitation, family and farm matters remained a constant topic in the correspondence. In 1794 the president appointed John Quincy to a diplomatic mission to the Netherlands. Younger brother Thomas Boylston went as his secretary. With a mixture of pride and concern the parents followed their sons' progress. In 1795 daughter Nabby presented her parents with their first granddaughter, Caroline Amelia Smith, and middle son Charles married and appeared to be settling into a career in the law.

John Adams to Abigail Adams

My dearest Friend   Philadelphia Feb. 4. 1794

The Mail of Yesterday brought me, a rich Treasure in your kind Letters of the 18. 24 and 25th of January. Ice in the Rivers or Snow or some other Obstructions on the Roads have delay'd the Conveyance of some of them and occasioned their Arrival all together.

Columbus and Barneveld were both written with Elegance and Spirit and the poor Wretches who so justly fell under their Lashes were never before nor since so exemplarily and so justly punished.

I hope my old Friend, will never meet the Fate of another Preacher of *Egalite*, who was I fear almost as sincere as himself. By The Law of Nature, all Men are Men and not Angells—Men and not Lyons—Men and not Whales Men and not Eagles—That is they are all of the same Species. And this is the most that the Equality of Nature amounts to. But Man differs by Nature from Man, almost as much as Man from Beast. The Equality of Nature is Moral and Political only and means that all Men are independent. But a Physical Inequality, an Intellectual Inequality of the most serious kind is established unchangeably by the Author of Nature. And Society has a Right to establish any other Inequalities it may judge necessary for its good. The Precept however Do as you would be done by implys an Equality which is the real Equality of Nature and Christianity, and has been known and understood in all Ages before the Lt. G. of Massachusetts made the discovery in January 1784.

I am pleased to hear that the Court appointed again their late State Attorney. Mr Dalton called on me a few Weeks ago to communicate to me a great Secret. The President had the Evening before took him aside and enquired of him very particularly concerning the Vice Presidents son at Boston: his Age, his Practice, his Character &c &c &c at the same time making great Inquiries concerning Mr Parsons of Newbury Port. From all which Mr D. conjectured that Mr Gore was to be appointed Attorney Gen. of U.S. and J. Q. Adams Attorney for the

District. I was somewhat allarmed and was determined to Advize my son to refuse it, if it should be so, though I did not believe it. I would not advize Mr J. Q. A. to play at small Games in the Executive of U.S. I had much rather he should be State Attorney for Suffolk. Let him read Cicero and Demosthenes, much more eloquent than Madison and Smith.

The rascally Lie about the Duke of York in a Cage at Paris and Toulon and all the English Fleet in the Hands of the Republick was fabricated on purpose to gull the Gudgeons and it completely Succeeded to my infinite mortifications. An Attempt was made to get me to read the red hot Lie in Senate in order to throw them into as foolish a Confusion as that below them: but I was too Old to be taken in, at least by so gross an Artifice the falshood of which was to me palpable.

You Apologize for the length of your Letters and I ought to excuse the shortness and Emptiness of mine. Yours give me more entertainment than all the speeches I hear. There is more good Thoughts, fine strokes and Mother Wit in them than I hear in the whole Week. An Ounce of Mother Wit is worth a Pound of Clergy—and I rejoice that one of my Children at least has an Abundance of not only Mother Wit, but his Mothers Wit. It is one of the most amiable and striking Traits in his Compositions. It appeared in all its Glory and severity in Barneveld.

If the Rogue has any Family Pride, it is all derived from the same source. His Pa renounces and abjures every Trace of it. He has Curiosity to know his descent and Comfort in the Knowledge that his Ancestors on both sides for several Generations have been innocent. But no Pride in this—Pomp Splendor, Office Title, Power, Riches are the sources of Pride, but even these are not excuse for Pride. The Virtues and Talents of Ancestors, should be considered as Examples and solem Trusts and Produce Meekness Modesty and Humity, least they should not be imitated and equalled. Mortification and Humiliation can be the only legitimate feelings of a Mind conscious that it falls short of its Ancestors in Merit.

I must Stop.

Yours affectionately

John Adams

John's mother, Susanna Boylston Adams Hall, who remarried five years after John's father died, had been widowed again in 1780. Already 85 years old in 1794, her many health crises remained a frequent topic in Abigail's reports. Abigail served as the prime caregiver for Mrs. Hall until her death in April 1797, six weeks after her son assumed his duties as president. Despite her long life there are no extant letters between John and his mother. The news concerning her health and other interests was usually conveyed by Abigail.

John Adams to Abigail Adams

private and secret

My dearest Friend   Philadelphia Feb. 4. 1794

The Indisposition of my ever honoured and beloved Mother gives me a very tender Anxiety. I hope she may yet get the better of her Disorder and enjoy a good share of Health. Remember me to her in the most affectionate and dutiful manner.

You ask me if I wish to give any Directions. I pray you not to let the good old Lady know that you have asked or I answered such a Question. But if the Melancholly Event should unhappily take Place, I desire to be at the whole Expence of a decent Funeral and pray My Brother to accept of all Claims from me of any share in whatever may be left. But if Health should be restored I pray you to Burn this Letter and say not a Word of it to any one.

Yours

John Adams

John Adams to Abigail Adams

My dearest Friend   Philadelphia Feb. 10. 1794

I have recd yours of Jan. 31.—And it has relieved me from a Melancholly which has hung upon me and been taken notice of by every body, since you wrote me of my Mothers illness. Present her my dutiful affection and tell her that I hope to enjoy the Pleasure of her Company yet for many Years—That I am of her Opinion that she has the best Daughter and that the best Mother ought to have such a Daughter.

It is Day about with the Newsmongers. France is in not so good a Way. Even Mr Butler told me this day that "he turned away his Face and thoughts from France with Disgust and Horror." A shambles is called a Republic. And if they would but have read the Discourses on Davila they would have seen all this foretold in plain Language. St. Bartholomews Days are there said to be the natural and necessary Consequence of such a form of Government. And St. Bartholomews Days will endure as long as the form of Government—aussi longtems qu'il plaira a Dieu.

I am weary of this eternal Indecision. I wish for the Times when Old Sam. and Old John conducted with more Wisdom and more success. This is Egotism enough to deserve the Guillotine to be sure but I cannot but recollect old scænes, and old Results.

The Rascals are now abusing the President as much as ever they abused me. And We shall see that A life of disinterested Devotion to the Publick is no more sacred in him than in another. In this Days Paper he is compared to Cosmo De Medicis to Sylla to Cæsar: and charged with arbitrary illegal Conduct in many particulars particularly in the Proclamation respecting Duplaine.

He cannot get out, any more than the Stirling, but I believe he desires it as fervently. I am determin'd to be saucy and I say that a Parcell of ignorant Boys who know not a rope in the ship, have the Vanity to think themselves able seamen.

We ought to authorize the President in perfect Secrecy to go as far as two hundred Thousand Pounds to obtain a perpetual Peace with the Algerines. Build a few frigates if you will but expect they will be useless because unmanned. But there is not a Member of either House who is not more master of the Subject than I am, so I should be modest.

Yours as ever.

Abigail Adams to John Adams

my Dearest Friend   Quincy Feb'ry 14th 1794

I received last Evening by my obliging Neighbour Captain Beals your kind Letters of Febry 4th, and before I reply to them I would inform you that our venerable Parent has appeard to revive for these two days past. Her disorder has proved a Lung fever. The dr advised to a puke two days ago. She was rather averse to it, wishing rather as she expresst herself to dye in quiet. She had labourd under a great sickness at her stomack which made her loath both food and medicine. It appeard to me likely to give her relief and I urged her to it promising to attend her through it. "Well she replied if you say so, it must be so. The Girls when they bring me any thing, do not say the dr says you must take it, but Aunt Adams says so, and then they are sure it will go down." We accordingly gave the puke, and it opperated kindly, since which she has rested better, expectorated freer, and for the present appears relieved. She inquired of me a few days since if I had written to you of her sickness. I told her that I had. She took me by the hand, and bursting into Tears, "give my Love and blessing to him. I shall never see my Dear Son again." I am happy in having so far anticipated your request as not to have given Your Brother occasion to expend a shilling upon her account. I have mentiond to you in a Letter already forwarded what I had done. Should the Melancholy event which we apprehend take place I shall punctually adhere to your directions. Such

I presumed they would be and that led me to ask them and further I had thought to remove the venerable Remains to this House, as it might be considerd an additional respect to them to have them intered from hence. These circumstances will remain in my breast only, unless circumstances call them into action.

I received by this Post 30 pounds. As the draught was forwarded to our son, and you made no mention of it in your Letter I am at a loss to determine whether you forwarded it towards the discharge of Pratts account, or whether you conceived I might have occasion for it, for purposes mentiond in your Private Letter. Having as you will see by a mem. inclosed discharg'd some debts upon the Receipt of the former Bills I have not at present sufficient to spair to make up the 20 dollors, more upon the account, without straitning myself more than I chuse, not because I have expended the other 30£, but because I have lent half of it. A vessel arrived from Germany loaded with 18 thousand calf skins, of a superiour quality and 2 shillings lower than they are to be purchased here. Boilstone was desirious of procuring a couple of hundred and for that purpose I lent him 50 dollars to make up his Sum. I wish it had been in my power to have lent him 500. Deacon Webb, purchased 18 hundred of the same skins, kept four hundred for his own use, in less than a week sold the remainder with an advance of only sixpence upon a skin, cleard his own four hundred and put a thousand crowns in his pocket. That is doing business to some purpose. I have laid by the money and if I should not be obliged to appropriate some of it, as I fear, it shall be paid to Pratt. The tarring of Trees will speedily commence. I must take Arnold into service. I pray your directions upon the subject of my two last Letters. I wrote to Brisler to inquire the price of oats and Rye. Belcher was in Town this week but he could not purchase oats at less than three shillings and Rye at 8. When you went away almost three months ago I had only three Gallons of Rum remaining of what Brisler bought. That has anwerd till this time, but as soon as my spring work commences I must make large recruits.

The political part of your Letters I must defer replying to till the next post. Mrs Field is upon the Recovery. Mrs Brisler and Family well, but sine I have returnd from Philadelphia so many persons have not been sick in Town. Aged and Children, appear to be voilently attackd with fevers. I have happily yet escaped any confinement. Am most affectionatly your

A Adams

John Adams to Abigail Adams

My dearest Friend   Philadelphia Feb. 17. 1794

I this day recd your favours of the 8. and 12th. but how this last could have leaped to this distance in five days I know not.

It is impossible to Say precisely when Congress will rise: but I will go home as soon as possible; I hope in April. I am very willing to confide all Arrangements to you. I like Shaw and his Wife: and I like Richards and Joy from your Account of them. We will try a dairy at each house: ten Cows at Thayers and Ten at Faxons, but they must all go to Pasture up Pens hill, till after, mowing the fresh Meadows. I wish you to buy as many Yearling Calves and two year olds as you can, and Cows to make up the N. 20 reserving two for our own home. I have sent an 100 Wt of Clover seed and twelve Quarts of herds Grass. Shaw may go into Thayers House the first of March if he will, and if you have not other Employment he may mow Bushes in the Pasture opposite. I shall plant again where Faxon planted last Year. The Fences should be put up as early as may be, and the manure carted in season.

My Mothers Indisposition continues to affect me most sensibly: I hope for her Blessing on you and me and on all our Posterity—and I thank you for your tender Care and watchful Attention to her, and I hope you will continue to supply every Want as far as may be in our Power. As We are not to live long in this earthly Residence, she has re-mained longer, and fullfilled every Duty of Life better than Mankind in general, and We shall again meet her I hope in a better World. This is scarcely worthy of Persons of her Character. She goes to the World where our Fathers are gone, and We must soon follow.

I am with every tender sentiment yours

J. A.

Abigail Adams to John Adams

my Dearest Friend   Feb'ry 26 1794 Quincy

Not receiveing any Letters on Saturday evening I was so impatient that I sent James to Town on Sunday afternoon, and he brought me home your kind favours of the 8th 9th and 10th of this Month; I do not omit writing to you once a week, and sometimes twice.

The late King of Prussia said that every age must commit its own follies, and that the experience of other was but of little benifit to them. "National corruption must be purged by National Calamities. A real reformation is not to be accomplish'd by ordinary means; it requires those extraordinary means which become punishments as well as lesson's," were the observations of a Great Politician: Whether France will ever emerge from the horrids Scenes, that deluge her with carnage, havock, and Blood, "is in the dark Gloom and abyss of Time." There present situation is well pictured in the following lines

> "The sacred arts of rule
> Turn'd to flagitious leagues against mankind
> And arts of plunder, more and more avow'd
> Devotion turn'd to a Solemn farce
> To holy dotage virtue; even to guile,
> To murder, and a mockery of oaths;
> Dishonour'd courage to the Bravo's trade
> To civil Broil; and Glory to romance
> Alass poor Gallia! What a bitter cup
> of vengeance hast thou drain'd?
> How many a ruffian form hast thou beheld?

What horrid jargons heard, where rage alone
Was all thy frighted ear could comprehend?
How frequent by the red inhumane hand
Yet warm with Brother's husbands, Fathers Blood,
Hast thou thy Matrons and thy virgins seen
To voilation dragg'd, and mingled death."

You ask me what mr Wibird says now to the French. He says that he believes that they will all go to the devil and that they deserve to, but still insists that they never would have gone to such dreadfull lengths if they had not been invaded and driven to desperation by foreign powers, and that future generations will be benifitted by their calamity. The abuse upon the President which you mention, but which I do not see, proves that the most virtuous and unblemishd Characters are liable to the Malice and venom of unprincipald Wretches. Such Virtues such disinterested Patriotism, when thus requited, has frequently become Tyranical, and unless mankind were universally enlightned, which never can be. They are unfit for freedom, nor do I belive that our Creator designd it for them. If such a Boon had been designd for them, all Ages and Nations from Adam to the present day would not have been one standing continued and universal proof to the contrary. Some were made for Rule others for submission, and even amongst my own Sex this doctrine holds good. History informs us that of the few Queens who have reigned for any length of Time as absolute Sovereigns the greatest part of them have been celebrated for excellent Govenours. Pliny, tells us that in Meroe, women rained for many successive ages. Among the Lacedemonians, the woman had a great share in the political Government; and that it was agreeable to the Laws given them by Licurgns. In Borneo, the women Reign alone, and their Husbands enjoy no other privilege than that of being their most dignified Subjects; but as Reigning and Ruling is so much out of fashion, at the present day, my ambition will extend no further than Reigning in the Heart of my Husband. That is my Throne and there I aspire to be absolute.

You will see in the Centinal a very vapid answer to a very vapid speech, and the estimation in which it was held, by the committee appointed to carry it. I have read with pleasure two very judicious papers in the Centinal taken from a Phyladelphia paper under the signature of Americanus. Such writers are wise and salutary;

> "Oh Peace! thou source and soul of Social Life
> Blest be the Man divine, who gives us thee."

I have deliverd your message to your Mother. She bids me tell you that she leaves you her Blessing, that she request your remembrane of her to the Throne of Mercy, that she is hastning to an other and a better Country, where she hopes one day to meet You, but that here she shall never see you more, and of this opinion I am daily more and more, as her decay becomes more and more visible. A few weeks if not days must put a period to a long and to a very irreproachable Life. My constant attendance upon her has very much lessned my desire of long life. Her fears least she should recover and become useless, her appearing to have out lived every enjoyment, shews that life at best is but a poor play, and the best that can come of it, it is a misirable Benediction. These Reflections exclude any further addition to my Letter, than the sincerest which I can make you of being ever Yours

A Adams

John Adams to Abigail Adams

My dearest Friend   Philadelphia March 11. 1794

I received Yesterday your kind Letter of Feb. 28. and March 1. I can never be sufficiently thankful to you for your constant unwearied Attention and tender care of my Mother. I hope that you will be very careful of your own Health and not suffer your Solicitude and Exertions to go beyond your Strength.

Our Selfish young Rogue at Boston is so taken up with his Business and his Fees, that he has not written me any Thing this Winter. However he has done a Public Service of more importance than is or ever will be acknowledged, by any Body but his father and Mother.

The Federalists must be in high Spirits to threaten Such mighty Things. But I doubt their Power, their Union, their Spirit too much. They are Seeking Popularity and Loaves and Fishes as well as the Anti's and find it inconvenient to act a decided open Part in any Thing. But for this, many Things would have gone better. But for this your Husband would not have been Sacrificed, nor the unrivalled unexampled Writings of your Son persecuted or neglected, as they have been. Let him listen to the Charge of a Father to mind his private Business and keep himself forever independent of the Smiles or Frowns of political Parties. A rigorous Frugality in Spight of all the Sneers of Bankrupts, Debauchees and Puppies, A solid Income from a landed Estate in the Country; an unwearied Attention to study and Business: and an Integrity inexorable to every temptation, will carry him, as it has his father, through Life with more comfort and Honour and enable him to do more good than hundreds of thousands of Reptiles and Insects by which he may be sometimes annoied.

You go on in the Conduct of your Farm with so much Spirit, amidst all your melancholly avocations, that it is a noble Regale to read your Letters. Plant the Ground which We broke up last fall with corn. Sow Barley where We had corn last Year. Plant again the lower Garden, Potatoes again at the Beach Meadow. Plant again Faxons last Years Corn field. Buy as many Cows and young Stock as you can keep in plenty. Send the sheep as soon as convenient to the Pasture by Harmans.

I shall send you some Money in a fort-night or three Weeks.

I know not whether John was at the Boston Town Meeting. Col Smiths Meeting at New York did not terminate so gloriously quite, as that at the Old South.

Most tenderly Your

John Adams

Abigail Adams to John Adams

My dearest Friend   Quincy March 28 1794

I last Evening received yours of March the 15 and 17th together with the Money you remitted. It was very fortunate in its arrival, for in half an hour after, I had two fine cows offerd me which I immediatly purchasd tho I gave 40 dollors for them. The sheep Lambd so early, and my cows came in so early that we have expended more english Hay than I could wish, and they Rob'd my Horses to feed the sheep; The oxen upon Faxons place will be very little able to work when he goes of. He has carted so constantly this winter and Spring that he has batterd the waggon wheels all to peices, but why should I perplex you with Domestick provocations, when you have so much trouble with the Political Machine. You are certainly what they Term the make weight in the Scale—which is a very important part, not so unimportant is your station as you have sometimes represented it. I believe from all I can learn that war is a very undesirable object with the people of the Eastern states. The Mercantile part, tho much opprest, became quiet, and determind to wait patiently the desision of Congress. The News of yesterday, has given spirits, and a spring to every thing. The prospect of having their vessels liberated, and their trade freed from the late embarressments together with the continuation of peace has defused a general joy.

I would fain believe that england will be too mindfull of their own interest to continue their abuse and they will be induced to make all reasonable compensation. I hope your constant and severe duty will not prove too hard for you. You may look forward to a charming Recreation and ample employ upon your Farms. I shall however do my best that nothing may essentially Suffer before your return, but I look round and feel as tho I could find employ for 20 Hands.

Your Mother continues to be gradually mending. My own Family is getting better.

I am too much occupied to have leisure to think myself Sick.

Mrs Brisler and Family are well. You will direct Brisler to give me Particular information with respect to the furniture. Yours Affectionatly &c &c.

A Adams

The war that Abigail and others feared would have been between Great Britain and the United States. Some of the issues that threatened to push the nations into conflict stemmed from the failure of the Peace of Paris, which ended the Revolutionary War, to resolve all of the problems and dispel the bad feelings between the two countries. In 1793 and early 1794, as the European war in which Britain and France were the major combatants expanded, and the challenge of new radical French ideas grew, British policy regarding America became increasingly inflexible. The British refused to give up fortifications clearly on American land, interfered with American shipping, and denied compensation to Americans for wartime losses. However, the war scare subsided later in 1794 and finally ended with the ratification of Jay's Treaty in 1795. Unfortunately, Jefferson and the opposition's dissatisfaction with that treaty increased the party spirit which the Adamses found so distasteful.

Abigail Adams to John Adams

My Dearest Friend   Quincy April 18th 1794

Your Letter of April 5th an 7th reachd me last Evening, and they fill me with more apprehensions of a War than any thing I have before heard. The Body of the people are decidedly against war, and if a War is madly or foolishly precipitated upon us, without the union of the people, we shall neither find men or money to prosecute it, and the Government will be Cursed and abused for all the concequences which must follow. I have many disputes with your Brother upon this Subject, whose passions are up, upon the insults, and abuses offerd us by Britain, and who is for fighting them instantly with out Seeing one difficulty in our way. In order to put a stop to too rash measures, Congress must rise. The people without are willing to wait the result of Negotiation as far as I can learn, and in the mean time we ought to prepare for the worst. Several vessels arrived here last week from Jamaca, where they were only carried for examination of their Papers, and immediatly dismist.

I most devoutly pray that we may be preserved from the horrours of war, and the Machinations of Man. You judg'd right of your Countrymen. The vote for mr Adams, notwithstanding all the Electionering was much more unanimous than I expected. In Quincy they were nearly divided between mr Cushing and him, in Braintree and Randolph they were nearly all for him. I am glad that we shall have a Govenour Elected by the people, and you will see by a Letter received from me before this time, how nearly we agree in sentiment upon this Subject, and I may adopt the words of mr Blount in a Letter to Pope, "that I have a good opinion of my politics, since they agree with a man who always thinks so justly." I wish it were in our power to persuade all the Nations into a calm and steady disposition of mind, while Seeking particularly the quiet of our own Country and wishing for a total end of all the unhappy divisions of mankind by party-spirit, which at best, is but the Madness of many for the Gain of a few. I Shall with pleasure upon this day particularly Set Apart by our Rulers, as a day of Humiliation and prayer, unite with them in wishing the temporal and eternal welfare of all mankind. How much more affectionatly then shall I do it for you to whom I am bound by the Strongest bonds of duty and affection. Ever yours

A Adams

John Adams to Abigail Adams

My dearest Friend   Philadelphia April 30. 1794

Your favours of 18th. and 19th instant are so full of your Plans and Labours in Agriculture, that I begin to be jealous you will acquire a Reputation as a Farmer that will quite eclypse my own.

I rejoice at length that all Tenants are dispossessed and that Land stock and Utensils are now at our own Disposal. I am glad you have bought a Yoke of oxen and hope you will buy a farm horse.

Our Thomas is fitted off with Horses saddle Bridle and Saddle Bags and on Monday last sett off upon the Circuit with Mr Ingersol. He will be absent Six Weeks. He goes to Chester Lancaster York Carlisle &c.

Mr Trumbull our Friend the Painter goes with Mr Jay as his private Secretary.

I send you an illiberal Party Pamphlet or two and am tenderly

John Adams

Abigail Adams to John Adams

my Dearest Friend   Quincy May 10th 1794

I received your's of April 27th and 30th together with the Pamphlets last Evening. Two of them from the spirit they breathe denote their origin to be of southern extract. They are a counter part with the attacks upon the Secretary made last year in the House. I have ever thought with respect to that Man, "beware of that Spair Cassius." This might be done consistant with prudence, and without the illiberal abuse in many respects so plentifully cast upon him. The writers however discover too plainly that envy. Pride and malice are the Sources from whence their opposition arrises, in stead of the publick good. They are written in the stile and spirit of Honestus, a Rancourous malice or a dissapointed ambition. At bottom you and I know that in two Instances the Letter writer Lies. "Most wickedly and from thence, if he could not be convicted in other instances." Yet we might safely conclude that many things which he alledges against the Secretary are equally false, and I shall Say of the knavish writer as the Son of Vattel says of Genet, that the Books which he abuses will outlive his malice and his Mushroom Letters; the North and South appear to be arranged very formidably against each other in politicks and one judas appears from this quarter too conspicuous for his honour, or reputation. Tis Said here that the Southern Members have promised him the vice presidency the next Election if the Southern States force us into a war. I hope their Negroes will fight our Battles, and pay these real and haughty Aristocrats all the Service due to them, from the Real and true Republicans. The Pamphlet upon Prophesy I shall send to mr Cranch who has some time been upon the subject, and told me not long since, that he was persuaded we were entering upon the third war Trumpet. He has borrowd the last volms of Gebeline lately which he is delighted with. When I have read the dreadfull Scenes which have past, and are still acting in France, when I behold so Numerous and powerfull a Nation overturning all their old established forms both of Government and of Religion opposing and baffeling so successfully so many powers, and that under no Government, that deserves the Name, I have been led to contemplate it, as no common or natural event, arrising from the pressure of any increasd burdens or any new infringment upon their priveledges, but the over ruling hand of providence fulfilling great designs. It is the Lords work and it is Marvelous in our Eyes. The skirt of the cloud will pass over us, and thankfull may we be if justice and Righteousness may preserve us from its Artiliry.

We are very dry, quite as much so as the last season. I aim at no rivalship. I only wish to fullfill my duty and pursue that which shall be for our mutual advantage. Yet I fear I shall be deemd an unprofitable Servant and that some things will be left undone; which ought to have been done. I have the satisfaction however of thinking that I am more usefull here than I could be by residing at Philadelphia.

I have very little hopes to give you respecting our aged Parent, who has had a relapse, and a very Severe one, but has Survived it, and is again better, tho mere Skin and bone, and unable to walk a step alone. Tis the decline of Nature aided by a long Sickness. Mr Cranch has accepted the post office. I check every rising wish and suppress every anxious desire for your return, when I see how necessary you are to the welfare and protection of a Country which I love, and a people who will *one day* do justice to *your memory* the reflection however of always having done what you considerd as your duty, will out weigh all popular Breath and virtue be its own reward. I am most Tenderly and affectionately your

A Adams

John Adams to Abigail Adams

My dearest Friend　　　　　　　　　　Philadelphia May 19. 1794

It is a fortnight to day Since I had a Letter from you but it Seems to me a month. I cannot blame you for one of yours is worth four of mine.

Three Bills, for laying Taxes are yet unfinished and there is little Reason to hope that they can be finished this Week, perhaps not before the End of the next. I cannot see much room to hope to get away before the first of June. A tedious Seven Months it has been and will be to me.

The Committee of Merchants Mr Norris of Salem and Mr Lyman of Boston, have Seen how the Land lays here. They have returned to Boston with more correct Views of Parties in Congress than they brought with them.

The Projects for War, have been detected and exposed in every Shape, and under every disguise that has been given them, and hitherto defeated. What another Year may bring forth I know not. Britain will not be in a very good condition to provoke a fresh Ennemy, in the Spring of 1795 with her 3 Per Cents Consolidated down at 55 or less;

and they will probably be as low as that, even if the combined Powers should have better Successes than they have had.

I have no Letter from Thomas last Week. He was at Lancaster.

Mr John, I hear rises in his Reputation at the Bar as well as in the Esteem of his fellow Citizens. His Writings have given him a greater Consideration in this Place than he is aware of. I am Sometimes told that I ought to be proud of him: and truly I dont *want* to be told this. He will be made a Politician too soon. But he is a Man of great Experience, and I hope sound Philosophy. He was a greater statesman at Eighteen, than some senators I have known at fifty. But he must learn Silence and Reserve, Prudence, Caution—above all to curb his Vanity and collect himself, faculties or Virtues that his Father has often much wanted. I have often thought he has more Prudence at 27, than his Father at 58.

I am, impatiently yours

J. A.

Abigail Adams to John Adams

Quincy 27 May 1794

Thanks to the Father of the Rain, and the Bountifull dispencer of the dews of Heaven, who has plentifully waterd the dry and thirsty Earth. The Fields recover their verdure, and the little Hills rejoice, the drooping vine rears its head and the witherd flower Blooms anew.

Join every living Soul

> "Beneath the Spacious temple of the sky,
> In adoration join; and, ardent raise
> one general song! To him ye vocal gales
> Breathe soft, whose spirit in your freshness Breaths:
> Soft rool your insense, herbs, and fruits and flowers
> In mingled clouds to Him; whose Sun exalts
> Whose Breath perfumes you, and whose pencil paints."

Indeed my dearest Friend it would rejoice your Heart to behold the change made in the appearene of all Nature, after one of our old fashiond Election storms as we used to term them. I hope we may be further blessd by repeated Showers.

I this day received yours of the 19th of May. I know not what became of the letter you mention. Such a one there was, nor do I recollect a Syllable of its contents, excepting asking your advise about the land which was the peice owned formerly by Margert vesey. I had 72 pounds bid for it, but it sold at 60 dollers pr acre and was purchased by dr Phips. I also mentiond that the Name of Adams might be supposed in high estimation, since by the returns received we had reason to suppose that our Govenour and Leiut Govenour were of that Name, but one and the same Man. Your Brothers too had that day been chosen Rep've for this Town of which I informd you, but I do not recollect any thing further. I might write a string of Blessings upon the Democrats their clubs, &c but as nothing I could say of them is more than they merrit, they are welcome to make the most of it, and Chronical it, if they get it.

"You caution our son to be reservd prudent cautious and silent." He is I believe all this. You bid him curb, his vanity. I know not whose praise would so soon tend to excite it, as one for whom he has so great respect and veneration, and whose judgment he so much relies upon. I will not say that all my Geese are swan. I hope however that I have no occasion to Blush for the conduct of any of my Children. Perhaps I build more expectation upon the rising Fame and Reputation of one of them, than of an other, but where much is given, much shall be required. I know their virtues and I am not blind to their failings. Let him who is without cast the first stone.

The Jacobines are very Angry that Congress leaves them at their Liberty, and permits them with their Eyes open to rush on to destruction. That they want Gaurdians is true enough, but no one obliges them to risk their property to French British or Spanish pirates.

Others I believe wishd the Embargo continued from real Patriotic motives.

Speculation, has been going on rapidly.

I understand the Term *impatiently yours* but I had a good mind to be a little Roguish and ask a Question, but I think I will only say that I am most Patiently Your ever constant and affectionate

A Adams

John Adams to Abigail Adams

My dearest Friend   Philadelphia May 27. 1794

It is proper that I should apprize you, that the President has it in contemplation to Send your son to Holland, that you may recollect yourself and prepare for the Event. I make this Communication to you, in Confidence, at the desire of the President communicated to me yesterday by the Secretary of State. You must keep it an entire Secret, untill it shall be announced to the Public in the Journal of the Senate. But our son must hold himself in readiness to come to Philadelphia to converse with the President, Secretary of state Secretary of the Treasury &c and receive his Commissions and Instructions, without Loss of time. He will go to Providence, in the Stage and thence to New York by Water and thence to Philadelphia in the Stage. He will not sett out however untill he is in form'd of his Appointment. Perhaps the Senate may negative him, and then his Journey will be unnecessary.

I shall go in the Stage on Saturday to New York, and be at home I hope by the 12 of June.

Adieu

J. A.

John Adams to Abigail Adams

My dearest Friend   Philadelphia Nov. 8. 1794

We took the Packet at New Haven, and arrived at N. York as Soon as the Stage. Although We Saved no time, We avoided some bruizes, at the Expence of a little of the Mal De Mer.

Mrs Smith and Children all well. Charity Smith married to Mr Shaw, Brother of the late Consul at Canton. Our Charles at Steuben after an Examination at Albany and an honourable Admission to the Rank of Councillor at Law. I was at his Office and Saw his Clerk who appears well pleased, and Says his Master has good Business. We arrived last night in this City and lodged at a Mr Alders opposite to Mr Binghams.

No Senate yet. The President returned, All Submission, in the Whiskey Counties. But a Force will be kept there to ensure their Obedience for some necessary time. Antifœderalism, Jacobinism and Rebellion are drooping their heads, very much discouraged.

Clark of N. Jersey and Comr. Gillon dead. Smith of Carolina elected with great Ecclat. Butler gone to Charleston last Week unaccountably. &c &c &c. Bradley left out, for a Man of different Politicks. Langdon in danger. These are Symptoms. If Ames fails The next Congress will be more fœderal than any that has yet assembled. But I Still hope better Things.

Fine Weather. I will write nothing as yet of Agriculture. Take great Care of your health which is pressious to me beyond all Calculation.

The Fall of Robespierre, has a great Effect on the Public Mind. It has Startled and terrified many, whose Confidence in him was excessive. I am as ever, yours without reserve.

J. A.

John Adams to Abigail Adams

My Dearest Friend   Nov. 19. 1794

The Presidents Speech is so important to the Public that I know you will be anxious to see it as early as possible. When the Answers of the two Houses come to be debated We shall, See whether there are any Apologists for Rebellion, in these Sanctuaries.

As Mr Edwards of Kentucky appeared in Senate to Day, We can do Business if one Member should be Sick, but it will be very inconvenient to have so small a Majority. Mr Potts of Maryland and Mr Taylor of Virginia have resigned. The Senate Seems really to be too small a Body for so important a Branch of the Legislature of so great a People.

I feel, where I am, the Want of the society of Mr Otis's Family, but much more that of my own. I pore upon my Family at Quincy, my Children in Europe, and my Children and Grandchildren in New York, till I am Melancholly and wish myself a private Man. That event however would not relieve me, for my Thoughts would be at the Hague and at N. York if I was with you at Quincy. Your Meditations cannot be more chearful than mine and your Visit to our afflicted sister will not I fear brighten your Views or soften your Anxiety. I hope We shall be Supported. But there is no Plan, that occurs to me that can relieve Us from our solicitude. We must repose ourselves upon those Principles in which We were educated and which I hope We have never renounced nor relinquished.

I would resign my office and remain with you, or I would bring you next Winter with me but either of these Plans, the Publick out of the Question, would increase our Difficulties perhaps rather than lessen them. This Climate is Disease to me, and I greatly fear would be worse to you, in the present State of your Health. Mrs Jay, poor Lady is more distressed than We are.

I pray you to take Care of your Health and of Louisa's too. She is a good Girl: but I Sometimes wish she would run about a little more if it was even to look at the young Men.

Adieu

J. A

Abigail Adams to John Adams

my Dearest Friend   Quincy December 6th 1794

Your kind favours of the 19th 23 and 26 of Nov'br came safe
to Hand, together with the pamphlet. The writer appears to have
ransakd Pandimonium, and collected into a small compass the iniquity
and abuses of several generations, "sitting down all in malice, and
Naught extermating." If the representations of our democratic Societies both of Men and Measures, for these two years past, were to be
collected into one pamphlet, and could obtain belief, some future Jefferson, might cry out, "that it containd an astonishing concentration
of abuses." In a Government like that of Great Britain, we know that
many abuses exist, both in the Governors and Governed, but still in no
Country, America excepted, has there ever existed so great a share of
personal Liberty and Security of property.

You ask what I think of France. I ruminate upon them as I lye a
wake many hours before light. My present thought is, that their victorious Army will give them a government in Time, in spight of all their
conventions, but of what nature it will be, it is hard to say. Men Warlike and innured to Arms and conquest, are not very apt to become the
most quiet Submissive Subjects. Are we, as reported, to have a new
minister from thence? I presume Munroe is to their taste. It will be
well if he does not take a larger latitude than his credentials will
warrent.

I am anxious for our dear sons. There prospects are not very
pleasent, even tho the french should not get possession of Holland.
This Whirligig of a World, tis difficult to keep steady in it.

It gives me pain to find you so lonesome in the midst of so many
amusements. I know you do not take pleasure in them, but you would
feel more cheerfull if you went more into society. The knitting work
and Needle are a great relief in these long winter Evenings which you,
poor Gentleman cannot use. Like mr Solus in the play, "you want a
wife to hover about you, to bind up your temples to mix your Bark and

to pour out your Coffe," but dont you know, that you will prize her the more for feeling the want of her for a time?

"How blessings Brighten as they take their flight."

The buisness of the Farm goes on, the plowing is all finishd and the manure all out, the yard full of sea weed, and a little wood.

The News of the day is that Mrs Hancock is going to take Captain Scot into her Employ, in plain words that she is going to marry him, an able bodied rough Sea Captain,

> "Frailty thy Name is woman
> We cannot call it Love; for at her age
> The hey-day in the Blood is tame, its humble
> And waits upon the Judgment, and what Judgment
> Would step so low?"

Alas Dorethy I never thought the very wise, but I thought the proud and ambitious.

Do you say I am censorious. It may be so, but I cannot but wonder.

Adieu. Pray write in good Spirits. You know I never could bear to hear you groan and at this Distance it gives me the vapours.

I am most affectionately yours

A Adams

Abigail Adams to John Adams

my dearest Friend   Quincy December 16. 1789 [*1794*]

Tomorrow will compleat three Months Since our dear sons saild, and this moment I have received a Letter from Town with this agreable intellegence, "on Sunday Evening the 14 Captain Joy arrived from England. Just before he saild from the Downs, a ship came too about 2 miles a head, of him. The Pilot who came on Board Captain Joy told him she was the Ship Alfrid in 32 days from Boston." Tho I have no letters; yet to know that the vessel is safe arrived, has given me a pleasure which you will easily conceive and participate, and I Seazd my pen instantly to communicate it to you. I pray God our dear Children may be safe and well.

I expect Letters from you tomorrow. Mr Brislers Letter came to day inclosing a Bill of Laiding. Our people have compleated covering the Medow with sea weed, which is all that can be obtaind untill a North East wind replenishs our shores again. Mr Brisler mentions a case and tells me it must not be brought up in a cart, but does not say what the contents are. Adieu. I am most sincerly and affectionatly yours

A Adams

John Adams to Abigail Adams

My Dearest Friend   Philadelphia December 16. 1794

I had flattered myself all the last Week with the Hope of a Letter on Monday: but when Yesterday came I found in the Door Keepers lodge of the senate, no Letter for me, though the Post was arrived, and the other Gentlemen had their Letters. Disappointed, mortified, sometimes half resentful, but more often anxious and apprehensive that you were sick, I passed but an unpleasant Morning: after dinner your Letter of the 6th. was brought to me in my Chamber, having been left with Mr Francis, I know not why, by one of the Presidents servants.

Callendars "Political Progress," is a Part of a great system of Reform or Sedition, which made a great Noise in Scotland, and has occasioned the transportation to Botany Bay of Muir, Margarot, and Gerald; a sentence of High Treason against Wat and Downie, &c &c.

Self created Societies are setting all Mankind together by the Ears. They will not cease in other Countries till they are laid aside in France, where they begin to be found inconvenient and to be thought dangerous. The popular Society of Caen resolved "We Acknowledge none but you for the Chiefs of the State: We own the national Representatives as the only point of rallying, and the People alone for sovereign. We Swear to be always faithful to the Convention. We will regard as the Ennemy of the People every Man who would rouse, near you, any Rival, insolent and usurping Authority." Bache's Paper tells Us it is The Spirit of the times to support the constituted Authorities against all self created, usurping rival Pretensions.

Whether The French or the Dutch are Uppermost in Holland our Sons have nothing to fear: I hope in a month or six Weeks We shall hear from them.

Solus has it right. I want my Wife to hover over and about me.

I hope Shaws Yard and Joys Yard, are or will be fill'd with sea Weed as well as mine. The Business has gone on charmingly. Dont forget your Daily or Weekly Chronicles of Farming.

As Dorothy has hitherto had only a peevish, fretful feeble Child for an Husband, I congratulate her on her opening Prospects of Advancement in the World, to the Arms of a generous, cheerful, good humoured, and able bodied Man. As the service of the People, according to modern Principles is no honour, Hopkintonianism in Politicks being the orthodox creed there can be no *distinction* between a Governor of a State and a Commander of a ship, except such as The Nerves confer. I suppose he has Property, which added to hers will make their old Age comfortable and that is enough. Literary Taste, intellectual Joys, Delicacy of the Sense of honour, and Reputation are about equal. I am not censorious. Not I. As Governors Wife, like her Husband, she has been an unprofitable servant and has no Merit. Why then should she have any Pride or Ambition?

The Weather has been so fine, that I hope Eames has arrived with your Flour seeds and Medallion. I hope you will consent to request Ceracchi, to give that Image to Harvard or the Accademy.

Love and Duty. Adieu.

John Adams to Abigail Adams

My Dearest Friend   Phila. Christmas Day 1794

This being one of the pleasant Days of the Week, Thursday the Post brought me your kind Letter of the 16th. The News of The Alfred was written me the Day or next Morning of its Arrival in Boston by our ever kind and attentive friends Dr Welsh and Mr Smith, and I should have instantly written it to you, with great Joy if I had not known, that you must have had it, much sooner than I from the same Sources. Although there is a feeling of Disappointment, accompanies the Intelligence, arising from not having any direct Account of our sons, yet the high probability of the Safe Arrival of the Ship, is a great Consolation. I congratulate you upon it, with cordial Sympathy, and join with you most Sincerely in your devout Ejaculation for the health and safety of our sons.

The Case mentioned in Brislers Letter contains the Marble Medallion, as brittle as it is elegant.

The Weather is as beautiful, as mild, soft clear and wholesome as can be imagined: but We had lately a North East Wind and Rain, which I hope has thrown up, on the shores of Quincy a fresh supply of Seaweed. I want to have the mowing ground opposite to Pennimans and Hardwicks upon Pens hill covered with it, if possible.

I am delighted with the Activity and Energy with which the affairs of the farm have been conducted, since I left you. A few years of such Exertions will make the Place productive of most of the Necessaries of Life for Us and I hope We shall be indulged with the quiet Enjoyment of it for as many Years as We can be useful to our Country our Friends or ourselves.

I have been to Church at Dr Ewings and heard a good sermon. Mrs Otis and Mrs Betcy are well.

The News of my Mothers Health and Activity is in a high degree delightful to me. My Duty to her.

Inclosed is a Book, a present for Louisa. A pretty Book it is—a good Book. I have very little fault to find with it, of any kind. His opinion of Grecian Taste in Art and Literature are so exactly like my own, that he makes me regret, deeply regret, that the Avocations of my Life, have not permitted me, to pursue it with so much Attention as I always desired: but still more than I have not had Opportunity to impress it upon my Sons, as I ought. They have better opportunities and Means than I had.

John Adams to Abigail Adams

My Dearest Friend   Philadelphia Jan. 16. 1795

The Travelling I suppose has retarded the Post of this Week, till to Day, when I received your two Letters of the 4th. and 8th.

I am happy to Day in the Company of our Charles, who arrived at my Invitation from New York as fat as a Squab or Duck. Mr Burr says he is a Steady Man of Business. He is gone to the Drawing Room and Play.

A Debate in Senate disappointed me of the female Commencement. Fenno has sent Mr Cranch his Paper from the 1st. of Jan.

Mr Bowdoins Morality is the same with that of the Livingston Family at New York, and of all other Men who have more Ambition than Principle. I have gone through a Life of almost three Score Years, and how few have I found whose Principles could hold against their Passions, whose honour could contend with their Interests, or even whose Pride could Struggle with their Vanity!

May I never have to reproach myself with faults which I have seen so often with Grief shame and Indignation in others. I know not that ever in my Life I gave a Vote against my Judgment. May I never deprive myself of the Power of saying this to my Wife and to my God in my last hour! I wonder that many of my Votes have not sent me home but here I am after a series of trying Years.

Four and thirty Years, the most of my Thoughts and Anxieties have been for the Public. Twenty Years have been wholly devoted to public Employments. My forces of Mind and Body are nearly spent. Few years remain for me, if any, in public Life probably fewer still. If I could leave my Country in greater Security, I should retire with Pleasure. But a great Cloud hangs over it yet. I mean a Cloud of Ignorance, Knavery and Folly. Whether a torrent can be stemm'd or not is yet uncertain. My Hopes however are stronger than my fears, and I am determined to be as happy as I can.

My head is not turn'd I hope, though my Paper is.

Nabby is not yet abed. She is well however. Mrs Otis and her sister are well and the little Girls too.

Don't say a Word of my coming home: but I hope to keep Thanksgiving with you. It is however uncertain. Perhaps Congress may rise perhaps not.

I must put Brisler and his Wife into our House next Winter, Louisa to board at Mr Cranches. I will pay with Pleasure for her, and take you along with me. What say you to this Project?

The greatest difficulty will be to find Lodgings.

May every Blessing and you and yours.

Adieu.

Abigail Adams to John Adams

My dearest Friend   Quincy Janry 21. 1795

We have had very severe weather through the whole of this week, but very little snow. Yet the Ground being hard froze, our people have been sledging stones. To day the wind has come round to the Southard, and Thaws. We cannot do half the buisness I want to have done. From here they go out early and spend no Idle time. The other Team does not work so hard, but looking after so Many cattle takes up much time.

You will see by the papers The Govenours speach. He has paid more attention to publick affairs than in any former speach. Mr osgood has really awakened him, and roused him to a Sense of his Duty. His Speach however is a pretty cold one and shews that he was constraind to say something, or look very unfeaderal.

The Connecticut News Boy is really cruel to the old Gentleman. I hope it will not be a Death Wound, as a similar insinuation from Burk killd good dr Price. He has given a sprig of Lawrel to embelish, (I am too much of a Democrat) to say *Crown* a Friend of mine. I think Congress had better have passd to the *order of the day* than have squabled so long to have made so much ill Blood, merely to give the Jacobines a Triumph. It was knowing the motives of the Mover, that raisd the indignation of the opposers. It was a Trap to catch those who scornd the Bate. It was done to allarm the credulous, and wound the feelings of those who possessd too much independance of Spirit to flinch at the trial. Having carried their point, I am sorry there was so much opposition to the yeas and Nays.

You will see by the papers that our sons had a fine passage. I am told that some private Letter informs that they left London on the 30 of october, for the Hague. I have written twice by way of London— tis strange that we get no Letters. Are there none from mr Jay? I hope it will not be long before I shall hear from them. Perilious are the Times into which they have fallen. I hope it may prove for their good and the benifit of their Country that they are called into Service in so critical a period. Many are my reflections upon it in the wakefull Watches of the Night, to an over ruling Providence I commend them. Adieu Ever Yours Yr

A A

References to Mr. Jay and "the treaty" concern the negotiations opened in June 1794 by Chief Justice John Jay in London. John Adams rightly predicted in a letter to Abigail on 9 February "A Battle royal I expect at its Ratification, and snarl-

*ing enough afterwards." The highly anticipated treaty did not arrive in Philadel-
phia until 7 March 1795. The contents, which failed to address the most important
maritime issues between the two nations and overwhelmingly favored the British,
were not revealed until Senate ratification took place in June.*

John Adams to Abigail Adams

My dearest Friend   Philadelphia Feb. 2. 1795

This Morning I received your favour of the 21st. of January. I am
sure your People do a great deal of Work, so dont be concern'd. I am
very well satisfied with your Agricultural Diary.

The venerable Governor made the best Speech he ever made, but
the old Leaven ferments a little in it.

I wonder you had not recd two Letters from Thomas which I
inclosed to you. I now inclose you one from Mr Jay, which shews
that our sons were arrived in Holland and had passed through their
Ceremonies at the Hague and gone to Amsterdam, to look as I Suppose after the imprudent Van Staphorst, and American Money in his
Hands.

The inclosed Postscript to Dunlap will shew you, that the expectation of a Treaty, hourly to arrive, will not allow me to leave my Chair
till the fourth of March. I shall be charged with deserting the President, forsaking the secretary of State, betraying my friend Jay, aban-
doning my Post and Sacrificing my Country to a weak Attachment to a
Woman and a weaker fondness for my farm, if I quit at this moment.
So be thou thankful alone, that thou hast a good Husband here, that
thy Children are safe and in Honour in Europe, and that thy Daughter
has given thee a fine Granddaughter; besides innumerable Blessings to
thy Country. I will be thankful and joyous here all alone.

We momently expect the Treaty: but it may not arrive this month.
When it does I expect to see wry faces as well as smiling ones. Perhaps
much Debate may take Place. Let Us know what it is first however before We oppose, or criticise or applaud or approve.

Your son John says it is better than War—that is all I know about it. Tenderly Adieu.

Keep all the Letters relating to our Sons.

John Adams to Abigail Adams

My Dearest Friend   Phila. Feb. 15. 1795

This is the coldest day We have felt this Winter, and if it were not for the hope I have of a Letter from you Tomorrow, I should freeze for what I know, to night. This Month has been all unpleasant Weather but none severe. You have had a North East storm I perceive which raised the Tides And I hope brought in a fresh and abundant supply of Seaweed.

It is the dullest time We have seen this Winter No Arrivals no News from abroad, nor from any Part of our own Country. The Treaty appears not and when it will, no Man can tell. Are We to wait here till May for it? I wont. There is not the smallest reason for my waiting. I can, in no possible Case have any Voice in its Ratification as two thirds of the Senators must agree. Nor will any opinion or Reasoning of mine have the smallest Weight with any one of the Senators. If I were disposed to wait how long must I wait?

I am tired of reading and writing: My Eyes complain: I want Exercise: I must have my Horse: and I must be at home.

Charles writes me that Nabby has got the better of her unfortunate Accident and is out of all Danger. I rejoice and am thankful.

We know not what to do with our Trunks and Flour and Porter &c &c. There is no Vessell here for Boston. We must store them and leave them with Some faithfull hand to be sent to Boston by the first Vessell.

You say I must stay a few Days at New York. But I shall be uneasy and impatient—No Business, No Books, no Amusement, No Society much suited to my Taste. Good Cheer is not enough for me. Balls Assemblies Hunting, are neither Business Pleasure nor Diversion for me.

What do you say shall I resign my Office when I am threescore, or will you come with me in a stage Waggon and lodge at a Tavern in fourth street?

I must contrive something new against next Winter. The old Routine grows too insipid!

I shall never be weary of my old Wife however. So declares your Affectionate Husband

John Adams

John Adams to Abigail Adams

My Dearest Friend   Philadelphia June 9. 1795

The Senate are now in Possession of the Budget. It is a Bone to gnaw for The Aristocrats as well as the Democrats: And while I am employed in attending the Digestion of it, I send you enclosed an Amusement which resembles it only in name.

I can form no Judgment when the Proscess will be over. We must wait with Patience.

I dined yesterday in the Family Way with The President. He told me that the American Minister, at the Hague, had been very regular and intelligent in his Correspondence. The whole Family made the usual Inquiries concerning You and Sent you the usual Compliments.

Be very carefull, my dearest Friend, of what you say, in that Circle and City. The Times are perilous.

J. A.

Abigail Adams to John Adams

my dearest Friend   N York June 10th 1795

I yesterday received yours of June 8th. and am happy to learn that there was like to be no delay from the absence of Senators. I wish and hope that there may be no unnecessary cavils respecting the Treaty. Mr Beauma came here last fryday, said he met you at Prince Town on thursday told us mr Fauchett was going to present a memorial againt the Treaty. Perhaps Adets arrival may prove a fortunate circumstance. Mr Jays Election seems to give great satisfaction here. I received a Letter yesterday from Louissa of June 4th. She says the news of mr Jays arrival was received in Boston with general Joy, desires me to tell her uncle that every thing respecting the Farm went on with great Harmony and allacrity and that it would do his Heart good to see his Farm. She tarried a week after we left home. Mrs smith send duty to you. Poor little John has got the Ague and fever to a great degree. I am at present much better in my Health for my Journey. I avoid the Evening air, and take Bark and drink porter and water as an Antidote to the Ague. The weather is very warm here, but I hope we shall not be detaind here longer than the present week.

Yours affectionatly

A Adams

Abigail Adams to John Adams

my Dearest Friend   N York June 15 1795

I have regularly received Your Letters and thank you for them. I have read the pamphlets. The Bone has much good natured Witt, contains many painfull facts, and Shows in a strong light what manner of spirit actuates the pretended Patriots. The writer has in some places taken, a poetical Licence. I have not offerd it where I am. Society and Interest and dissapointed ambition will have their influence upon most minds. Be assured I am remarkably cautious upon the Subject of Politicks. I am satisfied mine would essentially clash with any one, who could call the Peace System, a milk and water system.

I hope and trust the decision upon the Treaty will be a wise and candid one. That it should not be Suddenly rejected or accepted will I believe be more acceptable to the people than if it was other ways. I hope however a fort night at furthest will be found Sufficient. My Health has been much mended by my Journey. Johns Ague after 3 fits of it, terminated by falling into his face.

You mention having read a part of the dispatches from the Hague. Are they made publick to the Senate?

My best respects to the President and Mrs Washington. Love to Mrs otis Betsy smith &c.

Most affectionatly yours

A Adams

John Adams to Abigail Adams

My Dearest Friend   Philadelphia June 23. 1795 Tuesday

Some Senators are confident We shall rise tomorrow or next day. If so, I shall be with you on Sunday. But these Conjectures are always uncertain. I shall write you every day so that you will be apprized of the time when you may expect me.

Both the public Dispatches and private Letters of our dear Boys are the delight of all who read them. No public Minister has ever given greater Satisfaction, than Mr Adams has hitherto. His Prudence Caution and penetration are as much approved as the Elegance of his Style is admired. Providence I hope and pray will make him a Blessing to his Country as well as to his Parents.

I went out to Lansdowne on sunday about half a mile on this side Judge Peters's where you once dined. The Place is very retired, but very beautiful a Splendid House, gravel Walks shrubberies and Clumps of Trees in the English style—on the Bank of the Skuylkill. Jona. Williams's House, which was once McPhersons is over the River. It is the first time I have trodden the new Turnpike Road which is a great Improvement.

I am affectionately your

J. A

After spending July through November with Abigail in Quincy, John returned to Philadelphia by way of New York City. He stopped at his daughter Nabby's home and visited his grandchildren. Son Charles, "The Lawyer," had married Sarah (Sally) Smith, Nabby's sister-in-law, in August. Louisa, to whom both John and Abigail frequently refer, was the daughter of Abigail's deceased brother William Smith. She lived with the Adamses for the remainder of their lives and served as a surrogate daughter for Abigail.

John Adams to Abigail Adams

My Dearest Friend   New York Decr 6. 1795

We have been favoured with fine Weather and tolerable Roads in such a manner that We reached Kingsbridge on Fryday night and came into N. York by Nine o Clock on Yesterday morning. If it had not been for the Desire of seeing my Children I should have gone immediately on with the other Passengers. The stage House was so near C. Smiths and I knew not where my Son lived: so that I put up at Cortland Street: but for the future I will drive to my Sons.

My Grandsons and Grand Daughter are all very well and very gay. The Girl is a fine Child and will have La peau d'un Ange as the Baron De Stael said her Mother had, and I hope will be fort Spirituelle as the same Ambassador said her Grand Mother was. Mr Paine the Senator from Vermont and Mr Freeman of Barnstable, were our only Companions in the Stage till We reached New Haven.

As soon as I had dressed myself I walked out to find Mr Adams The Lawyer. I was told he lived in Front Street No. 91. I went through Broad Way and Wall Street to Mr McCormicks who was complaisant enough to take his hat and Cloak and conduct me to the House in Front Street No. 91. The House is new near the River among the Navigation. The Windows on the back side have a fine View of a forest of

Masts The sound and long Island. It must be a very good stand for Business. Accordingly They say he has twice or thrice the Employment he ever had before. I found him in his office, which is large and commodious and well stored with Book Learning at least, with three Clients about him in very deep and earnest Consultation. He lets part of the House for half the Rent.

Charles acquired the Character of a Wit, at the Time of the Epidemic Matrimony here. Some Gentleman asked him in the Country "How is the Fever Sir in Town?" Which Fever do you enquire after Sir? The Yellow Fever or the Smith Fever? said Charles. The Gentleman told the story in the City and it flew through the streets quicker than either of the Fevers.

The Lady of the Baron De Stael has lately published a Work under the Title of Reflexions on Peace, which Mr D'Ivernois has answered by another under the Title of Reflections on the War which he has sent me in French and another for the President in English. The Author has given some Account of "The Defence &c" and gives it the Preference, to all other Writers upon Govt. But all his Recommendations will have little Effect.

I wish, if it is possible, that our Men, after carting out the Manure upon the old Clover at home, would cart out that whole heap of limed manure in Mr Joys Cowyard, upon Quincys Meadow, as well as the heap already in the Meadow. These two heaps will give the Meadow a good dressing. They should be careful to mix the Lime with the other Ingredients as thoughroughly as possible. The other heap upon Penshill should be mixed in the same manner when that is carted out, and the whole very carefully spread.

Tomorrow Morning at Seven I cross the North River for Philadelphia. I am as I ever have been and ever shall be your affectionate

John Adams

Abigail Adams to John Adams

my dearest Friend   Quincy December 20 1795

The day I wrote you last, I received your Letter written at Nyork. Neither of my Neighbours Black or Beals went yesterday to Town, so that if any Letters came by saturdays post, I must wait till Thursday for them which I do not so well like. I should like you to write me by the wednesday post, then I should get my Letters of a thursday.

The account you gave me of Charles situation, and increasing buisness was very agreable to me. You did not mention Sally. Gentlemen are not half [as] particular as the Ladies are in their details. I recollect when C. L[*ivingston*] was minister for foreign affairs, he found fault because you was not minute enough in your description of the looks, behaviour &c of those with whom your buisness connected you. Accordinly in a Journal you sent, you related Some conversation and speaches, and even handing Madam La Comtess, to Table. I cannot but figure to myself how immoveabl and like the Marble Medallion you ought to keep your countanance whilst differing parties address you. The Speach of B. in support of M's motion, which the centinal informs us Bache has retail'd must have been one trial amongst many others. Is your Senate Chamber crowded? Parkers politeness is execrated. It is imposible for the President to have given a severer rebuke to the Jacobins than he has done, by the particular detail of the flourishing and prosperous state of our Country.

> To virtue only, and her Friends a Friend
> Faction beside, may Murmur, or commend
> Know all the distant din, that Fiend can keep
> Roll's o'er Mount Vernon and but; Sooths my sleep.

Those Lines of Pope occurd to me upon reading the speach fraught with so much benevolence; after all the abuse and scurility so wantonly display'd by, a decaying dying Junto, As I hope they now are, symptoms of Mortality appear in all their Limbs.

I suppose you take Bache paper upon the same principal that you wanted the Chronical, as their is no wife to prevent it. I should like to see Butlers speach, pray inclose it to me.

Are the reflections upon Peace by Madam de Stael, to be had here? If so be so kind as to send them.

Our people began the buisness you mentiond, but were driven of by bad weather. We are like to have snow enough. Adieu Ever Ever yours

A Adams

John Adams to Abigail Adams

My dearest Friend   Monday Morning Decr 28. 1795

I have just recd from the P. Office your Letter of the 20th. by Brisler who went to carry one for you. I write by every Post i.e by Mondays and Thursdays which are the only ones on which Mails are made up for any Place beyond N. York, and the only ones on which Letters arrive here from any Place beyond that City.

Mrs Adams your new Daughter behaves prettily in her new Sphere. I dined with them one day and promised, to take my Lodgings with them the next time. Mrs Adams shewed me an elegant bed which she politely said she had made up for me. As to the details in which you say the Ladies excell Us, I have not Patience. I who have the Patience of Job, have not Patience to write Letters in the style of Grandison and Lovelace.

You would admire to see with what Serenity and Intrepidity I commonly sett and hear. Not all the Froth can move my Contempt not all the Sedition stirr my Indignation, nor all the Nonsense and Delirum excite my Pity. If Dignity consists in total Insensibility I believe my Countenance has it. B. however tells me he can always perceive when I dont like any Thing. It must be by reasoning from what he knows to be my Opinions. My Countenance shews nothing for the most part. Sometimes I believe it may be legible enough.

The Reflexions upon Peace by Madam De Stael are not here.

The President and Presidentess always send their Regards to you. Madam invites you to come next Summer to Mount Vernon and visit the Fœderal City. I am almost afraid to write it to you for fear it should turn your head and give you thoughts and hopes of accepting the Invitation. I told Madame La Presidante, that after the Year 1800 when Congress should sett at Washington And that City become very great I thought it not impossible that You and your sister Cranch might seriously entertain such a Project, for the sake of making a Visit to Mount Vernon as well as seeing Mrs Cranches Grand Children.

Always write me how Mrs Brisler and her Children are. It makes the good Mans Countenance shine so bright when I tell him of it, that I take a great Pleasure in reading these Paragraphs to him.

My Mother I am anxious to hear of. My Duty to her and Love Compliments &c &c to whom you please.

Always yours

J. A

The First Couple

"My Ambition leads me not to be first in Rome, and the Event you request me to contemplate is of so serious a Nature that it requires much reflection and deliberation to determine upon it. There is not a beam of Light, nor a shadow of comfort or pleasure in the contemplation of the object."

—*Abigail Adams*

"You know what is before you, the whips and scorpions, the Thorns without Roses, the dangers anxieties and weight of Empire."

—*Abigail Adams*

"You complain that you are Solitary. I know that must be your lot frequently. It is then you want the relief that your talkative wife cared to afford."

—*Abigail Adams*

"Before I end my Letter I pray Heaven to bestow the best of Blessings on this House and all that shall hereafter inhabit it. May none but honest and wise Men ever rule under this roof."

—*John Adams*

"I Am Heir Apparent"

JANUARY 1796–JANUARY 1797

In January 1796, word began to circulate in Philadelphia that George Washington intended to retire, making John the heir apparent. This development changed the temper of Abigail and John's correspondence and caused them to weigh the consequences for both of them of his possible election.

John knew that the opposition had treated the great Washington scandalously during his second term. He did not delude himself that he possessed the stature or personality of the first president. And while he stated that he had no "desire to be the Butt of Party Malevolence," he could not resist seeking the position. This would be the culmination of his career in service to the nation—recognition that his eight years as vice president never provided. Much of his agonizing in letters to Abigail was merely exercise; the opportunity to hold the highest office was in fact irresistible.

Abigail, less driven than her husband in this case, appears to have been more realistic about the burdens they would bear. Aside from the torments the presidency would inflict on her thin-skinned husband, she had her own anxieties. Away from the capital for four years, she lived in Quincy "calm and easy, mixing very little with the World." She understood the social role the "First Lady" must play and doubted she possessed the patience, prudence, and discretion that Martha Washington had exhibited.

John Adams to Abigail Adams

My dearest Friend   Philadelphia January 5. 1796

There is a dead calm in the political Atmosphere, which furnishes no Event worth relating. The House of Reps is wholly taken up with two worthless Agents of Corruption.

I have this day however heard News that is of some Importance. It must be kept a Secret wholly to yourself. One of the Ministry told me to day that the President was solemnly determined to serve no longer than the End of his present Period. He mentioned such Circumstances of solemn Asservation as left him no room to doubt. Mrs W. said one thing to me lately which seemed to imply as much. Others, Men of the first Weight, I find consider the Event as certain. You know the Consequence of this, to me and to yourself. Either We must enter upon Ardours more trying than any ever yet experienced; or retire to Quincy Farmers for Life. I am at least as determined not to serve under Jefferson, as W. is not to serve at all. I will not be frightened out of the public service nor will I be disgraced in it. You will say that he will be over persuaded. You know what Jemmy said of Elijah. "His poor soul would have no chance for salvation for he had sworn most bitterly."

The Weather is mild as last Winter—No snow No frost—Farmers may plough.

I received Yesterday your favour of the 27. Who Randolphs four mighty Men were, I know not. I am much mortified to reflect that I ever had any Opinion of that Creatures head or heart.

There are Letters from John as far as 5th of October in the office of state. His public Correspondence is still very punctual and quite Satisfactory.

Randolphs Intrigues to defeat the Treaty defeated him of the honour of going to England but I dont regret it. I am with the tenderest affection your

                                        J. A.

John Adams to Abigail Adams

My Dearest Friend   Philadelphia Jan. 20. 1796

This is one of my red Letter Days. It is the Anniversary of the Signature of the Declaration of an Armistice between The U.S. and G. Britain, in 1783. There are Several of these Days in my Calandar, which I recollect as they pass in review, but which nobody else remembers. And indeed it is no otherwise worth my while to remember them than to render an Ejaculation of Gratitude to Providence for the Blessing.

We are wasting our Time in the most insipid manner waiting for the Treaty. Nothing of any Consequence will be done, till that arrives and is mauled and abused and then acquiessed in. For the Antis must be more numerous than I believe them and made of Sterner Stuff than I conceive, if they dare hazard the Surrender of the Posts and the Payment for [Spoteations?], by any Resolution of the House that shall render precarious the Execution of the Treaty on our Part.

I am as you say quite a favourite. I am to dine to day again. I am Heir apparent you know and a Succession is soon to take Place. But whatever may be the Wish or the Judgment of the present Occupant, the French and the Demagagues intend I presume to set aside the Descent. All these hints must be Secrets. It is not a subject of Conversation as yet. I have a pious and a philosophical Resignation to the Voice of the People in this Case which is the Voice of God. I have no very ardent desire to be the Butt of Party Malevolence. Having tasted of that Cup I found it bitter nauseous and unwholesome.

I hope Copland will find his six Loads to compleat the Meadow— and take the first opportunity to cart or sled the Manure from the Yard at home up to the Top of stony field Hill. The first season that happens fit for ploughing should be employed in cross ploughing the Ground at home over the Way.

The News of my Mothers Arm growing better, has given me great Pleasure. Of the four Barrells of flour I have shipped to you, present one of them to my Mother from me with my Duty and Affection.

Tell my Brother I hope he has seen his Error and become a better friend of Peace and good Government, than he has been somewhat inclined to be since the Promulgation of the Treaty.

I am with Affections as ever your

J. A.

The "memorable day" to which Abigail refers in the letter below is the anniversary of the execution of the French King Louis XVI on 21 January 1793, charged with conspiring against the people's liberty and general safety. His death led to an expanded European war and was followed in a few months by the so-called reign of terror, resulting in tens of thousands of executions, which made the guillotine the symbol of that unstable age. The French Revolution and the reaction to it, both in Europe and America, influenced the entire decade of the 1790s and beyond.

Abigail Adams to John Adams

my dearest Friend   Quincy Jan'ry 21 [*1796*]

A memorable day in the Annals of France; God forgive them, I would say, yet upon recuring to my Heart, I had a Doubt whether the petition was sincere. The Scripture tells us that we must pray for our Enemies, but it does not say that we must pray, that they may not be punished according to their deserts.

The post of this day brought me the Letters of two posts viz yours of Jan'ry 2d 5th 7th 8th and 12th. The transcript from our Sons Letter, as well as his Letter gave me sincere pleasure. I hope you communicated it to the President. If he needed any further proof to convince him of the corrupt system, and of the agents employd to abuse and calumniate him, this Letter is a key to him. Every thing there predicted has taken place exactly as foretold.

Some communications in your Letters are a source of much anxiety to me. My Ambition leads me not to be first in Rome, and the Event you request me to contemplate is of so serious a Nature that it requires much reflection and deliberation to determine upon it. There is not a beam of Light, nor a shadow of comfort or pleasure in the contemplation of the object. If personal considerations alone were to weigh, I should immediatly say retire with the Principle. I can only say that circumstances must Govern you. In a matter of such momentous concern, I dare not influence you. I must pray that you may have superiour direction. As to holding the office of V P. there I will give my opinion, Resign retire. I would be Second under no Man but Washington.

At Length you have the speach of a poor weak old Man, Superanuated indeed and fearing a shadow. The Virgina resolutions had been sent him, and it seems he was in favour of them as far as he dared to avow them, and declares in his speach, that the Treaty is pregnant with evil that it controuls some of the powers specially vested in congress for the Security of the people, and he fears that it may restore to great Britain such an influence over the Government and people of this Country, as may not be consistant with the general welfare.

How came the President of the united states and the 20 Senators not to make this discovery? Surely they would no more have ratified such a Treaty, than mr Jay have made it, if they had viewd it in this light.

I think he had better have left it, unnoticed than have come out in this manner, but it shews fully that the powers of his mind are unequal to enlarged views, and that he is under the influence of the Clubs. The Senate would not commit the virginia Resolutions, and in the House 56 to 24 were against commiting them. I am told the house will be Fœderel.

I hope you will write to our sons by every opportunity, and send them all the intelligence you can.

We have had a fine fall of snow which will enable our people to compleat getting home wood if it last. I have not read peter yet, because I sit down to write you immediatly. My finger is recovering, and my Health as usual. I hope we shall soon get more Letters from abroad. I have my Eye upon Sieyes. I believe I construed his refusal to be one of the five, right. When we see the intrigues the Ambition the Envy the malice and ingratitude of the world, who would not rather, retire and live unnoticed in a country village, than stand the Broad mark for all those arrows to be shot at placed upon a pinicle.

But I have done. Upon my pillow I shall reflect fear and tremble, and pray that the president of the united states may long long continue to hold the Reigns of government, and that his valuable Life may be prolongd for that purpose. I am most affectionatly your

A Adams

John Adams to Abigail Adams

Philadelphia January 26. 1796

Yesterday I came to Senate as usual on a monday morning pleasing my Imagination and my heart with the hope and reputation of a Letter from—my dearest Friend. No Letter for The Vice President says Mathers!

All Day in bad humour—dirty Weather—wet walking—nothing good—nothing right.

The poor Post offices did not escape—it was some blunder—some carlessness of theirs—in Philadelphia—New York or Boston.

Or Perhaps Mam is sick—Oh dear! Rhumatisms—Oh dear! Fever and Ague! Thus peevishly fretfully and unphilosophically was Yesterday passed. Yet to devert it I read a Number of Books in Cowpers Homer and Smoaked I know not how many Segars.

I have had the Agreable Society of Josiah Quincy and Martin Lincoln, to assist in consoling me a little of late.

There is absolutely nothing to write public nor private but such as the above.

Adieu.

J. A

John Adams to Abigail Adams

My Dearest Friend   Philadelphia Feb. 15. 1796

This Morning I have your favour of the 3d which raised my Spirits again after the mortification of passing the whole of last Week without one.

Benjamin has grown very dull—No Abuse—No lies no Terrors no Panicks no Rant—in comparison of what he used to have.

The Subject which you think will excite all their feelings is well known to every body in public Life, but is talked of by nobody: but in Confidence.

I could name you however as good Fœderalists and as good Men as any, who think and say that he will retire and that they would, if they were he. And who would not? I declare upon my honour I would. After 20 Years of such Service, with such success, and with no Obligation to any one, I would retire before my Constitution failed, before my Memory failed before my Judgment failed—before I should grow peevish and fretfull—irresolute—improvident. I would no longer put at hazard a Character so dearly earned at present so uncontaminated, but liable by the Weakness of Age to be impaired in a Moment. He has in the most solemn manner Sworn, before many Witnesses at various times and on several occasions, and it is now by all who are in the Secret considered as irrevocable as the Laws of Meads and Persians. Your Comments to Knox were perfectly delicate and perfectly wise. You need not tremble to think of the subject. In my Opinion there is no more danger in the Change than there would be in changing a Member of the senate and whoever lives to see it will own me to be a Prophet. If Jay or even Jefferson and one or the other it certainly will be, if the Succession should be passed over, should be the Man, the Government will go on as well as ever. Jefferson could not stir a step in any other system than that which is [begun?]. Jay would not wish it. The Votes will run for three Persons—two I have mentioned. The third being the Heir apparent will not probably be wholly overlook'd.

If Jefferson and Jay are President and Vice President, as is not improbable, the other retires without Noise, or Cries or Tears to his farm. If either of those two are President and the other Vice President, he retires without Murmur or Complaint to his farm, forever. If this other should be P. and Jefferson or Jay V. President, four Years more if Life lasts, of Residence in Philadelphia will be his and your Portion, after which We shall probably be desirous of imitating the Example of the present Pair: or if by reason of strength and Fortitude Eight Years should be accomplished, that is the utmost Limit of time that I will ever continue in public Life at any rate. Be of good Courage therefore and tremble not. I see nothing to appall me and I feel no ill forebodings or faint Misgivings. I have not the Smallest dread of private Life, nor of public—if private Life is to be my Portion my farm and my Pen shall employ the rest of my days.

The Money of the Country the Paper Money is the most unpleasant object I see. This must have a Remedy, and I fear it will be reserved for me to stem the Torrent, a worse one than the Western Rebellion or the opposition to the Treaty.

This is all in Confidence and Affection.

J. A

Abigail Adams to John Adams

My dearest Friend   Quincy Feb'ry 20 1796

Yours of the 6 8th and 10th came to me by the last Post. I too Sometimes get dissapointed but I always lay the Charge to the post where I know it ought to fall, but not usually writing untill after thursday post arrives here. I have not the advantage of the office here unless I wait for the next week, and a storm will sometimes, as last week, prevent my getting my letters to Town, but my conscience acquits me of Sins of omission. In that respect, I can seldom find more to say than one Letter contains. Upon some subjects I think much more than I write. I think what is Duty, to others and what is duty to ourselves. I contemplate unpleasent concequences to our Country if your decision should be the same with the P[*resident*]s for as you observe, whatever may be the views and designs of Party, the chief of the Electors will do their duty, or I know little of the Country in which I live. Shakspears says, "some are born great, some atchive greatness, and some have greatness thrust upon them." You write me fully assured that the P is unalterably determind to retire. This is an event not yet contemplated by the people at large. We must be attentive to their feelings and to their voice. No Successor, can expect such support as the P. has had. The first ministers have retired, and a man without intrigue, without party Spirit, with an honest mind and a judicious Head, with an unspotted Character may be difficult to find as V P. This will still render the first station more difficult. You know what is before you, the whips and scorpions, the Thorns without Roses, the dangers anxieties and weight of Empire.

> And for the day of trial is at hand
> With the whole fortunes of a mighty land,
> Are stakd on thee, and all their weal or woe
> Must from thy good, or thy misconduct flow;
> Have you Familiar with your Nature grown
> And are you Fairly to yourself made known?

and can you acquire influence sufficent as the poet further describes

> To still the voice of discord in the land
> To make weak Faction's discontented band
> Detected, weak and Crumbling to decay
> With hunger pinch'd, on their own vitals prey;
> Like brethren, in the self same intrests warm'd
> Like diff'rent bodies, with one soul informd
> To make a Nation, Nobly raisd above
> All meaner thoughts, grow up in common Love;
> To give the Laws due vigour, and to hold

That sacred balance, temperate, yet bold
With such an equal hand that those who fear
May yet approve, and own thy Justice clear;
To be a common Father, to secure
The weak from voilence, from Pride the poor
To make fair plenty through the Land increase
Give Fame in War, and happiness in Peace.

This is the bright and desireable light of the picture. This tho a hard and arduous Task, would be a flattering and a Glorious Reward, and such a reward as all good men will unite in giving to Washington, and such a Reward as I pray his Successor may merrit and obtain, should Providence allot the task to my Friend. But think not that I am alone anxious for the part he will be calld to act, tho by far the most important. I am anxious for the proper discharge of that share which will devolve upon me. Whether I have patience prudence discretion sufficent to fill a station so unexceptionably as the Worthy Lady who now holds it. I fear I have not. As Second I have had the happiness of stearing clear of censure as far as I know. If the contemplation did not make me feel very Serious, I should say that I have been so used to a freedom of sentiment that I know not how to place so many gaurds about me, as will be indispensable, to look at every word before I utter it, and to impose a silence upon my self, when I long to talk. Here in this retired village, I live beloved by my Neighbours, and as I assume no state, and practise no pagentry, unenvy'd I sit calm and easy, mixing very little with the World.

You need not be apprehensive least I should shew your Letters or divulge What is committed to me. All rests within my own Breast. Not the least lisp has escaped me to any one for tho I love Sociabily, I never did or will betray a trust. Affectionatly Yours

A Adams

Abigail Adams to John Adams

my Dearest Friend   Quincy [*28*] Feb'ry 1796

Thursday is my Red Letter Day. Then I usually get your favours, and a package of papers. The last thursday was particularly so. I received yours of the 10 13 15 and 17th of Febry. and two Letters from our Dear Sons one dated Helveotsluice Novbr 7th from the minister, the other of the 9th from the Hague. The wind had been contrary for near three weeks, and he poor fellow cooped up in a paltry Inn, and cut off as he says from all humane communication almost as intirely as if he had changed worlds but this he ought not to regreet as it saved him from the dangers of the perilious Nov'br Storm which proved fatal to so many poor Souls. A Letter from Thomas to J Quincy of a later date 25 Novbr says he heard that his Brother arrived in London on the 10th. Neither of their Letters are political, to avoid I presume the fate which some others have met with, of being retaind when captured. Possibly Letters may have gone on to you from mr Adams for Thom as apology for writing only a short Letter, was, that his Brother for want of better Employment, had amused himself during his detention by writing and sending him to Coppy a great Number of Letters of no moderate Length, which added to the buisness of a publick nature entrusted to his care, prevented him from writing to many of his Friend's. I do not know whether I ought to send you Johns Letter. It is in answer to one you wrote him, or rather to that part of it, in which you mentiond to him Charles marriage and express a wish that at an early period he might return home, and assume in like manner the cares and enjoy the felicities of a Family. He observes that tis a Maxim of Rochefoucaults, that we sometimes pass from Love to Ambition, but that we never return from Ambition to Love. If this Maxim is true, he says, what respite is to be expected by one who has past from Love, not indeed to ambition, but at least to its concerns. He proceeds and much more fully than he ever before did, lays open what had been the state of his Heart, "to Sacrifice the choice of the Heart, was all that prudenc or duty can require. It cannot it will not receive from my own controul, or from any other, the imposition of a different choice. If it can choose again, its Election must be spontanious, without receiving any direction from the Will."

I hope we shall soon get Letters from him by way of England. You will see by the Centinel that the Presidents Birth day was celebrated, with more than usual Festivity in Boston, and many other places. In the Toasts drank, they have for once done justice to the V P. It is a Toast that looks, I conceive to a future contemplated event. I am glad that your mind appears so well setled for what ever may take place, but who in their senses could suppose that you would continue to serve in your present station with any other than Washington. Who could wish or desire it must be destitute of your feelings or mine. To be the private citizen would not mortify me, but there remains not a Man in America, whose publick Services entitle him to the office, what ever his own opinion or that of his Friends may be.

> "All envy power in others, and complain
> of that which they would perish to obtain."

I am happy to learn that You enjoy your Health so well. The season is approaching when colds are prevelent. You are so subject to them that I daily expect you to complain. Every Body far and near are suffering with them. I have my Share, but hope it will not lay me up.

Ever your affectionate

A Adams

John Adams to Abigail Adams

My Dearest Friend   Philadelphia March 9. 1796

I recd on Monday your two favours of 28. Feb. I am very glad you employed Pratt to cutt the Timber, for it is high time I had a Barn to shelter my Hay that the Cattle may not complain of it so much, as they do this Year, with Justice. I shall build only the shell this Year—Raise the Barn and Board and shingle it.

The limed Manure upon the Hill I mean to have Spread upon the Grass Ground where it lies.

I join Copland in his Request that the Thatch Bank may be let, to either French or Burrell.

Priestley preaches once on a Sunday to a crouded Congregation, on the Evidences of Religion and is much Admired.

I sent your Message to Mrs Green.

Alass! Poor John! But his Father and his Mother too know what it is, to be cooped up in Taverns Waiting for Winds. Aye and the Boy too has had more Experience of it than a Million of old Men. Many a Week and many a Month as he been detained with me waiting for Winds and Waves and ships both political and Physical. He has resources within to amuse and employ him.

I dont believe All the Points of Rochefaucaults Thought. Ambition and Love live together very well. A Man may be mad with both at once. Witness Cæsar and Anthony with Cleopatra and many others.

If the Young Man really loves, I will not thwart him. I have been anxious lest my sons by early and indiscreet connections should embarrass themselves and Companions in Poverty Distress and Misery from which it would not be in my Power to relieve them. I have seen Instances enough to Ruin from early Marriage. Azariah Faxen and Sam Quincy were two among many.

The Birth Day has been celebrated very sufficiently. I have much doubt of the Propriety of these Celebrations. In Countries where Birth is respected and where Authority goes with it, there is congruity enough in such Feasts: But in Elective Governments the Question is more doubtful. Probably the Practice will not be continued after another Year.

In the Case you suppose, Blair McClenican Swears with great Oaths before Giles and all of them that he will vote for no Jefferson and no other Man, but his old Friend of 1775. But there is no Certainty of any

Change more than there has been for six months. Every Body takes it for granted there will be. But my Opinion is it will kill the Resigner. Affectionately

J. A

Abigail Adams to John Adams

My Dearest Friend   Quincy March 28th 1796

Captain Beal was in Boston on Saturday and he prevaild on the post master to let him take up the Saturday Mail by which means I got those Letters which ought to have come on thursday Letters of the 11th 12th 13 15 and 16th. The greatest comfort which I derived from them was hearing that you were well. The prospect of sitting till June is not a very agreable one, and the cause less so. What ever the Jacobinical party may think, if they should be so Head Strong and wicked as to carry their measures; they will find a ten fold clamour excited against them. I have heard it said, that those of them who belong to this state, would be torn to peices. The warmth excited by the debates is greater here, than I believe it is in congress. Even your B who you know never was reconciled to the Treaty, says that it *should* be complied with. There is not any circulation of the debates in any paper printed in Boston, but the Chronical, and that you may be sure will hold up, but one side of the Question. I cannot suppose that there will be a majority in Congress hardy enough to overturn the constitution, tho there is a party who *dare* what ever they think may succeed.

My last Letter containd some foreign intelligence which look'd like Peace, but the last arrival brings us no News of the kind. All Breathe War and Hostility. The powers must be exhausted e'er long. I am no Friend to Club Law, Yet I cannot but own that I have been gratified with the behaviour of our American seamen, in repelling the Lawless insolence of British Tyranny. Nor can the Britains be displeasd with a spirit and valour which proves the Legitimate descent of their opposers. The loss of so many seamen renders them more eager to supply their place at any rate.

I rejoice at the opportunity Thomas has of shewing that he is equal to the trust reposed in him. As Private Secretary he could only be a coppyest. I think we have great cause of pleasure and satisfaction in our Children. I hope you feel very proud of them; I do I assure you.

The Georgia purchaser or rather the repurchasers are giving up all their Notes, and part with their Ideal gains with much composure. Serious concequences may however be experienced by some of the Hot Spurs of Gorgia from whose proximity to their Savage Neighbours, they appear to have derived a portion of their ferocity, and infidelity.

I have not yet engaged any Hand. Billings has been at work for your Brother. I desired him to talk to him for me. He told me last Evening that he held himself very high and talkd quite wild about price, that he would not let himself but for a few months at a Time. I cannot hear of any body yet. It is scarcly time of year. I expect Copeland to top him self as he has become a Teams Man he thinks. One hundred dollors is like a drop in the Bucket. 33 for two loads Hay 25 for clover Seed 20 and 65 cents for Braintree Taxes, and 15 to Joy and his wife. Herds Grass seed the doctor has bought. We have Tard but do not find any woorms or milliars yet.

Those certainly get through the World best who trouble themselves least, but a foresight prevents many, evils and vexations. As to the wall upon the Hill Amphions harp must be set to a Golden cord before the Sound will compose the Walls of Pens Hill. I sent to the undertakers three weeks ago to request them to go about it, but they say they were not engaged to compleat it untill the first of June. I do not know whether the dr is like to get the other done. I think it fortunate that we are like to get the places out. I am sure I know not where we could have procured help without paying three times the value of the produce. I shall be obliged to purchase Burrel a load of English Hay for His cows. I did not bring away all from there, tho more than I wish I had. I hope his Salt and fish will answer for the young stock, tho he says it is not good. I am sure we never had so much English Hay as last year, but our salt was damaged, and the creek thatch they use only for to litter the horses with, the fresh, Tons of it, will go to make manure. I can not answer for the use of it. The cattle they Say are in much better order than last year, and so indeed they ought to be for they have not workd half so hard, and have been fed with English Hay in lieu of corn. When I talk to Copeland, he says Sir likes to have his cattle look well, and So does Mam, but not to have to purchase Hay for such a Stock. Well why should I torment you. Why because when one feels fretted, it is an ease to the Mind when it has cast it of.

Adieu adieu. When the wheels get in motion I shall be in a better Humour, but chopping and changing makes a bustling world. I detest still life—and had rather be jostled, than inanimate. Yours for aye

A Adams

The action taken in the House of Representatives on 30 April, to which John alludes below, was the funding of the commissions provided for in Jay's Treaty. The Jeffersonians had extended the partisan debate over the treaty even after the Senate had ratified it and President Washington had signed it the previous summer. John's frustration with the opposition's interference in approving the final appropriation certainly was intensified by his anger at having his regular spring departure for Quincy delayed.

John Adams to Abigail Adams

My Dearest Friend   Philadelphia May 3d. 1796 Tuesday

The Result of Saturdays Debate in the H. of R. removes all Anxiety for the Remainder of this session, and leaves me at Liberty to ask Leave to go home. The state of my own Health which requires Relaxation and the Sickness in my Family and Neighbourhood, would have well justified me, if I had retired even before the great Question was decided. I shall ask Leave this Day, unless something unforeseen should happen to prevent me. If I should obtain Leave of Absence after Thursday next I shall be at New York on Sunday. Whether I shall go by Water or Land from thence will depend upon Circumstances. Sometime in the Course of the Week after next I hope to see you, but there are so many Circumstances of Wind and Weather as well as other Things which may intervene, that I cannot make any Disposition by which I can calculate to a day or a Week when I shall get home.

It is a Mortifying Consideration that five Months have been wasted upon a Question whether National Faith is binding on a Nation. Nothing but the Ignorance and Inexperience of this People can excuse them. Really We have not a right sense of moral or national Obligations. We have no National Pride—No National sense of Honour.

I Suppose the Decision of The H. has determined The P.'s Resignation and Retirement. And The Question who shall Succeed him may occasion as much Controversy and Animosity as The Treaty with Great Britain, which was ultimately determined by no proper Considerations of Merit, but merely by fear of Constituents in many.

If My Plan should be altered in any respects I shall write you an Account of it. I must spend a little time, with the Children At New York. I have been five Months, without once mounting a horse and without one long Walk so that altho I have walked every day more or less, I am under some fears of the Effects upon my Health of a Journey of an 100 miles a day in a stage.

The inclosed Letters please to file away carefully with the others. With the tenderest affection I am

J. A

Abigail Adams to John Adams

my dearest Friend   Quincy Novbr 27 1796 Sunday Eve

Winter has caught you on the Road I presume, for a colder day than this we seldom have in Jan'ry. You will want to hear how the Farming goes on. The Letters inclosed which I received last evening have put it all out of my Head, and almost put out my Eyes to read. No other than the printed duplicate has come to Hand. I send you both yours and mine, both of which are important at this time when the plots are unfolding. They are a clue to all the whole System of Electionering under foreign influence which in a greater or less degree pervades every state in the union. They will afford but Sorry comfort to you whether destined to publick or private Life. If to private, "O! Save my Country Heaven." If we are to receive a President from the French Nation, What is to be our Fate? To accept the Presidency with such an opposition, and to know that one is rushing upon the thick bosses of the Bucklar requires the firmest mind and the greatest intripidity. Heaven direct all for the best.

You will see by the Centinal that poor Samuel has no opinion of his own. The House and Senate have however been firm. Inclosed is a curious extract from the Washington Gazzett taken from a paper calld the new world.

I presume the Fate of America will be decided by the time I get a Letter from you. We are told here that under the Jeffersonian ticket the voters distinguishd themselves by wearing the National cockade. Can they have become so openly dairing and bold? I saw Burks paper calld the Star. It ought to be termd the Chronical Rival, a Hireling wretch, in French pay I doubt not, a whineing and canting because the French Minister has *suspended his functions.* Our sons Letter is a key to the whole buisness. I have worn out my Eyes to day in coppying it; The Wall progresses, and the Barn yard has not been neglected. The rails are all brought home and I am reflecting that there is no small probability that you may spend the next Summer at Home. I hope peace Feild will not suffer a French invasion. I am not however terified. I say Gods will be done, and hope we are not yet given up to destruction.

Adieu let me hear often from you. You know how anxious I am at the events passing before me. Poor Johns pride was a little touchd that you should name cooper as a rival in Fame. Where will you find a man of his Age of his Prudence judgment discernment and abilities?

My best my Sincerely affectionate Regards to the President and mrs Washington. If any people on earth are to be envyd they are the ones, not for what they have been in power and Authority, but for their transit.

Once more adieu ever ever yours

A Adams

John Adams to Abigail Adams

My Dearest Friend   New York Decr. 1. 1796

I Spent a pleasant Day before Yesterday with Mrs Smith and her Children at East Chester where they now live. At night the Col and his two Brothers came home from hunting Patridges and Quails an Amusement which had engaged them two Days. Halcyon Days are over, at that house but Horses are still very plenty. Yesterday I came to Town and have been happy with My Son and Daughter here. The Baby is pretty and has the Small Pox very lightly. Miss Carloline Nabbys Baby is as fat and rozy and hearty as a Country Girl can be. Charles has a great deal of Business, and looks and dresses respectably: keeps good Company and minds his office.

Mr Jay and I met last Evening on our Anniversary 30 of Novr. and were very happy.

I go on this afternoon for Philadelphia, tho threatened with a Snow Storm.

I can tell you nothing about Elections, only that the Fed's appear to be sanguine and the Antifeds too in reality or appearance. There is some anxiety lest Pinckney should be Smuggled in, unintentionally, to the first Place. I hope he will not come in to any. I wrote you from Stratford and shall write next from Philadelphia.

We have had a cold uncomfortable Journey. Prices risen since May both of Travelling and Subsistence, and Publicans less Attentive and obliging.

The Federalists in Pensilvania prevailed in two of their Ticket the Antis in the rest. New York is said to be unanimous.

The French Minister is fulfilling your Sons Predictions with astonishing Exactness but it is said he has disgusted and alienated Friends from France. How this will appear in Congress, Time will discover. I Shall be mistaken in my Guesses, if Americans in general are very Servile.

I have as yet no Letter from you and am uninformed of the History of Agriculture. But I presume That Firewood and Stock have had the chief Attention since I left you.

Duty to My Mother, Love to Brothers and sisters and Couzens, Compliments to Neighbours &c.

J. A

John did not know the outcome of the election of 1796, the first real contest for the presidency, when he returned from Quincy to Philadelphia at the beginning of December. During the month reports from the states where the electoral votes were first counted assured his success, and Jefferson wrote a congratulatory note on the 28th. When the Senate, over which Adams still presided as vice president, officially tallied the electoral ballots on 8 February 1797, Adams announced that he had received 71 votes, Jefferson 68, and Thomas Pinckney 59. The Adams-Jefferson friendship that had cooled as partisan passions rose during the previous administration now ended. Not until 1812, after both men were securely retired from public life, did they re-establish their old relationship, and then only in correspondence. Abigail too became disenchanted with their old friend. She ex-

changed a handful of letters with Jefferson in 1804 after the death of his daughter Mary, but the correspondence ended after a few months.

John Adams to Abigail Adams

My Dearest Friend   Philadelphia Decr 7. 1796

I have recd your Letter of the cold Sunday on which I wrote you one from Stratford. In N. York Charles gave me the original Letter, the Duplicate of which you transmitted me. I communicated it to the P. with five preceeding Numbers. After reading them The P. was pleased to say that "Mr Adams's Intelligence was very good, and his Penetration and foresight very great. At least Things appeared to him in Europe exactly as they did to himself here." He communicated to me T. Paines impudent Letter.

This is the very Day the which. I laugh at myself twenty times a Day, for my feelings, and meditations and Speculations in which I find myself engaged. Vanity Suffers. Cold feelings of Unpopularity. Humble reflections. Mortifications. Humiliation. Plans of future Life. Economy. Retrenching of Expences. Farming. Return to the Bar. Drawing Writs, arguing Causes. Taking Clerks, Humiliations of my Country under foreign Bribes, Measures to counteract them. All this miserable Nonsense will come and go like evil into the Thoughts of Gods or Men, approved or unapproved.

Cousin Smith is said to have written Phocian and Murray the Pieces from Maryland. The Election is a Lott at this hour and if my Reason were to dictate I should wish to be left out. A. P. with half the Continent upon his Back besides all France and England old Tories and all Jacobins to carry will have a devilish Load. He will be very apt to Stagger and stumble.

If the Southern states are as unanimous as the Northern are supposed to be I shall be left out. But it is Said there will be 3 in Virginia and one in N. Carolina against Jefferson. In Pensilvania the Rebells in the West and the corupt Mob of Philadelphia aided by frightened Quakers gave a Majority of from 20 to 100, against the great Agricultural Counties of Lancaster York and Cuberland.

It really Seems to me as if I wished to be left out. Let me See! Do I know my own heart? I am not Sure. However all that I seem to dread, is a foolish, mortifying, humiliating, uncomfortable Residence here, for two tedious months after I shall be known to be Skimmed, as my Wallmen Speak.

I can pronounce Thomas Jefferson to be chosen P. of U. S. with firmness and a good grace. That I dont fear. But here alone abed, by my fireside nobody to Speak to, poreing upon my Disgrace and future Prospects—this is Ugly. The 16 of Feb. will soon come and then I take my Leave, forever. Then for Frugality and Independence. Poverty and Patriotism. Love and a Carrot bed.

Duty to My Mother and Love to all.

J. A

The Federalists are all very confident however of a small Majority. I say and believe that small Majority worse than none, and wish there could have been a large Majority any other Way.

Dont show this stuff.

John Adams to Abigail Adams

My Dearest Friend   Philadelphia Decr 16. 1796

I recd this morning your kind Letter of the 7th. and wonder you had not recd a Letter. I wrote from Stratford and New york and twice a Week since I have been here.

Your Anxiety for your Country is amiable and becomes your Character. Elevated Expectations of Grandeur and Glory as well as Prosperity have accompanied me through Life and been a great source of my Enjoyment. They are not diminished by the present Prospect.

It seems to be now certain, that Unless Mr Jefferson has Votes in N. Hampshire, Vermont or Rhode Island he can not be President. But it is not improbable that Mr Pinckney may be—unless N. C. should be of Opinion with Virginia that J. A. had better be P. than Pinckney.

The Northern Members have kept their Promise better than the Southern. They have got a great Number for Pinckney but the Southern have got none for A.

The English Party have outgeneraled the French and American both. That is the Construction I put upon it though others would make me beleive if they could that it is an insidious Maneuvre of Hamiltons individual Ambition. I care not whose Maneuvre it is; nor who is the Dupe, nor whether it is foreign Influence or private Ambition: so long as I am not guilty of any sin of Omission or Commission in the Business. The whole system is utterly repugnant to my Judgment and Wishes. I wish Patrick Henry had 138 Votes and would Accept them. Pinckney has no Pretensions to any of them more than Dr Jarvis. If Chance and Trick are to decide, it had better be decided by french Influence for aught I know or even by English, for either Jefferson or Hamilton had better Pretensions and would have made better Presidents than Pinckney.

I shall not suffer so much in retiring as the P. whose tender feelings are excited both by Kindness and Unkindness. I shall retire without much of either to harrow up my soul. It is rather a dull Prospect to see nothing but ones Ploughshare between one and the Grave but I am confident I can bear it as well as the P. My Misery will all be over by the Ninth of Feb. if I am released. But that is too long.

Yours most affectionately

J. A

Abigail Adams to John Adams

my dearest Friend   Boston December 23 1796

I received by the last post your favours dated 7h 8th and 12 of the
present Month together with Pains Letter and the counter part Jasper. I
tremble when I look forward to the scene opening before me. My own
reflections and meditations are similar to yours, except that I do contemplate a return to the Bar. Retirement at Peace Feild I think would
be a much more Eligible Situation than to be fastned up Hand and foot
and Tongue to be shot at as our Quincy Lads do at the poor Geese and
Turkies, and like the frog in the fable, sport to the Boys was death to
the frogs. Since I came to Town some curious Annecdotes have to me.
Judge daws after the Election was over, went to visit the Govenour so
said the G. To answer their own ends, I say to answer *their own ends*
Judge. They sit up Your Father and me Electors in opposition to each
other. If I had been Elected, I should have done something that should
have cemented the Friendship of my kinsman or severd us for ever. I
hope sir it will make no breach between your Father and me. Our
Friend Mrs Storer Says that the conduct of the Govenour in erasing
his Name from the Law respecting Electors, putt her in mind of some
lines in a little Book of the Childrens.

> There was a man in Thessaly
> and he was wondrous wise
> He jump'd into a quickset hedge
> and scratchd out both his Eyes
> And when *he saw* his Eyes were out
> With all his might and main
> He jump 'd into another hedge
> and scratchd them in again.

A Country Man this Week who lives about 50 miles back was in mr
N Austins shop, and began to talk with him upon politicks. Why says
he, they tell me that mr Adams, tho a Clever Man will not do for Pres-

ident. They say he can't talk. Aya says mr Austin, he can't talk Nonsense, but do you or can you believe that a Gentleman who was many Years in the full practise of the Law cannot talk?

Very harmless was that report in comparison of a thousand others which I dare say have come to your Ears. Dr Walter call'd to see me a day or two since. He said there were many people in this Town who almost wisht you might not be Elected that they might have you for their Govenour next year. To this speach I could make no reply, but bow'd. It is considerd here as a Matter setled that you are Elected, yet no person speaks of it, but what seem to commisirate the Station and to be fully sensible of its dangers and perplexitys.

I inclose to you an Aurelias, the reputed Author Young Gardner of Milton. It is *certain* that he corrected the press, and does not deny the peice. I cannot but Suspect however that he has consented to Father it for some other person.

Tell mrs otis that her Friends here are well, but in affliction for the sudden Death of Mrs Robbins, Nabby Saltmars that was, who on one Sunday was married and before a fortnight was a Corpse. "O Blindness to the future kindly given."

Tomorrow I return to Quincy where I hope to hear often from my dearest Friend to whom I am with the sincerest affection His

A Adams

John Adams to Abigail Adams

My Dearest Friend   Philadelphia Decr 27. 1796

I recd yours of the 14 on Fryday: but had no Letter on Monday.

According to present Appearances, Jefferson will be Daddy Vice, and between you and me I expect you will soon see a more ample Provision made for him, that he may live in Style and not be obliged to lodge at Taverns and ride in Stage Coaches. I See plainly enough that when your Washingtons and Adams's are stowed away our dear

Country will have a gay Government. I cannot help these injudicious Extreams into which People will run, nor these invidious Partialities.

The Rumours of Peculation and Want of Probity as well as want of Fidelity to Trusts are allarming and afflicting. My Old Friends Mifflin, McKean Ewing, exhibit despicable and detestible Phenomena for Governors Judges and Heads of Colledges, as their Conduct is represented daily in public Companies. I know nothing more. McKean indeed is only charged with a little too much Madeira and Infidelity to Friendship and political Principle.

Whatever the French may Say without stammering or with Swaggering, the American People will not be frightened by them.

Swan came to visit me, as well as Tenche Coxe. What a Puppy this last? He left his Card. I was at home when the other came and had a Conversation with him civilly enough.

The Prospect before me, opens many Questions and Inquiries concerning House, Furniture, Equipage, Servants and many other Things which will give me trouble and occupation enough and the more because you will not be here—Luckily for you. I should tremble for your health if you had all the Visits and Ceremonies to go through and all the Preparations to make.

71 is the Ne plus ultra. It is now certain that no Man can have more and but one so many. If no irregularity appears to set aside Votes 71 will carry the Point. I know of no irregularity. The suggested one of Vermont appears without foundation. I am affectionately

J. A

John Adams to Abigail Adams

My Dearest Friend   Philadelphia January 1. 1797

I wish the new Year may be the happiest of your Life. Last Night I had a Visit from Dr Rush, whose Tongue ran for an hour. So many Compliments, so many old Anecdotes. To be sure, My Election he said, he had vast pleasure in assuring me since it had been made certain had given vast satisfaction in this City and State. Even those who had voted for another had a great affection for me. Mr Smilie himself had told him this very day that he had an affection for me. He met Mr Madison in the Street and ask'd him if he thought Mr Jefferson would accept the Vice Presidency. Mr Madison answered there was no doubt of that. Dr Rush replied that he had heard some of his Friends doubt it. Mr Madison took from his Pocket a Letter from Mr Jefferson himself and gave it to the Dr to read. In it he tells Mr Madison that he had been told there was a Possibility of a Tye between Mr Adams and himself. If this should happen says he, I beg of you, to use all your Influence to procure for me the Second Place, for Mr Adams's Services have been longer more constant and more important than mine, and Something more in the complimentary strain about Qualifications &c.

The Dr then ran on with his Compliments to me and Sarcasms upon W. This Country would rise in the Estimation of the World and of all Europe, from the 4th. day of March next &c &c &c. It hurt me to hear this. But his old Griefs and Prejudices Still hang about him. He got disaffected to Washington during the War.

He has conversed with Dr Edwards and Edwards has told him that Washingtons Character is wholly prostrate in France—that Mr Monroe has been very active and industrious in behalf of his Country, that when his Letters come to be published, they will do him great honour &c. I heard all this with perfect Composure. I only asked if Dr. Edwards had not been Speculating in french revolutionary funds? Oh no was his answer—he beleived not. He confessed he had never read the Treaty with England nor one thing in favour of it or against it. He knew not whether it was a good or a bad one. He only disliked the Secrecy with which it was formed negotiated, and ratified.

All this Chaos, I heard in Silence, lamenting to see that the Southern Politicians had got so fast hold of him, he knew not why.

With regard to my Election he had taken no Part. He had been neutral. But he had made it a Rule, whenever either Jefferson or myself had been traduced in his Company to vindicate Us both.

Jefferson and I should go on affectionately together and all would be well. I should Settle all disputes with the French well enough. These are confidential Communications.

I have recd no Letter from you the Week past. What Say you to coming along to Eastchester in February and joining me in March? I cant live without you very well till next July.

I am most tenderly

J. A

John Adams to Abigail Adams

My dearest Friend   Philadelphia Jan. 9. 1797

I received to day, together, your Favours of the 31st December 1796 and 1. Jan. 1797.

Our H. of R. boasts that We are the most enlightened People in the World: but We behave like the most ignorant Babies, in a thousand Instances. We have been destroying all Terror of Crimes and are becoming the Victims of them. We have been destroying all Attachment and Obligation to Country and are Sold in Consequence by Traitors. We have been opening our Arms wide to all Forreigners and placing them on a footing with Natives: and Now foreigners are dictating to Us if not betraying Us.

Hamilton I know to be a proud Spirited, conceited, aspiring Mortal always pretending to Morality, with as debauched Morals as old Franklin who is more his Model than any one I know. As great an Hypocrite as any in the U. S. His Intrigues in the Election I despise. That he has Talents I admit but I dread none of them. I shall take no notice of his Puppy hood but retain the same Opinion of him I always had and maintain the Same Conduct towards him I always did, that is keep him at a distance.

The Constancy and Fidelity of Mr Gerry contrasted with the Weathercockism of McKean and the Rutledges and the Hypocricy of others touches the inmost feelings of my Heart. I will not explain all I know till I see you.

Your black Balls and flashing Guns are proofs of an Anxiety that is very needless. I never felt easier in my Life. My Path is very plain, and if I am not supported I will resign.

The Defence has been read by many others as well as the Deacon. In an 100 years it would not have been so much read, as it has been during the late Election. A new Edition of it is coming out here with an immense subscription and I expect it will be got by Heart by all Americans who can read.

The Extract from T's Letter is very clever. I went on Saturday to see the Globe Mill of Mr Davenport. Carding Spining and weaving are all performed at the same time by Water. It is in Some respects like the silk Machine which you saw with me at Utrecht.

Alass poor Billings—Madness or Sotting I fear will be the End. Reclaim him however if you can.

My Duty to my Mother and Love to Brothers and C[. . .]ts to all.

J. A

Abigail Adams to John Adams

my dearest Friend   Quincy Janry 15 1796 [*1797*]

The Cold has been more severe than I can ever before recollect. It has frozen the ink in my pen, and chilld the Blood in my veins, but not the warmth of my affection for Him for whom my Heart Beats with unabated ardor through all the Changes and visisitudes of Life, in the still Calm of Peace Feild, and the Turbelent Scenes in which he is about to engage, the prospect of which excite, neither vanity, or pride, but a mixture of anxiety and Solisitude, which Soften, but do not Swell the Heart.

By the last Post I receivd Yours of December 27th and 30. Janry 1 and 3d. The extract from mr Madisons Letter I believe to be the genuine sentiments of mr Jeffersons Heart. Tho wrong in Politicks, tho formerly an advocate for Tom Pains Rights of Man, and tho frequently mistaken in Men and Measures, I do not think him an insincere or a corruptable Man. My Friendship for him has ever been unshaken. I have not a doubt but all the discords may be tuned to harmony, by the Hand of a skillfull Artist. I see by the paper of to day that the extract is publishd in the Centinel, not through Eve, I assure you, for I have not disclosd it. It has gaind as most storys do, that mr J. declares he would not have taken the vice Pressidency under any other Man. The writer adds not unaptly, from shakspear,

> "The Event we hope will
> unite the Roses Red and white together
> That on one kind and Friendly stalk,
> they both may flourish."

My Authority for the Author of Aurelias, was william shaw who going one day into Nancreeds Book store saw a young Gentleman correctting the press. Nancreed introduced him to William as the Writer of Aurelias and gave him one of the Books; notwithstanding this, he may only, as he has on former occasions for our son be the Channel only, to convey and foster the ospring of an other. You ask me what I think of comeing on in Febry? I answer that I had rather not if I may be excused. I have not for many Years enjoyd so good Health as this winter. I feel loth to put it to risk by passing a spring in Philadelphia. I know not what is to be done. I think an inventory ought to be taken of what belongs to the united states. A House ought to be provided and furnishd in such a manner as they chuse, or a Committe appointed to do it, if a Sum Should be granted for the purpose. I desire to have nothing to do with it. There are persons who know what is both necessary and proper. If this is done I should not be against going to assist in the arrangement of the Household.

I will make the necessary inquiry respecting a Carriage and write you word as soon as I can obtain information. My old Chariot, I have purchased Runners and put it on. Dr Tufts says it must never be hung again. It has long been too shaby for use. I was beholden to my Neighbours for a conveyance before I got them. It answers very well for that purpose. The Sleighing is remarkable fine and has been so for more than a Month. I have had one succession of visiters and company, more than for any two years past. Every Body who ever knew one comes to pay compliments and visit who would not have been so forward perhaps. . . . a little prematurely too, but it shews their good wishes.

I see no prospect of the fall of any article. Grain is as high as ever and all west India articles risen beyond bounds. Such Sugars as were purchased last winter at 12 dollors pr hundred are now 18. Loaf sugar 2/6 pr pd. Tea Coffe Chocolat risen in proportion. At this rate we must be Starved if the House of Reps have not a sense of Justice before their Eyes.

What is to be done with our places? I have not advertized, nor have I seen Vinton or French since you went away. Burrel I believe will stay on if we find him a yoke oxen and cart. He has not had a drop of water since last july. Billings is getting steady. He had but a small flight this last time, but he wants his money as fast as he earns it.

I have been so much hinderd by company that I have not been able to write for these ten days only one short Letter to you.

I took up the Note and destroyd it. I inclose you a Letter from an old Friend. It contains some just sentiments. I need not say to you how necessary it is to lay ones finger upon their Lips, and to be upon our gaurd with *all* foreign Characters, and most domestick ones. I want to acquire an habit of silence, or of saying unimportant things.

We have had a wedding in our Family too in the last week which has occupied some part of my Time. Nancy Adams was married on thursday last, and to day the New married pair dinned with me. Mr and Mrs Shaw are here upon a visit to keep Sabbeth with me, and desire their Respects to you. I am Sitting up after all are a bed to write you that tomorrows post may not go without a Letter. You will write me, and inform me what I must do, or what you wish. Cabot says I must go on or all the wheels will stand still, but I know better.

Yours most affectly

Abigail Adams

Return the Letter when read.

Abigail Adams to John Adams

my dearest Friend   Quincy Jan'ry 22. 1797

I have not received a Line from you of a later date than the 3d Instant. The last week is the only one which has past since you left me, without Letters. I hope it is not oweing to any other cause than the difficulty of passing the North River. We have had this day Something very like a snow storm. It has Bankd Some tho not very deep. It is two months tomorrow since you went away, and we have had only one part of a day in which any Rain has fallen, and intensely cold the greater part of the Time.

I have something to propose to you on the part of your Mother. I think the remainder of her days ought to be renderd comfortable and respectable, that she is not now in such a situation as she ought to be placed, taking into consideration the station you will soon be call'd to fill. There is but one Grandaughter left. She has necessarily the whole Family care upon her which will prevent that constant care and attention which the Age and infirmities of your Mother require. She ought to have a lower Room, and not be obliged to mount up stairs, at the risk of falling. Mears has in His House a Handsome Room which I would furnish for the Good Lady, and Mrs Mears has no children and could attend alltogether to the care and necessary attention of her. If I should be calld away and Mears should agree to come and take care of this place we could easily remove her here. I should have proposed taking her here, but we have so little House Room and company would be urksome to her. I think she would be more agreabley placed in a Room which she should consider as her own, and with Authority to call for every assistance she wants. She told me since the marriage of Nancy, that if I went away she should have nobody to take any care of her. I assured her that she might make herself easy for she should certainly be provided for to her comfort and satisfaction, and that I would not leave her untill she was. I was sure it was your desire, and that I had in my Mind Such accommodations as would make her so. If you approve of this I will propose it to her, and engage Mrs Mears to undertake the Charge, and I will see every thing done to make her Comfortable.

There is much talk with the Merchants upon pettioning Congress to lay an Embargo. The Piracys of the French are very provoking and insulting. We have very few arrivals. Young Beals got home last week, but was near being lost in comeing upon our coast. We appear to be quiet here. The Election of Mr A. and mr J seems to have quieted for a Time the Spirit of Party. I have not had any further advises from our sons. Are there any publick Letters from them? I have read Peters censor. He is a full Blooded English Man. I want to see him craking Pains Bones. That Wretch has however written a Book which even the Jacobines will blush to advocate. I think he has done his buisness in this Country. There are more Persons who will detest him for his abuse of washington than for his infidelity. Adieu my dear Friend. I will not ask when I may hope to see you, for if you cannot come to me, I will to you, in the Month of May. I am my dearest Friend ever, Ever Yours

A Adams

Abigail Adams to John Adams

My Dearest Friend   Quincy Janry 28th 1797

I received by the post on thursday the whole Mail containing your
Letters of the 5th 9th 11th 14 and 16th. I began to be very impatient at
rude Boreas for laying an embargo upon that intercourse which alone
mitigated the pain and anxiety of Seperation.

Genll Lincoln had call'd upon me the beginning of the week and
informd me that you was well. The steady cold weather has been more
favourable to my Health than any winter we have had for years past,
and since I have been equiped with Runners I have not faild to take
the Air almost every day. In one of my late Letters I inclosed you
Frothinghams estimate of a carriage but as you have orderd one it will
not do to apply to him and you will want one sooner than he could
make one. I have been thinking that we shall want a light travelling
Carriage for me to go to and from Philadelphia, as you cannot be left
without one, and would it not be best for to sit Frothingham to make
one something upon the same plan with that which we formerly Had?
"You say your Farm appears very differently to you now from what it
did, and that it seems to you as if you ought not to think of it."

The greater reason there is for me to turn my attention to it, I consider it as our *Dernier* resort, as our Ark of safety. I think it ought not
to be sufferd to fall into decay, and I shall not regreet any pains which
I can bestow upon it to render it a retirement eligible to us when we
are four Years older if we should live to see the day. We have been doing, and undoing all our days. I would aim at making such arrangements as would tend to make it better rather than worse even tho I expended twice its annuall income. Billings has returnd to his senses and
conducts very well. He is going to sled stones next week, but it is impossible to dig them. We have had a covering of snow and Ice impene-
trable to every tool, the finest Sleighing I ever knew. The snow very
level so that there has been no difficulty in turning out of the road, but
for six weeks no rain and so cold as not to Thaw at all. The price of

flower which is good superfine has been in Boston from 11/2 to 12. I have inquired divers times, and I gave 12 about a month ago. It is to be had now for 11/2 which capt Beal has just told me he gave last week, but it is not of concequence whether any is sent. I can purchase it here.

In one of your Letters you mention having seen enough at East Chester. In an other you exclaim alass poor Nabby, and say you have written to the col. but get no answer; I received a Letter from Mrs Smith in December, in which she expresses a state of anxious suspence, and a willingness to submit to her Lot with resignation if she could but know that all just demands were satisfied, speaks of a col Walker as a Man very Rigirous and disposed to take ungenerous advantages. Mrs Shaw came here on a visit and spent the last week with me. She told me of many things which I did not before know of, and which I must give credit to. Some of them you had heard before from Charles. The Col is a Man wholy devoid of judgment and has deceived himself with visionary schemes, and run risks which he ought not to have done, and led his Family into a stile of living which I fear his means would not bear him out in.

You have I suppose before this Time received a Letter from me which inclosed an other proof of your old stuanch Friends confidence and attachment.

> "The Friend thou hast, and their adoption tried
> Grapple them to thy soul with hooks of Steel."

Mr Black told me the other day on his return from Boston, that col H. was loosing ground with his Friends in Boston. On what account I inquired. Why for the part he is said to have acted in the late Election. Aya what was that? Why they say that he tried to keep out both mr A[dam]s and J[efferso]n, and that he behaved with great duplicity. He wanted to bring in Pinckney that he himself might be the dictator. So you see according to the old adage, Murder will out. I despise a Janus tho I do not feel a disposition to rail at or condemn the conduct of those who did not vote for you, because it is my firm belief that if the people had not been imposed upon by false reports and misrepresentations, the vote would have been nearly unanimous. H[*amilto*]n dared not risk his popularity to come out openly in opposition, but he went secretly cunningly as he thought to work, and as his influence is very great in the N England states, he imposed upon them. Ames you know has been his firm Friend. I do not believe he suspected him, nor Cabot neither whom I believe he play'd upon. Smith of S C was duped by him I suspect.

Beware of that spair Cassius, has always occured to me when I have seen that cock Sparrow. O I have read his Heart in his wicked Eyes many a time. The very devil is in them. They are laciviousness it self, or I have no skill in Physiognomy.

Pray burn this Letter, dead men tell no tales. It is really too bad to Survive the Flames. I shall not dare to write so freely to you again unless you assure me that you have complied with my request. I am as ever most affectionately your

A Adams

John Adams to Abigail Adams

My Dearest Friend   Philadelphia January 31. 1797

I have recd yours of January 22d. I know not the reason you had not recd Letters for a Week. There has not been a Week Since I arrived in Philadelphia that I have not written you twice or thrice.

I agree with you that Something must be done for my Mother to make her Condition comfortable and respectable. A Horse and Chaise must be at her Command and I like your other Plan very well if she approves it. But I believe She will never think of leaving my Brothers Family. If she should prefer Staying with him I will be at the Expence of the Wages and Board of a Maid or Woman to live in the House and be wholly under her Direction. If Mears will take our House, or if he does not, if Mrs Mears will take the Care of her and she is willing to go to Mrs Mears's, I shall be willing. But I think she will prefer some

Provision for her at my Brothers. I shall leave it to you and her to digest and determine the Plan and any Expence for her Comfort and respectability I will chearfully defray.

There are no public Letters from our Sons later than the latter part of September.

An Embargo, which you say the Merchants talk of petitioning for, would not perhaps answer the End. It would give a shock to us which our People would impatiently bear and hurt the English so much more than the French, that perhaps they would persevere in their system as a Measure of Hostility against their Enemy.

If you come to me at all, the earlier in the Spring the better: for We must go to Quincy for the hot Months. The Plague has got into this Country and I will not remain here, nor shall you during the Season of it. But my Dearest Friend We must consult Œconomy in every Thing. The Prices of Things are so extravagantly high that We shall be driven to Extremities to live in any decent style. I must hire and maintain secretaries as well as servants and the purchase of Horses Carriage Furniture and the Rent of a House 2666 Dollars and 2/3 a year will Streighten Us and put Us to all manner of shifts. I have a great Mind to dismiss all Levees Drawing Rooms and Dinners at once. Dinners upon Washingtons Scale I will dismiss and only entertain a few select Friends. They shall have a Republican President in earnest.

A Committee of senate have reported in favour of an Augmentation of salaries but I dont expect it will pass the House if it does the Senate, and if it should what are 5000 Dollars. An Addition of Fifty thousand Dollars would not much more than restore the salary to its original Value, as Prices are tribled in most articles and doubled in all. In another Week or so The Point will be legally settled.

I fear you will not persuade Mears to take our House and I know not who else to think of.

Alass my Poor Country! Divided in herself insulted by France, and very frequently by Englishmen even since the Govt have assumed an Appearance of Moderation. Witness the cruel tyrannical Treatment of Capt Diamond at st. Eustatia.

The Fœderalists themselves are divided and crumbling to Pieces. Allmost all the ablist and best Men are discouraged and many of them retiring. And this has been brought about by Tom Paine prophecying Clergymen and French Finesse and Intrigue. But I must stop to assure you of my tenderest and never failing Affection.

J. A

"The Chief Majestracy of a Nation"

February 1797–February 1801

Abigail and John knew by early *1797* that he had been elected the second president and only awaited the electoral vote count for confirmation. The ensuing four years tested John. The same problems that frustrated him as a powerless vice president pursued him through his presidency. His attempts to avoid party politics sometimes isolated him and made Abigail's wise council more important than ever.

Problems in international affairs consumed his energy for the entire term and eventually led him to unwise domestic decisions. His efforts to prevent open war with France resulted in a blow to his popularity and permanent damage to his historical reputation. During the fall of *1797* the French snubbed the negotiators he sent to Paris in the infamous XYZ Affair. Anti-French sentiment swept the United States and in early *1798* John's popularity temporarily surged as war with France appeared imminent. Within months, however, he fell from grace.

Fearing that foreign influences were invading and subverting the country, he signed the Alien and Sedition Acts in June and July *1798*. The extreme restrictions on freedom of the press and the constraint of political opposition resulting from the legislation are remembered even today as one of the most important threats to individual liberties in the nation's history.

Eventually the hysteria that allowed the enactment of the Alien and Sedition Acts passed. Despite numerous provocations the United States did not declare war on France, and in *1799*, the president, with Abigail's later endorsement, nominated an old Adams family friend, William Vans Murray, to negotiate the treaty that settled the long Franco-American conflict.

Abigail Adams to John Adams

Quincy Febry 8 1797

"The Sun is drest in Brighest Beams
To Give thy Honours to the Day."

And may it prove an auspicious prelude to each ensuing Season. You have this day to declare yourself Head of A Nation. And now O Lord my God thou hast made thy servant Ruler over the people, give unto him an understanding Heart, that he may know how to go out, and come in before this great people, that he may descern between good and bad, for who is able to judge this, thy so great people? were the words of a Royal Soverign, and not less applicable to him who is invested with the Chief Majestracy of a Nation, tho he wear not a Crown, or the Robes of Royalty.

My Thoughts, and my meditations are with you, tho personally absent, and my petitions to Heaven are that the things which make for Peace, may not be hiden from your Eyes. My feelings are not those of Pride, or ostentation upon the occasion. They are solemnized by a sense of the obligations, the important Trusts and Numerous Duties connected with it, that you may be enabled to discharge them with Honour to yourself, with justice and impartiality to your Country, and with satisfaction to this Great People shall be The Daily prayer of your

A Adams

John Adams to Abigail Adams

My dearest Friend   Phila. Feb. 9. 1797

The Die is cast, and you must prepare yourself for honourable Tryals.

I must wait to know whether Congress will do any Thing or not to furnish my House. If they do not I will have no House before next Fall, and then a very moderate one, with very moderate Furniture.

The Prisoners from Algiers arrived Yesterday in this City, in good health and looking very well. Captn. stevens is among them. One Woman rushed into the Crowd and picked out her Husband, whom she had not Seen for 14 years. I am and ever shall be yours and no others.

J. A

Below is a curious letter that reveals the persistence of racism in Massachusetts even after that state abolished slavery. Abigail's father had owned a slave, Phoebe Abdee, but freed her in his will. Phoebe remained close to Abigail's family and is often mentioned in their correspondence. When Abigail celebrated Thanksgiving in November 1798, she noted that Phoebe, "the only surviving Parent I have," joined them.

The Adamses wrote frequently about their good and poor servants and took a personal interest in their well-being. James, a black youth who seems to have been an indentured hand, became one of Abigail's favorites. John, however, did not want him in Philadelphia, believing he had become too spoiled.

Abigail Adams to John Adams

my Dearest Friend   Quincy Feb'ry 13. 1797

It is now the middle of Feb'ry. It will be the 20 by the Time this reaches you. The whole months has been a Thaw so that to present appearences we shall have an early Spring. Billings has been several day at work upon the wall. He tells me he shall want help to cart and digg. Veseys time is just expiring, and as he is a bird of passage, he does not incline to tarry longer, So that I have to seek a Hand, and to hire occasionally, for I think this wall which Billings computes at 30 days, ought to be compleated as soon as possible. The Hill must however be ploughd in a week or ten days. Unless the weather changes, it may be done. Write if you are like to Send seed. French was with me a Day or two Since, to know if I had received an answer from you respecting his remaining upon the place. I told him that there was no doubt he might have it. He proposed breaking up 3 or 4 acres upon Belchers side adjoining to dr Phips. He says that will be sufficient, and that the manure will be required upon the gound which is to be sown so that much corn will not be profitable. I conversd with the dr upon the subject. He proposed letting French take the place for two years as an inducement to him to carry on Manure, but this is as you please.

I wish you to make provision in march for the payment of Haydens Note. His Brother call'd a few days since and ask'd me if I would take it up. I told him I was not prepaird then, but if he wanted the money I would procure it for him in a few days. He replied that he would not give me the trouble to do that. If his Brother was really in want he would let me know. I then told him I would take it up by the middle of March, but still I would get the money immediatly if he would send me word. I have not heard since so presume he will wait till March. My Rates were sent the first of this Month. They amount to 178 dollors and half the Farm tax upon which French and vinton are to 24 dollors, 16 Burrels. They have taken it upon them to Rate your personal estate at 90 dollors. I know of no one article of living which does not exceed in price this year the last; during 8 weeks of as good travelling as ever was known in the winter, there was a plenty, but no glut of the Market or fall of prices. I am disposed with you to curtail every expence which the Parsimony of our Rep's require, and I would calculate for a surpluss of Revenue too. It will be there disgrace, not ours, but they will bring their Government into contempt by it. They cry out, the high prices are but temporary, but they will starve out their officers whilst that temporary continues, which has been annually proving worse for these Six Years.

I have been much diverted with a little occurence which took place a few days since and which serve to shew how little founded in nature, the so much boasted principle of Liberty and equality is. Master Heath has opend an Evening School to instruct a Number of Apprentices Lads cyphering, at a shilling a week, finding their own wood and candles.

James desired that he might go. I told him to go with my compliments to Master Heath and ask him if he would take him. He did and master Heath returnd for answer that he would. Accordingly James went. After about a week, Neighbour Faxon came in one Evening and requested to speak to me. His errant was to inform me that if James went to School, it would break up the School for the other Lads refused to go. Pray mr Faxon has the Boy misbehaved? If he has let the Master turn him out of school. O no, there was no complaint of that kind, but they did not chuse to go to school with a Black Boy. And why not object to going to meeting because he does mr Faxon? Is there not room enough in the school for him to take his seperate forme. Yes. Did these Lads ever object to James' playing for them when at a dance. How can they bear to have a Black in the Room with them then? O it is not I that object, or my Boys. It is some others. Pray who are they? Why did not they come themselves? This mr Faxon is attacking the principle of Liberty and equality upon the only Ground upon which it ought to be supported, an equality of Rights. The Boy is a Freeman as much as any of the young Men, and merely because his Face is Black, is he to be denied instruction. How is he to be qualified to procure a livelihood? Is this the Christian Principle of doing to others, as we would have others do to us? O Mam, you are quite right. I hope you wont take any offence. None at all mr Faxon, only be so good as to send the young men to me. I think I can convince them that they are wrong. I have not thought it any disgrace to myself to take him into my parlour and teach him both to read and write. Tell them mr Faxon that I hope we shall all go to Heaven together. Upon which Faxon laugh'd, and thus ended the conversation. I have not heard any more upon the subject. I have sent Prince Constantly to the Town School for some time, and have heard no objection.

I think you will excuse my attendance at Philadelphia till october. I hope however you will be able to come on in june. I talkd with Dr Tufts on the subject of building a Barn. He says he should advise to

Building only a coach House for the present and appropriate the whole of this Building for the Hay. He thinks some alteration may take place in the course of an other year which perhaps may render it less expensive. Inclosed is a line which I received from mr Bracket a day or two since. I fear your more serious occupations will put out of your mind all personal concerns. Adieu my Dear Friend. Do not let any thing put out of your Mind your ever affectionate

A Adams

John Adams to Abigail Adams

My dearest Friend   Philadelphia March 3. 1797

The Congress have passed the Law allowing 14,000 d to purchase furniture. The State Legislature have done nothing about their new House: so that I shall take the House the President is in, at a £1000 or 2700 dollars rent, nothing better can be done.

Mr Jefferson arrived Yesterday and came to visit me in the Evening.

Tomorrow will be a worse day than the 8th. of Feb. was. We are to take the oaths, and P. Washington Says he will be there.

I shall purchase little furniture, before you come or give directions. All the World are of opinion that it is best for you not to come till next fall. I will go to you as Soon as I can but that is uncertain.

We shall be put to great difficulty to live and that in not one third the Style of Washington.

Mr Malcom Charles's Clerk is with me as a private Secretary.

Oh how I long to go and see you. I am with everduring and never ending affection your

John Adams

John Adams to Abigail Adams

Philadelphia March 5. 1797

My dearest Friend, your dearest Friend never had a more trying day than Yesterday. A Solemn Scene it was indeed and it was made more affecting to me, by the Presence of the General, whose Countenance was as serene and unclouded as the day. He Seem'd to me to enjoy a Tryumph over me. Methought I heard him think Ay! I am fairly out and you fairly in! See which of Us will be happiest. When the Ceremony was over he came and made me a visit and cordially congratulated me and wished my Administration might be happy Successful and honourable.

It is now Settled that I am to go into his House. It is whispered that he intends to take french Lave tomorrow. I shall write you, as fast as We proceed.

My Chariot is finished and I made my first Appearance in it Yesterday. It is Simple but elegant enough. My horses are young but clever.

In the Chamber of the House of Representatives, was a Multitude as great as the Space could contain, and I believe Scarcely a dry Eye but Washingtons. The Sight of the Sun Setting full orbit and another rising tho less Splendid, was a novelty.

C. J. Elsworth administered the oath and with great Energy. Judges Cushing, Wilson and Iredell were present. Many Ladies.

I had not Slept well the night before and did not sleep well the night after. I was unwell and I did not know whether I should get through or not. I did however. How the Business was received I know not, only I have been told that Mason the Treaty publisher Said We should loose nothing by the Change for he never heard such a Speech in Publick in his Life.

All Agree that taken all together it was the sublimest Thing ever exhibited in America.

I am my dearest friend most affectionately and kindly your

John Adams

John Adams to Abigail Adams

My dearest Friend   Philadelphia March 22d. 1797

Last night for the first time I slept in our new House. But what a Scene! The Furniture belonging to the Publick is in the most deplorable Condition. There is not a Chair fit to sit in. The Beds and Bedding are in a woeful Pickle. This House has been a scene of the most scandalous Drinkenness and Disorder among the servants, that ever I heard of. I would not have one of them for any Consideration. There is not a Carpet nor a Curtain, nor a Glass nor Linnen nor China nor any Thing. Dont expose this Picture.

This morning I recd your favours of March 12 and 13th. I am highly pleased with your Criticisms and Observations on my Adieus to the Senate, their Answer and my Reply. Before now you have a long Speech, which I hope you will descant on as learnedly and ingeniously.

As to the farms I must leave all to you and Dr Tufts. Let Trask clear all the Bushes in Curtis's Pasture. I want to have clean Work made there. You have not mentioned My Mares nor Colts. Are the Mares in a Way to breed Us Horses?

I have procured five Horses, which with my little fellow at home, will be all I shall keep.

As to Public affairs all is Suspence at present. Nothing can be determined till further and more Authentic Accounts arrive.

I never wanted your Advice and assistance more in my Life. My Country will not always oblige her Public Men to make Brick without Straw. As soon as I shall be out of the Question, their Presidents will go on Swimmingly whoever lives to See it. But it is wicked to complain.

I have not been able to receive any Company. And the House will not be fit for some time.

I am with all affection and ardent Wishes for your Society

J. A.

John Adams to Abigail Adams

My dearest Friend   Philadelphia March 27. 1797

You will See by the Proclamation in the Public Papers that I have been obliged to convene Congress on the 15th of May, and as it is probable they will Sitt till the Middle of July, this measure must make an entire change in all our Arrangements.

There are so many Things to do in furnishing the House in which I want your Advice, and on so many other Accounts it is improper We should live in a state of seperation that I must intreat you to come on, in your Coach with Louisa, Mrs Brisler and her Children. You must hire four Horses in Boston and a Coachman to bring you here, upon as good terms as you can. James may ride my little Horse and Anthony you must give away. I am very unwell—a violent cold and cough, fatigues me, while I have every Thing else to harry me: so that I must entreat you to come on as soon as you can. I shall send you some Post Note in a day or two.

Prince's Time is out and he will be discharged. James may come on with you, and return immediately to New York. I will not keep him a day. You may leave him at New York and hire some one to ride on the Horse to this Town. I will not have my Family here ruined by them turbulent blacks. Give them their Cloaths handsomely and dismiss them.

My Expences are so enormous, that my first Quarters salary will not discharge much more than half of them. You must come and see for yourself.

The French Executive Directory, will take Care to make our public Path thorny enough and our Country men will make our private one uneasy enough. So We need not expect Beds of Roses nor Walks of Flowers.

I have been obliged to decline Brother Cranches farm. It will involve me, and I cannot increase my Cares. I have and shall have quite enough. You will be Surprized to see hurry of Business in which I am daily and hourly involved.

                  J. A

Abigail Adams to John Adams

My dearest Friend   Quincy April 6 1797

I received an hour ago your Letters of the 22d and 27th. I have been
anxious enough for you, since I saw the proclamation. I advise'd you
to take for your cough Rhubarb and calomil. Do not omit it, but take it
immediatly. It will serve you for the complaint which usually afflicts
you in the spring as well as for your cough. I will obey the summons as
soon as possible but there are many arrangements to make, or deliver
all up to destruction, at once. I Shall endeavour to send mrs Brisler on
first by the Stage with her Children. I will See her tomorrow, and consult with her about it. I must find a Family which I can place here.

I expected you would find every thing in disorder in the House, tho
not so bad as you represent. I have as I wrote you, had three hundred
Dollors, of Gen'll Lincoln for the purposes mentiond, and one Hundred more I was obliged to take, to enable me to pay my Laboures as I
went on. O I had got a going so cleverly. Billings will compleat his circle of Wall in two days more, and it is a Beauty. Stutson in the Garden,
and Tirril and Bracket have been carting manure and plowing. I had
employd Pratt to compleat and finish a cart begun by Billings. It is
done and painted. I had got new ploughs and tools, and a Man to come
next week, for the season. I expected to have got all things in order for
your reception when you should be able to return to the domestick
joys of Peace Feild.

All these pleasing Ideas must yeald to new arrangements. I will do
the best I can and come as soon as I can. I write this now only to assure you that I shall tomorrow take some measures for executing the
System proposed.

Yours most affectionatly

A Adams

John Adams to Abigail Adams

My dearest Friend   Philadelphia April 22. 1797

I had no Letter from you Yesterday. As You intended to commence your Journey on the 24th. it is not probable this Letter will meet you, till it returns to this Place. But as it is possible you might not be able to set out so soon, you may receive it at Quincy. Brisler is at Quincy before this, I hope.

Charles is just gone, for N. York. I have communicated to him my Plan of sending my Coachman and Horses to Paulus Hook for You. I shall be obliged to send a Man or Boy with the Coachman and that Man or boy may ride my little Horse, which James rides to N. York. I Suppose you will give James his Time, with his Cloaths &c. I however shall leave it to you. I fear he will Spoil our whole House, if he comes here. He has been so indulged like a Baby.

Let me know when you shall be at N. York. You may write me indeed from New York. The Letter will come to me in a day. But it will take two days for my Horses to go from hence to Paulus Hook. If however you should by any Letter I may receive next Week, inform me on what day you shall arrive at N. York I could send my Horses early enough to be at Paulus Hook as soon as you will be in the City.

If you have Sold all at Vendue, that is proper to sell and let the Place at any reasonable Price, it will prove the most economical Measure for Us that could have been taken.

I am your ever Affectionate

J. A

Two deaths in Abigail's extended family delayed her departure for Philadelphia. John's mother Susanna Hall finally passed away on 17 April at the age of 88. Five days later, Abigail and John's 21-year-old niece Mary Smith died. She was

the daughter of Abigail's brother William and the sister of Louisa, who lived with the Adamses.

Abigail Adams to John Adams

My Dearest Friend   Quincy, April 23, 1797

I think through all the most trying conflicts of my life, I have been called to pass through them separated from the personal condolence and support of my bosom friend, I have been taught to look for support and aid from superior power than man: there is a state of mind, when affliction dries up the source of tears, and almost bids the swollen heart burst. I have left one of those distressing scenes, and come from the house of sorrow, and bitterness, and wo, to the house of silent mourning. The venerable remains of our parent, yet lie uninterred, and the distressing pangs of dissolution of an agonizing nature, are separating the soul from the body of my dear niece, whilst her senses are perfect, and alive to every attention, willing to go, praying to be released, yet requesting her friends and sisters not to leave her dying bed; but to remain by her until she breathes her last. O it is too much to bear! my heart is too big for my bosom; it rends my frame, and you will find me, when I reach you, more emaciated than with a fit of sickness. To-morrow I have the last duties to pay to our venerable parent. I have taken upon me the care and charge of the funeral; and to-morrow she will, for the last time, enter our doors. I have requested Mr. Whitney to attend. It is not for me to say when I will leave here; the will of heaven has detained me; I must not complain.

By the mistake or misarrangement of the mails, you will not receive my letters as I wish, but the detention will only spare you pain. I am, my dearest friend.

Your very afflicted,

A. Adams

Abigail Adams to John Adams

My Dearest Friend   Quincy, 26 April, 1797

This, I hope, is the last letter which you will receive from me at Quincy. The funeral rites performed, I prepare to set out on the morrow. I long to leave a place, where every scene and object wears a gloom, or looks so to me. My agitated mind wants repose. I have twice the present week met my friends and relatives, and taken leave of them in houses of mourning. I have asked, "Was all this necessary to wean me from the world? Was there danger of my fixing a too strong attachment upon it? Has it any allurements, which could make me forget, that here I have no abiding-place?" All, all is undoubtedly just and right. Our aged parent is gone to rest. My mind is relieved from any anxiety on her account. I have no fears lest she should be left alone, and receive an injury. I have no apprehensions, that she should feel any want of aid or assistance, or fear of becoming burdensome. She fell asleep, and is happy.

Mary, in the prime of life, when, if ever, it is desirable, became calm, resigned, and willing to leave the world. She made no objection to her sister's going, or to mine, but always said she should go first.

I have received your letters of April 16th and 19th. I want no courting to come. I am ready and willing to follow my husband wherever he chooses; but the hand of Heaven has arrested me. Adieu, my dear friend. Excuse the melancholy strain of my letter. From the abundance of the heart the stream flows.

Affectionately yours,

A. Adams

John Adams to Abigail Adams

My dearest Friend   Philadelphia May 4, 1797

Your Letters of the 21. 22. 23. and 26 of April are all before me. They have inspired me with all the Melancholly in which they were written.

Our Mother and our Niece are gone to rest. The first a fruit fully ripe the last but a blossom or a bud. I have Suffered for you as much as you have Suffered. But I could give you no Aid or Amusement or Comfort. I pray God that these dispensations may be for ever good. My Mothers Countenance and Conversation was a Source of Enjoyment to me, that is now dried up forever, at Quincy. Our Ancestors are now all gone, and We are to follow them very Soon, to a country where there will be no War or rumour of War, no Envy, Jealousy Rivalry nor Party.

You and I are now entering on a new Scene, which will be the most difficult, and least agreable of any in our Lives. I hope the burthen will be lighter to both of Us, when We come together.

I am, as long as Life lasts your ever affectionate

John Adams

The year 1798 proved to be a trial for the Adamses and the entire nation. French attacks on American neutral vessels and other provocations resulted in military and naval preparations that took the United States to the brink of war. John and Abigail traveled to Quincy to escape the Philadelphia summer and the relentless stress of the presidency. Despite the burdens of the office they were especially eager to return to Peacefield because two new rooms had been added in their absence—a parlor for Abigail and a library-office for John. Rather than finding relief, however, they had to endure an additional burden: Abigail fell sick on the journey, suffered an extended illness, and did not return to Philadelphia until November 1799.

Abigail Adams to John Adams

my dearest Friend   Quincy Novbr 13 1798

Mrs Smith appeard so anxious and unhappy tho she said nothing, that seeing it, I advised her to follow you, and sent Micheal to Town hoping she would overtake you tomorrow. She appeard so rejoiced at the proposal that in half an hour, she was gone. I hope she will overtake you by tomorrow night.

I slept well last night and tho I feel very low spirited, I shall strive to be content. I will follow you when I am able if you want me, but must leave it to future contingencies. I congratulate you upon the News which is now thought Authentic of the Capture of the French Fleet by Nelson. I inclose you some Letters received to day. The contents of one of them will remain as tho it had never been seen by me. I think it however uncandid and severe. Forgive me that I opend it. It was in hopes of finding a Letter from Brisler. Mr storer being here on his return to Hingham, I request him to address them and put them into the post office for you to be sent to N york. Mr Cranch remains very sick indeed the dr says. Love to William Shaw and to all who feel interested in the happiness of your

                                                                    A A

John Adams to Abigail Adams

My Dearest Friend   Stratford Nov. 16. 1798

From Rileys in Berlin, We went to Newhaven 26 miles to dinner at your Friends Mrs Smiths who were very respectfully inquisitive after your health, and very sorry to hear an Account of it from me, not so flattering. A Visit from Dr Dwight detained Us agreably for a short time but We found enough to cross the Ferry over the Housatonnoc by sunsett and soon reached Lovejoys in this Town. We had our Fire made in our Bedchamber and our Tea and Oysters Served up, When behold a Vision of the Night in the Forms of Mrs Smith and the fair Caroline bolted in upon Us without the least previous notice or Suspicion. The first Sight convinced me that you was better than When I left you. The Ladies have born the Journey to Admiration, and Mrs Smith is convinced as I am that the Stage is the easiest mode of travelling. I shall take them in my Carriage the rest of the Way which is not more than fifty five or sixty Miles to East chester. We shall not however reach Col Smiths before Monday night, for my Horses have been pushed too much already.

I rejoice to hear you are better, and now my most immediate Anxiety is for my dear Brother Cranch, who is represented by my Daughter to be very sick. I pray for his Recovery as well as yours.

Generals Washington, Hamilton and Pinckney are at Philadelphia, not waiting for me, I hope.

Envoy Logan is said to be returned, for any Thing that I know Ambasador from the Directory to ——.

I wish you a good night.

J. A

John Adams to Abigail Adams

My dearest Friend   Phil. Nov. 28. 98

I have recd yours of 18th and none later. Your Company here is much desired by every body: but by none so much as me. My Occupation in Business is so incessant, that I could have little time to pass with you, but that little every day would be prescious and invaluable. You express a Willingness to come on: but the thought of your attempting it without consulting your Friends and Physicians, distresses and terrifies me least it should prove fatal to a Life that is dear to me beyond all Expression. If however your Physicians are of Opinion, that you can come on by easy Journeys, in any Way you can think of, your Arrival here will be an inexpressible Satisfaction to me. But if you Attempt to come without a fixed Resolution to take Care of your Health and renounce those fatigues of public places Drawing Rooms, great Dinners &c I am very apprehensive that this Winter will be your last. A Constitution so wrecked and exhausted as yours has been by a three months confinement, may be easily oversett.

We are all well, and every Thing goes on very well. We had the Ministry and General Officers to dine on Monday and all agreable.

I am with tenderness inexpressible ever yours

J. A

Abigail Adams to John Adams

My dearest Friend   Quincy Nov'br 29 1798

This is our Thanksgiving day, when I look Back upon the year past. I perceive many, very many causes for thanksgiving, both of a publick and private nature. I hope my Heart is not ungratefull, tho sad; it is usually a day of festivity when the Social Family circle meet together tho seperated the rest of the year. No Husband *dignifies my Board,* no Children add gladness to it, no Smiling Grandchildren Eyes to Sparkle for the plumb pudding, or feast upon the mincd Pye. Solitary and alone I behold the day after a sleepless night, without a joyous feeling. Am I ungratefull? I hope not. Brother Cranchs illness prevented Him and my sister from joining me, and Boylston Adams's sickness confineing him to his House debared me from inviting your Brother and Family. I had but one resource and that was to invite mr and mrs Porter to dine with me: and the two Families to unite in the Kitchin with Pheby the only surviving Parent I have, and thus we shared in the Bounties of providence.

I was not well enough to venture to meeting and by that means lost an excellent discourse deliverd by mr Whitman, upon the numerous causes of thankfullness and gratitude which we all have to the Great Giver of every perfect Gift; nor was the late Glorious victory gained by Admiral Nelson over the French omitted by him, as in its concequences of Great importance in checking the mad arrogance of that devouring Nation.

And here let me congratulate you upon the event, as now made certain. I hope it will prove of great advantage to us, as well as to all the powers Whom France has abused debased and insulted.

I cannot speak of them in the stile of Gov. Henry, tho I like his Speech, and belive he made it without the aid of Laudanum, the address from thence I like, make a good answer to it.

I presume you reachd Philadelphia on saturday. I wrote to you twice to N york to the care of Charles and twice I have written to you addrest to Philadelphia. I hope you received the Letters.

I am as ever your truly affectionate

A Adams

Abigail Adams to John Adams

my dearest Friend   Quincy December 15 1798

I last Evening received yours of Novbr 28th. If oceans do not rool between us, mountains have arrisen. The late sevear snow storm has shut me in, as close as a mouse in a trap, and that so early in the Season, that no probability appears, of any comfortable travelling this winter. The Banks are so high, so hardly compacted together that they will not be removed untill Spring; I am well persuaded, so that I must sigh at Quincy, and you at Philadelphia, without being able to afford each other any personal comfort, or Genial warmth; you say you are fractious; you will have causes enough for vexation I doubt not. The Military arrangment is an ample Feild if you had no other; I see by the paper of to day, that Genll Brooks has resignd. It reminds me of a story of a certain Irishman who observing that his outer rows of corn were not so good as his others, determined that in future he would have no outer Row. It is very difficult so to place the outer row as to satisfy those which succeed, but nothing tends so much to render a Man Fractious as living without Femals about him. Even tho Sometimes they may be glad to lie low and let the sand fly over, they know how to temper the wind to the shorne Lamb and to Sooth into good humour, the jaring Elements. You see I am willing to keep up my self concequence, as well as the honour and dignity of the Sex. I have on Authority in point, our minister at Berlin in his last Letter Speaking of his wife says, "her Lovely disposition and affectionate heart, afford me constant consolation amidst all the distresses, cares and vexations which the publick concerns, as well as my private affairs so thickly strew in my way." I hope you can sleep a nights. I find it such a comfort to have my rest returning to me, that I know not how to prize it sufficiently. It restores the little indispositions of the day but I find tranquility of mind so necessary to my rest, that a little matter agitating me is sufficient still, to rob me for the night of that slumber which is indispensable for my Health.

Brother Cranch is getting better. He sees a fullfillment of the Prophecies in the report of the Russians being permitted to pass through the Dardenells an Event he has been long looking for, that once obtaind the door will never be closed untill the Turks are driven out and their citys destroyed, according to holy writ.

I shall write to mrs otis from whom I received a kind Letter last Evening, next week, but I rememberd you warnd me against writing much yet it is all my amusement. I want to know how the world passes, tho I cannot gain admittance now into the Cabinet.

Remember me to all my old Friends and acquaintance who inquire after me, and tell them that I very much regreet, that I have it not in my power to shew them those attentions which I should take pleasure in manifesting, if my Health had permitted me to have accompanied you to Philadelphia. A Good repose to you. I hope I shall enjoy the Same. Ever yours

A Adams

The frustrations that John and Abigail felt concerning their children accumulated over the years. John Quincy, who had married Lousia Catherine Johnson in London in July 1797, remained the apple of his parents' eyes, serving as the American minister in Berlin. By contrast, Charles, despite all the encouraging reports of his attending to business and family, succumbed to alcoholism and spiraled to his death in November 1800. Before that he mismanaged some of John Quincy's investments, resulting in significant losses. Nabby, the "Unfortunate Daughter," had three children and a husband who could not provide for them. Thomas Boylston returned to his unsuccessful Philadelphia law practice in January 1799 after four years in Europe. He moved to Quincy in 1802, where he again proved a failure as a lawyer and eventually helped oversee his parents' farms. Like his brother Charles, he too suffered from alcoholism.

John Adams to Abigail Adams

My Dearest Friend   Phyl. Dec. 17. 98

With a great deal of snow upon the Ground it is now plentifully snowing. There must be an unusual Quantity upon the Earth. I suppose you have it very deep.

Our Men and Teams must have had a terrible Jobb to get the Lumber home: but I hope it is all compleated e'er this.

To Day at two Dr Ewing and Mr snowden are to dine with me and tomorrow at four about 30 senators and Reps. I have not had as yet any Tuesdays or Saturdays Parties: and I believe I will not have any. There is too much familiarity at them: they Sit too late.

The last Letter from you was dated the 9th. I admire your taste for Weddings. I hope you will marry Louisa and Betcy Howard and all the single ones, who are ripe. I am sorry for Louisa at Berlin: But I have Grand Children more than enough. I dont want any more. Yet I should like that John should have a son and a Daughter. But I cannot bear the trouble of Children at my Age. In short I have enough of

Children as well as Grand Children. My Daughter and one son, will bring down my Grey Hairs with sorrow to the Grave, if I dont arrouse all my Phylosophy. The Daughter too without a fault. Unfortunate Daughter! Unhappy Child!

I begin to doubt whether I was in the Way of my Duty in ever engaging in public Life. With my Family of Children ought I not to have staid at home, minded their Education and sought their Advancement in Life! It is too late for this Cemistry now. The Die is cast and I am not far from the End of my Life. I have done all for my Children that I could: and meant all for the best. What have I not suffered? What have I ever enjoyed? All my Enjoyments have been upon my farm. Oh that my Children and Grand Children were all Farmers!

I am anxious and impatient to hear of the arrival of Thomas.

Is Master Cleverly dead? And Mr Burrell? How is Mr Cranch and Boylston Adams?

J. A.

Abigail Adams to John Adams

my dearest Friend   Quincy Fryday december 28 1798

On twesday Evening I received the Mercury, and read in it, the arrival of capt Jenkins in the America, on Sunday. You may well suppose I felt greatly rejoiced expecting from Thomas's Letter, that he was undoubtedly a passenger. No mention was however made of him in the paper: I expected for two days to hear of him. Then I conjectured that not knowing of my being here, was the reason of my not receiving a Letter to notify me. In this Suspence I wrote to mr Smith requesting him to get intelligence for me. I received an answer from him last Evening that he had seen one of Capt Jenks owners but that he knew not of any passengers comeing in her. He supposes mr Adams is on Board the Ship Barbara Capt Clark who saild at the same time for Boston, the 30 of october, but I have not been yet able to learn any thing further. I can only pray for his Safety. I watch'd the weather all last week, and tho threatned with a snow storm, it past off, with a small slight portion and ended in a Thaw, by which the travelling is again impeeded. It had just got passible, and the Roads were lively. The weather is now moderate and fine. I last Evening received your Letter of December the 19th. I cannot say that it added to my spirits, or Rest. The dissapointment from Thomas's not comeing had already depresst me, and the reflections and observations respecting our Children calls up so many painfull Ideas, that I cannot be otherways than unhappy when I reflect upon them. In Silence I do reflect upon them daily. I wish it was otherways with them. For mrs Smith I feel more keenly; because I know She is innocent of the cause of her misfortunes; she is and always was a dutifull and affectionate Child. I hope better days are reserved for her, tho at present the prospect is dark. With respect to what is past, all was intended for the best, and you have the Satisfaction of knowing that you have faithfully served your generation, that you have done it at the expence of all private Considerations and you do not know whether you would have been a happier Man in private, than you have been in publick Life. The exigencies of the times were such as call'd you forth. You considerd yourself as performing your duty. With these considerations, I think you have not any cause for regreet. What remains to us of Life, we must expect to have checkerd will good and evil, and let us patiently endure the one and rejoice in the other as becomes those who have a better hope and brighter prospects beyond the Grave.

Much is said in the Philadelphia papers respecting the united Irishmen. Is there any reason to think them so formidable as there represented? I know there is a banditty of unprincipeld wretches who are employd as emissaries to keep us at varience. A passage struck me in Fennoes paper last Evening, that the Democratic Society of N york were summoned to meet, by one davis when some communications of importance are to be made.

I took the more notice of it, from having read a preface written by one John Davis the translator as he calls himself, of General Buonaparte Campaign in Italy, a work of 300 pages, printed in N york at the Argus office in 98, written by a Genll officer of his Army. I am now reading it, but the stile of the preface struck me as the most conceited Bombastical thing I ever read. "He says he came to this Country the middle of last march, *with no other recommendation* than a *Love of literature*. He had caught the Bliss of publication in England, which will ever constitute my Supreme felicity."

As a specimin of this superb translator work, he is transported with joy, to have executed the translation of a work that records the actions of one of the Greatest warriours the world ever produced; compared to whom Hannibal was a stripling, Alexander a holiday captain, and Caesar a mere candidate for military Fame. I would recommend to him to translate Buonaparty Campaign into Eygypt. Query is not this the same fellow probably?

The Book belongs to Nat'll Austin the Brother of Honestus. You will wonder how I came by it. For the good of the publick it was put into the circulating Library in Boston, taken out by mr D Greenleaf, and by him lent to me.

Master Cleverly is still living. Mr Burrel who was sick when you was here recoverd, but a younger Brother of his who lived, with him took the fever and dyed with it. Mr Cranch is getting well I hope, so is B Adams.

I have not heard yet whether Richard Dexter has arrived.

I had a Letter from mrs Smith in which she expresses her anxiety at hearing you were unwell and fears you took cold in going on in the storm. She says she has been greatly afflicted with an Eruption upon her hands which the Dr pronounces the Salt Rhume—the same which afflicts you. She complaind of its itching intollerably—Sulpher and cream of Tarter she took: you have always found that of service to you, and I would again recommend it to you.

I inclose to you a Sermon. Dr Eckley was so polite as to send me two. It is a good performance. I see that the yellow fever has not purified the Northern Liberties. What a wretched crew!

Adieu ever yours

A Adams

John Adams to Abigail Adams

My Dearest Friend   Phil. Jan. 5. 1799

Three Vessells have arrived from Hambourg Since Thomas was there. The inclossed will shew you that he chose the Alexander Hamilton of New York. By this means he will escape the Dangers of our Massachusetts Bay; and I hope soon to hear of his Arrival.

The General Officers nominated Smith for the command of a Regiment. I nominated him to the senate who, after a warm opposition and a day or two's debate consented to his Appointment. His Pride is capable of stooping very low, or he would not have consented to be nominated. Let him run for Luck. All the Actions of my Life and all the Conduct of my Children have not yet disgraced me so much as this Man. His Pay will not feed his Dogs: and his Dogs must be fed if his Children starve. What a Folly! Yet he is brave and capable as an officer: and faithful to his Country as I believe, tho no Politician.

J A

Abigail Adams to John Adams

my Dearest Friend   Quincy Jan'ry 12 the 1799

I received your Letters of Decbr 31 and Jan'ry the 1st. I am sorry that it should fall to your Lot to nominate Col Smith again, and that to a lower Grade than, as a Soldier he merrits. I think however that he was placed in a difficult Situation. If he had rejected the offer, those who have stiled him a Jacobin, would have attributed it to motives unfriendly to his Country, but as a Man particuliarly calculated for the Millitary department, and having Served his Country with honour and approbation in the Feild, he deserved [a mu]ch Higher Grade of Rank. The New Modelling the Army [may] tend to reconcile him to the arrangment, but I think as an officer, he ought not to have Submitted to the Nomination, disgraced as he was by the senate, some of whom I shall always remember for their consistancy, of conduct.

The Idea which prevails here, is that Hamilton will be first in command, as there is very little Idea that Washington will be any thing more than, *Name* as to actual Service, and I am told that it ill suits the N England stomack. They say He is not a Native, and beside He has so damnd himself to everlasting Infamy, that He ought not to *be Head* of any thing. The Jacobins Hate him and the Federilists do not Love him. Serious People are mortified; and every Uriah must tremble for his Bathsheba; I do not consider G W. at all a happier man, because he has not Children. If he has none to give him pain, he has none to give him pleasure, and he has other Sources of anxiety, in full proportion. As to conjecturing what is to be the Lot, and portion of the next generation; my only anxiety is that they may have good and virtuous Educations, and if they are left to struggle for themselves, they will be quite as like to rise up virtuous and distinguished Characters as tho they had been born to great expectations. Vicious conduct will always be a source of disquietude to me. If my wishes are blasted I must submit to it, as a punishment, a trial, an affliction which I must bear, and what I cannot remedy I must endure.

Since I wrote you last mr Smith has seen capt Jenkins. He informs him that Thomas [applied] to him for a passage on Board his vessel, but captain [. . .] advised him not to come in her. Tho a fast sailor, she was a very wet ship, and a winters passage in her would have been very uncomfortable. He went with Thomas to examine the vessels there, and found the Alexander Hamilton Capt Clark for N york, in which he advised him to take passage, as she was a good vessel, and a Good captain. She was to sail in a few days after Capt Jenkins.

It is now two Months since you left me, and two more I hope, will return you Here again.

Our General Court are in Session. We shall see the Govenours Speach in tomorrows Paper I trust. I have met with Some of the Numbers addrest to Genll Marshall in the Chronical. They appear to me to be the common place stuff of the party, the same low invective and abuse of the Government for which the Faction are distinguishd. They will not injure Marshall so much as he injured himself. Gallitin and Nicholas have thrown asside, even the veil they used to wear. Harpers observations were good, but too lengthy, and his sarcasms very pointed.

After the dismall cold week we have had, last night came a strong south wind, and with out any rain, Swept away all but our Banks, broke up the sleighing, and left half the ground bare.

We are all well, but your Brother, who has his Eyes constantly Bad, one bunch gathering after an other. I am really affraid he will be Blind. He is too inattentive to the concequences.

I cannot write to day to william.

I send you a Green House.

Yours affectionatly

A Adams

John Adams to Abigail Adams

My Dearest Friend   Phyladelphia Jan. 16. 1799

Yesterday, Tuesday when the Levee Room began to be thin Brisler came running in, with the delightful sounds "Sir, Mr Adams is up Stairs." I was not long in mounting the Escalier and had the high Pleasure of embrasing my dear son Thomas after an Absence of four Years and an half. We had a very happy Evening and he has had a good nights rest after the fatigues of his Voyage and Journey. He seems in good health and is very little Altered in stature, shape or Feature. His Mind is well stored with Ideas and his Conversation entertaining. This Evening he goes with me to the Ball. I had rather spend it with him at home.

Inclosed is a beautiful Morcell from the Minister, Worth Gold. It is the best elucidation of the Character of the K. of Prussia that I have ever seen. Louisa I wish you were here to dance to night. I dont wish for your Aunt because one such Evening would kill her.

J. A

Abigail Adams to John Adams

my dearest Friend   Quincy Febry 14 1799

Upon the 12th. our dear Thomas reachd Quincy to my no small Joy! I am as happy in his company and Society, as you have been before me, and I bless God that he has returnd to his Native Country, an honest Sober and virtuous citizen. I hope he will continue an honour and a comfort to his Parent's tho it is allotted them to experience different Sensations with respect to one, of whose reformation I can flatter myself, with but faint hope's. It is so painfull and distressing a subject to me, that what I suffer is in silence. I cannot write upon it, but to him; and that I consider my duty; a painfull one it is. I wish however some means could be devised to save him, from that ruin and destruction with which he must soon be overwhelmd, if he is not allready.

I endeavourd as early as possible to save the Property of J Q A: that is as soon as I knew he had entrusted any to him, and I also endeavourd to get out of the hands of Dr W[*elsh*] what was in his. I have not written to you before upon it, because I did not wish to add private and domestic troubles to those of the public with which I knew you must be fully oppressd.

Early in the Month of December I was informd that two Hundred dollors were due upon the Shares in the Canal, that the dr had been frequently requested to make the payments, had always promised, but had not performd, and that the Shares must be advertized immediatly for sale. I wrote the dr and requested the papers and a transfer of the power to dr Tufts as I found immediate attention must be given to the buisness. Still I got no answer. I then wrote to mr Smith, and stated to him the buisness, requesting him to obtain the papers for me. He did so, and finally I received them, but not till after the quarters Rent of December was received by him, for the House. With the papers no Receits appear, of monies paid by him, or any account. A Letter accompanied them, stating, that an account had been renderd mr Adams by his son when he went to Berlin. I was indebted to mr Adams 25 Guineys which I had withheld not chusing to pay it, to either of his Agents. This money I immediatly paid to dr Tufts and made up the remaining Sum which he paid to the Treasurer, and stop'd the sale of the shares in the canal. I find however by the account stated by mr Adams, that exclusive of three quarters of a years Rent of the House which the dr has since received, there was a balance due to him of 200 90 dollors in the hands of the dr, which with the House Rent will amount to between 4 and 500 dollors, for all of which, he will never see as many pence; Comments are unnecessary.

I received by the last Mail yours of Feb'ry 1st. I have made inquiry respecting the light in which the report of the Secretary is viewd in this quarter, and find it is highly spoken of. It is considered as a measure approved and warrented by the president, but if you will permit a sausy women to make her comments, she will say, that upon reading of it the sentiments and Remarks are such as the dispatches, and the duplicity and knavery of citizen Minister, fully warrant, the conclusions are just; and if the Legislator approve them it may save them some long speeches, the Subject being amply discust ready to their Hands; but the Qustion which occurs to me is, was it a part of the Secretarys buisness, thus to teach the National Legislature what to think, and how to think upon matters of fact. Was not this implied. "You are not competant to judging of this buisness, without my Aid." I never have heard any person make an observation of this kind. I only say how the buisness struck me.

Have you any thoughts of going to the City of Washington before your return Home; it is said your Presence is indispensable.

Inclosed is the Report of our Senate and House, upon Virgina resolves and Kentucky resolutions.

I am with the utmost affection your

A Adams

John Adams to Abigail Adams

My dearest Friend   Phyladelphia Feb. 25. 1799

I have just recd yours of 14th. It has laid in the Post office I suppose
since saturday.

The subjects of Mr J. Q. A's Agents are horrible to me. I will therefore dismiss them.

Thomas's Predilection for Phyladelphia, I suppose will determine
him. Alass! Nelly is married poor Boy! and I suppose some of the Six
sisters will catch the Child in the Trap without a Groat and without
Connections! This is to be my fate, throughout. Three are gone already that Way—the fourth will go. Blind thoughtless, Stupid Boys
and Girl!

Frederic, Franklin and other Soidisant Phylosophers, insist that Nature contrives these Things with others to reconcile Men to the
thought of quitting the World. If my Phylosophy was theirs I should
believe that Nature cared nothing for Men, nor their follies nor their
Miseries, nor for herself. She is a mighty Stupid Wretch, according to
them, a kind of French Woman, sometimes beautiful and clever but
very often diabolical. A kind of French Republic, cunning and terrible:
but cruel as the Grave and imjust as the Temptor and Tormentor.

I believe nothing like this of Nature: which to me is a Machine
whose Author and conductor is wise kind and mighty. Believing this I
can acquiesce in what is unpleasant expecting that it will work out a
greater degree of good. If it were possible that I should be mistaken, I
at least shall not be worse than these profound Phylosophers. I shall be
in the same case hereafter, and a little, a great deal better here.

The Report, was not at last as it should have been: But it is very different from the Report made to me. I Scratched out, a little. I wanted no Report. In short it is one of those Things, that I may talk of, when I see you. After I sent that Report to Congress, I recd a Letter, which has favoured Mr Gerrys opinion and made against the Report. I have instituted a new Mission: which is kept in the dark, but when it comes to be understood will be approved. Oh how they lament Mrs Adams's Absence! She is a good Counsellor! If she had been here, Murray would never have been named nor his Mission instituted. This ought to gratify your Vanity enough to cure you. Love to Thomas, Brothers Cousins &c Louisa especially.

J. A

Abigail Adams to John Adams

my dearest Friend   Febry 27th 1799. Quincy

Yesterday afternoon mr Greenleaf returnd from Boston, and as he, as well as my others Neighbours; are particuliarly attentive and kind, in bringing Letters and papers to me as well; as of communicating all New's, he came full fraught, with the appointment of mr Murrey Minister Plenipo to France, a measure which had astonishd all the Federilist; and was a subject of great speculation in Boston. Soon after Thomas returnd from Boston, thinking to bring me great New's but found himself forestall'd. He however got a Good story in Boston. Some of the Feds who did not like being taken so by surprize, said they wisht the old woman had been there; they did not believe it would have taken place; This was pretty Sausy, but the old woman can tell them they are mistaken, for she considers the measure as a master stroke of policy; knowing as she did that the pulse had been feeling through that minister for a long time. Beside's the appointment shows that the disposition of the Government is still pacific, and puts to the test the Sincerity of the directory, who if they are really inclined to accommodate, have the door held open to them; and upon them rests in the Eyes of all the world, the responsibility. It is a measure which strikes in the Head Jacobinism. It come as unexpected to them, as to the Federilists. It will also prevent the directory sending a French minister here which was not desirable, knowing the Nature of the animal. It cannot be considerd as a degradation restricted as I lean the appointment is, that no negotiation shall commence, but with a minister of equal Rank specially appointed to treat; I have not heard an opinion upon it, but revoleving the Subject upon my pillow, I call it a master stroke of polocy. Even tho it should terminate in a buble it brings the directory, to the touch stone.

I was vext however to see our House of Rep's stop in the midst of a wise measure, and take for granted, what they had no buisness to consider; not a cord should be relaxed in concequence of the appointment. To ensure any kind of success to the negotiation, they should be prepared at all points for War, if it fails.

Pray am I a good politician?

We have had for the last ten days winter as severe as any before. It has frozen the Rivers and bay more than any time before, and it is now snowing with voilence. As to my own Health, it has its up's and down's. As soon as I feel any thing tolerable, I get out, and will not lose the air then. I get housed a day or two; but I endeavour to keep up my spirits, and take what comfort I can; as I go along comforting myself, that it will be better by and by.

In my last I mentiond to you leaving clinker for Thomas but I did not calculate that he was the only Saddle Horse you had, untill afterwards—when I recollected the loss of one, and that I had two here.

You mention that dr Tufts might draw upon you for any sum within Reason. The sum which he will draw for will be 500 dollors, unless you should give orders that any further sum should be laid out in public securities; I know not the reason, but the funds are allways a shilling in a pound higher here than at Philadelphia. They are now 6 pr cents, at 16. and 4 pence, fallen a shilling in a pound since the new loan. As to defered stock, there is not any to be had. The 6 pr cents are the most advantages, only that two pr cent is annually paid off.

I wrote you that French would give with Belchers place, 52 pound ten shilling.

It looks so like the depdth of winter, that Spring appears far off. I hope you will be at home before much is wanted to be done.

I am my dear Friend affectionatly Your

A Adams

John Adams to Abigail Adams

My dearest Friend   Trenton Octr. 12. 1799

We arrived on the 10th. I, much oppressed by one of my great Colds, which is now going off. I could obtain only one little Room and one little bedroom, but We can make a shift. I came here more loaded with sorrow than with Rheum. Sally opened her Mind to me for the first time. I pitied her, I grieved, I mourned but could do no more. A Madman possessed of the Devil can alone express or represent. I renounce him. K. Davids Absalom had some Ambition and some Enterprize. Mine is a mere Rake, Buck, Blood and Beast.

To go from a private Calamity to a public the Fever in Phyladelphia is still bad, from ten to fourteen in a day. The great black frosts which freeze an Inch, are not come and they are necessary. They seldom come before the Middle of Novr.

If the Weather has been as wett in New England as here, you will have a damp Journey and not pleasant Roads.

I must be seperated from you a whole month, which will appear to me long enough.

John Adams to Abigail Adams

My dearest Friend   Trenton October 27. 1799

I have recd yours of 24th and thank you for your relation of our little domestic affairs at Quincy. Brisler did not arrive last night as you callculated. His Children may detain him longer than you expected. Some of the public Offices are about removing to Phyladelphia this Week. I can Send James with my Horses and Charriot to meet you at Hoebucken Ferry or Elizabeth Town or any other Place you may appoint and at any time you will appoint, if you can be sure of your Planns and measures. If Mrs Smith and Caroline come on, you will want more room and more horses. Write exactly your determination.

I have been forenon and afternoon to Church to hear Parson Waddell, who gave Us two Discourses good and wholesome for soul, Body and Estate. He is a good Picture of "Stalled Theology" and is said to have a good Estate. Last sunday I went to the Presbyterian Church and heard Mr Grant an ingenious young Gentleman. There is Something more chearful and comfortable in an Episcopalian than in a Presbyterian Church. I admire a great Part of the divine service at Church very much. It is very humane and benevolent, and sometimes pathetic and affecting: but rarely gloomy, if ever. Their Creeds I could dispense with very well because, the scriptures being before Us contain the Creed the most certainly orthodox. But you know I never write nor Talk upon Divinity. I have had more than I could do, of Humanity. Benevolence and Beneficence, Industry, Equity and Humanity Resignation and submission, Repentance and Reformation are the Essence of my Religion. Alass, how weakly and imperfectly have I fullfilled the Duties of my own Religion! I look back Upon a long Life very poorly Spent in my own Estimation. Busy as it has appeared to some, to me it appears to have been very much too idle, inactive, slothful and sluggish. I fear it is too late to amend. My Forces are far Spent and by too much Exertion I should soon exhaust them all. I am not in the Vapours but in very good Spirits notwithstanding this penetent Confession of my faults. Write me every day.

J. A

Abigail Adams to John Adams

my dearest Friend East Chester october 29th 1799

I received last Evening yours of the 25, with a Heart filled with gratitide, for the many Blessings I have enjoyed through the 35 years of our union; I would not look upon a single shade in the picture; for if according to Rousseaus philosophy, abstinence from what we delight in, is the Epicurism of Reason; I have had my full proportion of enjoyment.

This day is very fine. I almost regreet to lose it; but as I cannot yet go into the city, I am certainly more comfortably and pleasantly situated here than at an Inn. I shall not be any expence to the Family, as I know you would not permit it, yet I had rather the expence should be here, than at an Inn.

Guion will supply me with a Horse to kinstone for 12 and half dollors, and a Boy to bring the Horse back. He does not keep any Stage Horses. I think this is high. He calculates upon 5 days absence of his Horse. I do not know whether I shall be able to do better. Farmer is so lame that I fear he is ruind for Life, tho he walks better than he did. As to getting any more horses unless you were to part with some you have, it Seems to me you will not know what to do with them all, and they are a great expence, but you will do as you think best. I am out of conceit of young Horses for journeying, tho this which Brisler bought, is a hardy Hearty cating Horse. I think you will be pleasd with him.

I make no calculation for going further southard. My inclination will lead me to Quincy if my Health will permit as Soon as the Roads are fit for travelling.

Caroline Eyes are so bad that she is obliged to be shut up in a dark Chamber. The rest of the Family are all well.

I am most affectionatly your

A Adams

In May 1800 Abigail left Philadelphia for Quincy and John went south to inspect the new capital in Washington, D.C. Although Congress had decided to move the seat of the national government to a location on the Potomac River nine years before, the work continued, far from complete. Many of the public buildings, including the executive mansion or president's house (later called the White House), remained unfinished when the official transfer took place in June. John visited widow Martha Washington at Mount Vernon before he headed home to Quincy on 14 June. He left Quincy again for the last time to serve the nation on 13 October. Abigail departed later in the month. As John notes in his 2 November letter, he was the first president to sleep in the executive mansion.

Abigail Adams to John Adams

my dearest Friend   Quincy June 2d 1800

Mr Gore came out this afternoon to see me; and informd me that mr dexter proposed to sit out tomorrow for Washington. By him I embrace the earliest opportunity of informing you of my safe arrival at Quincy on Saturday the last day of May, in good health tho some thing fatigued. I got on very well, met with no accident, Horses all in good order. I found our Friends here well. The Hill looks very well. Mr Porter says those parts which were manured will have a good crop of Grass. We have had very plentifull rains grain and grass promise well, but our verdure here, is not so deep, nor our grain so forward by any means. We are three weeks later. The building progresses, but not so fast as I wish.

Mr dexter can give you a more accurate statement of Parties and politicks than I am able to. I met with judge Hobart upon a visit at Fairfield. He came and spent the Evening with me at Penfields. Upon the subject of a late removal he said there had been some considerable sensation in that state at first, but that thinking people agreed that the President was certainly right in calling to his aid men who would act with him. The Jacobins in Boston say: or rather certain persons who call themselves federilists say, that it is an Electioneering measure. Others say that the federilists as well as Jacobins want to get a man whom they can manage. Burr means to be voted for in N york and says that it will be of no use to sit up Pinckney. Several people are disgusted with Harpers letter to his constituents. They consider it as a luke warm buisness, that part of it where in he appears to think it quite a matter of indifference whether mr A or mr Pinckney is elected. I have not got a line from you or mr shaw since I left new york. I hope to hear from you this week. I say to every body who inquires, that Gen'll Marshall will accept his appointment. I should sorry to believe that he would not deserve as well of his Country as mr Dexter. Good old Gen'll Lincoln call'd on saturday Evening to inquire, if they had not kill'd you yet. I told him no that you would live to kill half a dozen more politically, if they did not stear steady.

Our old Neighbour and tennant Elijah Belcher dyed yesterday morning. A kind remembrance to all Friends.

Affectionatly yours &c.

Mrs Smith is at N Wark with the cols Mother. She could not come on when I did having arrangements to make, and being uncertain what the col would do this Summer. If he goes up to the Miami with his Brother, she would be glad to come with you when you return to Quincy. Mr shaw can take the stage.

John Adams to Abigail Adams

My dearest friend   Washington June 13. 1800

I recd your favour of the 2d by Mr Dexter and this morning from Mr Gerry an Account of your health on the 4th, which have relieved me from some Anxiety as I had recd no Letter from you Since you were in N. York.

I have seen many Cities and fine Places since you left me and particularly Mount Virnon. Mrs Washington and her whole Family very kindly enquired after your health and all your Children and Louisa; and send many friendly Greetings.

I like the Seat of Government very well and shall Sleep, or lie awake next Winter in the Presidents house. I have Slept very well in my Journey and been pretty well. An Abundance of Company and many tokens of respect have attended my Journey, and my Visit here is well recd. Mr Marshall and Mr Dexter lodge with me at Tunnicliffs City Hotel, very near the Capital. The Establishment of the public offices in this place has given it the air of the seat of Government and all Things seem to go on well.

I am particularly pleased with Alexandria. Mr Lee lives very elegantly neatly and agreably there among his sisters and friends and among his fine Lotts of Clover and Timothy. I scarcely know a more eligible situation. Oh! that I could have a home! But this felicity has never been permitted me. Rolling rolling rolling, till I am very near rolling into the bosom of mother Earth. I am as ever your affectionate Husband

                                                        J. Adams

Abigail Adams to John Adams

My dearest Friend   Quincy october 27 1800

After a sleepless night I begin my journey, with an anxious mind, tho not a desponding one. My dear sister is I hope out of danger, tho so low and weak as not to be able either to stand or walk. Mrs Norten whom we had all buried in our expectations, is getting up again. Thus have I cause of comfort that death has not enterd their doors Whilst in my own family I have cause to mourn the death of poor Jackson whom last week I burried. The two shipleys were also threatned with the same fever and mrs Porter. To all of them and to Mrs Smith the doctor administered Emetic's and calomil. They are all better. Shipley however is not yet out.

I have been anxious that I have not heard from you. I have made all the haste I could under the circumstances of distress in which my sisters family have been, for others having the fever bad. My own weak state of body, and the agitation of my mind from the Sudden death of Jackson, and the apprehension of the fever upon others has distrest me greatly. New cases daily occur.

Shipley and the two Girls I send off tomorrow. Becky I hope will deliver you this. My journey is a mountain before me, but I must climb it. Mrs Smith I take to N york. Ever yours,

A A

P S I will write you upon the road.

John Adams to Abigail Adams

Presidents house,

My dearest friend   Washington City, Nov. 2. 1800

We arrived here last night, or rather yesterday at one O Clock and here We dined and Slept. The Building is in a State to be habitable.

And now We wish for your Company. The Account you give of the melancholly State of our dear Brother Mr Cranch and his family is really distressing and must severely afflict you. I most cordially Sympathize with you and them.

I have seen only Mr Marshall and Mr Stoddart General Wilkinson and the two Commissioners Mr Scott and Mr Thornton.

I shall Say nothing of public affairs. I am very glad you consented to come on, for you would have been more anxious at Quincy than here, and I, to all my other Solicitudines Mordaces as Horace calls them i.e. "biting Cares" Should have added a great deal on your Account. Besides it is fit and proper that you and I should retire together and not one before the other.

Before I end my Letter I pray Heaven to bestow the best of Blessings on this House and all that shall hereafter inhabit it. May none but honest and wise Men ever rule under this roof.

I shall not attempt a description of it. You will form the best Idea of it from Inspection.

Mr Brisler is very anxious for the arrival of the Man and Women and I am much more so for that of the Ladies. I am with unabated Confidence and affection your

John Adams

John did not need to wait until the 11 February electoral vote tabulation to realize that he had failed to win a second term. By mid-December he knew that his long service was coming to an end. In an extraordinary election in which both parties attempted to "manage" the outcome, Jefferson, who would eventually emerge with the prize, tied for first in the electoral vote with Aaron Burr at 73 votes apiece. Adams followed with 65.

John Adams to Abigail Adams

My dearest Friend   Washington Feb. 16. 1801

Saturday night 9 O Clock and not before I recd yours of 13th. and the Letter to Thomas with it, brought here no doubt by mistake. I regret very much that you have not a Gentleman with you. The Skittish young Colt with you, is always timorous, but no harm will befall you or her I trust. The Weather and roads here, on Saturday Sunday and to day are the finest We have seen this year.

The Election will be decided this day in favour of Mr Jefferson as it is given out by good Authority.

The Burden upon me in nominating Judges and Consuls and other officers, in delivering over the furniture, in the ordinary Business at the Close of a Session, and in preparing for my Journey of 500 miles through the mire, is and will be very heavy. My time will be all taken up. I pray you to continue to write me. My Anxiety for you is a very distressing addition to all my other Labours.

Our Bishop gave Us a good discourse yesterday And, every body enquired after you. I was able to tell them you had arrived on fryday night at Baltimore. I sleep the better for having the Shutters open: and all goes on well. I pray God to bless and preserve you.

I give a feast to day to Indian Kings and Aristocrats.

Ever

J. A

Abigail, eager to leave Washington, set off on 13 February and wrote this last surviving letter of John and Abigail's forty-year correspondence while en route to Quincy. The mixed reaction she reported from Philadelphia was to Jefferson's successful election, after thirty-six ballots in the House of Representatives broke the tie with Aaron Burr, on 17 February. Abigail's interest in public affairs continued to the end—her last sentence refers to the many judicial appointments John would make in his final weeks in office.

John accepted defeat but feared that the abrupt transition to a less active life might be too jarring for his health. He wrote a friend that "rapid motion ought not to be succeeded by sudden rest." Unlike George Washington, who had remained in Philadelphia to witness his successor's inauguration, John chose to leave the capital early on the morning of 4 March before Jefferson assumed the office. By the evening of 18 March, he had arrived at his Quincy home, from which he would never again stray very far.

Abigail Adams to John Adams

My Dear Sir   [*Philadelphia, 21 February 1801*]

I write you once more from this city. The Trenton River is impassable, and has prevented my sitting out. We hope however that the Rain may clear it. I sent Townsend of to day; I have heard Some of the democratic rejoicing Such as Ringing Bells and fireing cannon; what an inconsistancy Said a Lady to me to day, the Bells of Christ Church ringing peals of rejoicing for an Infidel President! The People of this city have evidently been in terror, least their Swineish Herd should rise in rebellion and seize upon their Property and share the plunder amongst them; they have permitted them really to overawe them; I foresee some day or other that N England will be obliged to march their militia to preserve this very state from destruction.

There is great uneasiness with the Merchants. They say the senate by rejecting the article in the convention to which they have excepted, have plunged them into great difficultys, that they know not what to do, that a better convention as it respects Commerce could not have been made and why it should be hazarded by the Senate they cannot conceive. The difference mr Breck told me it would make to this Country in one Year, would be nine Millions of dollors. The Chamber of Commerce meet this Evening, and send off an express tomorrow to the Senators of this state, hopeing that something may yet be done; that the President may be requested to return the convention to the Senate with his reasons, and by means give the Senate an other opportunity of accepting it. Mr Breck says that he wrote the Sentiments of the merchants of this city to Secretary otis requesting him to communicate them to mr Bingham and others. Whilst the convention was before the Senate; they regreet that they did not exert themselves more.

I could not help smiling when mr Breck told me he had conversed with mr Wolcott, but could get no satisfaction. Only mr Wolcott Said that there was no faith to be placed in French promises treaties or conventions.

I shall leave this city tomorrow. I believe there is scarcly a Lady who ever came to the drawing Room but has visited me, either old or young, and very many Gentlemen; as to a return of their visits, they cannot expect it; I believe they have made a point of it; who publishd my arrival in the papers I know not, but the next morning by ten oclock rainy as it was, they began to come and have continued it by throngs ever since. I thank them for their attention and politeness, tho I shall never see them again.

Adieu my dear Friend. I wish you well through the remainder of your political journey. I want to see the list of judges.

With Love to William. Yours affectionatly

A A

Epilogue

The Death of Abigail

In the years that followed John's election defeat, and John and Abigail's return to Quincy, the Adamses continued to be active intellectually and socially.

Their retirement years were not always easy. They had no income beyond what their farms produced and they lost most of their savings as a result of a bank failure in 1803. Happily John Quincy had resources to help them maintain financial security. But that could not protect them from personal tragedy. Their beloved daughter Nabby died at her parents' home in Quincy in 1813 after a lengthy battle with breast cancer. Three years earlier, Richard Cranch, Abigail's brother-in-law and the man who had originally introduced John to the Smith sisters, had died in October. His wife, Abigail's sister Mary, passed away a mere day later after a long illness. And in 1815, Abigail lost her other sister, Elizabeth, who died suddenly in the spring.

Abigail herself survived several illnesses but continued to enjoy life at Peacefield, especially when her children and grandchildren joined her. She and John remained pillars of the community, and Abigail persisted in the practice of charity toward her neighbors for which she had long been known. In the fall of 1818, however, she became dangerously sick with typhoid fever. On 28 October, in the early afternoon, she died; John was with her at the end.

John Quincy Adams to John Adams

My ever dear and revered Father   Washington 2. November 1818

By a Letter from my Son John, I have this day been apprized, of that afflictive dispensation of Providence, which has bereft you of the partner of your life; me of the tenderest and most affectionate of Mothers, and our species, of one whose existence was Virtue, and whose life was a perpetual demonstration of the moral excellence of which human nature is susceptible. How shall I offer you consolation for your loss, when I feel that my own is irreparable? Where shall I intreat you to look for comfort, in that distress, which Earth has nothing to asswage? Ten days have elapsed, since we received in a Letter from Harriet Welsh, the first intimation of my Mother's illness, and in every anxious hour, from mail to mail, I have felt that I ought to write to you, and endeavour to soothe by the communion of sorrows, of hopes and fears that anguish which I knew was preying upon your heart. Do not impute, my dear, and only Parent, the silence that I have kept, to the neglect of that sacred duty, which I owe to you. If I have refrained even from good words, it was because in the agitation of my own heart, I knew not how to order my speech, nor whether, on receiving my Letter, it would come to you seasonably to sympathize with your tears of gratitude or of resignation.

The pangs of dissolution are past; and my Mother, I humbly hope is a Spirit, purified even from that little less than heavenly purity, which in her existence here was united with the lot of mortality. I am advised that you have endured the agony of her illness, with the fortitude that belongs to your character—that after the fatal event that fortitude rose, as from you I should have expected, with renewed elasticity from the pressure under which it had been bowed down. Will the deep affliction of your Son, now meet in congenial feeling with your own, without probing the wound which it is the dearest of his wishes to alleviate? Let me hear from you, my dearest father; let me hear from you soon. And may the blessings of that God whose tender mercies are over all his works, still shed rays of heavenly hope and comfort over the remainder of your days.

Your distressed, but ever affectionate and dutiful Son.

John Quincy Adams

John Adams to John Quincy Adams

Quincy November 10th. 1818

My ever dear, ever affectionate, ever dutiful and deserving Son

The bitterness of Death is past. The grim Spector so terrible to human Nature has no sting left for me.

My consolations are more than I can number. The Seperation cannot be so long as twenty Seperations heretofore. The Pangs and the Anguish have not been so great as when you and I embarked for France in 1778.

The sympathy and Benevolence of all the World, has been such as I shall not live long enough to describe. I have not strength to do Justice to Individuals. Louisa Susan Miss Harriet Welsh, have been with us constantly. The Three Families of Greanleafs, Mrs John Greanleaf, has been, (your Mother Said it to me, in her last moments "a Mother to me"). Mr Daniel Greenleaf has been really the good Samaritan.

Louisa Harriet and Mrs John Greanleaf have been above all praise, Mr and Mrs Quincy have been more like Sons and Daughters than like Neighbours. Mr Shaw and your Sons have been all you could desire.

Your Letter of the Second is all and no more than all that I expected. Never was a more dutifull Son. Never a more Affectionate Mother. Love to your Wife. May you never experience her Loss.

So prays your Aged and Afflicted Father

John Adams

John joined Abigail again on 4 July 1826, the fiftieth anniversary of the American independence they had labored so long together—and apart—to create.

Chronology

Index

Chronology

1735

30 Oct.   John Adams is born at Braintree (19 Oct. O.S.).

1744

22 Nov.   Abigail Smith is born at Weymouth (11 Nov. O.S.).

1759

Spring–   Abigail and John meet for the first time, probably at the
summer   Smith home in Weymouth.

1762

Oct.   Abigail and John begin their correspondence.

1764

April–May   John undergoes inoculation for smallpox in Boston.

25 Oct.   Abigail and John marry.

1765

14 July   Abigail Adams 2d (Nabby), 1st daughter of Abigail and
          John, is born.

1767

11 July   John Quincy Adams, 1st son of Abigail and John, is born.

1768

April   The Adamses move from Braintree to Boston.

28 Dec.   Susanna Adams, 2d daughter of Abigail and John, is born.
          She dies 4 February 1770.

1770

29 May   Charles Adams, 2d son of Abigail and John, is born.

Oct.–Nov.   John successfully represents several British soldiers in the "Boston Massacre" trial.

1771

April   The Adamses move back to Braintree.

1772

15 Sept.   Thomas Boylston Adams, 3d son of Abigail and John, is born.

Nov.   The Adamses again move to Boston. They return to Braintree in June 1774.

1774

Aug.   John travels to Philadelphia to represent Massachusetts at the First Continental Congress. He returns to Massachusetts in November.

1775

19 April   Battles of Lexington and Concord.

April–May   John returns to Philadelphia for the second session of the Continental Congress.

May   Colonial forces lay siege to the British Army in Boston.

17 June   Battle of Bunker Hill. Abigail and John Quincy watch from Penn's Hill, near their home.

Aug.   John returns home briefly to attend the Massachusetts Council in Watertown; he goes back to Philadelphia in September.

Late summer and fall   Abigail contends with an epidemic of dysentery, which eventually kills her mother, Elizabeth Quincy Smith, on 1 Oct., among other family members.

Dec.   John again returns home to attend the Massachusetts Council.

1776

Jan.–Feb.   John travels to Philadelphia to again serve in the Continental Congress.

17 March   The British evacuate Boston.

June–July	John participates in the drafting of and debate over a declaration of independence, which is finally adopted on 4 July.
July	Abigail takes her children to Boston to be inoculated against smallpox.
Oct.	John obtains leave from Congress and comes home to Braintree.

1777

Jan.	John returns to the Continental Congress, now meeting in Baltimore. It will relocate to Philadelphia in March.
11 July	Elizabeth Adams, Abigail and John's 3d daughter, is stillborn.
Nov.	John returns to Braintree planning to resume his law career. He learns he has been appointed by Congress a joint commissioner to France.

1778

Feb.–March	John and John Quincy sail to France aboard the frigate *Boston*. In April, they join Benjamin Franklin at his house in Passy.
Sept.	Congress dissolves the joint commission and names Franklin sole minister to France.

1779

June–Aug.	John and John Quincy sail home to Boston.
Aug.–Nov.	John is elected to represent Braintree in a convention to draft a new state constitution. His draft is adopted, with alterations, by the convention in June 1780.
Nov.–Feb. 1780	John, John Quincy, and Charles sail from Boston to Spain, then travel overland to Paris, where John assumes his new position as minister with sole powers to negotiate treaties of peace and commerce with Great Britain. The commission will be revoked in summer 1781.

1780

June	John is commissioned by Congress to negotiate a Dutch loan. In the winter of 1780 he will also be elected minister to the Netherlands.

1781

June John is elected, along with four others, a joint commissioner to negotiate peace with Great Britain.

Aug. Charles begins his journey home to America; he arrives in January 1782.

1782

April The Netherlands formally recognizes American independence and John as minister plenipotentiary. In the coming months, he negotiates a treaty of amity and commerce with the Dutch and obtains a loan for the American government.

Oct.–Nov. John participates in the negotiation of the Preliminary Treaty of Peace, signed at Paris on 30 November.

1783

3 Sept. John signs the Definitive Treaty of Peace with Great Britain.

1784

June–July Abigail and Abigail 2d sail from Boston to England and meet John Quincy in London.

Aug. The family settles in Auteuil, France.

1785

Feb. John is elected the first American minister to Great Britain.

May John Quincy leaves France for America; John, Abigail, and Abigail 2d leave Auteuil for London.

1787

2 April William Steuben Smith, John and Abigail's first grandchild, is born in London.

1788

April–June Abigail and John sail home to Braintree. Abigail 2d sails to New York with her husband, William Stephens Smith, and their son.

Nov.–
Jan. 1789 Abigail travels to New York City to attend Abigail 2d in the birth of her second child.

1789

April	John is elected vice president and travels to New York City to assume his post. Abigail joins him in late June.
Oct.–Dec.	John visits Braintree during the congressional recess. George Washington tours New England to promote American unity.

1790

Nov.	John and Abigail move from New York to Philadelphia, the new seat of government.

1792

22 Feb.	The northern precinct of Braintree incorporates as the new town of Quincy.
Nov.	John returns to Philadelphia from a visit at Quincy; Abigail remains in Massachusetts.

1793

13 Feb.	The electoral vote is counted; John wins a second term as vice president.
March	John rejoins Abigail in Quincy. He returns to Philadelphia alone in November.

1794

June	John travels to Quincy during the congressional break; he returns to Philadelphia in November.

1795

Feb.	John visits Quincy again. He returns to Philadelphia in June; Abigail accompanies him as far as New York.
July	John travels to Quincy. He returns to Philadelphia alone in December.

1796

May	John travels to Quincy, returning to Philadelphia in December.

1797

8 Feb.	The electoral vote is counted; John is elected the second president of the United States.

May   Abigail travels from Quincy to Philadelphia to join John in the executive mansion there.

1798

July–Aug.   Abigail and John travel to Quincy from Philadelphia. Abigail becomes seriously ill. In November, John returns to Philadelphia alone.

1799

March   John returns to Quincy. He goes back to Philadelphia in October.

Oct.–Nov.   Abigail travels from Quincy to Philadelphia to join John there.

1800

May   Abigail goes home to Quincy.

2–14 June   John visits Washington, D.C., to inspect the future seat of government before returning to Quincy.

Oct.–Nov.   John and Abigail travel to Washington, where they become the first occupants of the unfinished president's house.

30 Nov.   Charles dies in New York City.

1801

11 Feb.   The electoral vote is counted; John is defeated for re-election to the presidency.

Feb.   Abigail departs from Washington.

4 March   John departs from Washington on the morning of Thomas Jefferson's inauguration.

1813

14 Aug.   Abigail 2d dies at the Old House in Quincy.

1818

28 Oct.   Abigail dies at the Old House in Quincy.

1826

4 July   John dies at the Old House in Quincy; it is the fiftieth anniversary of American independence.

Index

Since the present volume is not intended as a research tool, the reader is referred for more detailed entries to the indexes in volumes 2, 4, 6, 7, and 8 of *Adams Family Correspondence* and to the index in volume 4 of the *Diary and Autobiography of John Adams*, all in the Belknap Press edition of *The Adams Papers*. The editors have tried (not always successfully) to supply forenames for persons who appear in the text with only surnames, and to identify by residence or occupation as many individuals as possible. People with identical names are further distinguished by birth and death dates. Passing references to Adams family members have not been indexed.

Gerry, Elbridge, 77, 135–36, 141, 145, 148, 151–52, 153, 166, 199, 281, 345, 424, 464, 471

Gibraltar, 275

Giles, William B. (of Va.), 409

Gill, John (Boston printer), 67

Gillon, Alexander (of S.C.), 249, 252, 374

Globe Mill (Penn.), 425

Glover, Jane. *See* Newcomb, Jane Glover

Goffe, William (regicide), 235

Goldsmith, Oliver: "Edwin and Angelina," 56; "The Deserted Village," 67

Gordon, Lord George, 237

Gore, Christopher (of Cambridge), 354, 469

Grant, Rev. (of Trenton, N.J.), 467

Gray, Ellis, 270

Great Britain, viii, 28, 69, 95, 205, 213–14, 266, 298, 365, 366–67, 370–71, 410–11, 433

Green, Joshua (of Boston), 210

Greene, Catharine Littlefield (wife of Nathanael), 409

Greene, Gen. Nathanael, 250, 253

Greenleaf, Benjamin (of Newburyport), 76–77

Greenleaf, Dr. Daniel (of Braintree), 457, 464, 479

Greenleaf, Elizabeth (wife of Daniel), 479

Greenleaf, John (of Braintree), 479

Greenleaf, Joseph (of Boston), 154

Greenleaf, Lucy Cranch (1767–1846, wife of John, daughter of Mary Smith Cranch), 132, 317, 428, 479

Guild, Benjamin (of Boston), 268

Guion, Mr., 468

Hague, The, Netherlands, 284, 289, 308

Hall, John (stepfather of JA), 241

Hall, Capt. John, Jr. (of Braintree), 100

Hall, Susanna Boylston Adams (1709–1797, mother of JA): AA-JA relationship and, 3, 11; advises JA on housekeeping help,

23, 24–25; JA and, 87, 363, 393; correspondence with grandchildren, 210; health of, 241, 250, 327, 342, 357, 358, 360–61, 365, 369–70, 380, 399; AA and, 303–4, 335; cheese-making of, 330; care of, 356, 358–59, 428–29, 432–33; death of, 356, 445, 446, 447, 448

Hall, Mr., 164

Hamilton, Alexander, vii, 198, 281, 336, 339, 340–41, 368, 369, 373, 419, 424, 431–32, 450, 459

Hancock, Dorothy Quincy (wife of John), 92, 377, 379

Hancock, John, 57, 60, 62, 92, 98–99, 110, 166, 191, 198, 229, 331, 333, 334, 337, 339, 379

Hancock, Thomas (Boston merchant, uncle of John), 333

Hannes (Hones, Adams family servant), 16

Hardwick, Mr. (of Braintree), 380

Hare, Mr. (Phila. brewer), 148

Harman, Mr. (of Braintree), 364

Harper, Robert Goodloe (of S.C.), 460, 470

Harrison, Richard (Md. merchant), 324

Harry (Bass family servant), 129

Hartley, David (Brit. peace negotiator), 240, 283

Harvard College, 140, 256, 282, 295, 296, 301, 319, 322, 323, 328, 379

Hawley, Joseph (of Northampton), 77

Hayden, Mr. (Adams tenant or farm hand), 30, 438

Haydon, Capt. William, 253

Health and illnesses: smallpox, ix, xvi, 8, 18, 75, 95, 104, 109, 124, 128, 129, 130, 133, 148, 188, 330, 338, 415; smallpox inoculation, ix, 8–11, 14–16, 17, 57–58, 92, 122, 128–29, 130, 131, 132, 136, 138, 139–40, 141, 148; dysentery, xvi, 72, 73–74, 77, 78, 79, 80–81, 82, 87, 88–89, 152, 188; as topic of conversation, xvi; medicines and treatments, 10, 75, 131, 150, 387, 444;